Sanctified Sanity

"Sanctified Sanity is a well-researched and written text by an author whose knowledge of Salvation Army history and theology is clearly established. The author places Brengle's teaching of holiness, principally the role of the Holy Spirit in the work of sanctification of the believer, within the historic context of Brengle's life and ministry. This book is invaluable for bringing to light the work of this great holiness teacher."

—Dr. Roger Green, Professor and Chair of Biblical
and Theological Studies, Gordon College

"The Brengle story is a powerful disproof of the enemy's lie. It reveals that true holiness is really a matter of freedom, light, joy, and love, and that Jesus can free one to live in it. You will not want to miss this story, and you will want to share it."

—Dr. Dennis F. Kinlaw, Founder, The Francis Asbury Society

"Dr. David Rightmire gives us a treasure trove of insight into one of the key voices of the Holiness Movement, Samuel Logan Brengle. The author's scholarly assessment of this man's life, ministry, and theology clearly demonstrates Brengle's fidelity to the heart of Wesleyan scriptural holiness. In the preaching, teaching, and experience of sanctification, this work is a remarkable resource for the serious pilgrim."

—Dr. Jonathan Raymond, President Emeritus, Trinity Western University

Samuel Logan Brengle
(1860–1936)

Sanctified Sanity

The Life and Teaching of Samuel Logan Brengle

——— R. David Rightmire ———

Revised and Expanded Edition

Foreword by Dr. Dennis F. Kinlaw

Published by The Francis Asbury Society
ISBN 978-0-915143-25-2
Printed in the United States of America

To order this book, go to www.francisasburysociety.com or contact:

Francis Asbury Society
PO Box 7
Wilmore, KY 40390-0007
859-858-4222

Scripture quotations taken from the Holy Bible, King James Version. All rights reserved.

The author wishes to acknowledge the Houston Metropolitan Research Center, Houston Public Library, for permission to use the photograph, "Staff Captain and Mrs. Brengle."

To Lt. Colonel Lyell M. Rader, O.F., D.D. (1902–1994)

Soul-winning saint and personal
guide into the life of holiness

Contents

Acknowledgements

Words cannot express the impact that immersion in the writings of Samuel Logan Brengle has had on me. This multi-year project has been a source of blessing, inspiration, conviction, and encouragement. It is my hope that others who read about the life and teaching of this Salvationist saint will likewise be challenged to self-examination and avail themselves of God's gracious provision in Christ.

For the title of this volume, I am indebted to Clarence Hall, who first coined the phrase "sanctified sanity" to describe Brengle's balanced spirituality. Special thanks are also due to the editorial department of The Salvation Army National Headquarters, especially to Lt. Colonel Marlene Chase (former Editor in Chief) for offering the invitation to write this book and Jennifer Williams (former Book Projects Manager) for her painstaking attention to the editing of the same. Research was greatly facilitated by Susan Mitchem (Director) and Scott Bedio (Archivist) of The Salvation Army National Archives and Research Center in Alexandria, Virginia; Major John Merritt and Michael Nagy of The Salvation Army Southern Historical Center in Atlanta, Georgia; and Robin Rader and Major Lorraine Sacks of The Salvation Army Brengle Memorial Library, located at the School For Officer Training in Suffern, New York.

This revised edition of *Sanctified Sanity* has been facilitated by Dr. John Oswalt and Jennie Lovell of the Francis Asbury Society in Wilmore, Kentucky. I am grateful for the opportunity to make this study of the life and theology of Samuel Logan Brengle accessible to the larger Wesleyan-holiness movement through Francis Asbury Press, and for Dr. Dennis Kinlaw's willingness to write the book's foreword. Major Allen Satterlee, Editor in Chief of *Word and Deed: A Journal of Salvation Army Theology and Ministry*, granted permission to re-publish two articles, which comprise chapters thirteen and fourteen in this expanded version of *Sanctified Sanity*. Also, Jack Kerr, Director of The Salvation Army's Heritage Museum in West Nyack, New York, was instrumental in providing additional photographs for use in this volume.

Over the years I have received encouragement to write a popular (nonacademic) work for the Army by many, including Commissioner Stan Cottrill and Colonel Henry Gariepy. My parents, Commissioners Robert and Katherine Rightmire, and my wife Dawn have also offered moral support along the way. Since the original publication of *Sanctified Sanity*, I have been privileged to present much of this material in a variety of Salvation Army venues, including the National Brengle Institute in Chicago, and am indebted to those whose comments have made this revised edition better. Ultimately, however, I give praise to the One who makes all things possible.

Soli Deo Gloria.

Foreword

In the goodness of God it was my privilege to get acquainted with the writings of Samuel Brengle quite early in my Christian life. I never had the opportunity to meet Brengle or to hear him speak. My mother told me that he was easily the greatest preacher that she had ever heard. I learned from him only from his writings. The gracious lady who introduced me to Christ began immediately after my conversion to give to me the small books on personal holiness that Brengle wrote after the tragic attack on him that almost took his life. I remember devouring *Heart Talks on Holiness, Helps to Holiness,* and *When the Holy Ghost Is Come* in my early and middle teens. God spoke to me through them. They appeared so simple at that time. It was only later that I realized I was absorbing an understanding of the possibilities of grace of a very profound nature.

As the years passed, I sought for ways to explain what I learned from that was so formative. I came to realize that the key is in the prepositions. The lady who led me to Christ gave me the concept of following Christ. Brengle's little books, without me realizing it, introduced me to the possibility of living *in* Christ. I now sit at my computer and smile as I think of what the technician is talking about when he tries to introduce me to the concept of the *default position* of the computer. He tries to explain the position that the computer assumes when I am not using it. He then explains that when I finish my work and am ready to close my computer that the computer returns to the default position. The default position is where I start every day with my machine and the position to which it returns when I finish my work at the end of the day. In other words, it is where the computer begins and ends, the point of reference at all times in every project as I work.

There is a life in the Spirit in which Jesus is *the default position* for the human spirit. He can be the alpha and omega of one's life, the beginning and the end, the point from which we start and the one with whom we end every venture. He should even be the source of the life in between. I found many people who believed that such a life was how one *ought* to live and that it was the *duty* of the Christian to try to live that way. From Brengle, I learned that it was not so much a duty as it was a privilege through the Spirit, that the obligation was not necessarily a burden but could be *freedom* itself. During those days I heard of the concept of choosing for oneself a life verse from the Bible. The text that seemed to say it all for me was Paul's half verse in Phillipians 1:21: "For me to live is Christ . . ." When I was in my teens, I could not have explained then what I was learning in such language as I use now. The reality though is that I was beginning to experience, to know, depths of truth, biblical and otherwise, to which the succeeding years have enabled me to find definition.

So, Samuel Logan Brengle was my mentor!

In these succeeding years I have learned that I am not the only one for whom this is true. I found myself the host of a retired university president who was on our campus for a series of lectures. In a delightful time of personal conversation, I was able to learn a bit about his spiritual journey. He told me how he was the pastor of a prominent Methodist Church in a major southern city and learned that an unusual man named Brengle was going to be speaking in some holiness meetings at the Salvation Center in his city. The Salvation Army was not really a part of his normal life, but some unusual circumstances forced him to feel that he should go and hear Brengle. My new friend told me that it was a time of revelation for him. The truth to which he found himself exposed gave him a completely new understanding of himself and his ministry. Brengle spoke of a *singleness of motive* in one's devotion to Christ. "I became very conscious," he said, "of the duality of motive in mine. I was serving Christ, but I realized that my motive was mixed with a heavy element of self-interest in it all. The desire for me to look good stained my concern for complete faithfulness to Christ. A lot of my service was on my terms, not Christ's." He was learning what Albert Orsborn would speak of with the words *"if my purposes have altered and the gold be mixed with dross."* The concept of a clean heart and true freedom in Christ came to him. Now, a man in his mid-seventies, he was joyously speaking to seminary students in some holiness lectures on *freedom* in Christ.

Another evidence of the influence of Samuel Brengle came to me in class at Princeton Theological Seminary. I was a graduate student working under Princeton's philosophy professor, Dr. Emile Cailliet, the Pascal scholar. The course was entitled the *Christian Pattern of Life*, and Cailliet had three lectures on the Reformed doctrine of holiness. He was explaining the difference between the Reformed doctrines of justification and sanctification. He described how the human mind normally learns one thing at the time. The first lesson that had been lost to the Church and had to be relearned was that of justification, how to enter the Christian life. The Reformers recaptured that truth for the Church with their doctrine of justification. Then the question came as to what difference this ought to make in a believer's life. The answer to that question came later in the progress of doctrine in the Church. He lifted a copy of Clarence Hall's life of Samuel Brengle and informed the seventy-two Princetonians in the class that he wanted to read for them a testimony of one who had discovered the secret of the holy life and had lived and preached it. He read Hall's account of Brengle's experience of being filled with the Spirit and the cleansing and filling love that marked not just that moment but the duration of Brengle's life. At the end he paused, then looked across his heavy horn-rimmed glasses, and in his rather heavy French accent said: "Gentlemen," (at that time there were no women in our classes) "this can happen to you!"

You can understand why I felt free after this to share with Cailliet my own personal experience and Brengle's influence on me. I never got over his simple response: "That is beautiful. Now can you intellectualize that?" His question to me has haunted me across the years. I have always felt a profound inadequacy when I have attempted to explain the richness of the depths of personal experience and sophisticated theology that are implicit in what is being affirmed here. That is why I am so grateful for David Rightmire, his interest is not just in Brengle but in the truth to which Brengle was a witness. He has eased my conscience just a bit. This work of his on Brengle is a very good response to Cailliet's question to me. My fervent prayer is that this volume will get wide circulation and serious reading.

—Dr. Dennis F. Kinlaw

Introduction

Curious is the fact that although many within the Wesleyan-holiness tradition acknowledge the influence of Samuel Logan Brengle (1860–1936) on the late nineteenth- and early twentieth-century holiness movement, very little theological reflection has been done on the teaching of this "Salvationist saint."[1] With the exception of a few hagiographic treatments of his life and thought, most of the secondary literature on Brengle is not only dated but is also bereft of any sustained treatment of his theology.[2] Even though many within The Salvation Army still recognize Brengle's name, fewer and fewer Salvationists appreciate the influence his teaching and preaching had on the development of the Army's holiness theology.

Partly responsible for this diminished recognition is the neglect of Brengle in several histories of the movement. For instance, in Herbert Wisbey's *Soldiers Without Swords* (1955), there is only a brief reference to Brengle in a self-proclaimed "objective history of the Salvation Army in the United States . . . of use both to Salvationists and to students of American social and religious history."[3] Paradoxically, Frederick Coutts' 1979 official history of The Salvation Army for the years of Brengle's greatest influence (1914–1946) only refers to him in two brief citations, despite crediting Commissioner Brengle with a "personal influence . . . greater than any rank he held or appointment he was given."[4] This trend in Army historiography has had some notable exceptions in the works of Arch Wiggins (1955) and Edward McKinley (1995), who recognize Brengle's importance and reflect such in their coverage of his contributions.[5] More recent evidence of neglect among historians is found in Diane Winston's *Red-Hot and Righteous: The Urban Religion of The Salvation Army* (1999) and, to a lesser degree, in Lillian Taiz's *Hallelujah Lads and Lasses: Remaking The Salvation Army in America, 1880–1930* (2001).[6]

To address this general trend of neglect, evident in the histories of the Army as well as in its more recent periodical literature, John D. Waldron not only edited a book on Brengle's writings (1976) but also called for a "fresh assessment" of Brengle's life and influence (1985).[7] Waldron encouraged the Army to recognize the importance of Brengle's theological legacy, claiming that:

> perhaps no Salvationist in our history (except Catherine and William Booth themselves) has been the subject of more books and articles than Samuel Logan Brengle. His nine books have been reprinted again and again, and are found on bookshelves around the world. . . . Probably no American Salvationist is better known by members of other denominations, especially those in the Wesleyan tradition.[8]

Another individual who attempted to renew interest in Brengle within the Army world is Sallie Chesham whose *The Brengle Treasury: A Patchwork Polygon* (1988) provides the reader with primary source material (consisting of articles, notes, poems, letters, etc.) collected since the publication of her Brengle biography, *Peace Like a River* (1981).[9]

Despite such attempts to revive interest in Brengle's thought, a new generation has arisen with little or no knowledge of his theological importance. To reacquaint the Wesleyan-holiness tradition in general, and the Army in particular, with the legacy of this holiness apostle, this work offers a theological reassessment of his life and thought. Emphasis is placed on Brengle's understanding of the work of the Holy Spirit in sanctification, this being the focus of his preaching and literary contributions. What follows is not a biography *per se* but an examination of Brengle's thought within the context of his life, spiritual journey, and global ministry. For a more strictly biographical account, the reader is directed to Clarence Hall's classic *Samuel Logan Brengle: Portrait of a Prophet* (1933), a foundational work for all later treatments of Brengle's life.[10]

Due to the practical nature of his preaching and teaching, Brengle's theology is not easily systematized. In order to better understand and assess his thought, it is necessary to gather and arrange his numerous theological pronouncements on holiness. Only in this way is it possible to evaluate properly his theological understanding and contribution. This work purposes, therefore, to make Brengle's thought accessible to those who are unfamiliar with his teaching and to provide an orderly account of his holiness theology, which may serve as a theological foundation for further assessment.

In light of these objectives, the work is divided into two parts. Part I provides the biographical context of Brengle's life and ministry. The first two chapters sketch the broad contours of his spiritual pilgrimage and identification with the Army. In chapters three and four, Brengle's influence as a holiness apostle is presented—in terms of his international ministry as well as in relation to personal and institutional challenges he faced in later years. The concluding two chapters of Part I examine the methods of Brengle's holiness evangelism and the character of his interpersonal relationships with others. Part II focuses on his holiness theology, providing qualified definitions of this key doctrine. Chapters seven and eight deal specifically with Brengle's experience of holiness as gift and inheritance, defined primarily in ethical terms. His treatment of both misconceptions about entire sanctification and hindrances to experiencing the blessing of holiness are covered in chapter nine. Chapters ten through twelve address Brengle's practical teaching on the appropriation, maintenance, and fruit of holiness. This revised edition of *Sanctified Sanity* has been expanded to include two additional chapters, dealing with Brengle's understanding of the relationship of evangelism and the holy life (chapter 13), and how holiness finds ethical expression in Brengle's eschatology (chapter 14). These were previously published as articles in *Word and Deed: A Journal of Salvation Army Theology and Ministry*, and are used by permission.[11] The final chapter provides a theological assessment of Brengle in terms of his relation to the nineteenth-century holiness movement and his influence on the development of Salvation Army holiness doctrine.[12]

Several photographs with descriptive captions can be found between parts one and two of this volume, representing various stages of Brengle's life and ministry. Most of these photos were provided by Susan Mitchem, Director of the Salvation Army National Archives and Research Center in Alexandria, Virginia. This new edition of *Sanctified Sanity* includes a few additional photographs not available to the author at the time of the original publication (2003). They were provided by Jack Kerr, Director of the Salvation Army Heritage Museum and Historical Society, West Nyack, New York.

In order to present the life and influence of this holiness apostle in the clearest and most direct manner possible, the author has intentionally included large portions of primary source material in the text, while relegating much of the supporting material and critical apparatus to notes found at the end of the book. It is hoped that the reader who wants to better understand Brengle will consult these endnotes, not only for citations of the numerous quotations and cross-references, but also for further discussion of points of significance and their implications. The bibliography of primary and secondary sources, also found at the end of the book, is divided into three sections: books and pamphlets, articles, and unpublished sources. Although not exhaustive, this bibliography reveals the prolific nature of Brengle's literary contribution while providing the reader with the first published source-listing of his numerous writings, which includes hundreds of articles.[13]

It is the hope and prayer of the writer that such a tool will aid further research and reflection on the life and thought of Brengle and also serve as a resource for those seeking to understand and experience the blessing of holiness.

Part I

Brengle's Life and Ministry

Chapter 1

Simple Faith: Seeking the Blessing

———————————

The Brengle family moved to Kentucky in 1763, although their colonial roots were in Maryland. George D. Brengle, Sam's grandfather, was a blacksmith in Fredericksburg, Kentucky. Of his eleven children, two became ministers (one Presbyterian; the other United Brethren), and one became a teacher. This educator, William Nelson Brengle, moved to the frontier of Fredericksburg, Indiana, where he was put in charge of a school. Finding no Presbyterian church in town, he joined the Methodist church and was soon elected Sunday school superintendent. William married one his students, Rebecca Anne Horner, a daughter of a Methodist pioneer family. A year later, Samuel Logan Brengle was born on June 1, 1860.[1]

When Sam was two years old, his father left to fight in the American Civil War, during which he was mortally wounded at the siege of Vicksburg. Returning home as an invalid, William died shortly thereafter. During the next two and a half years, Sam and his mother lived alone, developing a close bond of mutual dependence. This relationship would suffer some major adjustments when Rebecca decided to remarry in 1865. The stepfather was a doctor with two children, and although Sam's relationship with him was far from perfect, he learned to appreciate the man who had "stolen" his mother's affections. Upon later reflection, he wrote:

> I would have been spoiled had she not married again and found in my stepfather a counterpoise to her tenderness. He was firm and unbending, and I stood in awe of him, much to my profit. . . . But while he was firm with us,

I felt in my boy-heart that he was not always just. He was hasty. He would fly into a passion. He was not patient, and did not always take time to find out all of the facts. . . . My sweet, lovely mother needed to firmly control the tenderness of her feelings and the floods of her affection, while he needed to control the unthinking quickness of his snap judgments and the nervous and passionate haste of his explosive temper. . . . I have no quarrel in my memory with his dealings, but only gratitude and affection.[2]

Unfortunately the medical profession was not very profitable, so in 1868 Sam's stepfather decided to try his hand at farming, moving the family first to Harrisonville, then to Shoals, Indiana, and later to Olney, Illinois. The whole family worked the farm, with only the winter months of the year devoted to the children's formal education at a one-room log cabin school. Life on the farm was difficult, but Sam learned the importance of hard work, as he daily put in long hours of physical labor. Although his appreciation for nature deepened through life on the farm, he experienced a certain degree of loneliness that was only abated by the exercise of his imagination, interacting with ideas and characters he encountered through the reading of such books as Bunyan's *Pilgrim's Progress*, Plutarch's *Lives*, Dickens' *Pickwick Papers*, Stephen's *History of Methodism*, Scott's *Ivanhoe*, and the works of Josephus. As Sam read and re-read the limited number of books to which he had access, he developed a love for language, resorting even to the perusal of *Webster's Unabridged Dictionary* for new words and their meanings.[3]

Sam was exposed to frontier revivalism in the churches he attended as a boy. He routinely witnessed the preaching of the gospel, resulting in individuals claiming to be "saved" after responding to an invitation to kneel at the mourner's bench (known by Salvationists as being at the penitent-form). At home, the saying of grace before meals, family prayers, and Scripture reading were part of Sam's experience. Reflecting on the spiritual nurture he received, he wrote:

Among the most sacred of my memories are those connected with the family altar of my childhood home. Owing to the somewhat stormy character and up and down religious experience of my step-father, family prayers were irregular in our home, but when we did kneel together in prayer, my soul was strangely and graciously stirred within me.[4]

Brengle's interest in the idea of conversion was first expressed at age twelve while attending a Methodist Episcopal church service in Olney, Illinois, during the fall of 1872. Sam's desire to become a Christian was deferred, though, due to the fact that the preacher did not offer an invitation to be saved. This opportunity, however, availed itself to him several months later while attending a revival meeting at the same church. Although Sam responded to the invitation to come to the altar to be saved, he felt as if nothing had happened to him. For the next five nights of the revival, Sam repeated his journey to the mourner's bench with the conviction that he needed to become a Christian. On the fifth night, Christmas Eve 1873, his mother knelt to pray with him and told him that since he had publicly given himself to God, he now needed to "trust" God. Sam left the church that night after testifying to having consecrated his life to God, but he still felt no assurance of acceptance by God. Several weeks later, however, while talking with his mother as they made their way to a prayer meeting, Sam received the witness of the Holy Spirit to his salvation.[5] In later years he reflected on the nature of this heart-warming assurance.

> For five nights I had been at the penitent form blindly seeking and waiting for the ecstatic thrill, the touch of fire, the vision, the rapture, or some other flaming emotion that others said had come to them, but I waited in vain. Then, without emotion I gave myself to God and rose from my knees. . . . The touch came later. . . . It was not a thrill, a vision, an ecstasy, a rapture—it was peace, assurance, blessedness, a sense of God's acceptance and favor which pervaded my whole inner being . . . like a gentle, diffused warmth. . . . "Blessedness" is the one word that best expresses my feelings at that moment.[6]

Over time, Sam recognized areas in his life that did not reflect the character of Christ. When responding in a fit of anger with his fists to a verbal attack from another boy, Sam lost the inward witness of the Spirit to his acceptance with God. Thus convicted of sin, he came to realize the ongoing effects of the sinful nature within. Although regaining a sense of peace and forgiveness after a period of prayerful penitence, Sam had been confronted with his need for further inward cleansing, which eventually caused him to seek holiness.[7] In the meantime, Sam got involved in the life of the church, being elected as assistant Sunday school superintendent. In 1874 he enrolled at Olney High School for a year, then spent two years in Claremont with Professor Hinman, a teacher of rhetoric. During this period Sam was too far from home to commute, although he did try to see his mother on the weekends. One day in 1875, he received a telegram informing him that his mother was dying. Arriving home an hour too late, Sam felt as if he had been orphaned. Throughout his life, he would reflect on his mother's love and the need to live in such a way that would not dishonor her name.[8]

Brengle suffered from melancholy following his mother's death. He decided that the best way to address his unhappiness was to apply himself to his studies. Professor Hinman encouraged Sam's thirst for knowledge and prepared him for a college education. Receiving a modest inheritance from the sale of the family farm, Brengle enrolled at Indiana Asbury (DePauw) University in the fall of 1877.[9] Not having enough high school credits to matriculate in the university, Sam spent two years in its preparatory school. Although he taught a large Sunday school class and was elected president of the college YMCA, his main interest was oration. Brengle excelled in this field, pursuing oratorical studies with a passion and becoming widely known on campus and within state competitions for his speaking ability. He particularly enjoyed participating in the Lyceum, a college discussion group which met regularly with invited area ministers. It was in this group that he first heard about the experience of entire sanctification.

Although Brengle reveled in opportunities to prepare and deliver public orations, his desire for material security guided him to a career in law, seeing this profession as the best place to exercise his skills. Many of his fellow fraternity brothers in Delta Kappa Epsilon were similarly motivated, some becoming famous lawyers, diplomats, or politicians.[10] Reflecting on this period, Brengle would later write: "In short, I was given over to selfishness and love of acclaim."[11] During his final year at the university, however, Brengle attended a revival and was convicted of the need to consecrate his life to God's service, even if it meant going to the mission field. Such consecration resulted in merely a degree of spiritual contentment: "I lived nearer to God after that and had peace with Him—but it was far from the peace of God *in me*."[12]

Ever since his conversion in 1873, Brengle had occasionally entertained the thought of becoming a preacher, partly because his parents had dedicated him to the ministry when he was an infant and partly because he viewed preaching as an avenue to use his oratory skills in the service of God. Although this call was sublimated during most of his university days, it resurfaced during his last term in the fall of 1882. Having been selected to represent his chapter of Delta Kappa Epsilon at their annual convention in Providence, Rhode Island, Brengle was to make an important speech before the assembled delegates. Feeling the weight of the world upon him prior to his opportunity to speak, Brengle spent time in prayer in his hotel room. When nearly overwhelmed with the burden of his task, he finally declared aloud: "O Lord, if Thou wilt help me to win this case, I will preach!" Immediately it seemed to him that the whole room was filled with light. His speech was tremendously successful. As a result, Brengle returned to Indiana not only with a sense of calling to preach, but also with the motivation to accept preaching invitations, applying his oratory skills to sermon preparation.[13]

Following the completion of his bachelor of arts degree from DePauw Asbury University in 1883, the Reverend Samuel L. Brengle embarked upon a yearlong circuit-preaching ministry in the Northwest Indiana Conference. Revival broke out in each of the four small rural churches he served, and in the process Brengle learned some important lessons about ministry. He later stated that it was "among the uncultivated farmers I learned the foundations of true preaching: humility and simplicity."[14] At the encouragement of Bishop Isaac W. Joyce, a prominent Methodist episcopal holiness advocate, he decided that further schooling in theological studies would enhance his ministerial qualifications. So, in the fall of 1884, Brengle moved east to attend Boston University School of Theology (also known as Boston Theological Seminary).[15]

Shortly after arriving in Boston, Sam became convinced of his need for holiness of heart and life. Being encouraged to seek the blessing by a fellow student, Brengle went to hear Dwight L.

Moody, who was conducting a series of revival meetings in town. Sam was "greatly stirred" by the power and simplicity of Moody's holiness messages, writing:

> He preached on the Baptism of the Holy Spirit. It was a revelation to me. I had looked upon that as an experience of the Early Church, but he told his experience and assured us that it was a present-day experience for all who, under the direction of the Spirit, put themselves in that relation to Christ which would enable Him to give them His Baptism with the Holy Ghost and with fire.[16]

What Moody had "stirred" within him was further explicated and refined while at seminary, as Brengle came under the influence of Dr. Daniel Steele, a professor of doctrinal theology at Boston University who was a leading proponent of the doctrine of entire sanctification during the late nineteenth-century holiness movement.[17] Steele personally led Brengle through an intensive study of Scripture with regard to the possibility of Christian perfection in this life. In addition, the reading of Hannah Whittal Smith's *The Christian's Secret of a Happy Life* made a deep impression on him, helping to vanquish some of his mental reservations concerning the life of holiness. Having been convinced of the theological justification for this teaching, Brengle began to seek after it experientially.[18]

Additional influences during this search were the writings of John Wesley, John Fletcher, Dwight L. Moody, William McDonald, and Catherine Booth (particularly her books *Popular Christianity* and *Godliness*).[19] Concerning Catherine Booth, Brengle later wrote: "I had read Mrs. Booth's books while a student at Boston University. Indeed, it was one of my teachers, Dr. Daniel Steele, who introduced these books into America, and a dear friend of mine, Dr. William McDonald, who published them, and they had been one of the compelling influences that led me into the Army."[20]

A further impetus on the road to holiness came through Brengle's membership in the Octagon Club, a group of eight university students who met daily for prayer and discussion of spiritual experience. Like the Holy Club, which both John and Charles Wesley were a part of at Oxford in 1729, this group served as a further catalyst for Brengle's search for holiness. He wrote that they "banded together like Wesley to seek the Lord until we were perfected in love and made clean within."[21]

Once convinced of the possibility and availability of this deeper work of God's grace, Sam sought for it earnestly over a period of several weeks, crying out to God with ever-increasing intensity of desire. Brengle relates the support he had in this search:

> A few of us students definitely set ourselves to seek and find the blessing, and one of these students proposed to me that he and I spend an hour a day praying and seeking and "confessing our faults one to the other" until we obtained the blessing. This confessing of faults was something new to me and became very searching and humbling to me until at last "the old man" in me, of which Paul writes, stood naked before me. The carnal mind was revealed and I saw there must be a death within me before I could have the blessing.[22]

During this time, he also became aware of a holiness meeting in the area. Attending this service, Sam sought the blessing through repentance and faith with mixed results. "I sought the blessing and was richly blessed but I did not get the blessing and the blessing I did receive leaked out."[23] For days Brengle agonized over his failure to "get the blessing," crediting such as a result of his unbelief. Through a period of self-examination and surrender, he came to realize that the experience he sought was not primarily one of empowerment for service, but one involving the purification of heart and life by the indwelling presence of the Spirit of Christ. Earlier in the search, he saw the experience of holiness as a means to make him a great preacher. "I was seeking the Holy Spirit that I might use Him, rather than that He might use me."[24] But coming under conviction for his self-centeredness when viewed in the light of Christ's character (as the standard of holiness), Brengle wrote:

> I saw the humility of Jesus and my pride; the meekness of Jesus and my temper; the lowliness of Jesus and my ambition; the purity of Jesus and my unclean heart; the selflessness of Jesus and my selfishness; the trust and faith of Jesus and my doubts and unbelief; the holiness of Jesus and my unholiness. I got my eyes off everybody but Jesus and myself, and I came to loathe myself. I

ceased to want to be a bishop. I was willing to take the littlest church and the meanest appointment that could be found. I was willing to appear a big blunder and failure if He would only cleanse me and dwell in me.[25]

Having come to the place where he realized the need to surrender himself fully to the cleansing presence of the Holy Spirit, Brengle finally relinquished control of his lifelong ambition and preparation, and prayed: "Lord, I wanted to be an eloquent preacher, but if by stammering and stuttering I can bring greater glory to Thee than by eloquence, then let me stammer and stutter!"[26] In later years, he characterized this surrender as an identification with Christ in His death: "I came to an end of myself. My whole being went over to Christ and Him crucified, to share in His cross, His reproach, His travail; to be His man, His slave of love."[27]

Now that his consecration was complete, Brengle expected to be filled with the sense of God's fullness. But nothing happened. Baffled by the seeming ineffectiveness of his self-emptying, he sought the Lord in prayer, during which time he was impressed by the words of 1 John 1:9: "If we confess our sins, He is faithful and just to forgive us our sins, and to cleanse us from all unrighteousness." Brengle noted that a "faithful and just" God promises to cleanse "from *all* unrighteousness."[28] What God requires, in order for this cleansing to be actualized, is "simple faith" in His character and promise. Coming to this realization, Brengle immediately prayed a prayer of faith in the grace and faithfulness of God.

In that moment, on the morning of Friday, January 9, 1885, in his room in Boston at 36 Bromfield Street, a great peace flooded over his soul. Questioning whether or not this was the promised blessing, Sam received a confirmation two days later through the witness of the Holy Spirit to the presence of Christ within.[29] Writing more than fifty years later, Brengle reflected:

The glory of that blessed experience has not faded through all the years. It was more than an experience—it was more than a blessing—it was the Blesser Himself that came in tender love and everlasting mercy and great kindness to dwell in my poor heart, making it clean, keeping it clean and promising never to leave nor forsake me. Hallelujah![30]

Brengle, as a student pastor, preached the following Sunday to his Egleston Square Church congregation on the theme of "going on to perfection" (Hebrews 6:1). He ended the sermon with a personal testimony concerning his own experience of holiness. This public profession helped confirm the inward impression of his experience. He had stepped out on faith, and there was no turning back. Two days later, God granted him a "glory experience" (which he later characterized as "the spiritual holy of holies in this life"), in which his religious affections were overwhelmed by divine love. "It was a heaven of love that came into my heart. . . . Oh, how I loved! In that hour I loved Jesus, and I loved Him till it seemed my heart would break with love."[31] Thus, four days after experiencing the inward peace of God's sanctifying presence, he received further assurance, through a baptism of love, that the work had been accomplished. Brengle wrote that "Christ was revealed not only *to* me, but *in* me."[32] At once, he began to testify to the experience of heart holiness and to preach of its possibility in this life. Although in subsequent years his feelings were, at times, less intense, Brengle faithfully witnessed to the transforming and purifying presence of the Holy Spirit.

> I have never doubted this experience since. . . . In time, God withdrew something of the tremendous emotional feelings. He taught me I had to live by my faith and not by my emotions. I walked in a blaze of glory for weeks, but the glory gradually subsided. . . . He showed me that I must learn to trust Him, to have confidence in His unfailing love and devotion, regardless of how I felt.[33]

The area of Brengle's life most affected by his holiness experience was his preaching. Many years later he wrote: "When He gloriously sanctified me, my knowledge and keen perception of truth were greatly enlarged and quickened, and my preaching became far more searching and effective."[34] No longer seeking acclaim for his abilities in oration, he sought to glorify Christ. "For he had forsaken preaching as a profession . . . and adopted it again as a calling, a life passion, that would have as its only object the saving of men and women from lowest sinfulness to highest sainthood."[35] This call was further clarified over the next several months, as Brengle sought to know God's will for his life's ministry. The process was aided by the arrival of William Booth in

Boston. Brengle went to hear the Founder of The Salvation Army speak at Tremont Temple one fall evening in 1886.[36] He wanted to find out about the General of this "strange religious army." Booth made an indelible impression on Sam that night, as he followed up his address with an "all night of prayer." Subsequently, he heard Booth speak at a lecture to Boston University School of Theology students and faculty on "that central doctrine of Methodism," Christian perfection.[37] Brengle was so impressed that he thought, "Here, certainly, is God's greatest servant upon earth today, the man bearing the heaviest burden of the world's sin and shame and woe."[38]

In the aftermath of Booth's visit, Brengle began to feel compelled to enter into full-time ministry. Along with this sense of calling came an offer to pastor a large Methodist church in South Bend, Indiana, recently built by the industrialist Clement Studebaker. The congregation was large and wealthy, and an appointment to this church would launch Brengle on a sure path of ecclesiastical notoriety. As he considered the offer, Brengle attended a holiness convention in Baltimore, and he was much blessed by the ministry of Dr. G. D. Watson (whose books he had previously read with profit) and others. While in Baltimore, he was invited to preach at the Eutaw Street Methodist Church (the oldest Methodist church in the city) with fruitful response. The combination of these events resulted in a greater sense of calling into full-time evangelistic work. Trusting the Lord to provide for his future, Brengle wrote a letter to Studebaker, declining the offer to pastor "the finest church in Northern Indiana."[39]

Feeling led by the Holy Spirit to be an evangelist, he settled on a course of lesser ministerial ambitions—a job that he had once referred to as "beneath the dignity of a full-orbed man." Resolved to be done with pastorates and seminaries, Brengle returned to Boston and moved out of school (not completing his divinity degree). He was asked to speak at Methodist Episcopal churches, camp-meetings, and holiness conferences around the Boston area during the ensuing months. Confirmation of his calling seemed to be evident everywhere he went, as hundreds were converted and sanctified under Brengle's evangelistic ministry. During this ten-month inauguration of his newfound calling, he served as an assistant to Dr. William McDonald, the president of the National Camp Meeting Association for the Promotion of Holiness, and also began writing. One of his first publications, an article published in C. E. Cullis' *Times of Refreshing*, later reappeared in tract form and sold by the thousands. As a result, Brengle became increasingly known around holiness circles, especially within the "National Association."[40]

Chapter 2

Embodied Holiness on the Pathway of Duty

Committing himself to an evangelistic ministry, in part due to the influence of William Booth, it was only a matter of time before Brengle realized that his association with The Salvation Army was meant to be more lasting. Previously he had become aware that the Army had "opened fire" in Boston, and had noticed newspaper accounts of the novel methods and evangelistic zeal of the Salvationists.[1] Brengle admired the courage these militant Christians exhibited in the face of persecution. In later years, when reflecting on these first contacts with the Army, Brengle wrote:

> Two or three things interested me when first I met the Army. One was their sacrificial spirit; another was their virility. I shall never forget going down to the Number 1 Corps hall in Boston and seeing the officer-in-charge, Major Gay, come in, blowing his trumpet, marching erect and with vigor, and preaching sermons with fire and bite in them. These Salvationists were so different from the theological students who were so soft and easy, so powerless as compared with men like Gay.[2]

What he detected in these "peculiar people" was an underlying commitment to a life of holiness. He found out about this dimension of the Army's message from two classmates (Briggs and Swartz), who at first visited the Army out of curiosity, but while attending one of the holiness meetings, found themselves at the penitent-form seeking the blessing. Upon their return to school, they told Brengle of the genuineness they had witnessed, declaring that "if any people on earth have the blessing of sanctification, these Salvationists have." Coming on the heels of his own experience of entire sanctification, these reports made Brengle aware of his need to make further contact with such "examples of the sanctified." His classmates made arrangements for Brengle to meet some Army officers by inviting them to a meal at the seminary. This contact convinced him that Salvationists were kindred spirits, who shared his newly found holiness priorities and missiological vision.[3] Contact with the Army became ever more frequent in subsequent months, as Brengle started attending the early morning "knee drill" at the Army #2 Corps on the way to his student pastorate every Sunday morning. He began attending other Army weekday meetings and not only read the Army's *War Cry* on a regular basis, but began to pass out copies of this periodical to strangers with whom he came into contact.[4]

What further attracted Brengle to the Army, however, was the meeting of a young woman Salvationist named Elizabeth Swift. A classmate, Doremus A. Hayes,[5] told Sam of having heard a Miss Swift speak at a parlor meeting in Cambridge. Another friend came back from church one Sunday and told Brengle of having heard her speak at the Clarendon Street Baptist Church. Following the recommendation of his two friends that he meet Elizabeth Swift, Sam attended one of her meetings at the Elliott Lower Hall in Newton on a summer evening in 1885.[6]

In later years, Sam would write about his first impression: "I can see her still . . . as she stood that night before that critical audience. . . a slender, delicate, cultured woman—she preached the truth, as I had seldom, if ever, heard preached. She preached in language simple, yet refined, and searching as fire to the conscience of men."[7] Following the meeting, he talked briefly with her. She was "warmly impersonal," but he was enchanted. Reflecting on this encounter, Brengle later expressed his feelings for Elizabeth, writing: "I fell in love with her at first sight, and lost my heart, but not my head. . . . My heart had the first innings, and I proposed to give my head a chance; so the next morning I wrote her a letter."[8] Over the next several months, they exchanged friendly correspondence and had the occasional visit whenever Elizabeth was in town for further speaking engagements.[9]

As time went on, Sam learned more about Elizabeth, affectionately known as Lily. Born on July 23, 1849, to George and Pamela Swift, Lily was raised in Amenia, New York. Her father, a graduate of Yale University, was a banker with a law background. The family lived in the country on a farm, where Lily learned to love nature, books, and poetry. She attended Vassar College until ill-health kept her from graduating. The concepts of death and hell were troubling to Lily, later recognizing that "the fear of death is an indestructible safeguard which God has set in our natures to protect the soul."[10] Although raised in the Reformed theological tradition, she began early to question the doctrine of particular election, and eventually turned away from the Christian faith.[11] After the graduation of her younger sister, Susie, from Vassar College in May 1884, Lily accompanied Susie and a college friend on a sightseeing tour of Europe. In Glasgow, they met The Salvation Army for the first time. Susie and her friend attended one of the meetings, while Lily stayed in the hotel, refusing to stoop to such association. When the two returned from the meeting to the hotel, they had not only been at the penitent-form but had fallen in love with the Army.[12]

Curiosity eventually got the best of Lily, who subsequently attended an Army meeting in Haymarket Square, Edinburgh. She was confronted with a crowd of six hundred men and women, who in her own words represented "every state and stage of poverty, vice and misery. Here was embodied before our eyes all the evil of which we had ever heard; here was sin so apparent in faces, looks, and uttered words, as to convince the most skeptical of the need of either a receiving hell or a reclaiming Gospel."[13] When the audience began to heckle the Salvation Army officer and his wife, Lily took it upon herself to address the raucous crowd from the platform, silencing them with a call for "fair play!" Her involvement in that meeting marked the beginning of Lily's association with the Army. She was attracted by the courage, self-sacrifice, and zeal of these Salvationists; nonetheless, she was still unwilling to submit to God's will for her life. Traveling on to London, the three young American women visited Salvation Army headquarters, where Susie and her friend conspired to have Lily meet "somebody like herself." Finding a French intellectual gentleman named Percy Clibborn available, they convinced Lily to meet with him to hear his testimony. As a result of this encounter, Lily committed her life to Christ and determined to respond to the divine call in the pathway of service.[14]

The Swift sisters decided to investigate the Army further. After attending 125 meetings in twenty-six different cities, Lily and Susie decided not to return to the United States, but to stay in London and offer their services to the Army as laypersons.[15] There they had a chance to meet with Catherine Booth and ask her questions regarding the theology and methods of the Army. Impressed by this contact, Lily desired to learn more about the training of officers and began to associate with the Clapton Training Garrison, where the principal, Emma Booth, put her to work teaching less educated cadets. At this time, Lily also began writing articles for the *War Cry,* while Susie was given editorial responsibility for the Army's fledgling missionary journal, *All the World*. It would appear that Lily and Susie were commissioned as officers in April 1885 prior to their return to America.[16]

In May 1885, Lily and Susie returned to Amenia, New York, and began to employ Army methods in attempting to convert their hometown. Susie returned to London at the end of the summer to carry on her literary work, and Lily was left alone in Amenia, where she established a Salvation Army corps.[17] She held meetings at the local Methodist church but temporarily moved them to the town hall because of space constraints. Initial success was due to the novelty of this woman-preacher's message and methods. Although effectively reaching the poor and disreputable persons of her town, Lily soon found it difficult to find a permanent place to meet, as churches shut her out. Nonetheless, her reputation as a female preacher began to spread, and when word of her pioneering work reached Army headquarters in New York City, Lily was asked to engage in an itinerant ministry to help establish Army work in other cities. This was the occasion for her preaching in Boston, where she met Brengle.

Following their initial encounter, Lily and Sam had an opportunity to visit with, and write to, each other over several months. During this time, Lily gave Sam a book she had written while in London titled *A Cradle of Empire*. This story about the London Training Garrison, with its emphasis on the consecration of the cadets to worldwide evangelization, had a profound influence on Brengle. It captivated his interest and laid the foundation for his future decision not only to join the Army, but also to enter into officer training.[18] He wrote later that "this little book finally tipped the scales and dropped me into the Army. I was a student in the theological school of Boston University, and the apostolic simplicity and spirit of devotion of the Army's school was so different from the scholastic spirit of the theological school that it broke my heart. Bursting into tears, I cried out, 'These are my people!'"[19]

Since experiencing the blessing of entire sanctification, Brengle had come to realize the need for divine guidance on the issue of whether he should marry. Surrendering control of this area of his life, he prayed that if God would have him marry, his future wife would be similarly committed to the way of holiness. Brengle recalls praying, "Lord . . . help me to find a woman who will love Thee supremely, for then I am sure she will always love me. . . . Choose for me, Lord."[20] In addition, Brengle's high regard for his own mother served as an unconscious standard for the qualities he admired in other women: "gentle sweetness and purity, and all womanly virtues which adorn a home and make it a haven of rest and a center of inspiration and courage and noble ambition."[21] Although he met several women in subsequent months who had these attributes, Brengle did not feel the Lord's confirmation for any of them to be his life partner—until he met Elizabeth.[22]

On the day that Sam went to hear this diminutive Salvationist preacher in Boston, his heart was smitten: "We met, and I fell in love. . . . Here she was, the sweet, gracious, cultured woman, filled with God's love, one my head and heart approved . . . and for whom I had prayed and watched and waited.[23] At first, Lily did not sense God's leading to consider Sam to be anything more than "a brother in Christ," but over time she warmed up to him. Developing a friendship initially, they gradually grew closer to each other. Sam remained convinced of God's will with regard to Lily becoming his wife, but he had to wait until she came to the same conclusion. During the spring of 1886, he spent three weeks with her in Amenia as a result of her invitation to have him conduct revival meetings in her hometown.[24]

While ministering in Amenia, Sam helped Lily see the need for "communion and waiting on God," which later found fruition in her entry into the "higher life," characterized not by the "faith of a servant," but that of a "friend." He remarked:

> She worked the limit, and she prayed fervently, but seemed to me to lack appropriating faith—the faith that

takes, receives, and is glad; the faith which rests as it works; the faith that drives the wrinkles from the brow, the burden off the heart, leaving the face sunny and the heart free; the faith that makes every prayer end in a burst of thanksgiving and which lingers with the Lord for sweet fellowship and communion when prayer is done.[25]

Lily concurred that there was something missing in her life, and while resting at a sanatorium for health reasons, she came to experience "abundant life." Writing to Sam about this breakthrough, Lily thanked him for his counsel.

Oh, Sam, you *have* helped me. You helped me when you showed me that Jesus wanted me for something more than a servant. I had never looked any higher. But I rose higher, and it was through you I did so, by keeping my promises to you of praying more in the way of communion and waiting on God. Sam, I feel His love about me like sunshine all the while. Ever since He gave me life more abundantly I have forgotten more and more my servantship though that was sweet and dear to me— and have come into the higher life of a friend.[26]

Brengle was thus instrumental in leading his future wife into a deeper experience of holiness, expressed in love for God and a closer communion with Christ by the power of the Holy Spirit. Yet, still he waited for her to respond to his love. When Lily was about to leave for England to do research on a book she was writing *(The Army Drum)*, Sam thought the time was right to propose marriage—only to receive a definite refusal. While in London through the winter months of 1886–87, however, Lily's heart began to incline toward Sam. At the same time, he felt led by God to offer himself as a candidate for officership in The Salvation Army. On Lily's return, Sam's renewed marital proposal was qualified by his newfound commitment to the Army, and two days later, after making it a matter of prayer, she consented to his request. They were married on May 19, 1887, at her family's farm in Amenia. The inscription in Lily's wedding band read, "Holiness unto the Lord," which served as a symbol of their foundational commitment to God and each other. Two days later, Sam sailed from New York City for London to enter the Clapton Training Garrison.[27]

Brengle arrived at the International Headquarters of The Salvation Army in London on June 1, 1887, to a lukewarm reception by William Booth. The Founder was not impressed with this new recruit, believing him to be of the "dangerous classes" (i.e., a man of education and culture) and hence unable to submit to Army discipline. Sam expressed his belief that the Holy Spirit had not only sanctified him, but had led him to offer his life in service within the Army. Brengle convinced the General of his sincerity by expressing his desire to join the ranks in order to minister self-sacrificially to the poor, stating: "I knew my only way up to heaven was by going down to the lowest of the low."[28] He had passed his first test but was sent to be interviewed by the Chief of the Staff, Bramwell Booth. Once again, Brengle was labeled a member of the dangerous classes and warned not to waste his time in joining an organization that he would probably leave in a year or two. Not to be rebuffed, the candidate persisted until Bramwell agreed to let him in on a trial basis. When issued his first uniform, Sam wrote to Lily: "I . . . half-way dread . . . going out for the first time with it on. I am not used to being stared at so curiously. But I shall trust the Lord to shut me in Himself and not let me feel a care for what man can do unto me." [29]

Sent to the Leamington field training depot, Brengle's first assignment was not soul-saving, but the cleaning and polishing of boots belonging to the other cadets. Initially suffering from a wounded ego, Sam was tempted to think such work was beneath him. He questioned: "Lord God, am I burying my talent? Is this the best they can do for me in The Salvation Army?" While in this frame of mind, he had a vision of Christ washing His disciples' feet, the very Son of God exercising the role of a servant on behalf of poor, unrefined, uneducated fishermen. Humbled by such self-sacrificial love, Brengle cried out: "Dear Lord, Thou didst wash their feet; I will black their boots!"[30] Later, Sam reflected on this experience in light of the humility of Christ:

> Jesus has a humble heart. Just a short time before His death, He took the menial place of a slave, washed His disciples' feet, and then said: "I have given you an example, that ye should do as I have done to you." How that did help me in the training home! The second day I was there, they sent me down into a dark little cellar to black half a carload of dirty boots for the cadets. The devil

came at me and reminded me that a few years before, I had graduated from a university, that I had spent a couple of years in a leading theological school, had been pastor of a metropolitan church, had just left evangelistic work in which I saw hundreds seeking the Savior, and that now I was only blacking boots for a lot of ignorant lads. My old enemy is the devil! But I reminded him of the example of my Lord, and he left me. Jesus said, "If ye know these things, happy are ye if ye do them." I was doing them—the devil knew it and let me alone, and I was happy. That little cellar was changed into one of heaven's own anterooms, and my Lord visited me there.[31]

Eventually, Brengle became known for his speaking ability, attending meetings each day of the week and as many as seven on Sunday. Between meetings he engaged in *War Cry* sales and home visitation, as well as scrubbing floors, cleaning windows, cooking meals, and washing dishes.[32] One of the earliest indications of Sam's future role as a holiness evangelist is evident in a letter he wrote to his wife from London on June 20, 1887, just two weeks into his experience as a cadet: "I don't know yet, of course, what kind of a little place God has for us in the Army, but I feel that my work will be particularly to promote holiness. I should like to be a Special to go about and hold half-nights of prayer just to lead people into the experience of holiness."[33] Later he would write about the expansion of this vision: "I have been led from the beginning to pray that I might be a blessing, not simply to some little corps, but to the whole Army."[34]

By July of 1887, Brengle was transferred from the Leamington Depot and for the next six weeks was assigned to preach at special holiness meetings in various corps and training stations. Overall, his ministry was a success, with many persons saved or sanctified, despite his apparent "long-windedness" and erudition. He was told of his need to emulate the Booths' preaching, characterized as "brief and 'Blood-and-Fire.'" A further step in his preparation for officership was his appointment to command the Stamford Corps for a month. This was one of the most difficult corps appointments in England, as reflected in his own words: "To me Stamford has been the nearest like hell of any place I ever got into. But I can rejoice that my Lord brought me off more than conqueror and enabled me to flash some light into dark hearts."[35] His time at Stamford, however, revealed Brengle's lack of administrative acumen.[36] This deficiency was one that he would never fully overcome, not because of lack of ability, but because of his all-consuming desire to call Salvationists into the experience and life of entire sanctification.

From Stamford, Brengle was sent to Clapton Depot for the rest of his training before being commissioned as a Salvation Army officer with the rank of captain. Leaving England with the blessing of William Booth, Brengle was eager to pursue his calling as an apostle of holiness within the American branch of The Salvation Army.[37] Writing to Lily about this calling, he stated: "My whole heart longs for the people there . . . above all to insist upon holiness of heart and life among them. That's my work. Wherever I am placed, in whatever part of the field, that is the one thing God asks me to do."[38]

Given the short-term appointment policy of the Army at the time of Brengle's return, he found himself in three separate corps in a nine-month span (from December 1887 to September 1888). In their first appointment in Taunton, Massachusetts, Captain and Mrs. Brengle found only one soldier claiming to be sanctified (from a congregation of about a hundred, of which twenty were soldiers). Filled with youthful idealism, Sam vigorously pressed the others to enter into the experience of entire sanctification. Not all were willing to measure up to his high holiness standard, which caused some degree of friction between the corps officer and his people.

During this five-month appointment, Lily fell ill and returned to her family home in Amenia. Brengle was next asked to fill in for an officer on furlough in South Manchester, Connecticut. During his three-week ministry in this large and vibrant corps, he realized the need to press home the call to holiness among the soldiery.

> They need holiness very much. . . . As I have but a short time to stay, I would much rather spend it in getting the soldiers sanctified and filled with the Holy Ghost, than to try to get sinners saved. . . . My heart yearns for the soldiers, that they may be "rooted and grounded in love" and established in the faith.[39]

As a result of his holiness campaign, nearly all of the corps soldiers were sanctified, and a policy was adopted that no person could be a member of the band unless they evidenced having been entirely sanctified.[40]

In May of 1888, Brengle was appointed to Danbury, Connecticut, where he was faced with his most challenging appointment to date. Since Lily was at home in Amenia, preparing to give birth to their first child, Sam went to this new location alone. He found a corps sadly in debt and just recovering from scandal with only an assistant and two soldiers. Brengle persevered by faith despite opposition from a number of quarters, including municipal authorities who denied outdoor meetings, local "toughs" who sought to disrupt services, and competition from schismatic groups such as the American Salvation Army (Moore's group) and the Christian Temperance Union (a group of dissenting former soldiers). From such meager and difficult beginnings, his ministry eventually bore fruit. After this three-and-a-half-month appointment, Brengle went to be with his wife for the birth of their son George (born October 12, 1888) before they were appointed to be in charge of the Boston #1 Corps on January 1, 1889.[41]

Being sent to Boston would test Brengle's commitment to the path of the cross in more ways than one. It was a difficult assignment from a missiological perspective since their corps and quarters were in a squalid area of town, right across from a saloon of ill repute. But a greater cross to bear was the fact that this appointment was in the same town where Sam knew a large number of prestigious friends from his student and pre-Army evangelist days. Wrestling with his pride about being perceived as a failure in the eyes of his former colleagues, Brengle remembered the faithfulness of the Apostle Paul in the face of death, and prayed: "Dear Lord, I, too, will be faithful. I am willing not only to go to Boston, and to suffer there if necessary, but I am willing even to die in Boston for Thee!"[42]

The stigma of association with the Army was not merely imagined but real. Almost a half century later, in a letter written to Dean Albert C. Knudson of Boston University, dated February 11, 1936, Brengle recalls the cost of such identification:

> Two of my teachers in the School of Theology refused to speak to me. . . . One of my dear friends who had been like a father to me, Rev. William McDonald, editor of *Christian Witness,* an eminent Methodist and author

of books, spoke rather sneeringly of my uniform when he met me. One of the professors of DePauw University came one thousand miles to Boston to plead with me to come back, saying there was nothing for me in the Army.[43]

This was a period of much soul-searching, when Brengle even admitted questioning God's calling on his life: "I confess there were times when I wrestled in an agony of prayer to make sure that I had not missed God's guidance and misread His call. Many of the Army people themselves looked upon me with some suspicion and it was years before the doors swung open to world-wide service and immeasurable opportunity."[44]

Sharing in Christ's sufferings not only involved a death to pride but also a degree of physical danger in ministry due to the many drunks that crowded into the tiny Army hall night after night, getting into fights and interrupting the services.[45] Apart from their attempts to evangelize these rowdy and often hostile visitors, the Brengles conducted regular soldiers' meetings for the purpose of discipleship training and held United Holiness Meetings to promote the experience of entire sanctification among their soldiery and people from other churches. These holiness meetings were all-day gatherings, held on a monthly basis, that not only attracted many non-Army church people but also served as a platform for some of New England's most prominent holiness teachers and preachers.[46]

The Brengles' appointment to the Boston #1 Corps came to an abrupt end one night when a "tough," who had been ejected from the Army hall, threw a brick and smashed Sam's head against a door frame. His life hung in the balance for several days, but eventually he recovered enough to be transported to a health resort in upstate New York. Following six weeks of treatment, he traveled to Amenia, where he spent the next eighteen months convalescing.

In June 1889, Lily suffered an emotional breakdown (diagnosed as *melancholia*) as she attempted to care for her sick husband and two frail children.[47] During this inactive period, Brengle took up the pen and wrote articles for the *War Cry* on the theme of entire sanctification. These articles were later collected and published as his first book, *Helps to Holiness,* which became part of the Red Hot Library of devotional classics personally selected by General Booth. Edward McKinley writes that this publication "established Brengle's reputation as the Army's leading exponent of the doctrine."[48] *Helps to Holiness*, as well as other books Brengle would later write, would serve as a blessing to many around the world. In retrospect, both he and his wife recognized God's providential hand in allowing the "brick incident" that almost took his life. Sam would often quip, "Well, if there had been no little brick, there would have been no little book!" Lily, for her part, saved the brick and wrote on it the words of Genesis 50:20: "As for you, ye meant it for evil; but God meant it for good to keep much people alive."[49]

Once strong enough to resume some activity, Brengle was asked to conduct an all-day holiness meeting at his old corps in Boston. The new divisional commander, who had only read articles by Brengle prior to this meeting, gave him the task of touring all the corps of the division for the purpose of conducting holiness meetings. A short time after complying with this request, Brengle was promoted to the rank of adjutant and appointed as district officer for Maine and New Hampshire in October 1892.[50] Brengle approached his new position as an opportunity to be a servant leader, traveling from corps to corps, conducting meetings and being a pastor's pastor. During this thirty-month appointment, he sought regularly to meet with his officers to encourage them in the way of holiness and "to bless and strengthen" them. He wrote to his wife: "I long to see just such times of revival all over Maine and New Hampshire. My heart is crying to God for a general revival and baptism of the Holy Ghost and fire all over the district."[51] In May 1895, Brengle was promoted to the rank of staff-captain and appointed as district officer for Western Massachusetts and Rhode Island. His one-year tenure in this position was marked by efforts aimed at cultivating spiritual maturity among his officers and soldiers.

Brengle's ministry would take a new turn in April of 1896, as he was called upon to help heal the breach in a schism within the American branch of The Salvation Army. In late February of the same year, General Booth's son, Ballington (and wife, Maud), had resigned from his position as National Commander as a result of a dispute with his father. His withdrawal threatened to divide the Army in America, as he drew away a number of Salvationists from the ranks to join his newly organized Volunteers of America.[52]

Brengle recognized the need to avoid the debilitating effects of this rift by keeping the Army ranks focused on their spiritual mission. He wrote to the Army leadership in London of the need to keep the officers and soldiers busily engaged in salvation warfare as the best way to divert their attention from the internal strife: "Lead them back to the old paths. . . . Make them mighty in God!"[53] In later years, Brengle reflected on the schism and his subsequent call:

> The worst storm that ever struck us in America had overtaken the Army. Our ranks were broken. Our people were full of distress and anxious questionings. Our battle-line from the Atlantic to the Pacific . . . was in confusion, and I felt, when in my office, a consuming desire to get out on the Field, to meet our people face to face, to hearten and exhort, to teach, to lead them, distraught and sore perplexed, into "the fulness of the blessing of the Gospel of Christ," and to win sinners to the Savior.[54]

The Army recognized Brengle's ministry as having a potentially unifying effect on the organization, and so he was sent to Chicago, a major center of schismatic dissent. In June 1896 he and his wife were promoted to the rank of major, and a month later he was appointed as the general secretary of the Northwestern Province (comprising Chicago, Southern Michigan, Wisconsin, and Indiana). In "Celebrating the Holy Life," John Waldron wrote:

> During the day he interviewed officers, talked with newspaper men, kept the province's books, straightened corps accounts, untangled legal difficulties, conducted officers' councils, wrote articles for publication, organized a . . . camp-meeting, and traveled throughout the command. His evenings and Sundays were taken up with public meetings, church services, more officers' councils, all-nights of prayer, holiness campaigns, etc.[55]

While Sam ministered in the Midwest for three and a half months, Lily stayed behind in Massachusetts as temporary district officer.[56]

Rather than addressing the themes of organizational schism and dissension within the ranks, Brengle focused his energies on spiritual matters, encouraging his officers and soldiers to do like-wise. Edward McKinley notes that

> For his part, Brengle used his energies almost entirely in speaking and writing on spiritual themes and counseling with wavering officers. His theme . . . was constant throughout the crisis: concentrate on the work God has given the Army—the salvation of the lost. Without ever referring specifically to Ballington, Brengle raised in a hundred ways the question of how it could matter to the rank and file who the National Commander was or why he had refused his orders when souls were dying all around for want of someone to speak to them.[57]

Brengle understood that "busy soldiers do not rebel," and so he sought to divert the attention of officers and soldiers from the schism by concentrating on spiritual growth and evangelism. In line with this emphasis, he wrote a series of articles for the *War Cry* on the topic of "soul-winning" (later combined with articles written during his eighteen-month recovery to create the book *The Soul-Winner's Secret*). These writings have been credited as being the principal means of encouraging Salvationists to focus on missional priorities, rather than the schism.[58] In this regard, Colonel George French later wrote: "This book probably did more to turn the minds of our people from self to souls, from the split to the Christ—thus saving them for The Salvation Army—than did any other person or agency."[59]

After successfully holding together the ranks in Chicago, Brengle was appointed general secretary for the central chief division in New York. Although serving in this capacity without Lily, who was back in Amenia taking care of her father, Sam tirelessly addressed the continuing effects of the schism by preaching holiness as the answer to the Army's problems. Although he consistently put his emphasis on the spiritual mission of his position, he found himself praying not only for "high spirituality" but also "high efficiency in business." In May 1897, eleven months into this demanding appointment, he was invited by Major William McIntyre, general secretary for the Pacific Coast chief division, to conduct a series of meetings in California.[60]

Brengle's west coast campaign started at the Trestle-Glen camp-meeting, which ran for two weeks, resulting in more than four hundred seekers. He then engaged in a number of shorter campaigns over a four-week period in various locations around the division. Officers wrote to the National Chief Secretary, Edward J. Higgins, suggesting that Brengle be given the opportunity to do this type of work full-time. These meetings served to confirm in Brengle's mind, as well, his calling to engage exclusively in holiness evangelism. Obviously his superiors agreed, for upon returning to New York, he was appointed by the Booth-Tuckers (National Commanders) to a new position, National Spiritual Special. The date was August 1, 1897, and Brengle had finally realized his ideal appointment—an apostle of holiness to the nation (1897–1904; 1911–1931) as well as to the world (1904–1910). He felt he was finally in the position to be the most help to the Army—as an itinerant evangelist, teacher, counselor, and friend.[61] "By nature domestically inclined"—this calling was not without sacrifice, as he found himself consigned to a life of worldwide itinerancy, spending long months away from his family and home.[62] Throughout these years, Brengle's influence was widely felt and officially recognized. He received regular promotion in officer rank, becoming a brigadier in 1898, a lieutenant colonel in 1901, a colonel in 1907, and a commissioner (the first American-born officer to attain this rank) in 1926.

Brengle was not only in demand as a Spiritual Special within the Army world but was also invited to speak to other Christian congregations, colleges, theological schools, civic clubs, and camp-meetings.[63] He was especially popular within Methodist circles, which he thought reflected divine irony in that he was being used to bless the Methodist Episcopal church through the Army. Brengle had regular speaking opportunities at Garrett Biblical Institute (part of Northwestern University) in Evanston, Illinois. He also held several revival services at Asbury College[64] in Wilmore, Kentucky, and John Fletcher College in University Park, Iowa. His speaking circuit included dozens of educational institutions as well as ministers' conferences and holiness conventions all across the country. Brengle was consulted by the leaders of other like-minded denominations because of his doctrinal expertise. John Waldron notes: "He was a major voice in the organization of the Christian Holiness Association . . . [and] was involved with the early days of the Brooklyn Holiness Convention," as well as the Lakeland (Florida) Holiness Camp Meeting.[65] Brengle's notoriety as a teacher of holiness led DePauw University (his *alma mater*) to confer the degree of Doctor of Divinity upon him in 1914.[66] In his travels he had opportunities to meet and enjoy the fellowship of other nationally known evangelists, notably Dwight L. Moody, Gipsy Smith, G. Campbell Morgan, Henry Clay Morrison, J. Wilbur Chapman, and D. Willia Caffray.[67]

Chapter 3

International Ministry: A Spiritual Special

Conducting campaigns in every state of the union between 1897 and 1904, Samuel Brengle's ministry was poised to take on international dimensions.[1] In June of 1904, while attending the International Congress in London, he was immediately inundated with accolades for his literary contributions by Salvationists from around the world. Brengle wrote to his wife:

> The Australian contingent swooped down on me the first meeting I got to, and crowded around and overwhelmed me with expressions of gratitude for my little books, and they have been followed by people from the continent, from Africa, Asia, Japan, Canada, Hawaii, and all over— till I wanted to get off in a corner and weep. I supposed there would be some to speak to me of the blessing, but I didn't expect them in such overwhelming numbers.[2]

Later in the week, Brengle was invited by William Booth to speak to the delegates. Clarence Hall notes: "Upon his appearance, Salvationists from all parts of the world joined in an ovation so resounding and prolonged that it was several minutes before he could get a hearing."[3] Before leaving for home, he conducted a series of public meetings in Paris. Following this campaign, he returned to London to meet with William and Bramwell Booth. The Founder first met with him in private and indicated that he wanted to extend Brengle's ministry beyond Paris to the rest of the continent. A few days later Bramwell Booth, Chief of the Staff, met with Brengle and outlined a plan to internationalize his ministry as a spiritual special. In a letter to his wife, Brengle described this interview:

> The Chief tells me the Army is lacking in devoutness, in fire, in the real fullness of the Holy Ghost, and he reiterated what the General had said, that they want me to do some traveling abroad. He thinks I have a message for the whole Army, and he wants to talk it over and if possible arrange for me to have a few months in Europe and, later on, possibly in other parts of the world. How wonderfully He has worked out, and is now working out, the answers to my prayers![4]

The prayers to which Brengle refers were first uttered during his days as a cadet when he asked God that he might be used "to bless the whole Army world."[5] This request was partly answered by having the opportunity to conduct campaigns in twelve foreign countries between 1904 and 1910.

Brengle arrived in Sweden in March of 1905 to contend with a rift brewing in the Swedish Salvation Army.[6] Clarence Hall writes of Brengle: "There was a significance about this, he felt. Indirectly, it had been a schism that had led to his appointment as a national revivalist. And now the first engagement launching his career as International Spiritual Special was to aid a land similarly affected."[7] Rather than directly addressing the controversy dividing the ranks and threatening organizational unity, Brengle focused on the primary need for holiness of heart and life, stating: "I shall stick to my spiritual work and only here and there drop a word of suggestion and hope and cheer regarding the difficulty."[8] Beginning his campaign in Stockholm, where he conducted a number of meetings and officers' councils, Brengle traveled for an additional five weeks visiting Salvation Army corps in several other cities. In each service, he called people to enter into the experience of holiness. A "sweeping victory with crowded halls" resulted, as many "disgruntled and dispirited officers and soldiers had readjusted their experiences at his penitent-form."[9]

In dealing with the schism, Brengle did not gloss over the problems within the Army that the "reformers" were reacting to. Instead, he proposed a more constructive way of reform: "These self-styled 'reformers,' who have split over here, see some of the Army's faults very plainly, but they haven't love enough to bear with them patiently till they can be corrected in a way that will conserve the good. . . . It is only as we get the beam out of our eye—self, lack of love—that we can see clearly to get the mote out of our brother's eye."[10]

Before leaving Scandinavia, Brengle attended the Danish National Congress in Copenhagen, where he was the featured speaker, and then returned to Stockholm to take part in the Swedish National Congress. He viewed the latter as a fitting conclusion to his campaign.

> It was a perfect victory. About a hundred officers were at the penitent-form. They shouted and wept and confessed and rejoiced in a way I never saw before. . . . They ended by carrying us around the hall twice on their shoulders, standing on their seats and laughing and praising the Lord like men drunk with new wine. Brotherly love prevailed everywhere.[11]

Thus, the mission of healing the breach within the Swedish Salvation Army was largely due to the ministry of this apostle of holiness.

Brengle returned to Sweden in January of 1906, where he conducted a campaign in several cities over a period of three months. Although the demands of the tour were rigorous, he was able to use his spare moments to work on a new book, *When the Holy Ghost Is Come*. Great missional success attended these services with "extraordinary manifestations of revival fire."[12] Leaving Sweden, he commenced a month's campaign in Norway, followed by another month of meetings in Denmark. By the conclusion of this five-month Scandinavian tour, there had been 2,405 seekers at the penitent-form (1,491 for holiness, 914 for salvation). In this, Brengle rejoiced:

> Having visited Sweden and Denmark last year, we found the people full of faith and joyful expectation for rich blessings on our return, and no doubt this eager expectancy on the part of the people helped to make possible the rich spiritual harvest that was gathered in. We were comparative strangers in Norway, and there we found the people expecting but little, but the Lord graciously surprised them by giving us between three and four hundred souls in the twenty-four days we worked among them, and . . . we received a most cordial and urgent invitation to return, if possible, next

year. . . . The Salvation Army is firmly established in the three . . . Scandinavian Kingdoms.[13]

On his way home, he stopped off in London to meet with Bramwell Booth and was promoted to the rank of colonel.[14]

After a few months at home, Brengle was back in Europe by the fall of the same year, where he conducted a three-month campaign in the Netherlands and Switzerland. Clarence Hall writes: "In these two little countries, he met with signal success in soul-saving, one thousand, one hundred coming to the penitent-form in Holland, and nearly two thousand in Switzerland."[15] Although he characterized the religious situation in the former as "a great mongrel mix-up of rigid Calvinism and defiant Unitarianism,"[16] Brengle's campaign met with positive response, particularly in the city of Rotterdam.[17] His time in Switzerland was marked with similar results, which he later characterized with words like "wonderful," "glorious," and "unheard of."[18]

Traveling to Scandinavia in January 1907, Brengle wrote to Lily from London about the upcoming campaign in Norway: "They are having a revival in Christiania [Oslo] among the Methodists and Salvationists, and people are professing to speak in tongues, etc. The General is fearful of it all. Pray the Lord to help me to guide them into 1 Corinthians 13 . . ."[19] A few days later, while attending the North European Congress in Stockholm, Sweden, he wrote to Lily with regard to the Army's concern about the Tongues movement in Norway: "[Bramwell Booth and Colonel Pvolsen] think it is of divine origin, but fear that the devil is trying to spread false fire. Our people welcome it as a release from the awful barrenness with which they have been afflicted so long."[20]

Revisiting Norway, Brengle campaigned there from February until May 1907, ministering primarily to Salvationists who had been caught up in two novel theological trends of the day: the Tongues movement based out of Christiania and the New Theology movement centered in Bergen. William Booth was concerned that Salvationists might be confused and led astray by these movements, but with regard to addressing the former, he cautioned Brengle to be careful not to quench the Spirit.[21]

Beginning his campaign in Christiania, Brengle was at once approached by representatives of the Tongues movement, who invited him to attend their meetings. Recognizing the need to better understand their teaching—speaking in tongues as "the essential evidence that the baptism of the Holy Spirit is received"—Brengle attended one of their services and wrote down his impressions: "One chattered. . . . One barked. . . . It seemed to me more like . . . meaningless sounds repeated over. Those affected seemed to be in a trance-like state. . . . I think it is a sort of hypnotic state caused by intense excitement and auto-suggestion. I could not feel the presence of the Spirit in it."[22] Later, in the meeting with some of the leaders of the movement, Brengle was encouraged to "get the gift and carry it around the world."[23] Rather than criticizing their position, and thus squelching the spiritual hunger he sensed was present in their revival, he sought to win them over by a winsome presentation of the way of holiness. Brengle later wrote about this encounter.

> It was just about time for my afternoon meeting, and I had no time to talk further. But I told them if they thought so, they must pray to the Lord to give me the gift, as I was perfectly willing and wanted all that God wanted me to have. So we prayed, and they all came to my meeting. I talked on the Holy Spirit and tried to show plainly the distinction between the Gift of the Holy Spirit and the gifts of the Holy Spirit. Then I spoke on love, and all at once it was as though I had touched an electric button. Nearly the whole congregation threw up their hands and shouted "Amen!" and "Hallelujah!" I told them my own experience, and when I pulled in the net they all came to the penitent-form.[24]

Brengle's ministry in Christiania bore fruit, as indicated in a letter he wrote to Lily: "We have had 620 for pardon and purity in the two weeks we have been here."[25]

His method of dealing with the Tongues movement is illustrative of Brengle's manner of engaging other theological controversies. Rather than denigrating his opponents and their theology, he sought to win them over through a biblically based exposition of the "more excellent way" of love, as validated in personal experience. Brengle explained his method:

> I expounded the twelfth, thirteenth, and fourteenth chapters of 1 Corinthians, laying special emphasis on the thirteenth, which shows the superiority of the *graces* of the Spirit over the *gifts* of the Spirit. . . . Many people,

who had been babbling around in tongues, when they
heard me came to the penitent-form for holiness. They
saw a great light, and they didn't indulge in Tongues any
more. It was swallowed up in a greater glory and a greater
blessing. The Lord is helping me to show how *practical*
the Holy Ghost is.[26]

He wrote to Lily from Christiania, indicating that this ironic
approach to the Tongues movement was reaping positive results:
"I think the Army is very wisely turning the tongues situation to
good advantage of the interest in spiritual things to get everybody
possible saved and sanctified; and it seems to me that our people
generally are in a healthy, sane, warm spiritual condition."[27]

Journeying on to Bergen, Brengle was asked by Adjutant
Theodor Westergaard to address a large crowd on the subject of the
New Theology. A prominent state pastor of the city had adopted
a form of Modernism, publicly denying such Christian doctrines
as the divinity of Christ and the inspiration and authority of the
Bible. Local pastors challenged this individual to public debate on
these important issues, meeting in a large auditorium on several
occasions. Brengle wrote to his wife about this new challenge: "The
'new theology' has broken out in Bergen and several ministers
have been lecturing pro and con on the Atonement. The officer
there has asked me to speak on the subject and I have agreed to do
so."[28] However, his reticence to engage in polemical debate is also
evident: "I have never considered myself so much an advocate as
a witness, and I did not wish to begin a few days' revival campaign
by getting mixed up in a controversy of which I knew so little, and
with gentlemen of whom I knew nothing."[29]

This was the setting of Brengle's famous address, "The
Atonement," arguably one of the most memorable oratorical
achievements of his career.[30] Brengle described his address as a
"simple presentation of truth that would win men to Christ and
reconcile them to God." He wrote that "the object of the address
was not so much to answer critics and to satisfy the demand of
scholarship, as to reach the hearts . . . of plain men and women
with the importance, the need, the nature of God's great gift of
love and sacrifice in His Son for the redemption of men."[31] Not
only did Brengle unmask the true nature of sin, but he showed
that while "God's holiness demands the condemnation of sin;
God's love and mercy demand the salvation of the sinner."[32] The

culmination of God's redemptive activity focused on the cross of Jesus, and the issue of the divinity of Christ was demonstrated to be absolutely necessary in order for salvation to be efficacious. Thus, to deny Christ's divinity was to forfeit the possibility of salvation. The ultimate proof for these assertions was grounded in the personal experience of Christ in the heart of the believer. As a result of this experience, Brengle claimed that

> our doubts shall vanish, our sins shall be forgiven, our guilt put away; we shall be born again, born of the Spirit . . . and have our hearts made pure to see God and discover who Jesus is. And then the Atonement, made by the shedding of His Blood, will no longer be an offence to our imperfect reason and a stone of stumbling to our unbelief, but will be the supreme evidence of God's wisdom and love to our wondering and adoring hearts.[33]

Following "The Atonement" address, great crowds attended his services at the Army corps. Clarence Hall records: "For the first meeting there were admitted into the hall built to accommodate four hundred fifty, more than one thousand persons—and that by ticket."[34] Indicative of Brengle's missional success in Bergen are his words in a letter dated May 11, 1907.

> We had a glorious finish to our campaign in Bergen. One hundred and sixteen souls for the day. The soldiers' meeting was a time of power. There must have been more than a thousand people in both the morning and evening meetings, half at least of whom stood for two hours and a half. But the most amazing thing was the crowd of between five and six thousand people who came to the boat at 11 p.m. to see us off.[35]

The effect of Brengle's ministry was expressed in the words of his officer assistant: "It is almost impossible to describe the interest manifested in connection with the Colonel's campaign."[36]

Brengle's next destination was Finland, where he campaigned for three months in the fall of 1907. Results of his efforts were good, but not as great as those experienced earlier in Norway. His correspondence with Lily reflects the fact that he considered his time in Finland a "trial of faith": "My disappointment in Finland was not due to a failure to see some most blessed results, but rather that I did not see all I had hoped for. Still it was good for me to have a trial of faith in that direction as all my trials of faith are good for me."[37] George Cooke, who chronicled Brengle's Scandinavian campaign, provided a different perspective:

> From the first meeting . . . to the farewell meeting on Sunday night, both the Finnish and Swedish meetings were characterized with marked manifestations of the Holy Spirit. . . . The afternoon holiness meetings were seasons of unusual blessing. The Colonel's plain yet powerful messages on the doctrine of holiness, and the importance of clean hands and pure hearts, attracted wide attention, especially among the better class of people. . . . This triumphant campaign closed with shouts of praise . . . for the 240 souls . . . .[38]

A little more than a month later, Cooke would report:

> Colonel Brengle's salvation and holiness campaign in Finland continues to attract wide attention, not only in our own ranks, but among all classes. . . . The Sunday morning holiness meeting was a time of unmistakable visitation of the Holy Spirit. The Colonel, in his unique, plain, yet powerful presentment of God's command to His people to be holy, powerfully gripped his audience, and forty-three people rushed to the penitent-form as the invitation was given. . . . Up to date about 1,350 souls have been forward for pardon and purity.[39]

While in Helsingfors, Brengle instituted a "soul clinic," providing the possibility of private interviews with him between meetings. This was such a popular idea that his appointment calendar quickly filled and remained full.[40] Another unique feature of his Finnish campaign was the adoption of a slogan adapted from Isaiah 7:9: "If you will not have trust, you shall not have rest." He reiterated this truth everywhere he encountered lack of faith, maintaining that unbelief hindered the appropriation of definite spiritual experience. This slogan took on mantra-like status in subsequent years among Finnish Salvationists.[41]

Brengle revisited Denmark in February 1908—two years after his first campaign there.[42] Beginning in Copenhagen, he traveled throughout the country for eight weeks until he was stricken with rheumatic fever. Slipping in and out of consciousness and experiencing intense pain, Brengle discovered new depths to his faith in God. In a letter to his wife, dictated during more lucid moments, Brengle wrote:

> I think I have made a great discovery: that there is a noble luxury and majesty in pain. . . . A great musician can discover great harmonies where an ordinary fellow would hear only discords; and I seem to sense there is, somehow and somewhere to be discovered, a great harmony in pain.[43]

During one of his bouts with intense pain, Brengle had a vision of the physical agony of Christ on the cross and saw his own pain as sharing in the sufferings of his Lord, even if in small measure. As a result, he began to see his pain as "a sort of blessing," which he was "glad" to have been "permitted to suffer for a while."[44] Although able to discover such blessing amidst physical suffering, Brengle was also prone to emotional distress during this ordeal,[45] as is indicated in a letter written by Lily to Sam in March 1908.

> All depressing emotions work havoc in your body, and it seems to me that these emotions are not of God, both because they hurt you, and because they are against faith. . . . Don't give way to these harmful emotions, my precious Sam. It will grow into a habit.[46]

Coming near death on Sunday, April 12, Brengle later described his experience in a letter to his wife.

> It was a desolate place down there on the shadow side of the gates of death. The glory was all on the other side. On this side there was distress, where the Devil mocks—for he was there. But I found Jesus, not by open vision, but in the way He appoints for us, *by faith*—and my heart was comforted. And I believe the Lord has helped me to bring back some spoil from that desolate place and He shall be glorified.[47]

His sickness elicited a great outpouring of prayer and concern throughout the Army world, and in retrospect, Brengle was able to see how his sickness had served to bring glory to God.

> Do not the Scriptures reveal that there may be such a thing as a sickness for the glory of God? The first and second chapters of Job seem to point that way, and Jesus says plainly that such was the sickness of Lazarus. And may it not be that God so means my sickness? I have wept

and prayed and preached and written and left home and crossed the seas again and again with my message, and may it not be that God has meant to put His emphasis upon it all by taking me down to the gates of death in the sight of my comrades? For the whole Salvation Army world has seen me here, four thousand miles from home, sick almost unto death. And judging from the letters I have received from Commissioners, Colonels, Majors, soldiers, and outside friends, they have been stirred to sympathy and prayer and, I doubt not, to a consideration of my teaching, which a half dozen more campaigns would not have aroused.[48]

After two months of recovery Brengle gained enough strength to make the journey home in late May, encouraged by the words of Genesis 41:52: "God hath made me fruitful in the land of my affliction."

Slowly recovering from his bout with rheumatic fever and a subsequent attack of appendicitis, Brengle's travels were curtailed for another eighteen months due to his weakened physical condition. During this time he participated in a few brief campaigns in Canada and New York, but it was not until January 1910 that he was able to venture forth on another overseas campaign. This time, his sights were set on New Zealand, Australia, and Tasmania, spending ten months in this region known as Australasia. Beginning his work in New Zealand, Brengle landed in Wellington in early March and proceeded to Australia and Tasmania in due course. This was the longest of Brengle's campaigns, and it proved to be successful from a missiological perspective.[49] What was most difficult for him was the protracted separation from Lily. Their correspondence, however, reflects joy in the spiritual fruit of his mission, in mutual love, and in concern for their children.[50]

Brengle spent two months in New Zealand, finding that the distribution of his book *Helps to Holiness* had preceded his arrival and had paved the way for a warm reception. His revival meetings there resulted in a total of eight hundred seekers.[51] During his five-month, thirty-city campaign in Australia and Tasmania, Brengle suffered "recurring attacks of his old rheumatic and gastric troubles, with complications of influenza . . . [which] he refused to allow to slow him down a whit, or cause, save in one instance, the cancellation of any meetings."[52] His lecture called "The Atonement," first preached in Norway, gained a wide hearing throughout Australia, as ministers throughout the country requested that he repeat it. Brengle recorded in his journal: "Think that God should have begun in Norway to prepare me to help His people in Australia? How little we know what God is doing. How far reaching are His designs!"[53] Traveling home by way of Ceylon [Sri Lanka] to conduct meetings with Army officers in the capital city of Colombo,[54] Brengle proceeded to London, where he met with William Booth before returning to America. Arriving back in Amenia, New York, in December of 1910, he wrote in his diary: "What a wonderful year this has been. . . . I have traveled thirty-three thousand miles, encircling the globe, preached and worked for Jesus in America, Australia, New Zealand, England, and have seen nearly three thousand souls seeking Him. Bless the Lord!"[55]

Brengle's Australasia tour would prove to be his last overseas campaign, with the exception of a five-week campaign to the Hawaiian Islands in 1921. The demand for his missional services was still high, but a variety of circumstances kept him from fulfilling the itineraries developed by International Headquarters for world-wide revivalistic work.[56] Nonetheless, Brengle's influence would continue to be felt around the world. Reflecting on his global ministry while on tour in Australia, he wrote to his wife: "If I had not followed Him [God] wholly I might have been a Methodist parson, known in a few towns and cities, but by taking up the cross and glorifying in its shame, he has made people to love me in every corner of the world."[57] His influence extended beyond the years of international itinerancy, however, through the wide circulation of his books. Writing to Lily from Tasmania in 1910, Sam noted how such influence was already apparent: "My books have certainly reached much farther than I had ever expected. How wonderful it is. . . . I wrote for the poorest and most ignorant little Salvationists, desiring with unutterable longings, to bless and help them, and lo! God has made my writings a blessing to all classes and churches. It proves this, that if we humble ourselves, He will exalt us."[58]

Chapter 4

Manifold Trials, Manifold Grace

Brengle experienced many trials during his life, and he understood them to come either as a means of divine correction or as a providential test of faith, patience, love, and steadfastness. He wrote: "I am a constant student in God's school, the University of Hard Knocks. I have forgotten much of my Latin, Greek, and Hebrew, but I will never forget the lessons I have learned in God's school. It is here that moral fiber is developed."[1] Reflecting on the nature of suffering in relation to the Christian life he often said: "Manifold trials call for manifold grace; manifold grace works for us manifold experience; manifold experience gives us a manifold testimony, enabling us to meet manifold needs."[3] Although having faith in the healing power of God in the context of physical distress, Brengle did not rule out God's use of suffering to accomplish the divine will and purpose. He understood the sufficiency of God's grace in the midst of suffering to be just as miraculous as divine healing. From his own experience, Brengle realized that "God does not make pets of His people. . . . His greatest servants have often been the greatest sufferers."[2]

Though he suffered a host of physical ailments during his lifetime, Brengle was not unconcerned about proper bodily care, as he sought to eat properly and maintain a regular physical exercise regimen throughout his lifetime. Most of his physical difficulties were either due to the rigor of his campaigns in all kinds of environmental conditions or to accidents experienced in the line of duty. But even the most life-threatening situations (like the brick incident in Boston during his early officership, an auto accident in 1924, and major surgeries in 1915 and 1928) were viewed in retrospect as "instruments of grace," being used by God as a means of blessing others.[4]

After a demanding campaign in 1914, Brengle was appointed as principal of the National Training School in New York.[5] What at first seemed like a rare opportunity to have an appointment in which he and Lily could minister together, training future Army officers, soon met with bitter disappointment. "During the very induction ceremony he was stricken with pain,"[6] and Lily fell ill in the weeks to follow. Granted several months of furlough, Sam underwent a series of operations for bleeding stomach ulcers, and Lily was ordered to bed with a condition that was initially diagnosed as "acute nervous prostration" but later thought to be either hardening of the arteries or a tumor on the brain. She fell in and out of consciousness for four months, and Sam was eventually strong enough to be allowed out of the hospital to visit her. Keeping vigil at her bedside during Lily's last hours on earth, Sam at last asked her: "Is Jesus with you?" She responded in the affirmative and then drew her last breath, dying peacefully on April 3, 1915. After witnessing his wife's departure from this earth, Sam wrote to Lily's sister Susie: "Then she fell asleep in Jesus as peacefully and unafraid as ever her tired babies fell asleep in her mother arms."[7]

A few days later, Brengle would write of his experience "in the valley of the shadow of death" for the *War Cry*. In an article titled "The Consolation Wherewith He Was Comforted" (later reprinted in pamphlet form), he wrote experientially of victory over hopelessness and despair in the face of death to those suffering bereavement. For Brengle, the secret of this "triumph over the worst that death can do" was the work of the Holy Spirit in the ongoing experience of entire sanctification. He wrote that ". . . a clean heart, filled with His Spirit, received and kept by obedient faith . . . brings immeasurable satisfaction and comfort, and uplifts in hours of stern conflict, of deepest sorrow, of unutterable bereavement."[8] Further, Sam believed that holiness provided him with a foretaste of the glory that Lily was experiencing in the presence of Christ. About her departure, he wrote that it was ". . . a passing out of weakness and pain into the fullness of life . . . out of our presence into the open vision of her Lord where I could not for the present follow, but the blessing of which I seemed, and still seem, in some indefinable and divinely consoling sense to share."[9]

Although comforted by God's love and at peace with regard to his wife's destiny, Brengle was greatly affected by her "promotion to Glory." He experienced a deep sense of loneliness and loss that would follow him the rest of his life. Not only did he lose direct contact with his soul mate, but he also experienced a sense of homelessness.[10] Sam persevered for another twenty years without the support of his beloved wife. During this time his loneliness was somewhat helped by the appointment of Captain Earl Lord in 1919 to be his traveling assistant and soloist for his campaigns.[11]

Even with the loss of his wife, and maybe because of it, Brengle threw himself into his work as a National Spiritual Special with new resolve, as he traveled across the country with the message of scriptural holiness.[12] In January 1923, he reflected on the spiritual challenges and victories of his ministry:

> The year just past has been one of the most fruitful I have ever known. We campaigned in twelve states . . . from ocean to ocean, and everywhere God gave us victory and made us more than conquerors. Over three thousand men, women and children were at the penitent-form seeking pardon and purity. . . . Everywhere we have seen people seeking and finding the Lord as Savior and Sanctifier. . . . During the year I had trials of faith, perplexities, conflicts, but without them I should have had no triumphs.[13]

The rigorous campaigning, however, eventually took its physical toll. In 1924, Brengle was hospitalized with the diagnosis of cancer. This caused him to return to New York, where a new team of doctors reached a different diagnosis. Brengle had "a very sick heart and a much impaired excretory system; a long-suffered duodenal ulcer [which] might quickly deteriorate to malignancy, and the least strain could end his earthly tour of duty."[14] His life was spared, and after a period of convalescence he resumed his ministerial duties, but now without his assistant and soloist. In 1925 Brengle wrote to Earl Lord:

> The Commander [Evangeline Booth] says no one wants me to retire, and the General [Bramwell Booth] writes me that he is not happy at the thought of my retiring and

that he thinks a rest will enable me to go on. So he is changing my work so that I shall write more and do long, heavy campaigns less. I like the arrangement.[15]

In 1926, Brengle became the first American-born Salvationist to attain the rank of commissioner.

During the mid-1920s, Brengle witnessed the growth of a reform movement within The Salvation Army in the United States. This did not take him by surprise. He was aware that the Army's organization would *eventually* need to be reformed, as the following record of a private conversation he had with another high-ranking officer indicates:

I do not expect the necessity for reform to come in the lifetime of the present General [Bramwell Booth]. He and the Founder were the creators of the Army, and their autocracy was, and is to an extent, essential to the development and direction of leaders in the organization.... But I feel sure that when the organization and expansion are complete, and the creators have passed away, and a new General—who is not a creator but a creature of the Army . . . takes over the reins of government, he will be confronted . . . with a demand for a restriction of his powers.[16]

Brengle saw the pitfalls associated with the Army's autocratic government, but he also saw the dangers in allowing reform to turn into revolution. When confronted on his travels with talk favoring reform, he urged patience and love. At the same time, he wrote several letters to General Bramwell Booth, urging that "autocracy might be allowed to decline in proportion to the growth of capacity for democracy" within the Army.[17]

The winds of reform soon were increasing in velocity, however, as a result of a series of documents circulated among high-ranking Army officials. In March of 1925, staff officers of the Army received an anonymous "manifesto" in the mail, describing itself as "the first blast of a trumpet, to be reiterated if necessary, against the assumption of infallibility and the exercise of arbitrary and despotic power by the present General of The Salvation Army."[18] The manifesto of 1925 was followed by two bulletins from a W. L. Atwood of Wichita Falls, Texas, in April and June of 1927. They spoke of "foreign dictators, . . . pseudo-generals, . . . I.H.Q. Imperialism, . . . [and] Americanism."[19] Brengle responded to these bulletins by sending out a letter of his own to leading officers, in which he cautioned against fragmentation and sought to reforge the bonds of unity and love. Remembering the damage done to the Army by the schism of 1896, he wished to encourage loyalty to the international Army:

> It is inconceivable in this day when all Protestant denominations are seeking for a basis of unity . . . that The Salvation Army (which has been so happy and blessed of God in its world-wide unity) should now be seeking to divide into separate parts. . . . Be it known to all these tempted brethren that, if there should ever be a split, I shall stick to the world-wide Salvation Army.[20]

Refusing to enter into "secret cabals" or "anonymous intrigue," Brengle had taken a stand against those who would, in the name of reform, divide the Army. Although recognizing the need for moderate reform measures, and having encouraged Bramwell Booth to consider such sooner than later, Brengle opposed attempts by the radical reformers to undermine the General's authority in such a way as to cause disunity. His loyalty to Bramwell Booth and the Army is evident in a letter to the General, in which Brengle wrote:

> I love you. I long to help you. I love the Salvation Army. I have given forty years of my life for it. I love its soldiers and officers and all the little, unknown, humble people in its ranks, who look to it for spiritual shelter, nourishment, fellowship and guidance to heaven.[21]

General Bramwell Booth became increasingly threatened by the popularity and power of his sister, Commander Evangeline Booth, in New York. Attempts to neutralize her power as National Commander of the Army in the United States were met with resistance by both Evangeline and American Salvationists. The tension between brother and sister was only exacerbated by a series of documents written by the mysterious Atwood.[22] In October 1927, Evangeline visited her brother in London and presented him with a document called *Notes for Interview with the General,* also known as *The Fifteen Points.* The primary thrust of this document was a call for constitutional reform, with particular concern for changes in the manner of appointing the General's successor.[23]

Bramwell sought to undercut the reformers by altering the Deed Poll of 1904. Several British commissioners reacted unfavorably to this obvious attempt to safeguard the General's autocratic control of the Army, both present and future. Opposition was so great that Bramwell realized that he must attempt to secure his position in a more indirect manner. He began removing or retiring dissenting commissioners and appointing new ones loyal to his agenda. In the meantime, he responded to the demands laid out in Evangeline's correspondence of February 9, 1928. In a letter dated April 23, 1928, to all the territorial commanders around the world (who had also previously received copies of Evangeline's communications with her brother), the General reiterated his concern about reforms that might undermine the Founder's intentions concerning the Army's system of governance. He also disclaimed any interest in changing the 1904 Deed Poll.[24]

In her attempts to push her brother toward needed reforms, Evangeline was backed by all four of the American territorial commanders, who sent cables indicating their support of her ideas. Brengle decided to write separately to the General, expressing his views in a letter dated March 19, 1928. Included in this lengthy letter were the following salient points:

So far as I can gather, there is an almost universal approval of the Commander's simplified plea for change in the method of the General's succession, and you are today not only in quicksands, as I said in your office two years ago, but you are now facing a rapidly rising and ominous tide. . . . May I earnestly suggest that you lift the whole subject out of the realm of controversy . . . by taking immediate counsel with representative leaders who are in touch with all ranks of officers throughout the world, inviting the fullest and frankest discussion and expression of opinion and conviction . . . weighing impartially all dangers . . . and then arriving at your final decision, based . . . upon accepted conclusions gathered from such exhaustive survey that will enlist the sympathy and hearty support of your representative leaders.[25]

Not heeding Brengle's advice, Bramwell Booth allowed the controversy to deepen. In response, Army leaders from around the world began urging the British commissioners to call a High Council to deal with the brewing leadership crisis. The convening of this assembly was not immediate, as some of the commissioners were hesitant to do anything that might weaken the Army or cause pain to an already physically infirm General. However, the news of Bramwell's rapidly deteriorating physical condition in November 1928 was the impetus needed for the calling of the Council. But as soon as the requisition for the High Council was issued, which temporarily removed authority from the General, Bramwell's health began to improve, and he was in no mood to relinquish control.[26]

This was the occasion for the calling of the High Council of 1929.[27] The requisitioning commissioners were not sure they had enough votes to render the General unfit for office, needing a majority of three-fourths votes of the sixty-four members. In the meantime, the General and his family (particularly his daughter, Catherine) used every means at their disposal to elicit support from the Army world.

This included articles in the *War Cry*, which was still under the General's control. Reaction from the public and the Army world to the calling of a Council was initially negative since they had been helped to perceive the events as the taking advantage of an old man's illness and weakness. To dispel these perceptions, and to offer a rebuttal to the General's press releases, the commissioners issued a brief statement, "The Why and Wherefore of the High Council"[28]

As a member of the Council, Brengle found himself in a difficult position. On the one hand, he loved his General and wished to be loyal to him. On the other hand, he loved The Salvation Army and desired to do what was best for the organization into which he had poured his life.[29] Likewise, the prevailing note of the Council's initial debate was with regard to duty versus affection. But as MacKenzie notes, "even from the point of view of affection, it was urged that consideration for the General should lead those who loved him to remove from him the great burden of leadership."[30] Writing from the High Council to an American officer friend, Brengle revealed his perspective.

> Catherine is putting up a stiff fight, but the High Council is almost of one mind that a change must come. . . . A letter was drawn up by a committee of which I was one, expressing the love and sympathy of the members of the High Council for him, and our firm conviction that at

his age, broken with the weight of years of vast labors extending over more than a half a century, of ceaseless anxieties for the world-wide flock he has shepherded, it was the only wise thing he could do both for himself and the Army.[31]

When it came to sending a delegation to speak with the General of the Council's concerns, the decision was made to send "some of those who had pleaded most ardently their love for their Leader."[32] A resolution signed by fifty-six of the sixty-three members on January 8, 1929, calling for the General's cooperation in retiring from office, was delivered along with the aforementioned letter by a seven-member delegation. Among those sent were Commissioners Gunpei Yamamuro of Japan (who had recently written a biography of Bramwell Booth) and Samuel Logan Brengle.[33] When the Council reconvened, the discussion first focused on the issue of the General's health. The seven-member deputation of the High Council was then dispatched to the bedside of the ailing Bramwell Booth with the charge of conveying the love and esteem of the Council as well as recommending his retirement due to his illness and advanced age.[34]

When the delegation visited the General at his seaside residence in Southwold, they were surprised with what they found. "The sight of Bramwell lying on his bed was a sad shock. He was evidently weaker than they had been led to suppose."[35] The delegation's eyewitness report confirmed the feeling that Bramwell's physical condition was not likely to improve. Yamamuro, who felt a good deal of affection for his General, stated, "It would be cruel, cruel to impose the burdens of his office on him again."[36] Brengle wrote, "He is certainly unfit at his age and in his helpless condition for his job. If he does not retire, and we have to adjudicate, I shall have to vote against him. There is no alternative."[37]

After hearing the Council's request, the General waited four days to respond. He steadfastly refused to retire on the grounds of duty.[38] The refusal came in written form and was accompanied by a threat to take the High Council to court (which was in direct violation of the Army's *Orders and Regulations* that Bramwell had himself helped to draft). This unforeseen development disillusioned many within The Salvation Army.

Edward McKinley writes: "His [Bramwell's] lawsuit damned the General in the eyes not only of the Council but almost all Salvationists who read about it in the *War Cry*."[39] Indeed, for many, it was the deciding issue in the controversy, as reflected in Commissioner Brengle's address before the Council. He told them of his love for the General, but also of the shock he experienced when reading his beloved leader's letter with its threat of legal action. He spoke of his disillusionment:

> When I was once in Italy I visited a picture gallery with a room dark, save for an illuminated portrait of the head of Christ. I treasured memories of that picture and sorrowed when later I heard that a vandal had slashed his knife across it. In my heart I long carried a darkened room, and in it an illuminated portrait of our General. But when I read the General's letter, this portrait was slashed.[40]

Thus, Brengle felt compelled to take a stand on his loyalty to the Army over its General. John Waldron writes, "Torn between his love for his General and a growing sense of duty, his address on the day of adjudication was declared to be the 'highest emotional point of the High Council' and profoundly influenced the eventual outcome."[41]

After further debate on January 16 that lasted into the early morning hours, fifty-five of the sixty-three members present passed a resolution to depose Bramwell Booth. The official bulletin, issued by the Council, read: "After conforming to all requirements of Deed Poll, High Council in session today arrived at adjudicating decision just after midnight, January 16–17, 1929, whereby the General was relieved of his office, votes in favor of resolution being fifty-five and eight against."[42] A court injunction, however, temporarily put the Council's deliberations on hold, as the General assembled legal counsel.[43] The court injunction prohibited any action on the resolution passed on January 17 until the General be given opportunity to make his case before the High Council.

The High Council met on February 13 to hear from the General's legal representatives. After several hours of testimony on behalf of the General, the Council voted once again to relieve Bramwell Booth of his command. Of the sixty-one members present on this occasion, fifty-two voted in favor of deposing the General. Later that evening, the Council elected Edward J. Higgins as General of The Salvation Army, beating out Evangeline Booth by a vote of forty-two to seventeen. Brengle, in a letter to Colonel Jenkins (National Secretary, USA) candidly related how Evangeline had attempted unsuccessfully to win the approval of the High Council by "flowery" and dramatic oratory. He further described how the outcome of the vote affected her: "Poor Commander! She is sadly cut up and feels humiliated by the smallness of her vote and she wants to lay it to anti-American feeling, but in that she is wrong. . . . They just didn't want the Commander."[44]

Brengle's saintly reputation and his role in the deposition of Bramwell Booth helped not only the Army world but the greater church accept the outcome the High Council.[45] With regard to his involvement in the crisis of leadership in 1929, Brengle later wrote: "We had . . . a painful time at the High Council. I loved Bramwell Booth, but I had to vote for his retirement. I saw him, and he was an utterly broken man, wholly unfit for the superhuman task of a General. I believe God led us in our voting."[46] In the end, he and Commissioner Yamamuro had the difficult task of relaying the Council's decision to the deposed General. Despite his involvement in this action, however, Brengle's love for Bramwell Booth continued, as reflected in words penned on the occasion of Bramwell's death.

> Yes, I believe God's hand removed our dear old General. I loved him. I grieve for him, and to me the world is lonelier now that he is gone. . . . We must hold fast to the things he preached and pray God to raise up workers. . . . I am urging our people to read Bramwell Booth's books. . . . These should be read by all our officers.[47]

In the fall of 1930, General Higgins called a Commissioners' Conference to be held in London to discuss wider reforms in Salvation Army government. Brengle, although scheduled to officially retire in June of that year, was given a one-year extension of active duty in order to include his input in the conference. Sam reluctantly agreed to participate in these meetings, even though he doubted that he had much to contribute to its administrative decision-making. Brengle's contribution to the conference, however, was invaluable, as he provided theological and philosophical principles to be considered in the process of reforming the Army's government. His address before the conference counseled balance in approaching reform, pointing out the strengths and weaknesses of Aristotle's three classifications of government: the autocratic, the aristocratic, and the democratic. His concern was that the Army, in its departure from an autocratic form of government, might fall prey to a spirit of "self-seeking," which was a danger of radical democratization. This warning against self-seeking, which he called "the Diotrephesian spirit," was further defined in an article written for *The Staff Review* in October 1930, titled "Who Among Us Is of the Tribe of Diotrephes?"[48]

Brengle retired on June 1, 1931, after almost forty-four years of officership. Retirement services were not held until October 4–5 in order to allow Commander Evangeline Booth to conduct the event personally.[49] These festivities included two parades, an open air meeting, and three public meetings at the Centennial Memorial Temple in New York City. The events allowed Brengle's "spiritual children" from around the world to pay tribute to this holiness apostle. Commenting on his retirement, Brengle said: "Well, they took plenty of time to get me retired, but I began all over again yesterday by preaching at the Christian Alliance Tabernacle, and I have engagements running up into the fall of 1933. It is a joke that I am retiring."[50] A sense of adventure mixed with retrospective reflection marked Brengle's thinking at this juncture of life, as is evident in words written on the occasion of his retirement:

> But let no one imagine for a moment that I am depressed or saddened by retirement. Not a bit. Fall and winter have their place and charm as well as spring and summer, and I am rounding out the seasons in my life. I am knowing life as a whole, and I do not shrink from it. It is all new to me, and I am finding the element of adventure and interesting surprise all along the way. . . . My life has not always been an easy one. I have suffered much from subtle temptations, from ill health, and piercing, dragging pains during these years. I have toiled and suffered and wept much. I have been bereaved and left lonely, oh, so lonely! Several times I have been at death's door, and friends doubted if I would recover. . . . At seventy-one, I am free from pain and count myself well. I have had much joy along the way, sweet fellowship with my Lord,

with loved ones, and dear comrades and friends. And the toils and sorrows and pains and narrow escapes are like a dream that has passed and is almost forgotten; like a tale that is told.[51]

Although officially retired, Brengle continued to minister both within Army circles and to those of other affiliations in numerous settings. Of particular note was his speaking in Chicago at the 1933 World Conference for the Promotion of Holiness. Sponsored by the National Association for the Promotion of Holiness, an interdenominational movement of which he had been a member for forty years, this conference proved to be "heaven upon earth" to Brengle. He witnessed a "unity of spirit" and love for Jesus that "refreshed" his soul.[52] In a letter to a friend after the conference, Brengle wrote:

> At times, the influence of the Spirit came in waves, and there was shouting, but never confusion—never any loss of what seemed Divine control of the meetings. . . . All these brought immeasurable blessing to my soul until it seemed to me that if I ever got much nearer Heaven, gravitation might turn the other way and I might not get back to earth. . . . All these manifestations of God's presence, in rich variety, and yet Divine unity, fill and thrill me with the hope for revivals in all parts of the earth.[53]

It is noteworthy that not only was Brengle blessed by his participation at this conference, but that such blessing gave impetus to a hope for worldwide revival and to the encouragement of the same through his writing ministry. In subsequent months he wrote a regular column in the *War Cry* (U.S.) on "Revival in Every Corps" and an article for the international *Officers' Review* on the need for revival in every corps of the Army world.[54]

In recognition of his lifetime commitment to holiness evangelism, Brengle was awarded the Order of the Founder by General Evangeline Booth (elected to office in 1934) in New York on September 23, 1935.[55] According to the General, this highest honor was in recognition of ". . . the inestimable service which he has rendered to The Salvation Army by the writing of widely circulated books on the saving and sanctifying power of our Lord and Savior Jesus Christ. To this service has been added a lifelong example as a true soldier of the Cross and unceasing toils for the benefit of mankind."[56]

In anticipation of entering the "abyss of retirement," Brengle had written an article on the importance of "prayerful forethought" before commencing this stage of life. Rather than an abyss, Brengle viewed retirement as a "peaceful slope on the sunset side of life," allowing for further kingdom work. In facing retirement, he reflected on the need to be properly prepared. "I am praying for grace and wisdom for that time, and already I am considering what seem to me to be possible dangers and arming my spirit in advance against them." A chief danger he had foreseen was the temptation of idleness. He wrote:

> There will still be abundant work for my head and heart and hands. . . . There will be plenty of knee-work to do. . . . I may find myself with more free time to watch and pray. . . . I shall meditate more . . . and read and ponder my Bible more. . . . I shall find plenty to do. If I can't command a Corps or a Division . . . or lead . . . great soul-saving campaigns, I can talk to my grocer and doctor and letter-carrier about Jesus crucified and glorified, and the life that is everlasting. I can wear my uniform and go to my Corps and testify, and can still take an interest in the children and young people. . . . And in doing this I shall hope to keep my own spirit young and plastic and sympathetic. Then there are letters I can write to struggling Officers on the Field—letters of congratulation for those who are winning victory; letters of sympathy and cheer for those who are hard pressed by the foe; letters to Missionary Officers in far-off lands; letters to those who are bereaved . . . letters to those who in pain and weariness and possible loneliness are nearing the Valley of the Shadow of Death. . . . Retirement will give my body a breathing spell, but I am studying how to satisfy my spirit and give it worthy employment. . . . Well, I shall find a way.[57]

Brengle weakened gradually during his retirement years. By 1932, his heart had shown signs of failure, and the doctors warned him that too much activity would be fatal. Nonetheless, he lived on, although not bouncing back very well from physical difficulties. Sam maintained his regimen of diet and physical exercise through the rest of his life, even jogging daily up until a few weeks before his death.[58] Physical demands on his heart eventually forced him to decline all public speaking invitations, although he maintained an extensive correspondence ministry. In addition to writing letters to struggling officers, Brengle committed himself to spending more time studying Scripture and interceding for others in prayer. He resided in St. Petersburg, Florida, during the winter and divided his time in the warmer months of the year between his two children, George and Elizabeth.[59]

Sam's eyesight gave out in the last years of his life, and with this experience of what he called the "abyss of physical darkness," he began to yearn increasingly for a brighter world. He wrote about his new condition and its effects to a friend.

> I am now rejoicing in a new affliction. My old eyes are all tangled up, and twisted about, so that I can neither read nor write except to write my name. . . . This trouble gives to me a new and rather poignant meaning to the words of our Lord: "The night cometh in which no man can work," but with the night the eternal stars shine out and I rejoice in the assurance that the morning also cometh, and then the vision of His face, Hallelujah forever. I am not a bit cast down by this trouble, and I feel confident that in some way it is going to work together for my good, and I trust in some way in the enrichment of my ministry to others. It has certainly quickened and enlarged the range of my sympathies.[60]

In a letter to Commissioner Gunpei Yamamuro of Japan, Brengle wrote further about his blindness: "My specialist has this week told me that so far as he can judge, my sight is rapidly failing and that the light will go out entirely in time, leaving me in darkness. . . . What a wonderful Savior we have and what infinite resources of grace He offers us. . . . Please pray for me."[61] Just prior to his death, Brengle wrote to General Higgins (R): "My eyes are bad, and I am getting weaker, but hallelujah! on I go to see my King in all His beauty and the Land that is afar off—and yet not far off! Glory to God in the highest!"[62]

As Brengle neared his seventy-fifth birthday, his physical condition deteriorated, as reflected in the following self-assessment in a letter to Earl Lord: "My eyes are very bad. I cannot see to read. I can write but a little. . . . My heart bothers me some too. . . . If it wasn't for my old heart, my stomach, my eyes, and my ears, I would be a very well man. Well, Hallelujah! 'The outward man perishes, but the inward man is renewed day by day, and I rejoice in my Savior!'" Of greatest concern to Sam was his vision impairment. He wrote: "This is a distinct loss to me. I can't read my Bible and songbook, but I am going on by the grace of God, to seek a way to get gain out of loss, and light out of the partial darkness."[63] This deprivation caused Brengle to urge his comrades to commit Scripture and Army songs to memory in order to maintain communion with God and His saints. In this way, Brengle could claim, despite his blindness, that "I have sweet fellowship at times in my own room. The saints of all the ages congregate there." Not only biblical representatives attest to God's faithfulness, but "Luther and Wesley and the Founder and Finney, and Spurgeon and Moody, and unnumbered multitudes all testify. Blind old Fanny Crosby cries out: 'Blessed assurance, Jesus is mine! Oh what a foretaste of glory divine.' So you see, I am not alone. Indeed, I can gather these saints together for a jubilant prayer meeting almost any hour of the day or night."[64]

Brengle spent his last days at peace, surrounded by his family, while visiting his son in Scarsdale, New York. A heart attack left him in a coma for a day and a half. He died at 1:30 P.M. on May 20, 1936. His daughter, Elizabeth, recalls the moment when he was promoted to Glory: "Just as his spirit departed on a soft little sigh, a smile came over his face and I believed then, and have ever since, that into that sunlit room, Jesus had appeared to him, and possibly little Mother, and his own mother."[65] Three days later, twelve hundred persons gathered for Brengle's funeral in the Centennial Temple in New York City, the service being conducted by Commissioner Alexander Damon and General Edward Higgins (R). Because General Evangeline Booth was unable to attend (being on campaign in Switzerland), Commissioner Edward Parker (National Secretary) read her eulogy, which included the following:

> None more tenderly beloved, none more greatly valued, our hearts are pained that he should have to leave us. I fain would have kept him longer. His faith and courage were unfailing bulwarks to me through the thirty years of my command in the United States, and even more so since being called to the high and sacred office of General. But his warfare is finished. Truly with the light

that radiates from Christ, his faith shone brighter and brighter until awakening in the dawn of the perfect day.[66]

General Higgins also eulogized the departed Commissioner, characterizing him as "... a friend; as a counselor— especially the counselor of four Generals of The Salvation Army; [and] as a great soul-winner."[67] An internment followed the funeral service at the Army's cemetery plot in Kensico, New York.[68] The closing words of S. Carvosso Gauntlett's tribute, titled "The Passing of a Prophet," expressed the feelings of many: "Thus, while his delightful personal presence will be missed, the Army praises God for Samuel L. Brengle's life, and rejoices that 'he, being dead, yet speaketh.'"[69]

Chapter 5

Communicating Holiness: Methods and Materials

In the words of George W. Ridout (1870–1954), a noted holiness evangelist, teacher, and writer, "Brengle became the greatest apostolic preacher of holiness throughout the whole world."[1] As this assessment bears out, Brengle was first and foremost a preacher, having surrendered his oratorical skills to God at an early age. Understanding the importance of study and reflection in the homiletical process, Brengle emphasized the importance of prayerful heart-preparation. He wrote: "The Campaigner must spend time and give all diligence to the preparation of his own heart. . . . Other things are important, but this preparation of the heart is the one thing without which all other things are empty and vain."[2] From his own experience, he recognized the danger of neglecting this proper approach to preaching, maintaining that "many make the mistake of giving more time to the preparation of their addresses than to the preparation of their own hearts, affections, emotions, and faith; the result often is beautiful, brilliant words that have the same effect as holding up glittering icicles before a freezing man. To warm others. . . a man must keep the fire burning hot in his own soul."[3]

Private devotion was part of Brengle's own heart preparation, which entailed daily, early morning communion with God in prayer and Scripture reading. Although he was regular in such devotional practices, such holy habits did not necessarily come easily. Brengle wrote: "I have not found a life of sustained prayer easy, and I gather. . . from the testimonies of many of the most devoted . . . saints of God and soldiers of Jesus Christ that they, too, did not find it so."[4] Writing about his lifetime Bible-reading regimen, he stated:

> For about sixty years I have been reading the Bible, and for nearly fifty I have been reading it through regularly, steadily, consecutively, year after year. When I have finished Revelation, I turn back to Genesis and begin over again, and day by day read my chapter or chapters with close and prayerful attention and never without blessing. In this way the Book has become very familiar, but not stale. It is ever new, fresh, illuminating.[5]

Often Brengle used *The Salvation Army Song Book* as an aid to meditation, comparing it to the Book of Psalms: "Like the Psalms, these songs were written to be sung, and it is through singing that we get most help and inspiration from them; but, like the Psalms, they may also be read with immeasurable blessing and profit."[6] He considered the song book to be not only a source of practical and experimental theology but also a means of heart-nurture and the development of religious affections.

> But while these songs enlighten, enrich and enlarge the mind, they more particularly enkindle devotion in the heart, and make us feel the reality and pull of things eternal when read with thought and prayer. . . . It is this devotional spirit—the spirit of love, of faith, of sacrifice, of spiritual worship—that is at the same time most important and most difficult for us to maintain. . . . But how shall we keep up this grace, this tenderness, this devotion of spirit? . . . The Bible and the song book are there to guide my thoughts and my utterances.[7]

One of the reasons Brengle felt it was important to be adequately equipped spiritually for ministry was because he viewed his evangelistic campaigns in terms of spiritual warfare. He recognized the need to do battle with principalities and powers in relation to the winning or sanctifying of souls: "I've got to do battle with the Devil. I have a pitched battle with him everywhere I go. But it is the battle for other souls I am fighting."[8] Not only did Brengle emphasize the need to "read and re-read and yet again read the Bible," he also valued the reading of devotional classics, doctrinal works, and spiritual biographies, concluding that "such books as these will equip your mind and soul for spiritual warfare, and fit you to win battles in your own soul and for the souls of others."[9] The importance of reading Scripture was also found in terms of its transformational quality.

> No one can live with the Bible, sense its passion for righteousness and holiness, its wrath against all wickedness and unrighteousness and its tenderness toward the weak, the needy, the penitent; no one can hide it in his heart, store it in his memory, believe its promises, practice its precepts—and remain a common person. The Bible will lift him above the common level into a new life, a heavenly realm . . . but above and beyond all, it will acquaint him with Jesus, Lord of Life and Glory.[10]

Scripture not only held an important place in heart-preparation but also served as the fundamental foundation for Brengle's preaching, as he sought to bring the Bible alive through graphic illustration and personal identification with the passages exposited. Edward Higgins maintained that Brengle's success as a preacher was directly related to "the place which the Bible occupies in his platform utterances." His sermons were not only Bible-centered, they were so saturated with scriptural quotations that he was described by some as "a walking, talking edition of the Bible."[11]

Brengle's sermons were more extemporaneous than memorized, as he preached with only a few notes. Although benefitting from many theological writers, he sought to depend more on the Holy Spirit for inspiration rather than to be a synthesizer of the thoughts of others. Over time, he developed a file of sermons that were most applicable for use in his evangelistic work. Although this pragmatic approach to preaching tended to restrict the expression of the broader range of his theological interests, Brengle's writing provided the opportunity to deal with such themes.[12] The latter outlet, combined with prayer and meditation, enabled him to keep spiritually fresh. Thus, Brengle sought to avoid the danger facing evangelists he had read about in George Adam Smith's *Life of Henry Drummond*, his copy of which has underlined in red the following words: "A few years of enthusiasm and blessing, then carelessness, no study, no spiritual fruit, too often a sad collapse."[13]

In contrast to other Army leaders, Brengle frowned on the use of sensational means to promote his spiritual campaigns.

Personally, I have never attempted anything spectacular, although I would not discourage this in others. Pageants, spectacular marches and uniforms, striking subjects, special music, all may be useful to reach the crowd. Cottage Prayer Meetings and Half-Nights of Prayer before a Campaign, with personal visitations, announcements, and invitations, I have found most helpful.[14]

He preferred a simple order of worship for his meetings with the minimum of announcements and introductions. He wrote to Lily: "I'm concerned about introductions. I want to get at the people, and elaborate introductions delay me and dissipate thought and time and energy."[15] Although using male vocal soloists on his campaigns,[16] he generally downplayed performance-oriented elements in worship services. He believed in the use of congregational singing to create the appropriate atmosphere—songs of praise being followed by more serious songs in line with the theme of the sermon. Brengle often exhorted the congregation to see, feel, or taste the song, recognizing the importance of proper preparation for hearing the Word of God.[17] His demeanor has been described as "grave, solemn but happy."[18]

Brengle's preaching was characterized, first and foremost, by simplicity. Due to his training in oration, Brengle found it rather challenging, at first, to communicate "vast things simply." Pragmatism, however, dictated the need to develop in this regard: "I carefully cultivated the conversational style, because I soon saw that it was the most effective in speaking to all classes of people."[19] Nonetheless, he realized the need for divine aid in the process of communication. Writing to his wife from an early campaign in Denmark, he stated, "I am sure that naturalness and simplicity, plus the Holy Spirit, are secrets of power."[20] In disclaiming the need to intellectualize the simple, yet profound, truths of the faith, Brengle wrote:

We may have to dig for the truth as men dig for gold, but when we have found it, shall we go and bury it again beneath a mountain of words, where common people can never find it? There is such a relation existing between the commonest of objects of everyday life, and the greatest mysteries of revelation, that the one illustrates the other. Indeed, he is the profoundest thinker and teacher who has so far mastered God's truth, and holds it so firmly and clearly in his own mind, that he can make it clear and plain to humble men and little children. And yet truth is not reached so much by the exercise of the thinking powers as by direct revelation. But revelations do not come to lazy people—only those who seek, who stir themselves up to think, to pray, to meditate. To them, and only to them, is truth made plain.[21]

Logic also characterized Brengle's presentations. He, like Charles Finney, preached in the fashion of a lawyer trying to win a case. Evidence was presented in a logical and compelling fashion in order to persuade the hearer to reach a decision.[22] Brengle, however, appealed not only to the head but also to the heart, and was often credited as being a "psychologist of the heart." His seeming intuitive knowledge of the soul enabled him to minister effectively to the deepest human needs. He derived such knowledge from Scripture and his own experience, stating:

The greatest book on psychology is the Bible. He who made the human heart knows it. . . . The Bible fits human needs and hearts like my two hands fit into each other. What I attack always in my preaching is sin in the heart. That is why men think I know their hearts. . . . When I came to know my own heart I got the key to every heart."[23]

General Evangeline Booth, writing in 1936, highlighted the therapeutic nature of Brengle's ministry to the heart: "In the pathology of guilt, Commissioner Brengle stood out a distinguished specialist. He did not attempt to be himself the Great Physician. He brought to bear on the patient a healing influence greater than all the resources of man."[24]

Although he preached lengthy sermons, Brengle was able to hold the attention of his congregations due to his ability to identify so effectively with his audience. Recognizing the need to shorten his sermons, Brengle humorously wrote: "My difficulty now is talking too long, but I am trying to reform myself at that point. The people will seldom help me by getting up and leaving."[25] His use of stories and experiential anecdotes was what made his addresses so meaningful. "His preaching and his writings . . . had a straightforward, conversational style and were anecdotal and full of stories and analogies to which the average Salvationist could relate," writes McKinley.[26] The communication of truth, he believed, was best achieved through such means. Sam wrote to Lily:

> You know I have sometimes wondered whether in my preaching I did not tell too many stories, but I read something from Tennyson yesterday that helped me. He is always helping me. No poet, I think, helps me so much. . . . Lowly people, and some who are not so lowly, cannot follow an argument, but they can grasp the truth of the argument when put into a story. So I shall go on preaching the word and illustrating it with my life stories.[27]

Lily, at times, offered constructive criticism with regard to Sam's preaching. In particular, she felt he was "far too demonstrative on the platform," fearing that he would wear himself out physically and emotionally.[28] That this had been an ongoing issue is reflected in a letter to Lily from his New Zealand campaign in 1910: "Don't fear about my roaring and wildly gesticulating. I do a bit, but thanks to you . . . not so badly as I used to do. The people here think I am gentle and quiet."[29] Lily remained unconvinced, writing back to Sam:

> I pray for you, that you may come home stronger than you went— that God would teach you the care of your body, so that you may conserve your vitality, and not come home wrecked, as you have done for so many years. And wherever I pray that prayer, I see you in my memory's eye, thrashing and darting and gyrating on the platform, like a swordfish on a hook and I see that the Lord has a hard opposition. . . . I think I'll repeat an opinion I expressed years ago— that your preaching would be more effective if it was absolutely quiet. Just try it once and see. When I first knew you, you were certainly filled with the Spirit, and yet you preached almost without motion. Go back to your first love.[30]

A few months later, Sam wrote again on this issue, making his case with Lily on the basis of a neutral observer.

> I have been entertained by an old college mate of mine for the last few days, the Rev. Dr. Savin. He has been filling some of the biggest pulpits in America. . . . So I asked him to tell me candidly whether or not he thought I used up vitality unnecessarily in my preaching. He said, "No,

you are just right. If you were more forceful, you would turn the edge of your sword. If you were less forceful, you would not drive home your point. You are just right." . . . One of the leading pastors of Australia . . . heard me and said, ". . . I wish I had your quiet and ease and poise in speaking." There now! Won't you trust me now? What more can I say to reassure your skeptical, exacting little heart. I am all right.[31]

Having trained his voice during his college years, Brengle had learned to use it to his advantage. It was observed by one of his contemporaries that "his voice has the tonal qualities of a great organ. In the course of his preaching, it runs the gamut of expression." Another observed, "His voice is of excellent tone, mellow, and exceedingly pleasing to the ear."[32] His eyes held the attention of those who attended his campaigns. Brengle's face was memorable for those who encountered him. Many commented through the years that they "saw Jesus in that man's face."[33] Described as possessing a "very outspoken, unpretentious genuineness," Brengle's preaching was marked by clarity and power, as reflected in the comments of his officer contemporaries. The *War Cry* of August 24, 1895, reported: "In his addresses is seen the rare combination of the teacher and preacher; for while the doctrine of holiness is most plainly put before his hearers, there are never lacking that warmth of feeling and liberty of expression which brings such strong convictions of the reality of both the speaker and the things he speaks."[34]

Exemplifying within his life his own preaching, Brengle added to the cogency of his biblically based messages. As mentioned above, he often drew on personal experience to illustrate his sermons. Thus, one of the secrets to Brengle's ability to communicate effectively was his use of anecdotal illustrations to make his theological points more memorable. Evangeline Booth recalled Brengle's skill as a communicator: "What anecdotes he could relate! How he could throw light on to deep truths by illustrations from his own experience. Doctrinal preaching is not easy preaching, but Brengle made it appear easy by his unique methods."[35]

Not only did he employ analogy and allegory to illustrate his teaching, Brengle presented his material in a dramatic way, often play-acting the part of a biblical character. He constantly sought to apply gospel truths to modern problems, emphasizing the relevance of Christ for the modern age. In addition, Brengle maintained that there were present ethical dimensions of eschatology, both in terms of blessing and judgment. The baptism of the Holy Spirit made possible "heaven on earth," while present rejection of God's grace would inevitably lead to final judgment. The sins of immorality, presumptuous refusals of God's mercy, and pharisaism, were favorite targets of his preaching.[36]

The pragmatic *telos* (end) to which all of Brengle's exhorting aimed was the penitent-form (altar, or "Mercy Seat"). It was at this place of closer communion with God, in response to the preaching of the gospel, that many found deliverance from the guilt and power of sin. It has been estimated that more than 100,000 individuals knelt at the altar during Brengle's evangelistic ministry within the Army.[37] In discussing the dynamics of penitent-form invitations, he makes clear his belief in a divine-human synergy: "We are to persuade men, exhort them, strive with them, and, in so far as we can, compel them to a decision, but always in dependence upon the cooperation of the Holy Spirit." He also believed that it was appropriate "to use all [sanctified] measures and methods . . . to bring men to decision."[38] Brengle not only called people to decision but also counseled and prayed with them. In fact, through such involvement, he gained a heightened knowledge of religious affections, as he witnessed the heartfelt convictions and desires of those with whom he prayed.[39] Although he felt it important to provide biblically based counsel for those who knelt at the altar, Brengle was also aware of the danger of over-dependence on human advice or methods:

> Give them an opportunity to listen to God's voice, and then let some wise soul go to them and say, "Is there anything I can do to help you, or do you prefer to pray in quiet yourself?" We must not hurry people into the Kingdom at the penitent-form. Give God a chance to deal with them. . . . If we help souls too much at the penitent-form, we may do them more harm than good. Give God a chance![40]

Brengle pursued his interest in attracting and ministering to children as well as adults. He had confidence in God's ability to work in their hearts, even if they lacked full comprehension of the gospel message.[41]

I fully believe in the conversion of children, and for a number of years a children's meeting has been an important part of my campaigns. . . . I believe that conversion is just as immediate a transaction with a child as it is with a grown person, only the religion of a child is the religion of a child. The child is an immature being, and he must be continually readjusting himself to the increasing light, and that readjustment makes it appear as though conversion is gradual —which it is not! The age of accountability varies in children; but I hold that as soon as a child knows it is disobeying its parents, and feels a sense of wrong for such disobedience, it is old enough to be won to the Savior.[42]

He produced a pamphlet for distribution titled *Can Little Children Be Really Saved?* in which was stressed the importance of child evangelism. Elsewhere he wrote: "Let us have faith in God for the little ones, surround them with an atmosphere of gentleness and love, and suffer them to come unto Him. . . . Oh, that every officer might see the spiritual treasure lying close to the surface in the hearts of the children all about us!"[43] When asked about how much little children could understand, Brengle replied:

It is not ours to know how far they understand. It is ours to explain the way, and to pray and to trust the Lover and Redeemer and Good Shepherd of these little ones to find His way into their hearts. . . . Shall we wait till they are old in sin and hardened in wickedness and fixed in unholy habits and bondslaves of the devil before we work and plan and pray for them and seek their salvation?[44]

Brengle maintained that divinely inspired simplicity was the key to communicating the gospel to children: "If you will pray to God for wisdom and love He will help you to make the deepest spiritual truths plain to the children."[45] John Waldron credited Brengle's holiness experience as that which enabled him to bridge the generation gap and love children:

He celebrated the holy life by his love for children and young people. There was never a generation gap with Brengle. . . . Stories about children abound in books by him and about him. . . . Sometimes skeptics, seeing his penitent-form lined with youngsters, would ask, "But do the children understand?" Brengle would . . . reply: "I am persuaded that the children often see the way more clearly than their teachers. They see God by faith, find Him not with heads, but their hearts." Brengle was an eloquent and passionate advocate of the children, and pleaded for their salvation.[46]

Brengle believed that teenagers were often neglected in many corps, and he was particularly concerned that "band boys" be handled carefully. He wrote to Earl Lord in 1935:

I am very much interested in what you tell me about the corps, and especially about the band boys. I know what a difficult situation they make for you. Our band boys are one of our greatest assets, and at the same time one of our greatest dangers. . . . Make each boy feel that you particularly want his aid, and that he can be a great help to you, or hindrance, and urge him to give his heart to the Lord, and be God's man.[47]

Although soul-winning was his passion and central concern, Brengle understood the importance of discipleship in order to help people grow in their love for God and neighbor.[48] Regarding spiritual nurture, he wrote: "If the world is to be saved, we must have converts and they must be guarded with sleepless vigilance, and followed with ceaseless and loving care."[49] To this end, he engaged in extensive correspondence with converts and those seeking spiritual counsel from all around the world. He would often skip meals or stay up late at night to find time for this important follow-up ministry.[50] A prodigious letter writer, Brengle believed his correspondence distracted him at times from other ministerial duties. In a letter to The Salvation Army's editor in chief, William G. Harris, he wrote: "I am greatly handicapped in writing for the [Army] press by a mass of correspondence that taxes my time and eats up my strength."[51] Nonetheless, such occasional frustration did not diminish his desire to communicate with those in need of spiritual guidance.

In his later years, Brengle was asked to comment on the reason he joined and remained faithful to the Army for so long. He replied:

I saw the lost sheep for whom the Savior died, the sinners unreached and unsought by the churches. I saw Salvationists struggling and suffering to win these, and so I became a Salvationist. Later, I saw how ill-equipped were many officers and soldiers for the great task. I saw the Founder and our leaders burdened with overwhelming administrative duties and unable to reach our poor people and struggling officers on the far flung battle lines, and so I prayed and preached and wrote and set myself with full purpose of heart to feed the lambs and sheep of Jesus. . . . And when sore tempted to leave the Army and seek an easier way and preach to a larger audience and more cultured than the few poor people who came to our little halls, I would reply to the tempter, "Who then will feed these sheep if I forsake them?" And I felt I could die for them rather than leave them. Little did I then see the worldwide ministry awaiting me. All I wanted was to be a servant of the servants of Jesus.[52]

In line with this ministry of discipleship, Brengle sought to be a blessing to his fellow officers, offering spiritual counsel and encouragement to his comrades wherever he went. The editor of the *Officers' Review* wrote: "He realized to the full, the vital importance of officers being sanctified, inspired, guided, if the Army was to march ahead. Thus, his thoughts were ever with us Officers—in all lands. With many, of high and low rank, the Commissioner corresponded personally, but he was interested in all, and sought to help them in every way possible."[53] Of particular note was Brengle's extensive correspondence with Catherine Baird—Army poet, hymn writer, and editor. He served as both a spiritual and literary mentor for Baird during her early officership, offering much-needed encouragement and advice.[54] He was also especially fond of opportunities to minister at the training colleges for officers. What made Brengle such an effective counselor was that his life was characterized by humanity, humor, and humility.[55]

Perhaps even more influential than the public ministry of this holiness evangelist were his published writings. Brengle wrote out of his own spiritual experience in a style that was marked by clarity and directness. "His articles and books are largely autobiographical," writes Clarence Hall. "Every word and every sentence is either reflective of his own life—and thus a transcript of his own heart—or of the needs of others, to deal with which he draws upon his own experience."[56] This experiential dimension of his theology is reflected in all his writing, as evident in his words to Bramwell Booth, written upon the completion of *Resurrection Life and Power:* "I have put in much of my own experience. I look upon God's dealings with my soul, not as something to be hidden in my own heart for my personal comfort and guidance, but as a trust for the tempted and hungry-hearted who will hear and read me." He further revealed that two of his books, *Helps to Holiness* and *Heart-Talks on Holiness,* ". . . grew largely out of the close personal work that I was doing with individual souls in my campaigns."[57]

What Brengle wrote touched his own heart as much as it did others: "My soul has often been deeply moved while writing. Again and again, as I have been composing an article, I have burst into tears as I have tried to display the love and mercy of my Lord and make it applicable to the deep needs of my readers."[58] Although Brengle experienced a degree of inspiration in his literary endeavors, writing never came easily to him: "I seldom have a thrill while writing. It is usually a throe. I get into an agony sometimes in trying to write a little bit of an article. I can't dash things off instantly. I sweat and labor over my subject, muse upon it, feel for just the right word, study to get just the right beginning. But, when I have put down a sentence, I seldom ever change it or throw it away."[59]

Much of the impetus for Brengle's writing came from demands placed upon him, first by William, then by Bramwell and Evangeline Booth. Persistent requests from Army editors kept Brengle busy trying to meet deadlines while maintaining a rigorous preaching itinerary.[60] During a campaign in Denmark in 1908, Sam wrote to Lily: "I think IHQ people feel my work is worth all it costs. It helps indirectly with the finance. I think too that they get considerable help from the sale of my books."[61] Although the Army was helped financially by the sale of his books, Brengle received no personal financial remuneration for anything he ever wrote, in accordance with Army regulations for officers.[62]

Not enjoying typing, Brengle wrote out his manuscripts in longhand. He was glad for the opportunity to write more in his later years, but the literary process was arduous for him. He lamented: "London wants me to write . . . though writing is the worst thing that I do. It tires me all over, while preaching if not to excess is good for me."[63] Although all of his writings dealt with some aspect of Christian living, he was once asked by Bramwell

Booth to consider writing biographies of David Brainerd and Jonathan Edwards. Lily dissuaded him from this task, writing to Sam on his 1906 European tour: "Biographies aren't in your line. . . . I don't want you to write a life of anyone, darling. Your *forte* is in didactic writing." Although later in life he considered writing an autobiography, and received the approval of Bramwell Booth to do so, it was never written.[64]

The bulk of Brengle's writing was for Army journals such as the *War Cry,* the *Officer,* the *Staff Review,* the *Officers' Review, All the World, Victory,* and the *Conqueror,* as well as for youth publications, such as the *Young Soldier,* the *Warrior,* and the *Counselor.* Many of the articles written were later gathered and published in book form.[65] Religious periodicals outside the Army and around the world requested permission to reprint his articles or chapters from books. His writings were of particular interest to other holiness movement publishers, such as Henry Clay Morrison, editor of the *Pentecostal Herald,* who wrote to Brengle saying: "Nothing you send will ever find its way to the *Herald's* wastebasket. All you write is well-beaten oil!"[66] C. W. Butler, president of the National Association for the Promotion of Holiness, requested permission to reprint a two-part *War Cry* article ("Fifty Years of Holy Living"), which appeared in pamphlet form as *Fifty Years Before and After.* In the foreword of this reprint, Butler wrote:

> I am asking senior members of the National Association for the Promotion of Holiness to prepare one tract each to be put out as one of a series. . . . We are presenting the present tract from the pen of Commissioner Brengle as Number One of this series. It will be found very useful among all classes and ages, but especially among the young people we wish to reach. It is not only sound theologically, but it involves a psychological explanation of temptation that is excellent. In addition to these facts it is rich in truth and personal experience.[67]

Brengle's writing career within the Army got its start during his eighteen-month convalescence following the 1889 brick incident in Boston. The articles written during this time appeared in various Army journals (especially the *War Cry*) but were eventually gathered together and published in book form. As a result, *Helps to Holiness* appeared in 1896 and has since gone through multiple editions in several languages. Conservative estimates exceed one million copies before his death.[68] This little book launched Brengle's literary career, as Salvationists around the world came to know and appreciate the insights of this apostle of holiness. Many outside the Army also learned to understand and appreciate the organization's theological position through Brengle's literary articulation of the same.

Readers the world over were blessed by Brengle's first book. His theological mentor, Dr. Daniel Steele, wrote to his former student after reading *Helps to Holiness*: "I have read your book, and I am delighted to find it has the red cord of testimony to the cleansing Blood and Fire of the Holy Ghost running all through. It's bound to be very useful."[69] Noted missionaries Paget Wilkes and Barclay Buxton distributed hundreds of copies of *Helps to Holiness* throughout Japan. The Oriental Missionary Society also promoted the book, as did holiness preachers and theologians worldwide. Numerous are testimonies of those from around the globe who entered into the experience of entire sanctification through the reading of this and other books by Brengle. Not only did his writings get translated into many languages, but in 1972 the Army issued a small book, *A Month with Samuel Brengle,* for use where English was a second language.[70] Although several of his articles later reappeared in booklet form (the most famous of which was *Fifty Years Here and After,* published in 1935), Brengle's books comprise nine volumes. First to appear in print, as noted above, was *Helps to Holiness,* which was based on articles written in 1889 and 1890 but published in 1896. *Heart-Talks on Holiness* followed in 1897, being another compilation of articles previously written on various phases of holy living. It has been characterized by Clarence Hall as "a clinical study of the Blessing of a Clean Heart." *The Soul-Winner's Secret* contains articles on the art and life of evangelists. Although not published until 1903, the articles that comprise this volume were written in 1896 and 1897, "during the 'Volunteer split,' for the express purpose of rallying the Army's forces by taking their attention from themselves and concentrating it upon soul-saving effort."[71]

The Way of Holiness, published in 1902, was Brengle's first book written as such. Composed in three weeks, it was produced in response to a request by Commissioner Bramwell Booth (Chief of the Staff) to provide a book on holiness for young people. *When the Holy Ghost Is Come,* a treatise on the person and work of the Holy Spirit, was written in 1906 during Brengle's Swedish campaign and published in 1909.[72] The content of *Love-Slaves* was first published as an article (appearing in the *Staff Review,* the *Officer,* and the *War Cry*) but was reprinted as a book in 1923. Its subject matter is more general than previous works and covers a greater variety of topics, but it shares a common emphasis on Spirit-empowered, Christ-like love.[73] Brengle's largest work, *Resurrection Life and Power,* also deals with a variety of topics and was first published in 1925. A compilation of unrelated articles, often thought to be his most interesting work, was published in 1929 as *Ancient Prophets (and Modern Problems).*[74] His final volume, *The Guest of the Soul,* was published in 1934. Apart from the reproduction of his famous address, "The Atonement," this work is a collection of writings from his later years.

Brengle's literary contribution was profoundly felt within the Army world and has been credited as partly responsible for his promotion to the rank of Commissioner. Brengle wrote of this unexpected honor: "It came to me as an utter surprise. . . . The writing that has brought this recognition to me was altogether a work of love and love never thinks about what it can get but only what it can give."[75] To account for this enduring literary legacy, Frederick L. Coutts (General of The Salvation Army from 1963 to 1969) credits the following strengths:

> First, he [Brengle] has the human touch. Perhaps his secret is that he wrote from his heart to the needs of the human heart. . . . A second secret is that Brengle saw that the doctrine of holiness is not the enemy of the heart's affections but their sanctifier. . . . Brengle deserves a monument for his acceptance of men and women as God made them. To quote: "All the appetites and desires of the body are normally perfectly innocent. The sexual desire is no more sinful normally than the desire for food and drink. None of these desires is destroyed by the grace of God, but they are brought under subjection to the law of Christ." . . . A third secret is that Brengle found the key to the experience of holiness in the word *Christlikeness.* There are many names for the experience of holiness. Our doctrine book lists more than a dozen. Each can be supported by texts—sometimes from the

Old Testament, more happily from the New. . . . Brengle found the thread through the yarns which some have darned by words without knowledge in the truth, that the same "Christ in you" who is the hope of glory, is also our hope of holiness.[76]

Brengle recognized that underlying all of the success of his ministry as a holiness evangelist and writer was his personal experience of entire sanctification and its ongoing effects. In a letter to his son George, dated January 9, 1923, Sam wrote to this effect.

It was thirty-eight years ago this morning at about nine o'clock that God sanctified my soul. I was sitting at my study table in Boston—almost in despair, hesitating to yield my will wholly to God. It was one of the blackest moments of my life, when suddenly I let go and said yes to God—said it from my heart, and instantly these words sounded in my soul like a whisper from God Himself . . . in great love He spoke them into my heart, "If we confess our sins, He is faithful and just to forgive us our sins, and to cleanse us from all unrighteousness" (1 John 1:9). That last was the revelation to me. I bowed my head in my hands and whispered, "Father, I believe that," and peace poured in, joy bubbled up and love began to burn and from that day God has been my portion. Jesus has been precious to me and the Holy Spirit has been with me and in me. . . . Out of that experience and from that moment has flowed my worldwide ministry, my preachings, testimonies, articles and books.[77]

Chapter 6

Brengle the Man

Despite being firmly committed to his own beliefs, Brengle consistently evidenced a sanctified tolerance of the doctrinal positions of others. He modeled with his life the words that he wrote on this subject: The Spirit-filled person

> is tolerant of those who differ from him in opinion, in doctrine. He is firm in his own convictions, and ready at all times with meekness and fear to explain and defend the doctrines which he holds and is convinced are according to God's Word. But he does not condemn and consign to damnation all those who differ from him.[1]

Throughout his ministry, Brengle's pragmatic spirit in combination with his commitment to holiness evangelism caused him to avoid controversial theological issues. Clarence Hall writes, "Doctrinal dissensions and ritualistic controversies occupied none of Brengle's time or thought . . . not because he doubted their worth or place, but because to him they were trivial, marginal, irrelevant."[2] Evangeline Booth paid tribute to Brengle by characterizing him as "a man of high principle," who had been claimed by love to a ministry of nondogmatic fundamentalism:

> The Commissioner was indeed an Apostle of the old-time religion—a fundamentalist. He believed in, he lived, he preached with matchless fervor the "faith of our fathers." From the teachings of the prophets and the apostles and The Salvation Army he never wavered. Nevertheless, he was not a bigot, neither was he narrow in his views, his interpretations of many of the vexed passages of the Bible indicated a true breadth of mind. In nonessentials he was never dogmatic. In essentials he was immovable. He could always be relied upon to state the doctrines of

The Salvation Army clearly and in such a manner that even a child could understand them.[3]

Brengle was far more interested in experiential or practical theology than in doctrinal speculation. Hall notes: "In his own message, only those doctrines which could be expressed in and through human experience were allowed a hearing. He was vitally interested only in those 'certainties in religion that are not settled by debate, but by tasting and seeing that the Lord is good.' For he knew that doctrine written in experience is the only doctrine that cannot be argued against."[4] Thus, experiential knowledge brings certitude and assurance, experience serving as "the proving-ground for the worth of the articles of faith."[5]

SANCTIFIED SANITY

Although staunchly supporting experiential religion, Brengle was concerned about the dangers of unbounded emotionalism. Recognizing the destructive potential of emotion, he likened it to fire—with both proper and improper uses. Brengle's "sanctified sanity" sought to keep the heart and the head in proper balance: "Let your love and your light keep pace. Keep them in equal proportion. Otherwise your love may lead you into fanaticism, or your light may lead you into cynicism."[6] He understood the importance of religious affection in the Christian life and wrote to his son George to be careful not to spurn such.

I wish you would read chapter seventeen—entitled "Preaching," in my book *[When the Holy Ghost Is Come]*. You are afraid of emotion and emotions and I think that chapter may help you a bit on the psychology of the subject. Our emotions and sensibilities are a part of us, as much as is our reason, and to neglect and dwarf and emasculate them is as ruinous as to neglect and dwarf the intellect and reason. When God appeals to us, He appeals to the whole man—in intellect, his sensibilities, his will, his conscience. God made us to love and hate and hope and fear, quite as much as to reason. A man is not all head, nor principally head; but he is, or ought to be part, and a large part, heart. God says, "Come, let us reason together," but He also says, "Son, give Me thine heart." We are not mere logic machines, we are a bundle of sensibilities as well, and all our joys come to us through our sensibilities regulated by sound reason.

Reason furnishes direction, emotion furnishes motive power.[7]

Brengle was also aware of the dangers of religious affection apart from spiritual discernment. He wrote: "Those who receive the Holy Spirit may fall into fanaticism, unless they follow the command of John to 'try the spirits whether they are of God' (1 John 4:1)."[8] Brengle recognized that many confuse the doctrine of holiness with fanatical irrationalism. In this regard, Clarence Hall rightly noted:

> In the early decades of the twentieth century, irrational emotionalism took a heavy toll of the holiness movement. To the popular mind, especially in America, a "holiness preacher" came to mean a fanatical bawler; Pentecostalism was associated with rolling on the floor to the tune of a sensuous chant and disorderly hullabaloo. . . . So confused had holiness become with its unscriptural variants that the Church as a whole, as well as the world, began to shy away from any mention of the doctrine. Brengle, to his deep sorrow, witnessed the words "holiness" and "Pentecost" being thus degraded from their proper and revered definitions in the ecclesiastical vocabulary to become terms used by many to denote religion on the loose.[9]

Brengle's relationship with Pentecostalism is reflective of the holiness movement's general reluctance to be too closely associated with their fire-breathing cousins. He believed that words like *holiness* and *Pentecost* needed rehabilitation in light of the contemporary misuse of these terms.[10] At the same time, he sought to redirect the misplaced emphasis on emotions to a proper expression in the doctrine of holiness, which he understood as *true* religious affection. "In dealing with those whose light had not kept pace with their love, and who had toppled over into fanaticism, it was not in him to slash and slay and denounce," writes Hall. "He realized with Fénelon that 'all maddest passions that transport mankind were only the true love gone astray from what should be its center.'"[11] Brengle's religion, however, was not devoid of emotive expression. In fact, he maintained that there was power in praise: "Nothing is more completely hidden from wise and prudent folk than the blessed fact that there is a secret spring of power and victory in shouting and praising God."[12] Although maintaining that the only religion worth having was a "red-hot religion," such fire was understood as the presence and power of the Holy Spirit, chiefly manifest in faith, hope, and love.

One of the reasons Brengle's popularity spread throughout the holiness movement was his reputation for "sane sanctity." He preached and lived holiness in such a way that he kept a spiritual balance between "glowing emotion and cool perception."[13] Brengle's reputation for sanctified sanity gained the respect of many including prominent churchmen. Indicative of such respect is the following endorsement from Dr. S. Parkes Cadman[14] in a letter written March 13, 1930: "In my humble judgment, Commissioner Brengle is one of the most competent and trustworthy guides of the spiritual life of the churches to be found in our country, or in any other, today."[15]

Brengle was his own best witness to the life of holiness, as he modeled in word and deed the blessing of a clean heart and Spirit-empowered, Christ-like living. His embodiment of holiness went a long way in serving to correct misunderstandings about the doctrine of entire sanctification. Brengle's growing reputation for saintliness, however, did lead some to perceive him as an austere mystic. An entry in Brengle's diary, dated October 4, 1907, records his ongoing dilemma: "Why are so many people afraid of me before they see me? They think that holiness makes my eyes like flames of fire, that I will have no mercy on their infirmities. . . . And when they find out what a human creature I am, that I can laugh and be happy, it is such a surprise and a relief to them."[16] Thus humor, as well as humanity and humility, marked Brengle's life, although it was often subtle and reflected more in the twinkle of an eye than in back-slapping guffaws. As Earl Lord recalls, "Brengle was a very human person. He had a sense of humor and could laugh at a good joke. He told some very witty stories, loved poetry and often quoted lines from his favorites."[17]

Brengle's "holy man" image, however, often made him seem unapproachable. His sensitivity to this impression is evident in his comments on the humaneness of holiness: "There is nothing about holiness to make people hard and unsympathetic and difficult to approach. It is an experience that makes a man preeminently human; it liberates his sympathies, it fills him with love to all mankind. . . . And while it makes him stern with himself, it makes him gentle with others."[18] Eric Coward notes that once people met Brengle, they realized that this "slim, bearded man, with gentle eyes, and love written all across his face" was indeed "humble, unassuming, [and] most approachable."[19]

Always the gentleman, Brengle was courteous to all, regardless of social status, gender, or rank. He was also characterized by an "unconscious humility" that was open to criticism and "invulnerable to flattery."[20] His indifference to rank is evident in his attitude toward his own promotions, which always came as something of a surprise to him. In fact, he had a concern for the potentially negative effect of his promotions on his approachability. He wrote: "When people have suggested during the past years that I should be made a Commissioner, my heart cried out: 'O Lord, if the rank of Commissioner would separate me from the lowest of the low, if I should cause a trusting or humble soul to shrink in reticence from me, don't let it come near me!' Now it has come. O Lord, don't let me lose contact with Thy sheep and lambs!"[21] Not unaware of his growing popularity as a holiness evangelist, Brengle recognized the need to depend on God, as the following diary entry states: "If I appear great in their eyes, the Lord is most graciously helping me to see how absolutely nothing I am without Him, and helping to keep little in my own eyes. . . . Oh, that I may never lose sight of this!"[22]

PERSONAL LIFE

Brengle spent at least an hour each morning in communion with Christ, searching the Scriptures and praying. In this way his soul was nourished and kept in tune with God. He ate a light breakfast (normally shredded wheat and milk) before beginning his day of speaking, visiting, and writing. He believed in physical fitness and sought to walk as much as his daily schedule allowed. As Earl Lord recalls, "He loved nature— the mountains, valleys, rivers, lakes. He was not a sportsman but loved to climb mountains and was an ardent walker. Although not strong physically, Brengle's endurance through many adverse conditions and illnesses was partly due to the attention he paid to exercise and diet. He often advised officers to take good care of their bodies, God's temples . . ."[23] This was based on the belief that the physical body should be under the control of the Holy Spirit, and holiness of life leads to temperance and self-restraint (not asceticism) for the sake of others. Accordingly, he wrote: "And so, all mighty men of God have learned to deny themselves and keep their bodies under, and God has set their souls on fire, helped them to win victory against all odds, and bless the whole world."[24]

Brengle is portrayed by his biographers as a model husband, his marriage to Lily described as "idyllic."[25] Over the

course of their twenty-eight years of marriage (only eighteen of
which they spent together), it has been said that "they grew more
and more into a perfect union." Ever since Sam's appointment as
Spiritual Special in 1897, he had spent long periods away from
home and family. Perhaps this partly explains why Sam and Lily
cherished their time together, and has prompted Clarence Hall
to characterize Sam as an "enthusiastic" lover.[26] What is more
certain, however, is the depth of intimacy they shared in spiritual
matters. Their correspondence consistently related the details of
their developing relationship with Christ, and the ongoing work
of the Holy Spirit in their lives. Writing to Sam in 1908, Lily
underscored the spiritual communion they shared, even when
apart: "I love you devotedly. I could miss you dreadfully, but I am
not going to. I shall find you daily, and hourly in that trysting place
of blood-bought spirits, the mercy seat."[27] These letters reveal
that the Brengles' deep affection for each other was based on a
common commitment to Christ, expressed in holiness of heart
and life. After Lily's death, Sam wrote about the relationship of
personal holiness to their marriage:

> Before we met each other we had met the Lord and
> entered into that secret [holiness], and when we met
> each other and talked of our experience our two hearts,
> we found, were one. . . . We set ourselves to practice
> "holiness unto the Lord" in all the common affairs and
> tender intimacies of our private life as well as our public
> ministry.[28]

Once on the road, Brengle would have little time to spend
with his family. On occasion, Sam even toyed with the idea of
requesting a home appointment, as indicated in a letter written to
Lily from Australia: "You wonder, darling, whether God means us
to be separated so much. . . . What shall I do? What can I do? Shall
I ask for a division or province? Or a position at headquarters? I
do not feel fit for any of those appointments, but I want you to be
happy, my darling."[29] Lily responded with a mixture of longing
and self-abnegation: "When I think about you personally, and
feel the awful 'accustomedness' to your absence stealing over me,
I hate to have you gone. It seems to me that you must come home
and stay. But when I read of the Holy Spirit descending under
your preaching, and making things new in worn-out desert cities
and corps, I feel the eternal bond between us strengthening."[30]
Thus, Sam and Lily became reconciled to the idea of extended

periods of separation out of a sense of the higher claims of salvation warfare. At the same time, Sam did not fail to realize the depth of his wife's sacrifice. Acknowledging this, he wrote: "It is true, darling, that you have never resisted the Spirit to prevent me from going where the Lord has wanted me, however great the sacrifice may have been, and you shall have your reward."[31]

The Brengle children, however, expressed disappointment with their father's globe-trotting itinerary. This is evident in a letter Sam wrote to Lily while on campaign in Finland in 1907:

> This morning I got your letter echoing the protests of the junior Brengles against India. . . . The Lord sends me. His people need me. Can we not make our sweet children see it? . . . The Lord put me into training for this work and now that I am trained would my sweet children have me fail my Lord? . . . I don't like to be away from home. I'm torn in two by the call to preach to the uttermost parts of the earth, and my love for you and the children and my desire to be with you, but I must work the works of Him that sends me.[32]

Lily would later write to Sam to reassure him of the family's love and support for his ministry: "You are most of all a blessing to me, who love[s] you so, and you are also a blessing to the children, in making them happy, and making them good. We all three love you, devotedly, and count you the biggest blessing the Lord has given us."[33]

Despite his absence, Brengle was very concerned about his children's spiritual condition and their commitment to God's kingdom, as his correspondence with them reflects. George and Elizabeth appreciated their father's efforts to keep in touch with them, especially considering the heavy demands of his itinerant ministry. Although they missed having their father around, they held him in high esteem, George even going so far as to remark: "It is a great thing to have a father who is one's ideal of a man."[34] Brengle's philosophy of parenting evidences his conviction about the importance of modeling holy living in the home:

> If parents have trained their children wisely . . . the character of the loved and esteemed parent will exert a greater authority to mold and fashion the child in righteousness than anything the parent can say or do. The commanding authority and chastenings of the law must yield to the more penetrating and purifying self-

discipline imposed by the recognized faith and hope and love of the parent, the disappointing of which the child feels will bring the deepest and most abiding pain to his own heart. This is God's way.[35]

Brengle also attempted to provide counsel to his children through letters. For example, he exhorted George to maintain moral courage while away at school:

You must have courage to be a Christian. . . . There are two kinds of courage—physical and moral. . . . Physical strength and good health are usually the basis of physical courage. So do not waste your nervous force by any kind of bad habit, nor laziness, by overeating and sleeping, or any sort of excess. Take religious care of your health. Be strong, and you will find it far easier to be brave. Moral courage is a thing of the spirit. Keep on good terms with God, with truth, with your conscience, if you would be truly courageous.[36]

In response to his son's desire to know the direction his life should take, Sam wrote:

The eighteenth chapter of my new book *[When the Holy Ghost Is Come]*, on the Holy Spirit's call to the work may help you. The Lord will help you to find the work He calls you to, if you will listen and obey. If He wants you to be a lawyer then I want you to be a lawyer. If He wants you to teach, I want you to teach. If He wants you in the Church or Army then that is my choice for you. Only be sure you are following His lead. Be sure you have His reasons on your side.[37]

Later, he would write to George about the need to be centered in the will of God: "Old St. Augustine said, and he was wholly right, 'Thou O God, has made us, and we are restless till we rest in Thee.' The soul finds its center in God. He is its true home, and when it finds Him it enters into peace, its unutterable longings are satisfied. I am praying for you daily . . . George, that you may know Him, love Him and delight yourself in Him."[38] Brengle wrote to his son not only about spiritual matters but also about academic concerns. This is evident in the following advice given to George, revealing Sam's literary appreciation and breadth of knowledge:

Your letter about authors in England has just come and I was much interested in what you say. I consider Ruskin by far the most interesting, and I think he would prove the most profitable, of any of the men you mention. To my mind he is in the front rank of masters of style, he is almost, or quite as much a prophet as Carlyle, and his range of subject, will, I think, interest you far more than any of the others you mention. . . . In forming your own style there is no author whom I would prefer you to take as a pattern before Ruskin. His studies in art will open to you a new world of beauty, while his studies in ethics and economics will, I believe, mightily stimulate you. I shall be mighty glad if you thoroughly study and master him. . . . When I laud Ruskin so highly, it is in comparison with other prose writers. Of poets I should put Tennyson first.[39]

Lily raised George and Elizabeth (nicknamed Duckie), cared for her aging father, and sought to minister to those around her during Sam's absence. Her speaking and writing abilities took a back seat to her family responsibilities. Sam and Lily regularly expressed their loving concern for their children's physical, emotional, and spiritual welfare in letters written to each other. George, although physically frail, went on to graduate from Wesleyan University in Middleton, Connecticut; then from Harvard Law School in Boston. Elizabeth, although crippled from infancy, went on to be educated at Centenary Collegiate Institute, and then was married. Writing to Duckie in 1908, Brengle stated: "Your life is as yet largely a blank book, but you are writing, writing over its white pages every day. Write *Veritas* [Truth] on every page. Let the basis of your character, your thoughts and desires be veracity, truthfulness."[40] Elizabeth's spiritual growth and evangelistic interest were, doubtless, a source of encouragement to her parents.[41]

George's decision to enter the legal profession, however, disappointed his parents, who had hoped that their son would become a preacher, especially an Army officer. In reaction to George's announcement, Lily wrote to Sam: "Well, my darling, there it is. It isn't the worst thing that could have happened, but it's a pretty heavy blow. I don't mind his studying law, but he hasn't an ear to hear God."[42] Sam responded in writing to Lily while en route to Sydney, Australia, in 1910:

> God can provide for our boy, so let's keep on believing that instead of filling his nostrils and lungs with the dust of old law books and the smoke of a law office, he shall fill himself with the fresh breezes of God's glorious ministry. . . . It seems to me such an utter waste of time and talent for George to be a lawyer. The world has no need of him in a law office, but it does need him as a preacher of righteousness. I can only pray that he may preach. But I want God to call him.[43]

Lily concurred with her husband's sentiments, writing back to Sam about her futile attempts to dissuade George from his decision:

> The one thing that I desire is his personal acquaintance with God. If God wants him to be a lawyer, I certainly do. But God has no chance with him. He doesn't listen. I told him that I believed God had called him over and again, only he had stopped his ears, and couldn't hear. Bless him! God loves him and is constantly seeking him and will not let him go.[44]

Writing to George directly, Sam addressed what he perceived to be his son's "spiritual defeat":

> I have just received letters from mother and in one of them she copies your letter in which you tell her you have decided to study law, with your reasons, also your reasons why you do not feel you can be an officer or a preacher. I fully respect your reasons, my precious boy, and am not surprised, nor particularly grieved by your decision, but I am sorry, so sorry for the failure and spiritual defeat that lie back of the decision.[45]

In the same letter, Sam identified the areas of defeat in George's life: "lack of courage," "lack of strong conviction," and "fear of hypocrisy." He exhorted his son not to stay defeated:

> Begin to serve God at once. Take your stand. Exercise what little courage you have and it will grow. . . . Don't shrink back for fear of being a hypocrite. Has it not occurred to you that one can be a hypocrite by living below his convictions, as much as by living beyond them? . . . Serve the Lord. Take your stand for Him. Read your Bible. Pray.

Testify. It may not be easy, but if you will yield yourself wholly to God He will fill you with His Holy Spirit, and it will become your supreme joy. Then I shall say a glad Amen! to your being a lawyer, if you feel that is what you ought to be. I don't care what your occupation is, if you only serve God with all your heart and do not allow your spiritual nature to atrophy. I have always wanted you to preach . . . but if you will not preach because you have no call, will you not set to work in real earnest, and at once serve God and your fellow men as a Christian layman?[46]

It is clear that Sam and Lily's chief concern for their son was that he be entirely sanctified and committed to serve the Lord whole-heartedly. In this light, once George had made the decision to pursue law, Sam and Lily, although disappointed, encouraged their son to be an ethically principled lawyer.[47]

In 1930, Sam tried to convince the Army to publish a collection of his correspondence with his wife, sending a sampling of letters, neatly typed, to the Literary Department in London. The following explanation accompanied those letters:

When I read a book that helps me in my spiritual life, I want to know what kind of man he was who wrote it—if his life, his temper, his faith, his love, match his words. These letters, written in the thick of the fight, in the smoke and dust and weariness and exultation and depression and joy and pain of homelessness in far-off lands and intense spiritual battles will answer many questions. . . . They also show Mrs. Brengle's self-sacrificing spirit. They are private letters, written with no thought of publication, therefore they are all the more self-revealing. They are without pose or self-consciousness.[48]

He believed this correspondence, covering a thirty-year period, would help illustrate and reinforce the message of his books. The letters were not published during Brengle's lifetime but were rediscovered at International Headquarters more than fifty years later and form the substance of *Dearest Lily* (1985), edited by William Clark.[49]

Reverend Samuel Logan Brengle, age 22, around the time of completion of his bachelor of arts degree from DePauw University in 1883. Following his graduation, Brengle embarked on a circuit ministry in the Northwest Indiana Conference, serving in four rural churches. He would move east the next year to attend Boston University School of Theology to enhance his ministerial qualifications.

Brengle's influence was widely felt and officially recognized. He received regular promotion in officer rank, becoming a brigadier in 1989, a lieutenant colonel in 1901, a colonel in 1970, and a commissioner—the first American-born officer to attain this rank—in 1926. This photograph was most likely taken upon his appointment as commissioner.

Elizabeth Swift Brengle, known as Lily, was born on July 23, 1849, and raise in Amenia, New York. She attended Vassar College but never graduated due to illness. Although once having turned away from the Christian faith, Lily met The Salvation Army in Glasgow, Scotland, while touring Europe with her sister. She attended her first meeting in Edinburgh, spontaneously addressing the raucous crowd in an effort to calm them. Lily committed herself to Christ soon after in London, where both sisters decided to stay and offer their service to the Army as laypersons. They were commissioned as officers in April 1885, prior to their return to America.

After she established an Army corps in her hometown, Lily's reputation as a preacher spread.. When word of her pioneering work reached Army headquarters, Lily was asked to engage in an itinerant ministry that allowed her to preach in other cities. While in Boston, she met Sam in the summer of 1885.

Sam's first proposal of marriage to Lily was refused, but a second attempt months later, qualified by his newfound commitment to the Army, was accepted. They were married on May 19, 1887, at her family's farm. Two days later, Sam sailed for London to enter the Clapton Training Garrison.

Brengle was promoted to the rank of staff-captain in May 1895 and appointed as district officer for Western Massachusetts and Rhode Island. His one-year tenure in this position was marked by efforts to cultivate spiritual maturity among his officers and soldiers. The photograph above shows Staff-Captain and Mrs. Brengle, Chicago, Illinois, 1896 (courtesy Houston Metropolitan Research Center, Houston Public Library).

Traveling assistants were appointed to accompany Brengle during his arduous campaigns as a Spiritual Special. Pictured here with him is one such assistant, Walter B. Mabee.

The death of his wife, Lily (1915), profoundly affected Sam. This photo is of Colonel Brengle at Lily's grave, Kensico Cemetery, Vahalla, New York.

Concerned with training others in holiness evangelism, Commissioner Brengle appears in this photo with cadets in their 'Torchbearer raid' on Greenwich Village, New York City (1928).

In recognition of his lifetime commitment to holiness evangelism, Brengle was awarded the Order of the Founder by General Evangeline Booth in New York on September 23, 1935. According to the General, this highest honor paid tribute to "the inestimable service. . . rendered to The Salvation Army by the writing of widely circulated books on the saving and sanctifying power of our Lord and Savior Jesus Christ. To this service has been added a lifelong example as a true soldier of the cross and unceasing toils for the benefit of mankind."

Seven members of the 1929 High Council arriving at Sunbury Court, England—(left to right) Alfred Cunningham, Brengle, Gunpei Yamamuro, James Hay, Trounce, Mitchell, and Haines. A special meeting with Commissioner Brengle and these international delegates was held on January 8, 1929, to decide whether General Bramwell Booth was still capable of leading The Salvation Army: Elaborate precautions were taken to provide the Council absolute secrecy. Brengle found Yamamuro to be a kindred spirit before, during, and after this time of crisis.

Commissioner Brengle holds the attention of a group of campers (Girl Guards) at Star Lake Camp in Bloomingdale, New Jersey, circa 1930.

"Have faith in God for the little ones, surround them with an atmosphere of gentleness and love, and suffer them to come unto Him." Brengle stressed the importance of child evangelism, confident in God's ability to work in their hearts even though they lacked full comprehension of the gospel message: "It is not ours to know how far they understand. It is ours to explain the way."

Commissioner Brengle stands with officer friends Colonel Alfred Chandler and Colonel and Mrs. Joseph Atkinson in Old Orchard Beach, Maine, September 17, 1934.

Brengle leads in song at an open air meeting held at the Kensico Cemetery in Valhalla, New York, 1931. William Parkins plays the cornet.

Brengle traveled extensively throughout his officership despite periods of illness, fatigue, and conflicting pressures to write. What was most difficult for Brengle in the early part of his career was his protracted separation from Lily. Their correspondence, however, reflects joy in the spiritual fruit of his mission, in mutual love, and in concern for their children. Although Lily died on April 3, 1915, Brengle persevered for another twenty years. Even with the loss of his beloved soul mate, or perhaps because of it, he threw himself into his work as National Spiritual Special with new resolve. Brengle (shown left with daughter Elizabeth) weakened gradually during his retirement years, although maintaining a regimen of diet and exercise. He resided in St. Petersburg, Florida, during the winter and divided his time in the warmer months between his two children.

Part II

Brengle's Holiness Theology

Chapter 7

Holiness as Gift and Inheritance

Samuel Brengle's holiness theology must be understood in the light of his personal experience of entire sanctification. Throughout his life, Sam constantly referred back to January 9, 1885, not only as his "day of days" but also as his entry into a dynamic life of spiritual blessing, characterized by purity, power, and above all, love. Of this experience he wrote: "One wondrous morning He sanctified my soul. He purified my affections; He cleansed my heart; He bent my will into loving harmony with His will. He captured and held my whole being until I adored and wondered and worshiped, and wept for love and joy. Glory to God!"[1] In addition to the purifying and conforming work of the Spirit, Brengle came to experience an abundant harvest of spiritual fruit manifest in his life. In later years, he would reflect on events leading up to and including this transformative encounter.

> I went to Boston to complete my theological studies. There I heard a sermon on the "Baptism of the Holy Ghost," and I began to cry to God for it. God searched me. I saw the corruptions of my heart as never before. I was humbled into the dust. I confessed. I hid nothing. I opened my heart to the light, I wept and prayed. . . . Day and night for weeks I asked, I sought, I knocked. . . . Then one glad, sweet January morning suddenly the door opened at which I had knocked so importunately; I received, I found what I so earnestly sought. It was far beyond what I received when I was saved as a boy. That was the day, dawn; this the broad day with the sun risen in my soul. That was "peace with God;" this was

"the peace of God." That was forgiveness and the new birth; this was cleansing from all sin, heart purity, and fullness of love and joy and peace and long-suffering. That was accompanied by the witness of the Spirit; this by the fullness of His indwelling. It was the fulfilment of that great group of promises and assurances of Jesus in John 14:15–23. He had fulfilled His promise and the Father had given me the "Other Comforter." . . . Christ was revealed in me, and, oh, how I loved it! It seemed I would nearly die of love. . . . My whole inner being was transformed. God had blessed my ministry before, but it now took on new forms and new power.[2]

Elsewhere, Brengle likewise characterized his holiness experience as a transition from darkness to light, with an emphasis on the witness of the Holy Spirit and the indwelling presence of Christ.

I passed from gloom to perplexity and almost despair to light and peace and sweet and instantly satisfying assurance. The Comforter had come. God spoke to my heart and my heart knew and responded to the Divine voice, and doubt and fear and perplexity vanished as the shadows of the night flee before the rising of a cloudless sun. . . . I found it [the blessing] was love made perfect. . . . It was Christ found within me, the hope of glory.[3]

Testifying to his experience of entire sanctification, Brengle used a variety of terms to express the nature of holiness. In 1922, he wrote:

Thirty-seven years ago this day God sanctified my soul. He cleansed my heart. He baptized me with the Holy Spirit. He revealed His Son to me, and the blessing and the Blesser abide with me still. . . . An unutterable desire possesses me to glorify my Master in my life and in my death, and to bless His people and help them discover the riches that are theirs by right as heirs of God and joint heirs with Christ.[4]

A year later, he reflected metaphorically on "the most memorable of all days," when God ". . . purified my heart and took undisputed possession of my whole being—body, mind and soul. Peace poured into my heart like a river. . . . Joy bubbled up within me like a fountain. . . . Love burned within me like a fire—the love of

God shed abroad in my heart by the Holy Ghost which was given unto me."5

Brengle maintained the importance of holiness as a doctrine to be believed and an experience to be enjoyed, but he also stressed the importance of testifying to the blessing. This was to be done not only at the earliest opportunity but on an ongoing basis—because it was possible to lose the blessing if one failed to testify to it. According to Brengle, those who have been entirely sanctified are "under a solemn obligation to let everybody know that Jesus is alive and that He can save to the uttermost."6 Public witness to the experience of entire sanctification played an important role in Brengle's own spiritual growth. Once again, we see this illustrated in his own account, titled "My Personal Testimony," which implicitly connects witness with further manifestations of God's sanctifying grace.

> On January 9, 1885, at about nine o'clock in the morning, God sanctified my soul. . . . The following day, I preached on the subject as clearly and forcibly as I could, and ended with my testimony. . . . That confession put me on record. It cut the bridges down behind me. . . . God saw that I meant to be true till death. So, two mornings after that, just as I got out of bed and was reading some the words of Jesus, He gave me such a blessing as I never dreamed a man could have this side of Heaven. It was a Heaven of love that came into my heart. I walked out over Boston Common before breakfast, weeping for joy and praising God. Oh, how I loved! In that hour I knew Jesus, and I loved Him till it seemed my heart would break with love. I loved the sparrows, I loved the dogs, I loved the horses, I loved the little urchins in the streets, I loved the strangers who hurried past me, I loved the heathen—I loved the whole world. Do you know what holiness is? It is pure love. Do you want to know what the baptism of the Holy Ghost is? It is not a mere sentiment. . . . It is a baptism of love that brings every thought into captivity to the Lord Jesus; that casts out all fear; that burns up all doubt and unbelief . . . that brings one into perfect and unbroken sympathy with the Lord Jesus Christ in His toil and travail to bring a lost and rebel world back to God. God did that for me, bless His holy name!7

It is clear, from Brengle's own experience of entire sanctification, that several elements played a role in the process of full appropriation of the blessing, including consecration, faith, peace, assurance, witness, preaching, and anointing. Writing about this a year before his death, Brengle recalled:

> On the ninth day of January, 1885, fifty years ago, I came to an end of myself. My whole being went over to Christ and Him crucified, to share in His cross, His reproach, His travail, to be His man, His slave of love, and in that moment I found it easy to believe. The word came to me, "If we confess our sins, He is faithful and just to forgive us our sins, and to cleanse us from all unrighteousness." God had spoken to my inmost soul in those words, and especially in the words "to cleanse us from all unrighteousness," and with my whole heart I believed and in that moment a deeper and more assured peace than that which came to me as a child on the wind-swept prairies took possession of my heart. I knew that I was clean, and my fellow students in the school of theology, who saw me immediately after, said that they recognized the inward work of the deep peace and light reflected on my face. I preached on the subject and testified, and then the great anointing came; the Comforter moved into my heart. . . . Such love as I never dreamed could fill a human soul flooded through all my being.[8]

FULL SALVATION

One of Brengle's favorite phrases to describe the experience of entire sanctification was "full salvation"—salvation in all its fullness.[9] The purpose of Christ's death on the cross was to reconcile sinners to God—and to make them holy.[10] Holiness "is the perfected work for which His blood was outpoured and the crowning work of the Holy Spirit." Salvation is thus viewed dynamically by Brengle to include both justification and sanctification, but even holiness has room for growth and development: "Conversion is not your rest. We rest a little bit here but soon find we must arise and press on. . . . Fullness of the Spirit is your rest. It is God you want. But even here you must, like Paul, 'forget the things that are behind' and press hard after Jesus. . . . Glorification is the final rest."[11] Since all Christians are in need of fresh spiritual renewals and filling, it was obvious to

Brengle that "all the lovers of Jesus should in these days seek fresh renewings and a greater fullness of the Holy Spirit."[12]

He also maintained that there was a biblical mandate for holiness: "Anybody who reads his Bible with sincerity . . . will see that it plainly teaches that God expects His people to be holy, and that we must be holy to be happy and useful here, and to enter the kingdom of heaven hereafter."[13] In further addressing the need for holiness, he wrote:

> We should be holy because God wants us to be holy. He commands it. He says: "As He which hath called you is holy, so be ye holy in all manner of conversation; because it is written, Be ye holy, for I am holy" (1 Peter 1:15–16). God is earnest about this. It is God's will, and it cannot be evaded. . . . To many, however, the command seems harsh. They have been accustomed to commands accompanied by curses or kicks or blows. But we must not forget that "God is love," and His commands are not harsh, but kind. They come from the fullness of an infinitely loving and all-wise heart. They are meant for our good.[14]

Thus, for Brengle, holiness is not optional. In fact, it is the reason for Christ's atoning sacrifice: "We should be holy because Jesus died to make us holy . . ." (Titus 2:14; Ephesians 5:25–27). From a utilitarian perspective, holiness is required for usefulness: "So long as there are any roots of sin in the heart the Holy Spirit cannot have all His way in us, and our usefulness is hindered. But when our hearts are clean the Holy Spirit dwells within, and then we have power for service." Holiness is also a safeguard against sin, for "sin in the heart is more dangerous than gunpowder in the cellar." Ultimately, holiness has eschatological implications: "We should be holy because . . . without holiness 'no man shall see the Lord'" (Hebrews 12:14).[15]

With his characteristic "sanctified sanity," Brengle viewed holiness as "reasonable":

> It is a duty to be entirely sanctified to God. Because God has commanded His creatures to love Him with all their hearts. . . . It is reasonable that every professor of religion be sanctified to God entirely. When you were sinners, you were all sin and no holiness; so now you are professors, it is but reasonable that you should be all holiness and no

sin. . . . It is but reasonable that the creature should love its Creator. It is certainly reasonable that the redeemed should perfectly love his compassionate Redeemer.[16]

Such reasonable relatedness to Christ, however, is meant to fit the believer to serve God's eternal purposes: "The baptism of the Holy Ghost is to bring us into union with Christ, into loving fellowship with the Heavenly Father, to fit us snugly into God's great, complex scheme of life, and equip us for such service or sacrifice as falls to our lot."[17]

Brengle, following the lead of his mentor, Daniel Steele, understood the Holy Spirit as the representative and executor of the Godhead, in that He "represents and executes the redemptive plans and purposes of the Triune God."[18] In addition to the roles of revelation, conviction, illumination, purification, and empowerment, Brengle emphasized the transforming presence of this "abiding Guest," in the conforming of the Christian to the image of Christ.[19] Holiness thus involves radical transformation:

> Glory to God! It's possible, right down here, when sin and Satan have once ruined us, for the Son of God to thus transform us, by enabling us to "put off the old man and his deeds," and to "put on the new man, which after God is created in righteousness and true holiness," being "renewed in knowledge after the image of Him that created him."[20]

In this light, it is important to note that Brengle's understanding of full salvation involved both a salvation *from* (negative) and a salvation *for* (positive) dimension with characteristic emphasis on the latter. Brengle's optimism of grace is evident in the way he understood God's redemptive purposes:

> His object is not alone to save them from hell, but to save them from sin, and not from its guilt and penalty only, but from its pollution and power and the love that they have for it. Nor is it merely to save men from sin, which is rather a negative work, but to save them into all goodness and love and holiness through a vital and eternal union with Jesus Christ . . . a union that gives perpetual vigor and energy and fruitfulness in righteousness and holiness to all the powers of the soul, filling it with grace and truth.[21]

HOLINESS AS CRISIS AND PROCESS

In line with his Wesleyan heritage, Brengle stressed that sanctification begins at regeneration—"initial sanctification." Simultaneous with justification, the new convert is born again by the Spirit of God and begins a lifelong process of growth in grace. However, Brengle also taught that no one experiences the blessing of a clean heart until a later point in time. This is necessarily so because until the Holy Spirit enters the believer's heart, there is no awareness of the depths of depravity within. Although the *guilt* of past sins is taken care of in justification, the *sin nature* (and its ongoing effects) remains in the believer and needs to be addressed:

> The fact is, that neither the Bible [n]or experience proves that a man gets a clean heart when he is converted, but just the contrary. He does have his sins forgiven; he does receive the witness of adoption into God's family; he does have his affections changed; but before he has gone very far he will find his patience mixed up with some degree of impatience, his kindness mixed with wrath, his meekness mixed with anger . . . his humility mixed with pride, his loyalty to Jesus mixed with a shame of the cross, and in fact the fruit of the Spirit, and the works of the flesh, in greater or less degree, are all mixed up together. But this is done away with when he gets a clean heart, and it will take a second work of grace, preceded by a whole-hearted consecration, and as definite [an] act of faith as that which preceded his conversion, to get it.[22]

Brengle pointed to New Testament evidence to support this claim, finding such not only in the Pentecostal experience of the apostles but, more particularly, in Paul's exhortations for *Christians* to "put off the old," and "put on the new" nature in passages like Ephesians 4:22–24 and Colossians 3:9–10.[23] Death to the old nature is something that "is not to be a slow, evolutionary process, but an instantaneous work, wrought in the heart of the humble believer by the Holy Ghost."[24]

Thus, entire sanctification as an instantaneous gift—given subsequent to justification, in response to consecration and faith—was Brengle's experience and his consistent message. In line with both John and Charles Wesley, he believed that although this divine gift is received in a moment in time, this only signifies the beginning of a lifelong growth in holiness. Brengle consistently emphasized both *critical* (crisis) and *progressive* (process) elements in his holiness teaching.[25] Often criticized for maintaining this position by those who understood holiness only as a growth process, Brengle would respond with analogy:

> Sanctification is an instantaneous act, as instantaneous as death. The approach to death may be gradual and prolonged, but there is a moment when a man is alive and the next moment he may be dead. So there is a moment when a man's heart is not pure, and the very next moment, through faith in the atoning work of Christ . . . the blessed work may be done. But we must beware of thinking that there is no further development. We are bidden to "grow in grace." We have entered into a rich grace through this act of sanctification and we are to grow in it, though we cannot grow into it. There is no end to the further development of the soul that is purified from sin. When you have pulled the weeds out of your garden, the vegetables do not cease to grow. So when the pride and jealousy and hasty tempers and inner corruptions of the heart are gone, the graces of the Spirit have room and opportunity for unlimited development.[26]

In light of later misrepresentations of his holiness teaching as all "crisis" and no "process," it is important to note that for Brengle, entire sanctification involves not merely the removal of "weeds" but the dynamic of an unhindered and unending growth of charisms.[27]

Brengle employed other metaphors to illustrate the importance of the critical, in relation to the progressive, dimensions of entire sanctification. For example, he maintained that a man does not grow into a coat, though he may grow in it. He must first put it on. In the same way, a man may grow in grace but not into it. Similarly, a swimmer may swim in water, but not into it.[28] In using metaphor, Brengle followed John Wesley's lead in responding to criticism concerning his stress on the critical dimensions of entire sanctification. Wesley maintained that "there is growth in the womb before birth and long, long growth after . . . but the birth itself is in a matter of moments."[29] Thus, holiness must involve both critical and progressive dimensions, but the important thing to recognize is that crisis plays a decisive role in the process of entire sanctification.[30]

Brengle sought to clarify the distinction between the purification experienced in the critical moment of entire sanctification and the maturation or growth process flowing from it:

> You must keep "looking unto Jesus, the Author and Finisher of our faith" (Hebrews 12:2). Look unto Him, not for immediate maturity. That is a process. It comes by growth. Look unto Him for purity, which you can have now by faith in the Blood which He shed for your instant cleansing from all sin; faith in God's love and willingness to make you clean and sanctify you now; faith in the presence and power of the Holy Spirit within you to burn out all selfish pride and temper and sin and make you all clean and Christlike within and to do it now. . . . The difference [is thus] between purity which is obtained by faith, and maturity which is attained by growth. . . . The youngest Christian may be pure in heart, perfect in love, but it may take years to arrive at maturity. . . . In 2 Peter 1:4–8, the Apostle writes to those who, through faith in the exceeding great and precious promises, have been made partakers of the divine nature. . . . They have been purified, sanctified, made clean. But now they are to go on unto maturity.[31]

He also believed that the growth in grace, which followed entire sanctification, included further critical moments of empowerment: "But while the Holy Spirit abides in the believer, there yet seems to be the need for frequent renewals of the power He bestows."[32]

Brengle taught that the experience of entire sanctification makes one progressively better—increasingly more like Jesus Christ. This process involves both "subtraction" and "addition" in that the holy life is evidenced by the removal of the works of the sinful nature and the ever-increasing fruit of the Spirit. In describing a form of subtraction, he often spoke about putting to death the evil temper. In terms of addition, he consistently delineated the nature of holiness as spiritual fruit-bearing with the emphasis on love. Furthermore, these characteristics of Christ, made possible in us by the Holy Spirit, must find their expression in the context of our association with others. In this regard, such holiness is not only ethical but also social in orientation.[33]

HOLINESS AND THE POSSIBILITIES OF GRACE

Brengle maintained that the experience of entire sanctification brings deliverance from the power of sin in the Christian life: "The converted man is bound to his inbred sin, Jesus looses him and he is free indeed. It is a complete deliverance, a perfect liberty . . . that Jesus gives, by bringing the soul under the law of liberty, which is the law of love."[34] In this regard, Brengle interpreted Romans 7:9–25 as a struggle of the regenerate Christian—the one who struggles with the sin nature that remains in the heart after conversion. Deliverance from this inner conflict between the new and old natures is possible in the experience of entire sanctification. Thus, holiness deals with the sin nature—not only with sins.[35] In light of 2 Peter 1:4, Brengle wrote ". . . the apostle speaks of being made 'partakers of the divine nature, having escaped the corruption that is in the world through lust.' That is holiness. To escape from the corruption of our evil hearts and receive the divine nature."[36]

Brengle reflected on the unsettled state of his own spiritual life prior to his experience of entire sanctification, referring to such as an irrepressible conflict with the carnal mind."[37] He maintained that in order for entire sanctification to be experienced, the "carnal mind" (sin nature) must be removed: "This evil within must die, this seed of all sin must be destroyed, and this is something that can and does take place just as soon after conversion as we can see the need and the possibility of its being done, and we come to Jesus with all our heart, and with perfect faith to have it done."[38] Entire sanctification involves the casting out of the "old man" and the enthronement of Christ within, thus resolving the warfare between flesh and Spirit.[39] Brengle wrote: "The Bible tells us that it is perfect deliverance from sin. . . . Not one bit of sin is left . . . for we are free from sin (Romans 6). And we are henceforth to 'reckon ourselves dead indeed unto sin, but alive unto God, through Jesus Christ our Lord.'"[40]

It is clear that Brengle, along with other nineteenth century holiness advocates, maintained an eradicationist position with regard to sin in the entirely sanctified. At times, he used graphic metaphors to describe the dynamic effect of entire sanctification on the sin nature. Once, he even likened holiness to dynamite applied to a stump:

> After conversion he finds his old sinful nature much like a tree which has been cut down, but the stump still left. The tree causes no more bother, but the stump will still bring forth little shoots if it is not watched. The quickest and most effective way is to put some dynamite under the stump, and blow it up. Just so, God wants to put the dynamite of the Holy Ghost [the word *dynamite* comes from the Greek word for power; Acts 1:8] into every converted soul, and forever do away with that old, troublesome, sinful nature, so that he can truly say, "old things have passed away, and behold all things have become new."[41]

In a letter to Rev. Charles G. Trumbull, editor of the *Sunday School Times,* written on April 6, 1934, Brengle defended his position against the Calvinist understanding of holiness as merely repression of sin.

> The term eradication is not a Scriptural term and I don't remember having used it; however, I cannot see that it differs radically in meaning from John's words where he says that "the blood of Jesus Christ . . . cleanseth us from all sin" (see 1 John 1:7). If all is cleansed away, no sin is left. Of course, the old Calvinistic view of sin is based upon the idea that we are still under the "Adamic Law" of absolute perfection, while I hold with Paul and Wesley, that we are no longer under the law, but under the law of love to Christ. . . . The carnal mind can be, and is, destroyed out of the heart that is made clean by the precious blood of Christ.[42]

In underscoring his commitment to the eradication of sin in the entirely sanctified, Brengle reveals the influence of Daniel Steele. Referring to Steele's *Mile-Stone Papers,* Brengle quotes from a chapter titled "Repression Not Sanctification" to make his point.

> It is a remarkable fact that . . . the Greek language richly abounds in words signifying repression, a half score of which occur in the New Testament. . . . Yet not one of these . . . is used of inbred sin; but such verbs as signify to cleanse, to purify, to mortify or kill, to crucify, and to

destroy. We have diligently sought in both Old Testament and the New for exhortations to seek the repression of sin. The uniform command is to put away sin, to purify the heart, to purge out the old leaven, and to seek to be sanctified throughout soul, body and spirit. Repressive power is nowhere ascribed to the blood of Christ, but rather *purgative efficacy*. Now, if these which signify to cleanse, wash, crucify, mortify, or make dead, and to destroy are all used in a typical or metaphorical sense, it is very evident that the literal truth signified is something far stronger than repression. It is *eradication, extinction of being, destruction.* The repressive theory of holiness is out of harmony with the divine purity. Holiness in man must mean precisely the same as holiness in God. . . . Who dares to say that God's holiness is different in kind from man's holiness save that one is original and the other inwrought by the Holy Ghost?[43]

Another issue relating to the possibilities of grace in this life was whether sanctification involves imparted or imputed righteousness. Answering those who believed imputed righteousness was all that could be expected in this life, Brengle wrote:

The people who hold this doctrine are still under the law, and live in the seventh chapter of Romans, and are perpetually sighing: "Oh, wretched man that I am, who shall deliver me from the body of this death?" Now it is true that the law makes no man righteous or holy, but Christ dwelling in our hearts does. . . . This is the glorious liberty of the Gospel. This is what Jesus came to do; not to impute righteousness and holiness to us, but to make us right and holy. . . . And so the entirely sanctified Christian sees that Jesus has imparted purity and love and every grace to him. . . . He is not holy in himself in such a sense that he no longer needs Christ, any more than the branch is fruitful in such a sense that it no longer needs the vine. . . . He needs Christ every instant, and he has Him every instant, and having Him he has holiness and power.[44]

Brengle recognized that there was a certain mystery concerning the gift of entire sanctification, yet he consistently urged others to share his 'optimism of grace.' "Don't be scared by the word sanctification," he invoked, "Do not be dismayed in the presence of that experience. Do not say 'impossible.'"[45] Although freely admitting that the mechanics of Spirit baptism are unknown, Brengle emphasized the transformative effects of the experience:

> If you ask how the Holy Spirit can dwell within us and work through us without destroying our personality, I cannot tell. . . . How can fire dwell in a piece of iron until its very appearance is that of fire, and it becomes a firebrand? I cannot tell. Now, what fire . . . do[es] in iron . . . the Holy Spirit does in the spirits of men who believe on Jesus, follow Him wholly and trust Him intelligently. He dwells in them and inspires them, till they are all alive with the very life of God. The transformation wrought in men by the baptism with the Holy Ghost, and the power that fills them, are amazing beyond measure.[46]

The extent to which such transformation changes the individual, without diminishing individuality, is illustrated in Brengle's essay, "Is Temper Destroyed or Sanctified?" It is clear from this piece that human faculties are cleansed and enabled, not diminished, in the experience of entire sanctification:

> Temper, as usually spoken of, is not a faculty or power of the soul, but is rather an irregular, passionate, violent expression of selfishness. When selfishness is destroyed by love, by the incoming of the Holy Spirit revealing Jesus to us as an uttermost Savior, and creating within us a clean heart, of course such temper is gone. . . . so, strictly speaking, sanctification does not destroy self, but it destroys selfishness—the abnormal and mean and disordered manifestation and assertion of the self. . . . he may still feel indignation in the presence of wrong, but it will not be rash, violent, explosive and selfish as before he was sanctified, but calm and orderly, and holy and determined, like that of God. It will be the wholesome, natural antagonism of holiness and righteousness to all unrighteousness and evil.[47]

Note the redirection of temper (natural energy) through the destruction of selfishness (subtraction) and the infilling of the Spirit (addition), thus having what John Wesley called "holy tempers."

THE HOLINESS HERITAGE

In line with Salvation Army doctrine, Brengle taught that entire sanctification was "the privilege of all believers," and that as such, it represented a divine heritage, birthright, or inheritance to be claimed. "The Pentecostal baptism is for an inner circle. It is a family affair. It is for the children who have become sons and daughters of God through penitent, obedient faith. It is part of their heritage. It is the portion of that immeasurable inheritance in Christ which is bestowed upon them while on earth."[48] Brengle maintained that all believers were called unto holiness, and the experience of the same "fits us for the enjoyment and the glad employment of the full heritage in Glory." As part of the Christian's inheritance, however, it must be appropriated in order to be enjoyed. Certain outcomes follow from failure to claim this birthright: "If we turn away from it, we disappoint our Heavenly Father, we frustrate His kindly and wondrous purpose and our portion is given to another."[49] Thus, for Brengle, rejecting heart holiness has serious consequences:

> The professing Christian who hears of heart-holiness and cleansing from all sin as a blessing he may now have by faith, and, convicted of his need of the blessing and of God's desire and willingness to bestow it upon him now, refuses to seek it in whole-hearted affectionate consecration and faith, is resisting the Holy Spirit. And such resistance imperils the soul beyond computation.[50]

Although he never preached a "holiness or hell" message, a few passages in Brengle's writings implicitly point in that direction. For example, he referred to the entirely sanctified as those who must ". . . guard the fire in their hearts as their sole protection upon earth and their passport to Heaven."[51] Elsewhere he wrote: "No time to be holy! We have all the time there is, and we are making our destiny of weal or woe as we use or misuse it."[52] Holiness, as a foretaste of heaven, is also viewed as an eschatological gift, an inheritance which ". . . will fit us for the final and full reward, but which, rejected or neglected, will leave us eternal paupers among those who weep and gnash their teeth in outer darkness."[53]

Not only did Brengle view entire sanctification as essential for the Christian life, both now and for eternity, he also saw the preaching and teaching of the holiness message as the chief legacy of the Army's message and mission. Reflecting on this priority in William Booth's ministry, Brengle quoted the Founder as publicly stating: "If ever The Salvation Army ceases to get men baptized with the Holy Ghost, I pray God He may then rid the world of The Salvation Army." Brengle maintained that, although the Army was Booth's life work, ". . . he cherished it only as a tool, a means of winning men to Christ, enthroning Him in their hearts, and making them temples of the Holy Ghost. He felt that if it ever ceased to accomplish this it would become a dead thing, a corpse, an encumbrance to the Master's cause, and he then wished that it might be buried out of sight."[54] Affirming the Founder's view of the centrality of the doctrine of holiness to Salvation Army mission, Brengle wrote metaphorically of its foundational importance:

> One of the Army's central doctrines and most valued and precious experiences is that of Heart-Holiness. The bridge which the Army throws across the impassable gulf that separates the sinner from the Savior—who pardons that He may purify, who saves that He may sanctify—rests on these two abutments: the forgiveness of sins through simple, penitent, obedient faith in a crucified Redeemer, and the purifying of the heart and empowering of the soul through the anointing of the Holy Spirit, given by its risen and ascended Lord, and received not by works, but by faith. Remove either of these abutments, and the bridge falls; preserve them in strength, and a world of lost and despairing sinners can be confidently invited and urged to come and be gloriously saved.[55]

Brengle believed that holiness was the secret to the Army's success, stressing the importance of both the doctrine and experience of entire sanctification. He discerned the keys to spiritual leadership from great biblical leaders. From such examples of those who had a personal encounter with God, and sought to maintain and deepen such an experience, Brengle drew a parallel for Army leadership: "Here we discover the importance of the doctrine and experience of holiness through the baptism of the Holy Spirit to Salvation Army leaders. . . . Nothing is so vital to our cause as a mastery of the doctrine and an assured and joyous possession of the pentecostal experience of holiness through the indwelling Spirit."[56] Brengle emphasized the need for Army leaders to perpetuate not only the doctrine but also the experience of holiness. In this, he reveals his interest in both "head" and "heart" holiness: "Simply to be skilled in the doctrine is not sufficient for us as leaders. . . . We must not only know and preach the truth, but we must be living examples of the saving and sanctifying power of the truth."[57] He exhorted these leaders in practical terms to model the life of holiness:

> We . . . must be holy, else we shall at last experience the awful woe of those who, having preached to others, are yet themselves castaways. . . . Our lives must square with our teaching. . . . However blessed and satisfactory our present experience may be, we must not rest in it. . . . If we have the blessing—not the harsh, narrow, unprogressive exclusiveness which often calls itself . . . holiness, but the vigorous, courageous, self-sacrificing, tender, pentecostal experience of perfect love—we shall both save ourselves and enlighten the world.[58]

Chapter 8

Ethical Dimensions of Holiness

When describing the work of God in entire sanctification, Brengle preferred the use of ethical terms, emphasizing heart purity, relational transformation, and Christlikeness.

HEART PURITY

Brengle often resorted to language of the heart, alternately equating the blessing with having a "perfect heart" or "an undivided heart."[1] He underscored the fact that purity of heart is no respecter of persons. What God desires are perfect religious affections, not perfect intellectual ability: "You may be ignorant and illiterate; your abilities may be very limited . . . but you can have an undivided, perfect heart toward God. . . . It is not the perfect head but the perfect heart which God blesses."[2] Although the Christian life is marked by growth in grace, Brengle insisted that purity of heart is the result of God's gracious work of cleansing, not the result of a process of maturation. "Holiness . . . is not maturity, but purity: a clean heart in which the Holy Spirit dwells, filling it with pure, tender, and constant love to God and man. . . . All that God asks is that the heart should be cleansed from sin and full of love."[3] He understood such heart cleansing to take place in a moment of time, as an instantaneous work of grace. This makes possible constant, closer communion with God, yielding dynamic growth in relationship.

Brengle's emphasis on the critical nature of God's sanctifying work was balanced by his understanding of the dynamic nature of perfect love. He illustrated the relationship between the critical and progressive dimensions of heart purity as follows:

> There is a plant in South America called the "pitcher plant" on the stalk of which is a little, cup-like formation which is always full of water. When it is very small, it is full; as it grows larger, it is full, and when it reaches its maturity, it is still full. That illustrates holiness. All that God asks is that the heart should be cleansed from sin and full of love, whether it be the tender heart of a little child, with feeble powers of loving, or of the full-grown man, or of the flaming archangel before the throne. This is holiness, and this only. It is nothing less than this, and it can be nothing more.[4]

Thus, for Brengle, holiness is dynamic and improvable: "But we must beware of thinking that there is no further development. We are bidden to 'grow in grace.' We may, and should, increase daily in knowledge, in good judgment, in understanding, in ever-increasing love and devotion to God and to the well-being of our fellow-men."[5] To further illustrate this point, Brengle wrote the following about the model spiritual life of the Apostle Paul:

> Purity comes instantly when the surrendered, pardoned soul intelligently and gladly, in simple faith, yields all its redeemed faculties and powers in an utter, unconditional, irreversible dedication to its Lord. But the ripe mellowness, the serene wisdom, the Christlike composure of maturity come through manifold experiences as we walk with Jesus in service, in sacrifice, and suffering, and learn of Him.[6]

Brengle viewed the heart as the place of God's habitation within the entirely sanctified: "When He baptizes us with the Holy Spirit, the holy of holies within us is then occupied, and out from that center of our being His life radiates through our affections, dispositions, tempers and activities."[7] God made the heart to be His home, but the Fall brought about a disordering of both the "will and affections," the will becoming "rebellious and selfish," the affections becoming "estranged from God." As "heirs of a sinful nature," humankind shares in a universal condition of "heart-depravity."[8]

Brengle maintained that holiness is a restoration of the "right heart relations to God,"[9] understanding redemption as involving not only the forgiveness of sin but also the restoration of "the lost moral likeness of God." Since God is holy, His children are meant to share in this nature. "God wants us to be like Himself, wants the lost image restored, the heart-likeness renewed." Thus, Brengle interpreted Jesus' command in Matthew 5:48 to "be perfect" as to be "perfect in love." Conceding that humankind cannot be like God in His "greatness" (His "eternity, power, wisdom, and knowledge"), he believed that it is possible, by God's sanctifying grace, to be like God in our heart "essence," namely, "in our goodness, holiness, love, humility, gentleness, meekness, and truth."[10]

Brengle's holiness theology placed a priority on the ethical dimension of heart purity when dealing with spiritual empowerment, since the power of the Holy Spirit cannot flow unhindered in the presence of sin. Accordingly, he wrote:

> Many have looked at the promise of power when the Holy Ghost is come . . . and they have hastily and erroneously jumped to the conclusion that the baptism with the Holy Ghost is for work and service only. It does bring power—the power of God—and it does fit for service . . . the proclamation of salvation and the conditions of peace to a lost world; but not that alone, nor primarily. The primary, the basal work of the baptism is that of cleansing. . . . The great hindrance in the hearts of God's children to the power of the Holy Ghost is inbred sin— that dark, defiant, evil something within that struggles for the mastery of the soul . . . and when the Holy Spirit comes, His first work is to sweep away that something, that carnal principle, and make free and clean all the channels of the soul. . . . This purification from sin is promised. . . . it is necessary. . . . [and this] deliverance is possible. . . . It is primarily for this that the Holy Ghost comes as a baptism of fire: that sin might be consumed out of us.[11]

Nonetheless, once the heart has been made clean, the resources of divine empowerment are available not only for service, ". . . but He is also given to us for power to live holy lives, to be patient under trial . . . power to love our enemies and the good people who try our souls, power to suffer patiently, power to sacrifice gladly, power for all manner of holy living and holy dying."[12] Thus, the cleansed heart receives power ". . . over the world . . . over the flesh . . . over the devil."[13]

RELATIONAL DIMENSIONS OF CHRISTIAN PERFECTION

It is clear that Brengle understood holiness in relational terms—as perfect love. Thus, the purpose of redemption is the restoration of such love: "When sin came man was estranged from God and filled with selfishness. Salvation is restoration to love. Holiness is restoration to perfect love through the baptism of the Spirit, which destroys everything that is against love."[14] In reflecting on his own experience of the baptism of the Holy Spirit, he described such in terms of God's gift of a "clean heart," when "a heaven of love . . . came into my heart." Brengle elaborated further on this restored love and its effects:

> Do you want to know what holiness is? It is pure love. Do you want to know what the baptism of the Holy Ghost is? It is not a happy sensation that passes away in a night. It is a baptism of love that "brings every thought into captivity to the Lord Jesus" (2 Corinthians 10:5); that "casts out all fear" (1 John 4:18); that burns up doubt and unbelief . . . that makes one hate uncleanness, lying, and deceit . . . that makes Heaven and Hell eternal realities; that makes one patient and gentle . . . that brings one into perfect and unbroken sympathy with the Lord Jesus Christ in His toil and travail to bring a lost and rebel world back to God.[15]

Brengle maintained further that "the human heart must have some supreme affection," and those who love God with all their heart have experienced holiness. Evidences of perfect love include: "obedience, patience under tribulation, peace like a river—perfect peace, abounding joy—not raptures, deliverance from sin—[the] expulsive power of a new affection, freedom from fear—fear being cast out, and a glorious sense of fellowship and communion with God."[16] Holiness is, for Brengle, a divinely enabled response to God's love in Christ:

> God loved us with a great and everlasting love, and with loving-kindness He is ever drawing us away from sin to Himself. He has loved us out of our sins, and He would love us into holiness. . . . The call to holiness is the wooing of a great Lover seeking to draw His loved one

into perfect love and fellowship with Himself. Holiness is love made perfect—love so filling the heart and mind and soul that sin is expelled and the great Lover is enthroned in peace and purity and power where sin had reigned.[17]

As "perfect deliverance from sin," such love expels from the heart "all hatred and every evil temper contrary to love," resulting in "a state in which God is loved and trusted with a perfect heart."[18] Understanding the Holy Spirit as love personified, reflecting the dynamic love between God the Father and God the Son, Brengle viewed holiness as a baptism into the love of the Father, as manifest in the Son, by the power of the Spirit. Brengle wrote about his own experience of this love:

Jesus was revealed to my spiritual consciousness, revealed in me, and my soul was filled with unutterable love. . . . This is the perfect love about which the Apostle John wrote. . . . In it is personality. This love thinks, wills, talks with me, corrects me, instructs and teaches me. And then I knew that God the Holy Ghost was in this love, and that this love was God, for "God is love."[19]

In viewing holiness in terms of heart purity, Brengle understood this "as a kind of perfection required of His people by God." At the same time, however, he realized the need to qualify the meaning of the word *perfection* in order to clarify the extent to which individuals can expect to be made perfect in this life. He did this by contrasting being made perfect in love with other types of perfection.

God alone is absolutely perfect in all His attributes, and to such perfection we can never hope to attain. Then there is a perfection possessed by the angels which we shall never have in this world. Adam also had certain perfections of body and mind which are out of our reach. There is, however, a perfection which we are given to understand God requires in us, and it is a perfection not of head but of heart; not of knowledge, but of goodness, of humility, of love, of faith. Such a perfection God desires us to have, and such a perfection we may have.[20]

Brengle further delineated the nature of Christian perfection in relation to characteristics manifest in Christ.

The perfection of heart, of purity, of goodness, was seen in Jesus in several particulars. *First:* perfect submission. We are to be perfectly submitted to God . . . in perfect submission to His will. . . . *Second:* like Jesus, we may perfectly trust God. We may possess a confidence in God that holds out in ways that we do not understand . . . that will trust with all the heart. . . . *Third:* God desires His people to be perfect in love; to love Him perfectly . . . to love with all our hearts—with all our power to love. . . . *Fourth:* there must be perfect loyalty. Love is not an emotion. . . . It is a deep principle, revealing itself in perfect loyalty to God. . . . *Fifth:* God also requires of us perfect obedience. Our performance may not always be perfect, while our spirit may be perfect.[21]

Paradoxically, such perfection in love leads to a form of servitude. This is what Brengle referred to as becoming a "love-slave." Commenting on the New Testament writers who wrote as servants of Jesus Christ "in an age when labor and service were a badge of inferiority and shame," he maintained that in the new era ushered in by Christ, service became a "badge of royalty" and a "distinguishing mark of the sons of God and the citizens of Heaven on earth." As servants, they considered themselves "slaves of God and of Christ." Recognizing the "harsh and forbidding" sound of such servitude, Brengle qualified this relationship as an "unbreakable bondage of love."

It was not the slavery of compulsion and law, but the willing and glad slavery of love. Jesus had won the apostles by love. . . . They had sat at the feet of the Great Servant of love, who came not to be served, but to serve, to minister to others, to give His life a[s] ransom for all. . . . Such bondage and service became to them the most perfect liberty [since they were now at liberty to] do always that which pleases Him. This is the freedom of the love slave.[22]

Thus, in this relationship of utter devotion and perfect love, "the love-slave does not fear the Master, for he joys in the Master's will." Such a relationship is realized "by the expulsive power of a new and overmastering affection and purpose" and affects the way the love slave relates to others: "The love-slave is gentle and forbearing and kind to all the children of the household and to all the other slaves for the sake of the Master. This slave of love counts not his life dear unto himself. It belongs to the Master."[23]

HOLINESS AS CHRISTLIKENESS

For Brengle, holiness consisted in being transformed into the image of Christ by the power of the Spirit. In this light, it is not surprising that he viewed the result of this decisive encounter as making the believer like Jesus:

> Holiness is that state of our moral and spiritual nature which makes us like Jesus in His moral and spiritual nature. It does not consist in perfection of intellect . . . nor does it necessarily consist in perfection of conduct. . . . But holiness does consist in complete deliverance from the sinful nature, and in the perfection of the spiritual graces.[24]

Brengle consistently emphasized that the effect of entire sanctification was "to be made like God . . . to be made partakers of 'the divine nature' (2 Peter 1:4)."[25] Such "conformity to the nature of God, . . . as revealed in Jesus," finds expression in the believer's "separation from the world, in purity, in love, and in the fullness of the Spirit."[26] Although Brengle considered Christ as "the perfect and unchangeable standard of holiness,"[27] he also recognized the impossibility of being like Jesus without the gracious impartation of a new heart.

> Now it is impossible for us to walk like Him, to live like Him, unless we have a heart like His. We cannot bear the same kind of fruit unless we are the same kind of tree. So He wants to make us like Himself. Now we judge trees by their fruit, and so we judge Jesus, and then we can find out what kind of heart He had. We find in Him love, therefore Jesus had a loving heart. . . . Now it is just this kind of love He wants us to have. . . . I know if we examine love we find that it includes all the other graces, but we will look into the heart of Jesus for some of them. Jesus had a humble heart. . . . Jesus had a meek and gentle heart.[28]

Therefore Christ, indwelling the believer by the presence of His Spirit, is the means by which the holy life is lived. "When He baptizes us with the Holy Spirit, that holy of holies within us is then occupied and out from that center of our being His life radiates through all our affections, dispositions, tempers and activities."[29]

Brengle emphasized the Spirit's mediatorial role in revealing the reality of the resurrected Christ in the experience of entire sanctification. Finding support in the experience of the disciples at Pentecost, Brengle wrote: "He had been revealed *to* them in flesh and blood, but now He was to be revealed *in* them by the Spirit; and in that hour they knew His divinity, and understood His character, His mission, His holiness, His everlasting love and His saving power as they otherwise could not, had He lived with them in the flesh to all eternity."[30] Brengle further characterized the life of holiness as one lived by the power of Christ's resurrection. The baptism of the Holy Spirit thus makes possible communion with the resurrected Christ in the heart.[31]

Brengle's Christocentric understanding of holiness is evident in his appraisal of Pauline theology. Although he claimed that isolated Johannine texts had led him ". . . into the holy of holies, into the experience of cleansing, and the spiritual vision and inward revelation of Christ," he also claimed that Paul was his "greatest teacher, my mentor, my most intimate spiritual guide . . . [and] patron saint."[32] In this light, Brengle often used Pauline categories to describe the life of holiness. He maintained that life "in Christ" was the secret to the apostle's purity, power, and perseverance. "Paul's secret" was that having identified with Christ's death and resurrection by faith, Christ now lived in him, and he lived in Christ (Galatians 2:20).[33] Holiness is thus understood as the manifestation of the characteristics, or the fruit, of Christ in the believer. God's sanctifying work not only includes a purification of "nature," "affections," and "thoughts" but also a filling of the soul with the presence of Christ. "And 'love, joy, peace, long-suffering, gentleness, goodness, faith, meekness, temperance,' are the fruit of His indwelling."[34]

The indwelling Holy Spirit (as "Holy Guest") makes possible the intimate fellowship and communion with Jesus, which Brengle called "the secret of happiness and holiness."[35]

> There is a union with Jesus as intimate as that of the branch and the vine, or as that of the various members of the body with the head, or as that between Jesus and the Father. . . . This union is, of course, not physical,

but spiritual, and can be known to the one who has entered into it by the direct witness of the Spirit; but it can be known to others only by its effects and fruits in the life. . . . It is a union of the will. . . . It is a union of faith—of mutual confidence and esteem. . . . It is a union of suffering, of sympathy. . . . It is a union of purpose.[36]

He further stated that such union is not only possible but *necessary* for sharing in eternal communion with God. The Holy Spirit is the means by which the triune Godhead dwells within the Christian: "When the Holy Guest abides within, the Father and Son are there too; and what finer . . . sanctifying incentive to holy living can one have than this indwelling presence of Father, Son and Holy Ghost, as Holy Guest of the Soul?"[37] This union, however, requires self-sacrificial identification with Christ. Such identification is the basis of "knowing Jesus." The essence of such knowledge is love. To know Christ is to be transformed into His image (which is love) by His indwelling Spirit.[38]

Brengle compared this intimate communion with Christ by the power of the Spirit to the marriage covenant: "The coming of the Comforter is a holy thing, a solemn act, and must be preceded by an intelligent and solemn covenant between the soul and God. It is a marriage of the soul to the Redeemer. . . . It is carefully considered, and it is based upon complete separation and consecration and the most solemn pledges and vows."[39]

Brengle also held that such intimate communion, once entered into, must be cultivated in order to be maintained. He wrote to his son, George, about the relational dynamic of holiness as knowing Jesus:

I have been praying for you this morning . . . that you might be baptized with the Holy Spirit, and that you might have the manifestation of Jesus. He manifests Himself to them that seek Him with all the heart. He comes to them and abides with them and in them and they know Him and their joy is full. . . . O, how I long for you to know Him and love Him as He is worthy of your love! His service will then be your joy. You do know Him dimly, but pray and press on to know Him fully, as fully as possible while you are in the body . . .[40]

According to Brengle, not only does the Holy Spirit reveal Christ to the heart,[41] but he also reveals Jesus through believers, displaying his character and disposition (what Wesley called "holy tempers"): "This is His chief work—to reveal Jesus to the spiritual consciousness of each individual believer, and by so doing to purify his heart, to destroy all evil dispositions, and to implant in the soul of the believer the very tempers and dispositions of Jesus Himself."[42] In addition, "He illuminates that soul, purifies, sanctifies, empowers it; instructs it, comforts it, protects it, adjusts it to all circumstances and crosses, and fits it for effective service, patient suffering, and willing sacrifice."[43] Holiness thus includes "a heart made clean of pride, of temper, of covetousness, of hate, of sloth, of envy, jealousy, malice, strife, vaulting ambitions, lusts, passions and unbelief, with Christ enthroned within. It is a clean heart indwelt by the Holy Spirit ungrieved. It is a life "hid with Christ in God" (Colossians 3:3), one that is "rooted and grounded in love" (Ephesians 3:17).[44]

Christ living His life in and through the believer, is the focus of an article Brengle wrote on "God's House of Flesh and Blood." Reflecting on this figure of speech used by Paul in Ephesians 2:22 and 2 Corinthians 6:16, he commented: "Wherever you find a man or woman, a boy or a girl, loving God, trusting and obeying Jesus, washed in His Blood and filled with His lowly, loving Spirit, there you find a temple of God, a house of God—God's habitation."[45] Brengle marveled at the privilege and responsibility of being Christ-bearers to the world:

> This is our glory here and our hope of glory hereafter— "Christ in you the hope of glory," wrote Paul. It is for this we labor. It is not to deliver so many addresses each week, offer so many prayers, raise so much money, get so many people to the penitent form, and simply build an organization. It is to build living temples of God, to get men and women saved from sin and filled with the Holy Ghost. This, and this only, is the end for which we labor. . . . So all our religious work is but labor lost if it does not lead men to Christ and constrain them to throw wide the door and receive Him into their hearts, so that they become His dwelling-place.[46]

Reflecting on Galatians 5:19 and the idea of Christ being formed in the believer, Brengle interpreted the conception of Jesus by Mary as symbolic of the mystical and spiritual conception of Christ by the Holy Spirit in the heart of the entirely sanctified believer. "It is 'the Jesus of history become the Christ of experience,' 'the Christianity of the New Testament' reproduced in the twentieth century."[47] Such a manifestation of Christ is thus an extension of the incarnation, as is evident in Brengle's reflections on Colossians 1:27: "Christ in you is not a gorgeously robed aristocrat, arrayed in purple and fine linen and gold and pearls, but is a lowly, peasant Carpenter . . . [who] became a Servant of all, that He might lift us to the bosom of the Father and make us partakers of the divine nature and of His holiness."[48]

Brengle viewed the Holy Spirit as the means by which God's redemptive plan in Christ is carried out in world history. In this light, he wrote, "Pentecost was both an end and a beginning. It was the end of an age-long preparation. It was the beginning of an age-long, world-conquering achievement." Brengle understood the Old Testament as a period of preparation culminating in the revelation of Christ, who further prepared His followers to receive the baptism of the Holy Spirit. On the Day of Pentecost, "the Comforter came, and the disciples were no longer bereft and orphaned by the absence of Jesus." With the coming of the Holy Spirit, Christ, who had been with the disciples, was now in them, empowering them for redemptive mission: "It meant that God had come to tabernacle in the hearts of men, that all Heaven was enlisted in a campaign for the salvation of the world."[49]

Further, Brengle viewed Pentecost as fallen humanity's "restoration to an Eden of blissful fellowship with God such as Adam never knew. It was the beginning of a new race . . . a new 'colony of Heaven' upon earth . . . a new world order." Holy Spirit baptism enables believers to enter into this fellowship and receive a "seal," "pledge," or first "installment" of their inheritance in Christ.[50] Thus, the work of God within the believer is carried out by the Holy Spirit, who makes Christ known, present, and available.

> But not only have we One to represent us, to be our Advocate at the "throne of grace" . . . but there is another Advocate who represents our Redeemer. Christ has His Advocate with us, at the throne of our hearts, at the bar of our conscience; and as our Advocate pleads *for* us, so this other Advocate pleads *with* us to win us wholly to Christ, fit[s] us for union *with* Christ and service and fruit-bearing *for* Christ. This August Advocate who

represents Christ is the Holy Spirit, the other Comforter whom Jesus promised to His disciples, and whom He sent to abide for ever with His people on the day of Pentecost. This Advocate is "the other self" of Jesus; in Him we have Jesus evermore with us in the Spirit, and without Him we lose Jesus as Savior and Lord. . . . It is of the utmost importance that we receive and know this other Advocate and Helper.[51]

Chapter 9

Heart Holiness: Misconceptions and Hindrances

————————————

T hroughout his officership, Brengle sought to disabuse people of their misconceptions about the experience of heart holiness. Chief among these was the confusing of regeneration with entire sanctification.

REGENERATION IS NOT ENTIRE SANCTIFICATION

Although he believed that the Holy Spirit came to dwell within the believer at conversion, when the individual was both justified and regenerated (born again), Brengle firmly maintained that regeneration was not to be confused with entire sanctification. Viewing the Spirit as active in the work of conviction, repentance, faith, forgiveness of sins, assurance of salvation, and empowerment for spiritual warfare, Brengle nevertheless held that such work was preparatory and partial. Regeneration is thus a "preparing of the house" for the indwelling fullness of the Holy Spirit.[1] He consistently emphasized the need for a deeper work of the Holy Spirit in the life of the believer, subsequent to their regeneration: "Do not, my dear Comrades, confound birth with baptism. A man is not necessarily baptized of the Spirit because he is born again of the Spirit. The baptism is subsequent to regeneration and it is the gift of Jesus to those who keep His commandments and earnestly seek in all ways and gladly [to] obey Him."[2]

Recognizing the danger of viewing entire sanctification as the result of works righteousness, however, Brengle insisted that holiness is an "obtainment, and not an attainment; an act, and not a process; a gift, and not a growth." He held that it is obtained not by good works, but by "putting ourselves in that attitude before God that will enable Him to bestow it upon us. It is a gift of God, 'a new creation,' and as such is received by faith."[3] Brengle thus underscored the subsequency of the gift of perfect love in relation to regeneration:

> It [holiness] is received in two installments. It is begun at conversion and regeneration, when the sins of the past are pardoned, guilt is removed, the power of evil habits is broken, the tide of corruption is stayed, the central purpose of the will is changed, and new affections are planted in the soul. . . . It is completed in the moment of entire sanctification by the baptism with the Holy Spirit, when all waywardness of the will is corrected. These new affections are made perfect, every contrary affection and desire is destroyed, and the whole being is brought into a sweet bondage of love, and every thought "into captivity to the obedience of Christ," the heart becoming a holy of holies, a little Heaven of heavens, in which Jesus forever abides.[4]

Although Brengle clearly recognized the fact that the Holy Spirit was the means by which regeneration occurred, and adoption as children of God was made possible, he also understood that there was something more that the Holy Spirit wanted to accomplish in every believer: "But, great and gracious as is this work, it is not the fiery pentecostal baptism with the Spirit which is promised; it is not the fullness of the Holy Ghost to which we are exhorted. It is only the clear dawn of day, and not the rising of the day-star. This is only the initial work of the Spirit. It is perfect of its kind, but it is preparatory to another and fuller work. . . ."[5] Once again, Brengle employs the symbolic distinction between regeneration (dawn) and entire sanctification (sunrise), which reflects his own spiritual pilgrimage. These metaphors are further elaborated in a two-part work titled, "From Dawn to Sunrise," in which he contrasted the "dawn day" of his conversion experience to the "sunrise" of his baptism with the Holy Spirit.[6] Some excerpts from this work reveal Brengle's powers of allegorization in relation to distinguishing between regeneration and entire sanctification:

> The dawn is only the herald of the full-orbed day, and so conversion is but a herald of Pentecost, as John

the Baptist was the herald of Jesus; and the glories of conversion, however great they may be, are only the gray dawn of the morning, and are to absorbed and lost forever in the sevenfold splendors of the rising of the Sun of Righteousness through the baptism of the Holy Ghost and the entire sanctification of the soul. . . . This figure of the day-dawn and sun rising is Scriptural [2 Peter 1:19]. . . . Now, there is usually not much time intervening in the temperate zone between the first dawning of day and the uprising of the sun; and so there should not be much time between the conversion and the entire sanctification of the soul. . . . In the tropics there is almost no dawn, so soon does the sun hasten to follow; in the temperate zone the dawn is longer, while in the frigid zone there is little light but that of dawn. So it is in the spiritual world. Souls converted in the tropical heat of red-hot churches and Army corps soon seek and find full salvation; while those poor souls that are converted in the frigid zone of worldly conformity and lukewarm profession, and surrounded everywhere by spiritual icebergs, never get beyond the dawn, or, if they do, it is probably late in the day of life. . . . Unfortunately, I was converted well up toward the frigid zone, and it was eleven years and more before I turned fully to Him, and the Sun arose in my heart.[7]

In a further development of this contrast between "dawn" and "sunrise," Brengle noted four differences. First, like the light of dawn, the knowledge of Christ in conversion is indirect and incomplete. Although "the darkness flees away" and "the soul sees now what it could not see before," yet Jesus is not fully revealed. "But when the sun comes up, all inferences and presumptive evidences are swallowed up in perfect knowledge. . . . So with the man who has had his Pentecost. . . . Jesus has shined directly into his heart, the Scriptures flame with light, and he carries around in his own soul the absolute knowledge of the truth as it is in Jesus."

Second, Brengle noted that just as there is little heat in the dawn, "so in conversion there is but little of the heat of love." He recognized that some may confuse "gushing and tender emotions" with spiritual heat, but Brengle characterized such warmth as "feeble and fleeting." Entire sanctification, however, produces more lasting and transforming effects: "But when the sun comes up, and his direct rays fall on the earth, all nature rejoices in his warmth. . . . So when Jesus is revealed in the heart, love reigns supreme."

Third, the light of dawn and sunrise differ in their effect on perspective. "In the dawn objects assume abnormal proportions. . . . So in the dawn of the Christian life, men and things are not seen in their right proportions." This results in the misperception of the scope and magnitude of difficulties, often leading the soul to despair. "But when the sun comes up . . . when . . . we are filled with the Holy Ghost, spiritual relationships and proportions are rightly discerned. The soul sees only Jesus."

Finally, Brengle noted how the light of sunrise provides a better view of "distant objects" or a proper eschatological perspective. "So in the beginning of the Christian life, death and judgment . . . and the eternal world are only dimly realized. But . . . when the Holy Ghost is come the soul lives 'as seeing Him who is invisible,' the Judge is realized as always standing at the door . . . and eternity is in full view."[8]

Like John Wesley, Brengle maintained that the process of sanctification begins at regeneration (what Wesley called "initial sanctification"). But just as clearly, Brengle recognized that in this process, the Holy Spirit brings to light the effects of the sin nature remaining in the believer's life, thus pointing to the need for a further cleansing. "But unless you have been sanctified wholly, you also feel that there are yet roots of bitterness within. . . . These must be taken away before your heart can be made clean, love to God and man made perfect, and the Holy Spirit have all His way in you."[9] Although maintaining the subsequency of the work of Christian perfection to regeneration, Brengle did not believe that the baptism with the Holy Spirit was necessarily the result of a long process.

> Every child of God knows that the Holy Spirit is with him; realizes that He is working within, striving to set the house in order. And with many who are properly taught and gladly obedient this work is done quickly, and the Heavenly Dove, the Blessed One, takes up His constant abode within them; the toil and strife with inbred sin is ended by its destruction, and they enter at once into the sabbath of full salvation. . . . Since the day of Pentecost, He may be received immediately by those who have

repented of all sin, who have believed on Jesus and been born again. . . . But often this work is slow, for He can only work effectually as we work with Him, practicing intelligent and obedient faith.[10]

FURTHER MISCONCEPTIONS ABOUT HOLINESS

Other misconceptions about entire sanctification addressed by Brengle included ideas that holiness results in an idyllic existence, one which is constantly "bubbling over with joy," that holy people "are never tempted," that holiness is unimprovable, and that it is a state from which one cannot fall.[11] Of particular concern to Brengle was the understanding of entire sanctification as merely an emotional experience. In response to this misconception, Brengle emphasized the place of the human will in holiness, without disparaging the proper role of religious affections. His balanced approach to these matters is evident as he wrote: "Sanctification to some of them seems to be an extreme emotional experience. We should get rid of this idea forever. The experience is usually volitional."[12]

Thus, in line with the holiness teaching of Charles Finney, Brengle consistently emphasized the importance of volitional response in the experience of entire sanctification. "Familiarity with what the Bible says, with the doctrine and that standard, will avail nothing, unless it is translated into conduct, into character, into life. It is not enough to know, it is not enough to approve, but with our undivided will, with our whole being, we must choose to be holy."[13] Salvation and holiness are matters of the will. "Once my will yields, there is fact. Salvation means . . . my affections are weaned from the world and placed on Jesus. Sanctification is Christ's complete enthronement in my will and affections."[14] Nonetheless, Brengle understood the need to keep religious affection as part of the holiness equation: "You cannot have any great inner experience without emotion. . . . One of the greatest dangers to religion today is the fear . . . of emotion. They are so anxious to be balanced and well poised that they cease to be vital and natural."[15]

Another misconception was the understanding of entire sanctification as "sinless perfection." On the contrary, Brengle maintained that Christian perfection is to be understood as a perfection of love. In a letter to Lily, Sam shared on this issue from an encounter he had while in New Zealand: "Then I told him God had taken us out from the Adamic law of perfection and put us under Christ and that we are now under law to Christ, the law of love to Him, a blessed loving, divine Person, and that this law of love was graded to the capacity and light of each individual soul."[16] Elsewhere he wrote of Christian perfection in terms of heart intentionality: "Holiness is not absolute perfection, which belongs to God only; nor is it angelic perfection. . . . But it is Christian perfection. It is a state of heart and life which consists in being and doing all the time . . . just what God wants us to be and do."[17] Like John Wesley, Brengle held a view of relative perfection in this life, qualified by the persistence of infirmities common to human existence. In this regard, he wrote: "But though the heart may be perfect, the head may be very imperfect, and through the imperfections of his head, of his memory, his judgment, his reason, the holy man may make many mistakes, yet God looks at the sincerity of his purpose, at the love and faith of his heart . . . and calls him a holy man."[18]

Because Brengle understood holiness as a state of conformity to the divine nature, the holy person is like God, "not in God's natural perfection of power and wisdom and knowledge and omnipresence, but in patience, humility, self-control, purity of heart, [and] love. . . ." Having established what holiness is, Brengle delineates what it is not:

> *First,* holiness is not necessarily a state in which there is perpetual rapturous joy. . . . *Second,* holiness is not a state of freedom from temptation. . . . *Third,* holiness is not a state of freedom from infirmities. It does not produce a perfect head, but rather a perfect heart. . . . *Fourth,* holiness is not a state of freedom from affliction. . . . *Fifth,* holiness is not a state in which there is no further development. When the heart is purified it develops more rapidly than ever before. Spiritual development comes through the unfolding revelation of Jesus Christ in the heart, and the holy soul is in a condition to receive such revelations constantly, and since the finite can never exhaust the Infinite, these revelations will continue forever and prove an increasing and never-ending source of development. . . . *Sixth,* holiness is not a state from which we cannot fall.[19]

Brengle was careful to address misconceptions about holiness from Scripture. Having established that God desires holy people, after the pattern of Jesus, Brengle declared that "holiness is more than simple freedom from condemnation for wrong-doing. . . . it is a state of union with God in Christ, in which the whole man becomes a temple of God and filled with the fruit of the Spirit." In this light, he once again cautioned against confusing purity with maturity. "Purity is a matter of the heart, and is secured by an instantaneous act of the Holy Spirit; maturity is largely a matter of the head and results from growth in knowledge and experience. In one, the heart is made clean, and is filled with love; in the other, the head is gradually corrected and filled with light." According to Brengle, Scripture teaches that holiness is not a state which we reach in conversion. "Purity of heart is obtained after we are converted. . . . the disciples were converted before they received this pentecostal experience, so we see that heart purity, or holiness, is a work wrought in us after conversion."[20] In this regard, he warns against equating entire sanctification with pardon for post-conversion sin: "If I fall into sin, I must first confess my sin with a penitent heart and trust for pardon through reliance upon the Blood of Jesus, and if I do this the peace of pardon will fill my heart, but I must not mistake this for sanctification."[21]

One further misconception about holiness that Brengle addressed was the notion that Pentecostal baptism was to be restricted to the experience and ministry of the apostles in New Testament times. In contrast, Brengle maintained that the Pentecostal baptism is available to all Christians throughout time. Although not always appropriated, the fullness of the Holy Spirit has been the catalyst for reform throughout church history and has provided the essential link with the early church.[22] In light of the fact that Holy Spirit baptism was not unique to Pentecost, Brengle wrote:

> Many people teach today that the Holy Spirit was outpoured once and for all on the day of Pentecost, but I wholly agree with Mr. Moody . . . who received the baptism of the Holy Spirit years after he was converted. He declared that he considered the Day of Pentecost just a sample day, and that God was waiting to give us Pentecosts all around the world when He could find

people who united in faith and love, in earnest prayer for the Spirit.[23]

HINDRANCES TO HOLINESS AND THE PATH OF THE CROSS

Brengle was fully cognizant of the difficulty concerning the doctrine of holiness. He recognized the existence of several "hindrances to full salvation." Some persons, he believed, were unaware of the doctrine: "Vast multitudes of professing Christians have never heard of a second work of the Holy Spirit that purifies the heart and perfects it in love." Others failed to believe in the possibility of this work for themselves: "Many are familiar with the Word of God, but they have not an appropriating faith." Still others have misconceptions about the experience and its results: "They expect the blessings of full salvation to bring deliverance from temptations, infirmities, natural consequences of broken law and the like." Another misconception is that the experience is only for the super-spiritual: "Holiness is not some lofty experience, unattainable except to those who can leap to the stars, but it is rather a lowly experience, which lowly men in the lowly walks of life can share with Jesus, by letting His mind be in them."[24]

Grieving and quenching the Holy Spirit are also hindrances to holiness in that they lead to further resistance to the Spirit. Brengle wrote: "Grieving the Holy Spirit is a very common . . . offense of professing Christians. . . . By getting in a rage, by loud, angry talking and evil-speaking and petty malice, by unkindness and hard-heartedness and an unforgiving spirit, we grieve Him. . . . The cure for all this is a clean heart full of sweet and gentle, self-forgetfulness, generous love."[25] But he also maintained that Christians are equally guilty of quenching the Spirit: "Just cease to rejoice, through fear of man of being peculiar . . . neglect to pray when you feel the gentle pull in your heart to get alone with the Lord; omit to give hearty thanks for all God's tender mercies, faithful discipline and loving chastenings, and soon you will find the Spirit quenched."[26] Thus, although often done unintentionally, grieving and quenching the Spirit can lead to intentional resistance to holiness.

Brengle realized the holiness message as one that often provoked opposition and related the unpopularity of holiness to the unpopularity of Jesus: ". . . do not think that you can make holiness popular. . . . 'Christ in you' is the 'same yesterday, today and forever'—hated, reviled, persecuted, crucified."[27] Brengle therefore understood the radicalism of the holiness message. He credited such to the opposition between holiness—understood as Christ in the believer—and the "spirit of the world." He wrote: "This spirit and the spirit of the world are . . . fully opposed to each other. . . . Fire and water will consort together as quickly as the 'Christ in you' and the spirit of the world."[28]

Chapter 10

The Appropriation of Holiness

Brengle, in urging others to enter into the experience of entire sanctification, often wrote about the practical steps of appropriating the blessing. He provided the following outline of conditions to be met in awaiting the Pentecostal baptism:

> 1. We must be rid of sin. There must have been that heartfelt repentance that leads us to turn forever from sin; confessing our sinfulness, acknowledging our faults and looking unto Jesus only for salvation, for pardon and peace and purity. Sin will forever shut Him out of the heart. We must be at peace with God if we would have the Spirit, and there can be no peace so long as we abide in sin.

> 2. We must be at peace with our fellow men. They may not be at peace with us. They may refuse to be at peace with us, but so far as in us lies, we must be at peace with them. . . .

> 3. In order to receive the Heavenly gift we must consent for Him to have His way with us, remembering that His love toward us is perfect and His way is best. . . .

> 4. We must have faith that He will grant us the Spirit; that He is more willing to give than we are to receive. . . .

> 5. Expect Him at any time, at any moment! If your heart is prepared to receive Him, He will come suddenly into His holy temple; but do not prescribe how He shall come. He may come as quietly as sunrise, or He may come like a rushing, mighty wind. . . . Let Him manifest Himself in the way He chooses, but have faith in God!

. . . This blessing is for you, if you will but meet the simple conditions; if you will have faith in God; if you will open your heart and receive. Do it now![1]

A divine-human synergy is evident in Brengle's understanding of how entire sanctification is appropriated: "God and man must work together both to save and to sanctify. . . . so to get the priceless gift of the Holy Spirit—a clean heart—we must work together with God. On God's side all things are ready, and He waits and longs to give us the blessing, but before He can do so we must, with His help, get ourselves ready; we must do our part." Although recognizing the fact that holiness is a divine gift, Brengle emphasized human responsibility in the appropriation of entire sanctification: "We must see our need of the blessing, and fully to see this need we must be justified." Then, we must confess our need of heart cleansing, believing that the blessing is a present possibility, and "take it by faith and wait patiently on Him for the witness of the Spirit."[2]

Perfection of heart must begin with total consecration, but it requires a work of God's grace. By the power of the Holy Spirit, the heart can be made pure, yielding Christlike characteristics. Such heart purity is available in the present as an instantaneous work of divine grace, conditioned upon an appropriating faith response.[3]

Brengle treated the divine-human synergy of entire sanctification as involving interactive responsiveness: "Sanctification has meant complete abandonment to the will of God, but not in such a way that my will has become passive in its functioning. It has had to be, and has been, active, firm, assertive in purpose, to be the Lord's. . . . God and man must cooperate, work together, both in the reception and continuance of the blessing."[4] Brengle viewed the gift of the Holy Spirit in entire sanctification as a divine response to a seeking heart: "Seek Him with all your heart, and you shall find Him; you shall indeed, for God says so, and He is waiting to give Himself to you."[5] Characterizing this synergistic relationship in terms of a voluntary submission of "love-slaves" to their Master, Brengle underscored the need for total commitment to God and a waiting upon Him for the gift of perfect love:

Do you ask, how shall I enter into this sweet and gentle and yet powerful bondage of love? I answer, by your own choice and by God's revelation of Himself to your own soul. . . . The choice must be complete and it must be final. Then like the love-slave you must wait upon the Master. When He speaks to you, listen. What He says to you, do. . . . He will reveal Himself to your longing, loving, seeking soul, and you shall know the sweet compulsion of the slavery that is love.[6]

In treating the conditions for experiencing entire sanctification, Brengle often focused on consecration, faith, and waiting on God:

To get this blessing, then, we must recognize that in this, as in all other steps of salvation, we are "workers together with God," that God cleanses the heart when we meet certain conditions. First, there must be complete consecration of all we have and are and hope to have to God. There is something absolute about this consecration. It differs materially from the surrender of the sinner. It is the utter identification of the soul in all its aspirations, its loves, its ambitions, its interests, with those of the Savior. There is a sense in which it is a death; it is a death to self-will, self-seeking, and side interests. Secondly, such a consecration as this usually makes faith easy, and faith is the second condition. At this point the soul that would be sanctified must be careful not to get the cart of feeling before the horse of faith. The order is, first faith, then fact, then feeling. After the soul has committed itself utterly to God, and rested itself fully upon His word . . . if the baptism does not come immediately, it must not cast away confidence but expectantly wait till the Comforter comes.[7]

Although acknowledging that some receive entire sanctification without a long period of waiting, Brengle maintained that others must wait "patiently, steadfastly, and expectantly" by faith before they experience "the holy experience of a pure heart, filled with a Heaven of love."[8]

With regard to consecration, Sam's own spiritual pilgrimage had taught him that in order to experience a deeper work of God's grace in his life as a Christian, what was required was an "inner crucifixion which enables one to believe unto holiness of heart."[9] This consecration of life was often expressed in sacrificial terms: "Just so, he who would be entirely sanctified must make an unreserved offering of himself to God. This act must be real, not imaginary—a real transfer of self, with all hopes, plans, prospects, property, powers, of body and mind; time, cares, burdens, joys, sorrows, reputation . . .[10] Such self-sacrifice was portrayed as an identification with Christ's sufferings and death: ". . . enter into a solemn and eternal covenant with Him. . . . Take up that cross before you *now,* and trust Him; trust Him to make you clean within, to sanctify you wholly. His Blood cleanses from all sin."[11]

The coming of the Holy Spirit is preceded by full consecration, understood as a rational covenant commitment: "This coming of the Comforter is a holy event, a solemn act, and must be preceded by an intelligent and solemn covenant between the soul and God." Brengle likened this consecration to vows of marital commitment: "We must covenant to be the Lord's 'for better or worse,' and we must trust Him."[12] Although important in the process of appropriating entire sanctification, consecration (as a divinely assisted human work) is not to be confused with the gift of perfect love (God's work). Brengle responded prophetically to the growing trend within the Army of his day to confuse the two.

> Brigadier J. N. Parker of Chicago has written me, calling my attention afresh to the fact that so many of our people in their teaching substitute consecration for sanctification. I have myself noticed this danger greatly increasing amongst us. We seldom see a report in the *War Cry* stating that people have come forward for the blessing of a clean heart, for sanctification, but rather for consecration or to offer themselves for service. There would have been no Salvation Army such as we have today if that sort of teaching had prevailed in the early days, and there would have been no Methodist Church. Consecration is not sanctification. Sanctification is man's work *plus* God's cleansing and the baptism of the Holy Ghost and of fire. . . . We shall wax weaker and weaker in faith, in world-conquering experience and in our joy in the Lord, if we do not return with full purpose of heart, with definite preaching and teaching, to the definite experience of cleansing through the Blood, and power and fullness of joy and love through the baptism of the Holy Spirit.[13]

There were other misconceptions that Brengle sought to address. In this regard, he identified two types of imperfect consecration:

> There are two classes of people who profess to consecrate themselves to God, but upon inquiry it will usually appear that they are consecrated more to some line of work than to God Himself. They are God's housekeepers, rather than the bride of His Son—very busy people, with little or no time or inclination for real heart-fellowship with Jesus. The first class may be termed pleasure-seekers. They see that sanctified people are happy and, thinking it is due to what they have given or done, they begin to give and to do. . . . The other class may be rightly called misery-hunters. They are always seeking something hard to do. . . . They wear themselves out in a hard bond-service. It is not joy they want, but misery. . . . But these people do not really make greater sacrifices than sanctified people, only they make more ado over them.[14]

Faith's role in the appropriation of entire sanctification was illustrated in Brengle's own experience, whereby his claiming of God's promise concerning being "cleansed from all unrighteousness" yielded an awareness of Christ's sanctifying presence. "Instantly, I, by faith, closed in with that promise. I believed as easily as I breathed and was liberated from every doubt and every fear. . . . In that moment I was more deeply conscious of the presence of Jesus than I have ever been of any living presence."[15] So, although holiness is dependent on God's gracious provision (present purification through the blood of Christ and the fire of the Holy Spirit), appropriation of the same is only by "simple faith," defined as "trust in the word of Jesus, simple confidence that He means just what He says in all the promises, and that He means all the promises for you."[16]

A synergistic relationship between divine gift and human faith-response was an integral component of Brengle's holiness theology:

> There are three points in teaching holiness that the Lord has led me to emphasize continually. *First,* that men cannot make themselves holy . . . that no amount of good works, of self-sacrifice and denial, of labors for the salvation of others can cleanse the heart, can take out

the roots of pride, vanity, temper, impatience . . . and in their stead put unmixed, perfect love. . . . *Second,* that the blessing is received by faith. . . . *Third,* that the blessing is to be received by faith now. The man who expects to get it by works will always have something more to do before he can claim the blessing. . . . But the humble soul who expects to get it by faith sees it is a gift, and believing that God is as willing to give it now as at some future time, trusts and receives it at once.[17]

Brengle was careful, therefore, to disclaim works righteousness in relation to holiness. Works are a fruit of, not a precondition to, entire sanctification. Holiness is not the result of a natural growth process but requires something to be removed and something else added: "Holiness consists in having something taken from us and in having our spiritual nature made over into the image of Jesus." The "old Adam" must be put off, and the "new Adam" put on. In fact, "new man" solidarity is only possible by putting to death the "old man." This is accomplished by God's grace and appropriated through "childlike faith."[18]

Brengle decisively noted the difference between faith, understood as assent (*assensus*), and trust (*fiducia*). He wrote of two types of faith: "1. That of the head—with this you assent to the truth of the gospel. You believe it is true but it does not give you victory over sin. 2. That of the heart—with this you rely upon Jesus for your salvation and you find in Him your victory over sin—peace and joy and comfort."[19] Elsewhere, Brengle referred to faith in Jesus as ". . . more than mere intellectual assent. It is a vital, throbbing, transforming moral assent that carries the soul into experimental fellowship and union with Christ."[20] As stated earlier, the role of the will in sanctifying faith was important to Brengle. He emphasized this, as well as the need to go beyond emotional assurances, in a letter to former classmate Martha Tarbell:

I will to believe. . . . Over fifty years ago, through the baptism of the Holy Spirit and the shedding abroad of God's love in my heart, such assurances were given me that I could no more doubt His being, His love, His Word, than I could doubt my own being; but, after a while, that intense emotional assurance faded away, leaving me to believe or to doubt. I chose the better part and my spirit is nourished and sustained in every tempest and swelling flood that would overwhelm me, by this faith.[21]

In this regard, he likened the experience of "the seeker after full salvation" typologically to the sacrifice of Abraham in the fifteenth chapter of Genesis:

> Just so, he who would be entirely sanctified must make an unreserved offering of himself to God. . . . He must, like Abraham, patiently, trustingly, expectantly wait for God to witness that he is accepted. . . . Now during this short or long period of waiting, the devil will surely send his birds of prey to snatch away the offering. . . . Look unto Jesus and pay no attention to your emotions; they are involuntary, but will soon adjust themselves to the fixed habit of your faith and will.[22]

Brengle thus emphasized the need to appropriate the blessing of entire sanctification by faith—apart from feelings. But in contrast to those who insisted that by faith the work is done, he stated: "I don't ask you to believe that He has done it, but that He is doing it, in answer to your present faith."[23] Nonetheless, present faith must wait for assurance that the work has been accomplished, and total consecration plus steadfast faith are the conditions that must be maintained as one waits on God's sanctifying work. "So then, there must be entire consecration, unwavering faith, and a frank, artless confession of both to Jesus. This is man's part, and, when these simple conditions are met and steadfastly maintained, against all contrary feelings, God will suddenly come . . . filling the soul with His presence, purity, and power." [24]

Brengle maintained that "hindrances in obtaining the blessing" included imperfect consecration, imperfect faith, and an imperfect conception of holiness. In writing to seekers about such, he denied "that any of these hindrances are in God, or in your circumstances, for they are not, but altogether in yourselves." He further exhorted them to "find out what these hindrances are, and by the grace of God . . . put them away."[25] Brengle believed that while many are hindered by lack of consecration or weak faith, some have a faulty understanding of the nature of holiness:

> Consecration and faith are matters of the heart, and the trouble with most people is there, but no doubt there are some people whose trouble is with the head. They fail

to get the blessing because they are seeking something altogether too small. Holiness is a great blessing. It is the renewal of the whole man in the image of Jesus. . . . There are other people who fail to get the blessing because they are seeking something altogether too great. They want a vision of heaven, of balls of fire, of some angel; or they want an experience that will save from all trials and temptations, and from all possible mistakes and infirmities; or they want a power that will make sinners fall like dead men when they speak. . . . They overlook the fact that purity and perfect love are so Christ-like and so rare in this world that they are in themselves a great, great blessing.[26]

Although laying the fault concerning hindrances to holiness squarely with the believer, Brengle also believed that these hindrances provided the devil further opportunity to deter individuals from entering into the experience of entire sanctification. In other words, the reason why many fail to experience holiness is because they listen to the "whisperer."

The devil fights against definite testimony and stirs up vague, subtle doubts in our hearts to hush our testimony. . . . A man should testify joyfully to the Lord that the Blood cleanses. . . . He should testify in private and public. . . . If we withhold our testimony, we rob Him of the honor which is His due, and we rob the people of the testimony which would encourage their weak and drooping faith and enable them to overcome the mocking whisperer who ever opposes them when they would believe unto full and joyful salvation. If we will give our Lord honor and glory by our humble, but definite testimony, He will give us the witness of the Spirit and help us to understand and outwit our old enemy and accuser, the devil, who is the mocking whisperer.[27]

As has been demonstrated, Brengle believed in the present possibility of the gift of entire sanctification by faith: "Believe it; believe it *now* for yourself, and invite the Holy Ghost to become the Holy Guest in the heart His Blood has made fit and clean for His indwelling. 'Behold, *now* is the accepted time.'"[28] Although staunchly maintaining the need for faith in the present working of the Holy Spirit, Brengle also stressed the need to wait for divine assurance concerning the work having been accomplished.

Such assurance is not to be confused with "unusual feelings" but is understood as an inner knowledge or witness of the Spirit.[29] When addressing the issue of the witness of the Spirit, Brengle reiterated Wesley's doctrine of the "two witnesses."

> How . . . shall I know that I am justified or wholly sanctified? There is but one way, and that is by the witness of the Holy Spirit. God must notify me, and this He does, when, despairing of my own works of righteousness, I cast my poor soul fully and in faith upon Jesus. . . . Unless He Himself assures me, I shall never know that He accepts me. . . . John Wesley says: "By the testimony of the Spirit I mean an inward impression of the soul, whereby the Spirit of God immediately and directly witnesses to my spirit that I am a child of God. . . ." When the Holy Spirit witnesses to me that I am saved and adopted in God's family as His child, then other evidences begin to abound also. For instance: 1. My own spirit witnesses that I am a new creature. I know that old things have passed away, and all things have become new. My very thoughts and desires have been changed. Love and joy and peace reign within me. . . . 2. My conscience bears witness that I am honest and true in all my purposes and intentions. . . . It is for our comfort and encouragement to know our acceptance of God and our rights and privileges and possessions in Jesus Christ, and the Holy Spirit is given for this purpose, that we may *know*.[30]

Brengle therefore emphasized the need to wait on the witness of the Spirit—not only in relation to conversion (including justification, regeneration, and adoption) but also for the revelation of God's love in entire sanctification.[31] Holiness is to be claimed by faith in the present, but one must wait for assurance with "a fixed determination to stand on the promises of God."[32] Such waiting by faith holds fast to the promise of holiness: "If you gave yourself to God in the very best way you knew of, but did not receive the Holy Ghost, I beg of you not to be discouraged. Do not take a backward step. Stand where you are, and hold fast your faith. The Lord means to bless you. Keep looking unto Jesus, and fully expect Him to satisfy your heart's desire. Tell Him you expect it, and plead His promises."[33]

What is the relation between appropriating faith and receiving the assurance that the work of entire sanctification has been accomplished? John Larsson uses Brengle's experience of entire sanctification as a paradigm for understanding this relationship:

> What in effect happens is that the seeker so trusts God to be true to His promises that he accepts *by faith* that the work is done, and thanks God and praises Him for fulfilling His promises, and then proceeds to live *as if* the work of grace has been wrought. Sooner or later the confirmation will come. . . . And let it be said, it was true to Brengle's own experience. He placed his all on the altar on the Saturday morning. It was an act of faith that brought him a measure of peace and joy. From the pulpit on the Sunday he witnessed to what he had done. But it was not until Tuesday morning that the fire descended from Heaven, consuming the offering and filling him with glory.[34]

At this juncture, it is important to note the distinction Brengle made between the grace and the gift of faith. The "grace of faith" is that which enables every person to come to God. This is in line with the Wesleyan understanding of prevenient grace. The "gift of faith" is subsequent to the bestowed ability. Thus, exercise of the "grace of faith" (as a condition of entire sanctification) enables one to receive the "gift of faith" (assurance and witness of the Spirit). Brengle viewed as dangerous any claiming of the gift before fully exercising the grace of faith. Although consistently urging people to pursue this grace, he insisted that one must wait for the gift—although the wait doesn't necessarily have to be long. He illustrated his point:

> A man seeking the blessing of a clean heart . . . says: "I believe there is such a blessing, and I believe God will give it to me." Now, believing this, he should at once seek it from God, and if he perseveres in seeking, he will surely find. But if someone comes up and gets him to claim it before he has by the grace of faith fought his way through the doubts and difficulties he has to meet, and before God has bestowed upon him the gift of faith, he will probably drift along for a few days or weeks and then fall back, and probably come to the conclusion that there is no such blessing as a clean heart. He should be

warned, instructed, exhorted and encouraged to seek till he gets the assurance. . . . Beware of urging them to claim a blessing God has not given them. Only the Holy Ghost knows when a man is ready to receive the gift of God, and He will notify that man when he is to be blessed. . . . Let no one suppose that the grace of faith will necessarily have to be exercised a long time before God gives the assurance.[35]

Brengle maintained that failure to wait on God by faith for the promised blessing is a hindrance to holiness: "Just when all is on the altar and there is not one thing more to do but to stand still and see God come, 'an evil heart of unbelief' draws back." He insisted that the seeking soul must wait for the Lord to indwell the heart: "It is in this attitude of unflinching watching and waiting that faith and patience is made perfect; and when this perfection is attained the Lord will come suddenly to His temple, even to the heart that has waited for Him."[36]

The importance of waiting on the Lord is a constant theme in Brengle's writings. As a general spiritual principle, Brengle emphasized the necessity of waiting on God's power and love, not just at critical points in the spiritual walk but in the everyday Christian experience of the entirely sanctified. He wrote of the high priority placed on such waiting.

If I were dying, and had the privilege of delivering a last exhortation to all the Christians of the world, and that message had to be condensed into three words, I would say, "Wait on God!" . . . Waiting on God means more than a prayer of thirty seconds on getting up in the morning and going to bed at night. It may mean one prayer that gets hold of God and comes away with the blessing, or it may mean a dozen prayers that knock, and persist, and will not be put off, until God arises, and makes bare His arm in behalf of the pleading soul. There is a drawing nigh to God, a knocking at Heaven's doors, a pleading of the promises, a reasoning with Jesus, a forgetting of self, a turning from all earthly concerns, a holding on with determination to never let go, that puts all the wealth of Heaven's wisdom, and power, and love at the disposal of a little man, so that he shouts and triumphs when all others tremble, and fail, and fly, and becomes more than conqueror in the very face of death and hell.[37]

Despite the synergistic emphases relating to salvation and sanctification, Brengle maintained that God's grace is sovereign and must be waited upon:

> We must not forget that "our sufficiency is of God"—that God is interested in this work and waits to be our Helper. We must not forget that with all our study and experience, and knowledge and effort we shall fail unless patiently, daily, hourly, we wait upon God in prayer and watchful faith or the help and inspiration of the Holy Spirit. He it is that opens the eyes of our people to see spiritual things in their true relations, He melts the heart, He bends the will, He illuminates the mind, He subdues pride, sweeps away fear, begets faith, and bestows the Blessing, and He makes the testimony, the preaching, and the written word mightily effective.[38]

In relation to receiving the gift of entire sanctification, however, there follows from complete consecration a waiting that is far from passive. Those who have yielded their all to God, "must wait on God and cry out to Him with a humble, yet bold, persistent faith till He baptizes them with the Holy Ghost and fire. He promised to do it, and He will do it, but men must expect it, look for it, pray for it, and, if it tarry, wait for it."[39] Brengle recognized that waiting is never easy—but a necessary part of the emptying and filling process of entire sanctification:

> Oh, this waiting on God! It is far easier to plunge madly at this thing and that, and to *do, do, do,* till life and heart are exhausted in joyless and comparatively fruitless toil, than it is to *wait on God* in patient, unwavering, heart-searching faith, till He comes and fills you with the Almighty power of the Holy Ghost. . . . Waiting on God empties us that we may be filled. Few wait until they are emptied, and hence so few are filled.[40]

He exhorted those who were impatient with the waiting process to exercise persevering and active faith: "And if we are not filled at once, we are not to suppose that the blessing is not for us. . . . But we should try all the more, and search the Scriptures for light and truth . . . humble ourselves . . . and never faint."[41]

Brengle asserted, however, that even after receiving the gift of entire sanctification, there is a *constant* need to wait upon God. This dynamic nature of his understanding of holiness was underscored by a recognition of the continuing need for divine anointing as necessary equipment for ministry.

> There is a spiritual bankruptcy. . . . I may be so eager to help souls that I give away all my spiritual capital. I talk and talk without waiting on God to fill me. This is folly. We should wait to be clothed with power from on high. We should take time to hear what the Lord will say; then speak so much as He gives us to speak and no more. Then again seek His face and be quiet and attentive before Him till He refills us. If we do not do this, we become weak inwardly; we draw on our reserve power, and become exhausted both spiritually and mentally. We may be so eager to give that we become impatient of waiting upon God to receive, forgetting that Jesus said: "Without Me ye can do nothing." Those who have blessed men the most, and blessed the most men, have taken time to listen to God's voice and to be taught of Him.[42]

For Brengle, waiting on God was more than a means of appropriating and maintaining holiness; it was an essential resource for serving others. "Take time to wait on God, and when God has come and blessed you, then go to the miserable ones about you and pour upon them the wealth of joy, and love, and peace God has given you. But don't go until you know that you are going in His power . . . unless we . . . are full of faith, and hope, and love in our own souls, we shall be unable to help others."[43]

Chapter 11

Maintaining Holiness

Brengle was concerned that people not only enter into the experience of entire sanctification, but that they persevere in the same. In this regard he emphasized conditions for maintaining the holy life, dealt with the relationship between holiness and temptation, offered advice on how to regain the blessing, if lost, and urged the Army not to forfeit, by neglect, its holiness heritage.

CONDITIONS FOR MAINTAINING THE EXPERIENCE OF HOLINESS

Just as there are conditions for entering into the experience of entire sanctification, Brengle believed there to be conditions for maintaining holiness. He outlined several of these conditions in an article titled "How to Keep a Clean Heart." After affirming the possibility of keeping a clean heart, Brengle addressed the means by which this experience is sustained. The key to this was found in Colossians 2:6—"As ye therefore received Christ Jesus, the Lord, so walk ye in Him." Brengle called this verse "one of the simplest and completest statements of how to keep the blessing. . . . [namely] the conditions of getting it are the conditions of keeping it." He delineated these conditions as the following:

Perfect Consecration—

"To keep it there must be continued joyful and perfect consecration. We have put all on the altar to get it. We must leave all on the altar to keep it."

Unwavering Faith—

"There must be steadfast, childlike faith. It took faith unmixed with doubt to grasp the blessing . . . and of course, this same faith must be maintained in order to keep it."

Constant Communion—

"We must pray and commune much with the Lord."

Bible Study—

"We must give diligent attention to the Bible. The soul needs the food of truth."

Witness to the Blessing—

"We must confess it, be aggressive, and seek to get others into it. . . . Testify, testify, testify—clearly, definitely, constantly, courageously, humbly—if you would keep the blessing."

Self-Denying Spirit—

"We must constantly live in the spirit of self-denial. By yielding to fleshly desires, to selfish ambitions, to the spirit of the world, we may lose the labor of years in an instant. . . . We must watch and pray, and keep low at Jesus' feet in profoundest humility, if we would keep it. It is all summed up in one word, 'walk in the spirit,' 'walk in love.'"

Continuous Growth in Grace—

"Finally there must be no resting in present attainments. The Lord has clearer revelations of Himself for us. We may be filled to the limit of our capacity today, but we should ever pray, 'Oh, Lord, enlarge our vessel,' and this we should expect . . . (Philippians 3:13–14; Ephesians 3:20)."[1]

Brengle emphasized, first and foremost, the need for complete consecration to be maintained in the life of entire sanctification. He warned of the danger of failing to maintain one's consecrated relation to the Lord. What often happened, he wrote, was that

By and by age comes on, with its cares and infirmities and weariness and insomnia, its deferred hopes and unfilled ambitions, its large knowledge of the complex and massed and seemingly invincible forces of evil, and now comes the temptation to slow down, to compromise, to question the wisdom of having burned all the bridges behind, to draw back or hold back "part of the price." No doubt Paul was so tempted, but if so, he met the temptation squarely, and in the open, and declared to the Philippians and to the ages: "I counted and I count." He counted the cost in the past, and he continued to count as he began.[2]

Brengle called for consecration that was "unconditional, complete and sustained to the end," claiming that only such consecration will satisfy the soul as well as the claims of Jesus and answer the awful needs of a lost world:

> It is only by such uttermost and sustained consecration that we can satisfy the imperious claims of Jesus—claims not of an arbitrary will but of infinite love. He does not compel us to follow Him; He invites us to do so, with the understanding that if we choose to follow, we must gird ourselves for lifelong service and uttermost devotion and sacrifice. "There is no discharge in this war." Jesus says: "If any man will come after Me, let him deny himself, take up his cross and follow Me." . . . Finally, it is only by an utter and sustained consecration that we can meet the needs of the world about us. . . . "Ye are the Light of the world," said Jesus. Men would stumble and grope in unutterable darkness but for the light of the Cross. . . . The Christian [must] be true, for he is the light bearer of Eternal Life, and he will stumble . . . and fall into a bottomless pit of outer darkness, and others will stumble and fall with him if his light goes out—if his consecration fail.[3]

Ultimately, however, Brengle's "simplest rule" for continuance in the state of entire sanctification is relational. He would have his readers "consider Jesus." By abiding in Christ, and allowing His words and ways to abide in them, Christians will not lose their way. "If we will consider Jesus, His precepts and promises for our direction and comfort, His way in the presence of duty . . . and His great and sufficient work of atonement, and considering Him, will trust and obey and steadfastly follow as He leads on, we shall not lose our way, we shall not be robbed of our blessing."[4]

Brengle often emphasized volition over emotion in maintaining holiness. Experientially, he had come to realize the volitional basis of assurance. He reflected on this near the end of his life:

> I have been asked again if the realization of sanctification has ever waned during those fifty years. Judging from my emotions, yes; judging from my volitions, no. There have been times when my emotional experience had ebbed out and I wondered if I had lost my Lord and my experience. . . . When deliverance came, for I was not cast away, I discovered that my will had not wavered in its purpose, that my volitions had held fast to Christ in the midst of the emotional storm and desolation that swept over my soul; and to all my tempted comrades I would say: Hold fast! Be faithful regardless of how you feel, for Christ will never leave His own.[5]

Brengle believed many to lose their experience of entire sanctification because they no longer walked by faith, but by feeling. He cautioned others to trust facts over feelings: "Do not think He has left you because you are not overflowing with emotion. Hold fast your faith."[6] Brengle also held that feelings might serve as a hindrance in regaining holiness, once lost: "When people lose the experience of full salvation . . . they will never get it again if they spend their time in continual self-examination of their feelings and in vain regrets over lost emotions. . . . Attention must be given to the volitions, not the emotions. . . . We must give our whole attention to willing and doing, not feeling."[7]

Thus, a synergistic relationship is evident in Brengle's understanding of both receiving and maintaining the holiness experience: "Sanctification has meant complete abandonment to the will of God, but not in such a way that my will has become passive in its functioning. It has had to be, and has been, active, firm, assertive in purpose, to be the Lord's. . . . God and man must cooperate, work together, both in the reception and continuance of the Blessing."[8] Such purposeful submission to God's will involves an active abiding in Christ. Brengle wrote: "Remember that the blessing is simply the result of His indwelling in your heart, and you are not to think so much about keeping the blessing as about keeping Him."[9]

HOLINESS AND TEMPTATION

Brengle regularly addressed the relationship between holiness and temptation, reminding his readers that sanctification does not preclude one from being tempted, nor is temptation to be equated with sin.[10]

> But we must clearly understand that temptation is not sin and it doesn't indicate sinfulness. Temptation is a solicitation to evil, and since we are in the body, since we are creatures, we shall probably always be tempted until God takes us into His unveiled presence and Satan and his hosts are sent to their final doom.[11]

In fact, Brengle asserted that those who are entirely sanctified do experience temptation at a new level as a result of their heightened spiritual awareness. In a letter to Dr. S. Parkes Cadman, he wrote:

> My very old friend and teacher, Dr. Daniel Steele . . . used to tell us that as the pure in heart see God, so the pure in heart and only those can distinguish the devil from the workings of their own minds. This corresponds with my own experience, following that wondrous day when God purified my heart by faith and anointed me with the Holy Spirit. I found myself in a new realm of temptation and was as conscious of a spiritual presence tempting me as I was of a sacred divine Presence reassuring and delivering me.[12]

Since no "negative inclinations" are left within the person, due to the destruction of the "roots of sin" and the inhabitation of Christ by the Holy Spirit, the entirely sanctified are able to discern Satan's temptations. Thus, for Brengle, temptation takes on a different meaning in relation to holiness:

> The fact is that the truly sanctified man, who is "dead to sin," doesn't have any inclinations in him that respond to the ordinary temptations of men. As Paul declares, "He wrestles not against flesh and blood," against the sensual, fleshly, and worldly temptations which used to have such power over him—but "against the principalities, against powers, against the rulers of the darkness of this world, against wicked spirits in heavenly places." . . . I do not mean to say that Satan will never hold up

any of these worldly and fleshly pleasures and honors to induce the soul to leave Christ, for he will; but what I do mean to say is, that the soul being now "dead to sin," having the very roots of sin destroyed, does not respond to the suggestion of Satan, but instantly rejects it. . . . But while Christ has set this sanctified man at liberty, and he no longer has to fight against his old worldly passions and fleshly appetites, yet he has a continual warfare with Satan to keep this liberty. This warfare is what Paul calls "the good fight of faith."[13]

For those who are entirely sanctified, old temptations are replaced with new ones. Satan's accusations seek to undermine faith, which is the means by which continuance in holiness is possible. Brengle wrote:

By faith the sanctified man is made an heir of God and "joint heir with Jesus Christ" of all things. . . . Now, in the very nature of the case, these things can only be held by faith, but so long as he thus holds them, Satan's power over him is utterly broken. This the devil knows quite well, so he begins a systematic warfare against the faith of the newly sanctified man. . . . When Satan has injured the faith of the sanctified man he will begin to blacken the character of God. He will suggest to the man that the Father no longer loves him. . . . As a further result of this wounded faith, the man's secret prayer loses much of its blessedness, his intense desire to deal with souls will grow dull, the joy of testifying for Christ will grow less . . . and the Bible will cease to be a constant source of blessing and strength.[14]

Although the entirely sanctified are more aware of the presence and power of evil in the world, Brengle also believed that sin was not invincible in this life. Victory over the power of sin was possible through the experience of heart holiness.[15] Nonetheless, the life of holiness was not devoid of spiritual warfare with the world, the flesh, and the devil.

The devil makes war upon this doctrine and experience. Let us resist him and he will flee. The world will mock or turn away. Let us overcome the world by our faith. Faithfulness to this truth and experience will sometimes require of us the endurance of hardness as good soldiers of Jesus Christ. The holy man does not love always in

> ecstasy. Sometimes he passes through an agony, and at such times the weakness of the flesh will test one's firmness of purpose, but we must be true and we shall "conquer though we die."[16]

Recognizing that Satan often tempts the entirely sanctified to doubt their experience, Brengle insisted that these doubts need to be countered by faith, witness, and full consecration. He once wrote in response to an officer who was not fully enjoying the blessing, "Unbelief . . . frustrates the grace of God." He further offered these three conditions for the continued enjoyment of the blessing—faith in the efficacy of the blood of Christ, testimony to the experience of a clean heart, and "uttermost consecration." In this, Satan is defeated.[17]

Reticence to testify concerning heart holiness was a temptation to be resisted since faithful profession of such is necessary for continuance in a state of entire sanctification. Accordingly, Brengle wrote: "But after you have taken the step of faith, God's plan is for you to talk your faith. . . . You must stand out before the world as a professor of heart purity. . . . Only in this way can you burn all the bridges behind you; and until they are destroyed, you are not safe. . . . You are not to 'keep the blessing' at all; but you are to boldly assert your faith in the Blesser, and He will keep you."[18]

Other common temptations for the entirely sanctified are either to doubt their experience or to think that the Holy Spirit has left them. For Brengle, walking by faith and yielding obediently to the presence of the Holy Spirit are keys to overcoming such temptation.

> After having received the Holy Ghost, many people get into confusion. In time of temptation, they think He has left them. Instead of trusting and acknowledging His presence, and thanking Him for stooping so low as to dwell in their poor hearts, they begin to seek as though He had not already come, or had gone away. They should stop seeking at once, and go to fighting the devil by faith, and telling him to get behind them, and go to praising the Lord for His presence with them. If you will seek light when you have light, you will find darkness and confusion. If you begin to seek the Holy Spirit when you already have Him, you will grieve Him. What He wants

is that you have faith. Therefore, having received Him into your hearts, continually acknowledge His presence. Obey Him, glory in Him, and He will abide with you forever, and His presence will be power in you. Do not keep seeking and crying for more power. Rather seek, by prayer and watchfulness and study of your Bible and the honest improvement of every opportunity, to be a perfectly free channel for the power of the Holy Ghost who is now in you.[19]

Brengle characterized an "evil heart of unbelief" as "Satan's stronghold" against sanctification. Thus, the struggle against doubt is understood in terms of spiritual warfare: "It is a fight of faith, in which the soul takes hold of the promise of God, and holds on to it, and believes it, and declares it to be true in spite of all the devil's lies, in spite of all circumstances and feelings to the contrary, and in which it obeys God, whether God seems to be fulfilling the promise or not."[20]

Brengle held that temptations, if approached by faith, can serve the entirely sanctified as occasions for growth in grace: "Your very trials and temptations will lead you into a deeper acquaintance with Jesus."[21] They can also provide opportunity for testing the genuineness of love for God. Giving many examples of the need for faithfulness by the sanctified Christian in the midst of apparent defeat, Brengle urged his readers to find victory through surrender: "Through loss comes richest gain. We reach the heights through abasement; the supreme victory is only achieved by what, at the time, often looks like defeat; and only as our joyous faith holds firm in the dark and 'works by love' can we come to know the tender love, faithfulness, and almightiness of God."[22] Brengle illustrates this from his own experience in times of testing: "He has taught me that sin is the only thing that can harm me, and that the only thing that can profit me in this world is 'faith which worketh by love.' . . . During the years since He sanctified me, God has enabled me to keep a perfect unbroken purpose to serve Him with my whole heart."[23]

Just as the life of holiness is not devoid of temptation, neither does it entail the suppression of natural desires. Brengle addressed this issue when he wrote the following:

I am told that many young people confuse temptations of the flesh with departure from the Blessing of Full

Salvation. . . . But this is not true. All the appetites and desires of the body are normally perfectly innocent. The sexual desire is no more sinful, normally, than the desire for food or drink. None of these desires is destroyed by the grace of God, but they are brought under subjection to the law of Christ, of purity and unselfish love, and are never to be indulged in sinful ways.[24]

Whereas entire sanctification does not yield freedom from temptation, Brengle held that it does make possible victory over temptation: "The sanctified soul is made clean of sin and free from sin. . . . But this does not mean that the sanctified soul is beyond the reach of temptation. . . . But thank God, we can have instant victory over temptation through the exercise of a sanctified will and simple trust in our blessed Lord and the presence of the indwelling Holy Spirit."[25]

HOLINESS LOST AND REGAINED

Due to the conditionality of maintaining entire sanctification, Brengle offered advice on how to regain the experience of holiness:

Failures in the life of holiness can generally be traced to two . . . root causes. First, to a vague, indefinite beginning of the life, due either to faulty teaching, or to imperfect consecration, or weakness of faith . . . Second . . . to improper or neglected use of the means necessary to nourish, sustain, and develop a holy life . . . [i.e.] the necessity for private prayer, communion with God, and Bible study for personal enlightenment, comfort, and help.[26]

The loss of holiness was not just a theoretical matter for Brengle. In a personal anecdote he shared his post-entire sanctification crisis, highlighting the seriousness of sin after Holy Spirit baptism:

I suspect there are many Peters among the disciples of Jesus today; many in our own ranks, who, somewhere in the past, since they began to follow Jesus, vowed they would do the thing, [which] He by His Spirit through their conscience asked them to do; vowed they would die for Him, and meant it, too, who when the testing time came, forgot their vows, denied Jesus by word or act and practically left Him to be crucified afresh and alone. I remember such a time in my own experience years ago, before I joined the Army, but after I was sanctified. It was not a sin of commission, but one of omission, a failure to do what I felt the Lord would have me do. . . . I felt I had grieved the Holy Spirit . . . forever and that I was lost, and so I threw away my shield of faith, I cast away my confidence in the love of Jesus for me, and for twenty-eight days I suffered, it seemed to me, the pains of hell.[27]

What, precisely, his sin of omission was—is not clear. Perhaps Brengle offered a hint when he wrote: "I am convinced that many people lose the blessing because they withhold their testimony, or give it vaguely, indefinitely, in general terms instead of constantly, humbly, and clearly."[28] Whatever the cause of his loss, in time he experienced the assurance of God's forgiveness and felt he had been given another chance. Like Peter, Brengle felt confronted with Christ's words: "Lovest thou Me?" Similarly, he believed that the Lord would have him feed the lambs (new converts) and sheep (entirely sanctified), and thus, in response to God's restoring love in Christ, he found what was lost (holiness).

Brengle advised those who had lost their entire sanctification to continue seeking after holiness. In fact, he wrote that holiness regained has the potential to be more complete and certain:

John Wesley stated that he believed people usually lose the blessing several times before they learn the secret of keeping it. You prove your real desire and purpose to be holy, not by giving up in the presence of defeat, but by rising from ten thousand falls, and going at it again and again with renewed faith and consecration. . . . Suppose you lose it? Then seek again. God will surprise you some day by pouring out such a full baptism of His Spirit on you that all your darkness and doubts and uncertainty will vanish forever, and you will never fall again.[29]

Note his conviction that once the secret of keeping the blessing has been learned, perseverance in holiness is possible.

Brengle maintained that although entire sanctification can be lost if temptation is yielded to, it can be restored the moment sin is confessed and faith is exercised in the cleansing blood of Christ: "If we have faith—ah! there is the rub. It is hard to get people to believe once they have lost the blessing, and yet

God bends over them in infinite and everlasting love as eager and willing to restore the blessing as He was to give it in the beginning."[30] In reply to a field officer's inquiry with regard to the possibility of being restored to the blessing of entire sanctification, once such an experience has been lost, Brengle wrote that "God never says 'no' to penitent, seeking, trusting souls. . . . He will restore the backslider . . . if he but seeks with all his heart, in simple faith and whole-hearted obedience. And He will restore the blessing of a clean heart filled with the Holy Spirit to one who has lost it. He surely will."[31]

Ultimately, however, walking by faith in Christ is the secret of unbroken communion and fellowship with God.[32] In this regard, Brengle wrote metaphorically of the need to keep the fire burning:

> Of course we must first get the fire—the fire of love and assurance. If we have lost it, we must wait on God until we obtain it again. And having the fire, we must keep the draughts open. That is, we must testify, not simply talk about religion, but testify to what Christ has done in our hearts. . . . Again, we must keep the ashes out of the way. The fire is continually consuming fuel and burning it to ashes. So our experience of yesterday is burnt out, and we must not depend upon it, but clear it out of the way in order that we may enjoy the blessed experience of God's love and fellowship today. Again, we must pile on plenty of fuel. We are to find out God's will for today and do it. We are to seek out His precious promises and believe them. We are to comfort ourselves with the assurances He gives us. We must seek out His precepts, and stir ourselves up to live by them and to fulfill them. If we do this, the Divine fire in our heart will never go out.[33]

MAINTAINING THE STANDARD OF HOLINESS

Brengle constantly reminded the Army of its holiness birthright and legacy, noting the sacred obligation and spiritual indebtedness entailed as bearers of the holiness standard. He insisted that such a holiness heritage was central to the mission and message of the Army and also the source of its continued life and power:

> And it is this Holiness—the doctrines, the experience, the action, that we Salvationists must maintain, else we shall betray our trust, we shall lose our birthright; we shall cease to be a spiritual power in the earth. . . . In this matter an immeasurable debt is laid upon us. We owe it to our Lord, who redeemed us by His Blood, not simply that the penalty of our sins should be remitted, and thereby we escape the just deserts of our manifold transgressions, but that we should be sanctified, made holy; that we should become temples of the Holy Ghost, and live henceforth not for our own profit or pleasure, but for His glory, and His bondservants and friends, ready for service and sacrifice, and prepared for every good work. . . . We must pay this righteous debt, my comrades; and we will. We must and we will maintain our Holiness standard in both our teaching and our experience, and in so doing we shall save both ourselves and them that hear us. . . . This will be our glory and our joy.[34]

Brengle emphasized the *experience* of entire sanctification as the incarnation of the Army's holiness standard and doctrine, stating: "Our Lord still baptizes with the Holy Ghost and fire. He has given us a doctrine, and He wants to give us an experience that shall incarnate both standard and doctrine in heavenly and all-conquering life."[35] In fact, Brengle believed there was a reciprocal relationship between doctrine and experience in maintaining the holiness standard: "Without the doctrine, the standard, the teaching, we shall never find the experience, or, having found it, we shall be likely to lose it. Without the experience we shall neglect the teaching, we shall despise or doubt the doctrine, we shall lower the standard."[36] He held that beyond experiential knowledge of doctrine, the holiness standard is maintained by gospel proclamation and holiness teaching: "If we are to maintain the Holiness standard we must not only know the doctrine and experience in our own hearts, but we must teach it, preach it, press it upon the people."[37]

Brengle was also convinced of the need to promote the reading of holiness literature within the Army. Accordingly, he wrote: "We shall greatly help ourselves and others if we carefully and constantly read and scatter Holiness literature. Wesley declared that the Methodists need not hope to grow in experience unless they became a reading people. That surely has been the feeling of our leaders with regard to Salvationists."[38] Brengle believed that the holiness standard was more than a doctrine to be taught. As exemplified in Christian living it convicts and inclines sinners to salvation. Hence, he saw the need for soul-winners to be sanctified, stating that

> The surest way to get sinners saved and backsliders reclaimed, as well as the only way to get Christians sanctified, is to preach Holiness plainly, constantly, tenderly. Then, not only do Christians see their need and privilege, but sinners lose their self-complacency, discover their desperate position, perceive the possibilities and joys of a true Christian life, and are inclined to surrender and be saved.[39]

Chapter 12

The Fruit of Holiness

Beyond emphasizing the nature of holiness and how to attain and maintain the experience of entire sanctification, Samuel Brengle gave attention to the abundant harvest of spiritual fruit and the overflowing of heart and life that results from fullness of the Spirit.[1] The Army's motto "saved to serve" found expression in his holiness doctrine: Not only is a clean heart requisite for personal growth in peace, joy, and spiritual communion; it is needed for a zeal for souls and perfected love toward others. Writing about "The Meaning of a Clean Heart" in 1899, Brengle stated that heart purification would result in the following outcomes:

Evangelistic Spirit—

"A clean heart filled with the Spirit makes a soul-winner out of one who receives the blessing. . . . It opens wide and clear the channel of communion between God and the soul, so that His power, the power of the Holy Ghost, works through him who has a clean heart, surely convicting and graciously converting and sanctifying souls."

Balanced Spirituality—

"The blessing results in a constancy of spirit. The soul finds perfect balance in God. Fickleness of feeling, uncertainty of temper, and waywardness of desire are gone, and the soul is buoyed up by steadiness and certainty."

Peace—

"There is perfect peace. The warring element within is cast out, the fear of backsliding is gone, self no longer struggles for supremacy, for Jesus has become all and in all." Brengle differentiates the "peace with God," experienced by the convert, and the "peace of God" enjoyed by those who have been perfected in love.

Perfect Joy—

"Joy is perfected. There may be sorrow and heaviness on account of manifold temptations, there may be great trials and perplexities, but the joy of the Lord . . . flows and throbs through the heart of him who is sanctified in an unbroken current. God becomes his joy." Brengle acknowledges that not all the entirely sanctified experience this joy, "but they may if they will take time to commune with God and appropriate the promises to themselves."

Perfect Love—

"To be born of God is to have Divine love planted in the heart. . . . When we are born of God we are made partakers of His nature" (2 Peter 1:4). In a new convert this love is weakened by "much remaining corruption in the heart . . . but when the heart is cleansed, all conflicting elements are destroyed and cast out, and the heart is filled with patient, humble, holy, flaming love." Brengle maintained that "love is made perfect," and as such, "it flames upward towards God, and spreads abroad toward all men. It abides in the heart, not necessarily as a constantly overflowing emotion, but always as an unfailing principle of action, which may burst into emotion at any time."

Biblical Illumination—

"The Bible becomes a new book. It becomes self-interpreting. God is in it speaking to the soul." Not that all passages become self-evident, ". . . but all that is necessary to salvation . . . [the seeker] finds and feeds upon in the Bible."

Humility—

"It begets the shepherd spirit, and destroys the spirit of lordship over God's heritage. . . . If the cleansed man is superior, it makes him patient and considerate. If a subordinate, willing and obedient."

Spiritual Discernment—

"Temptation is quickly recognized as such, and is easily overcome through steadfast faith in Jesus."

Courage—

"Divine courage possesses the heart" of the entirely sanctified.

Dependence on God—

"There is a keener sense than ever before of the weakness of the flesh, the absolute inability of man to help us, and of our own utter dependence on God for all things."

Discretion—

"The cleansed man makes a covenant with his eyes, and is careful which way and how he looks. . . . Likewise he bridles his tongue and seasons his words with salt, not sugar. . . . He does not despise the day of small things, and he can content himself with mean [common] things."[2]

Elsewhere Brengle wrote that entire sanctification brings comfort, instruction, guidance, and power. The coming of the Holy Spirit also issues in heart "rest . . . certainty and confidence," love-induced service, and victory over temptation.[3] The indwelling of the Holy Spirit is therefore instrumental as well as transformative in effect.

When Jesus came, a body was prepared for Him and through the body He wrought wondrous works; but when the other Comforter comes, He takes possession of those bodies that are freely presented to Him, and He touches their lives with grace. . . . He kindles a fire of love in their hearts, and lights the flame of truth in their minds. They become His temple, and their hearts are a holy of holies in which His blessed Presence abides. From that central citadel He works, enduing the man who has received Him with power.[4]

Brengle insisted that holiness comprises both body and soul. Against those who held merely to an inward working of the Spirit, his proof-text for bodily sanctification was 1 Thessalonians 5:23. Since the body is the "temple of the Holy Spirit," holiness is manifest through the proper use of its parts.[5]

Brengle further emphasized the need of the perfecting work of the Holy Spirit for Christian living: "We each and all need the Blessing of Pentecost, not simply for service, but for holy, worthy living, for the perfecting and completing of character from which flow influences which often are more effective than the busy activity which we call service." He urged his readers to manifest a spirit of humility, obedience to the will of God, and self-sacrificial love—all characterizing "the spirit of Jesus still abiding in man." Notably, Brengle maintained that the fruit of the Spirit does not reach its full maturity apart from the holiness experience: ". . . only the Pentecostal Blessing can produce this fruit unto perfection in our lives." The "full, rich, and ripe" fruit of the Spirit manifests "the life of Jesus on earth." Once again, he underscored the nature of holiness as Christlikeness—the manifestation of the life and character of Christ.[6]

PEACE

Of the many above-mentioned fruit manifest in the life of the entirely sanctified, one of the most important for Brengle personally was the peaceful heart. Holiness, characterized as "perfect peace," was based upon communion with Christ by the presence of the Holy Spirit: "To exercise this mighty faith which brings 'perfect peace,' we must receive the Holy Ghost into our hearts. . . . He will make us know Jesus, and understand His mind and will, and realize His constant presence, if we trust Him."[7] As stated earlier, Brengle experienced "peace like a river," a great peace flooding over his soul on the morning of January 9, 1885, upon entering into the experience of heart holiness.[8]

LOVE

The chief fruit of holiness, for Brengle, was love. This is illustrated throughout the years, as he testified to his personal Pentecost experience:

> It is over fifty years ago that I received the baptism and I loved and loved and loved until it seemed to me I would nearly die of love, and I wept and wept and wept and sorrowed to think I had ever sinned against my blessed Lord. And that baptism has been an abiding blessing and has given me power to continue unto this day, loving and serving God and my fellow-men, and to do it gladly.[9]

The nature of perfect love is not incompatible with reverential fear since the holiness of God yields holy fear. In fact, Brengle asserted that such holy fear, as the fruit of holy love, is "the great need of the world and of the church today."[10] In this regard, he wrote:

> But men who understand the unchangeable holiness of God's character and law tremble and fear before Him at the thought of sin. . . . And this is not inconsistent with the perfect love that casteth out fear. Rather, it is inseparably joined with that love, and the man who is most possessed of that love is the one who fears most, with the reverential fear that leads him to depart from sin. For he who is exalted to the greatest heights of divine love and fellowship in Jesus Christ, sees most plainly the awful depths of the divine wrath against sin and the bottomless pit into which sinners . . . are running. This vision and sense of the exceeding sinfulness of sin and of God's wrath against wickedness, begets not a panicky slavish fear that makes a man hide from God as Adam and Eve hid among the trees of Eden, but a holy, filial fear that leads the soul to come out into the open and run to God and seek shelter behind the blood of "the Lamb of God, which taketh away the sin of the world."[11]

In contrast to fallen humanity's submission to the carnal nature, spiritual humanity follows the new nature and submits to the law of the kingdom, which is love. Brengle believed that such self-sacrificial love is perfected in those who have been filled with the Spirit.

> The natural man is a fighter, it is the law of his carnal nature. . . . His kingdom is of this world, and he fights for it with such weapons as this world furnishes him. The Christian is a citizen of Heaven, and is subject to its law, which is universal, whole-hearted love. . . . This is the narrow way which leads to life eternal.[12]

Thus, true spirituality is marked by meek and lowly sacrificial love.

> When the Holy Spirit finds His way into the heart of a man the Spirit of Jesus has come to that man, and leads him to the same meekness of heart and lowly service that were seen in the Master. Ambition for place and

> power and money and fame vanishes, and in its place
> is a consuming desire to be good and to do good, to
> accomplish in full the blessed, the beneficent will of
> God.[13]

Even spiritual power is subordinated to perfect love, in that holiness is chiefly characterized by the love of Christ—not signs and wonders. Accordingly, Brengle maintained that religious ecstasy without a lowly heart is not holiness. He asked: "You who have visions of glory and rapturous delight, and so count yourselves filled with the Spirit, do these visions lead you to virtue and to lowly, loving service?"[14]

Brengle held that entire sanctification expresses itself in love-service: "We are sanctified not by works, but by faith which works by love."[15] Therefore, the baptism of the Holy Spirit enables the graces of love and faithfulness in ministry. Brengle wrote that "this combination of love and faithfulness . . . is a [D]ivine thing. . . . But that is the standard we should set for ourselves, and which, by the baptism and the indwelling of the Holy Spirit, we may attain."[16] He believed that self-sacrificial love for others in the pathway of the cross of Christ was evidence of the Spirit's sanctifying and empowering presence.

> If thou dost love Him who died for thee, who entrusts His
> honor and His cause to thee, prove thy love, O my soul,
> by feeding and watching over His lambs and sheep. Love
> thy comrades as He has loved thee; and as He laid down
> His life for thee, so, if needs be, lay down thy life for the
> brethren, and so shall all men know that thou ar[t] His
> disciple.[17]

In this regard, Brengle was careful to emphasize the social dimensions of holiness. The redemptive love of Christ, expressed through the entirely sanctified life, is the only proper motive for our relationships with others. Such love, he believed, compels social action: "The social gospel is none other than the gospel of love, of good will, of service to the uttermost for our fellowmen. But, remember and press it home hard upon the hearts of these ministers that the social gospel of Jesus springs out of the redemptive gospel of Christ and that we are simply beating the air when we talk about a social gospel without Christ."[18]

POWER

When Brengle wrote of the power of the Spirit at work in the entirely sanctified, his interest was primarily in the ethical dimensions of divine enablement: "The Holy Spirit is given for power or service . . . but it is also given to us for power to live holy lives . . . power to love our enemies . . . power to suffer patiently . . . power to sacrifice gladly . . . power for all manner of holy living and holy dying."[19] Christ's "resurrection life and power," he maintained, are available to all those who have been baptized by the Holy Spirit, evidenced in the fruit of the Spirit, which are the very characteristics of Christ.

> Through the faith perfected in them [the disciples] by the resurrection of Jesus they were led to wait for and receive His baptism with the Holy Ghost, and Christ was revealed in their hearts. . . . In Him was sacrificial, deathless love, and this love was reproduced in them also. . . . Joy, the very joy of Jesus was perfected in them. . . . Yes, He did also leave them His peace. . . . Now, too, longsuffering was perfected in them. Eternity was in their hearts. . . . the gentleness, the goodness, the faith, the meekness and temperance, or self-control of their Lord, all these were reproduced in them, and made manifest in word and deed, it was Christ living His life in them.[20]

Brengle believed that Christians experience the power of the Holy Spirit in regeneration, but in a relatively "weak" form. Rather than being simply "children in grace," the entirely sanctified are "men in Christ Jesus, and therefore they are proportionately strong."[21] For Brengle, holiness results in "power for service or sacrifice, according to God's will."[22] Such power makes the entirely sanctified more useful for God's kingdom purposes: "When a person is born again, sanctification is begun, and the person is proportionately useful; but entire sanctification makes us more holy, and consequently we shall then be more useful."[23] He maintained that usefulness is contingent upon the purifying of the heart of all that would hinder the fullness of the indwelling Spirit: "But when our hearts are clean, the Holy Spirit dwells within, and then we have power for service . . . ."[24] It is important to note that such usefulness, understood by Brengle as fruitfulness, is not based on ability, but on sanctified availability: "Oh, how God wants to use you! But before you ask Him again to do so, see to it that your heart is 'perfect toward Him'. . . . See to it that you are 'filled with the Spirit,' and Jesus will see to it that out of your life shall flow rivers of holy influence and power to bless the world."[25]

SELF-DENIAL AND HUMILITY

For Brengle, holiness also leads to humility and self-denial. To exemplify this, he found a model of simplicity, heart purity, and self-sacrificial service—worthy of emulation by all who wish to live a holy life—in St. Francis of Assisi. This "thirteenth century Salvationist," as Brengle referred to him, ". . . wrought a great reformation by love, by simplicity, and self-sacrifice. He was a kindred spirit of George Fox . . . John Wesley and William Booth." The life of Assisi evidenced a vital union with Christ and purity of heart, which found expression in sacrificial service. Brengle wrote:

> Francis had found the secret of joy, of power, of purity, and of that enduring influence which still stirs and draws out the hearts of men of faith, of simplicity, of a single eye. . . . He found hidden reservoirs of power in union with Christ; in following Christ; in counting all things loss for Christ; in meekly sharing the labors, the travail, the passion, and the cross of Christ.[26]

The work of the Holy Spirit in the entirely sanctified life produces lowliness of spirit, humility of mind, tolerance of those who differ from them, unity of spirit, and holy love. With regard to discerning these characteristic evidences of holiness, Brengle noted:

> When the Holy Spirit comes in His fullness, He strips men of their self-righteousness and pride and conceit. . . . A humble, teachable mind marks those in whom the Holy Spirit dwells. . . . Again, the man who is filled with the Spirit tolerates those who differ from him in opinion, in doctrine. He is firm in his own convictions . . . but he does not condemn and consign to damnation all those who differ from him. . . . The Holy Ghost begets a spirit of unity among Christians. . . . Divine love is the great

test by which we are to try ourselves and all teachers and spirits.[27]

To those who claimed that the doctrine of entire sanctification leads to spiritual pride, Brengle responded: "Holiness goes down to the root of all pride and digs it up utterly. . . . And so long as he [the entirely sanctified individual] keeps the blessing he is deeply humble."[28]

With regard to self-denial, Brengle related that he found deliverance from the "bondage of selfishness" through a baptism of Divine love. He maintained that such love, as a fruit of holiness, must find expression in relation to the needs of others. He recalled from his own holiness experience that with "love to Him came a love for the whole world."[29] Similarly, covetousness (which Brengle characterized as "a common yet subtle sin") can be avoided "by following Jesus in daily, resolute self-denial . . . by utter surrender to the Holy Ghost . . . [and] by keeping the heart clean."[30] The self-denial that flows from holy love is what Brengle emphasized:

> There are four kinds of self-denial: 1. There is compulsory self-denial, where we deny ourselves because we are forced to it by necessity. There is no virtue in this. 2. There is the mere formal self-denial, where it is done purely as a form, because it is the fashion, and it would not be good taste or policy not to deny ourselves. There is no virtue in this. 3. There is a self-denial that springs from principle, where we deny ourselves because we know it is right, and we choose to do the right thing at whatever cost. This is well-pleasing to the Lord, and will surely have its reward. But best of all, there is a self-denial that is joyous, springs from love—love to God and man. This is its own reward.[31]

Only through self-denial and "cross-bearing" living, he maintained, will Christ be manifest in and through His people: "This is the great task of . . . all the people of God—so to live and love and labor as to unveil the face of Jesus Christ, and let the world see the glory of God, the glory of His sacrificial love."[32]

TRIUMPH THROUGH SUFFERING

Brengle believed that holiness affects the way the individual experiences suffering in this life. Victory in the midst of trial and testing is possible by the power of the indwelling Spirit. He asserted that despite the inevitability of suffering, God can providentially transform us through such circumstances.

> The Lord enables the man filled with the Spirit to thus triumph over suffering . . . by giving the soul a sweet, constant and unshaken assurance through faith: *First,* that it is freely and fully accepted in Christ. *Second,* that whatever suffering comes, it is measured, weighed and permitted by love infinitely tender, and guided by wisdom that cannot err. *Third,* that however difficult it may be to explain suffering now, it is nevertheless *one* of the "all things" which "work together for good to them that love God," and that in a "little while" it will not only be swallowed up in ineffable blessedness and glory, but that in some way it is actually helping to work out "a far more exceeding and eternal weight of glory." *Fourth,* that though the furnace has been heated seven times hotter than was wont, yet "the Form . . . like unto the Son of God" is walking with us in the fire. . . . This is faith's triumph over the worst the world can offer through the blessed fullness of the indwelling Comforter.[33]

While acknowledging that not all Christians experience such triumph in the midst of their difficulties and sufferings, Brengle viewed such victory not only as possible but also as a fruit of entire sanctification: "This is God's standard, and they may attain unto it, if by faith, they will open their hearts and be filled with the Holy Spirit."[34]

UNITY

Along with John Wesley, Brengle upheld that the only true holiness was social holiness. This is evident in his comments on the prayer of Jesus in John 17, which focuses on the unifying dimensions of the sanctifying work of God in the hearts of the disciples:

> The religion of Jesus is social. It is inclusive, not exclusive. We can have the glory only as we are united. We must be one in spirit with our brethren. Let division come, and the glory departs. Let the unity of brotherly love continue, and the glory abides. . . . Let us beware of the leakage of love, of the loss of the spirit of unity, of

the subtlety and snare and death of the spirit, of distrust, and division![35]

Brengle believed that holiness manifest in loving relationships was the secret to the unity in the New Testament church.

> Their unity began in the heart and extended to the head, and worked itself out in deeds of loving fellowship and service. . . . Like the coat of the Master, the infant Church was "without seam." . . . The rending of this seamless robe can always be traced back to lack of love. The great heresy of the ages is not manifested so much in false doctrine as in failing love and consequent false living. . . . Heresy begins in the heart, not in the head. The heretic of the Early Christian society was the loveless schismatic.[36]

With all of his emphasis on personal holiness, Brengle was also careful to recognize the corporate dimensions of Christian life: "The religion of the Lord Jesus is social, and His promise is specially given to those who meet together in His name for worship, prayer and religious conversation and study of His Word."[37] Brengle underscored the responsibility placed on the entirely sanctified within the Body of Christ ". . . to foster the unity of the Spirit and to beware of the pride and jealousy and envy and suspicion and unholy spirit of lordship that leads to division." Further, humility and self-sacrificial service are called for to promote such unity: "Let us be content to wash each other's feet and be ambitious only to be servants of all."[38] Focusing on Jesus' prayer in John 17, Brengle saw that not only was holiness the foundation for oneness within the Body of Christ, but it was only such sanctified unity that would enable the church to fulfill its role as an instrument of God's redemptive purposes.

> Jesus prayed, "Sanctify them." Set them apart, consecrate them to thyself and to Thy service. Seal them and make them holy. Not only keep them from the evil that is in the world, but save them from the evil and corruption that is in their own hearts. Make them clean. Refine them as fire. Purify them until no spot of sin remains upon them, until they are "all glorious within." "Sanctify them through thy truth: thy word is truth." Let thy truth search them till they are wholly conformed to Thy nature and Thy will, until their lives match Thy truth, and in them the truth lives incarnate, walks among men. Not for these alone,

however, did He pray, but for all who should through
their word believe on Him. His thought was girdling the
globe and embracing the ages. Wherever and whenever
a penitent, trembling soul believes on Him through their
word, that soul comes within the desire and purpose of
this prayer. He wanted them all to be one . . . that they
might be the habitation of God upon earth, and that the
world, seeing this, might believe on Him.[39]

SPIRITUAL ILLUMINATION

Brengle viewed entire sanctification as also affecting
the intellect in its knowledge of God and His revelation—not
that the sanctified are recipients of new revelation, but that they
truly discern the spiritual meaning of Scripture and the person
and work of Christ.[40] The Holy Spirit, he believed, illuminates
Scripture, reveals the Father and the Son, provides guidance, and
gives strength to resist temptation and to do good works: "He will
make the Bible a new book to us. He will make Jesus precious to
us, He will make God the Father ever real to us. We shall not walk
in darkness, but shall have the light of life. We shall not be weak
in the presence of duty or temptation, but 'strong in the Lord, and
in the power of His might' (Ephesians 6:10). We shall be ready to
[do] every good work" (Titus 3:1).[41]

Thus, Brengle's "sanctified sanity" is apparent in his
understanding of the effects of holiness on the knowledge of divine
things. Sanctified intelligence enables the individual to pray better
with his mind, but it also allows him to increase in knowledge
of spiritual realities as revealed in Scripture: "Knowledge and
wisdom must take the place of foolish ignorance. . . . Now,
when the Holy Spirit comes there pours into the soul not only
a tide of love and simple faith, but a flood of light as well, and
prayer becomes not only earnest, but intelligent also. And this
intelligence increases as, under the leadership of the Holy Spirit,
the [W]ord of God is studied."[42] Since holiness results in closer
communion with Christ, prayer in perfect alignment with God's
will is possible. As a result of such "vital union and partnership
with God," the prayers of the sanctified, "inspired by the Holy
Spirit, move all Heaven in their behalf."[43]

Chapter 13

Evangelism and the Holy Life

Equally important to Brengle's influence as a holiness teacher was his lifetime commitment to holiness evangelism. "Soul-winning" was directly related to his concern to lead people into the experience of entire sanctification, believing that holiness was the ultimate goal of salvation. In his practical advice to soul-winners, Brengle underscored the ethical dimensions of the holy life as providing impetus and motive power for effective evangelistic work. Emphasizing the need for revival in the church, he addressed the conditions and hindrances of such, viewing evangelism ultimately as a means of personal and societal transformation.

THE IMPORTANCE OF SOUL-WINNING

Of all Salvation Army activities, Brengle believed in the priority of evangelism. He wrote:

> We may be sweet singers, eloquent and moving preachers, skillful organizers, masters of men and assemblies, wizards of finance, popular and commanding leaders, but if we are not soul-winners, if we do not make men and women see the meaning and winsomeness of Jesus, and hunger for His righteousness and purity, and bow to Him in full loyalty, then one thing, the chief thing. . . we lack.[1]

He maintained that the role of the evangelist involved "winning souls from sin. . . and the binding of them in vital union to Christ. . . making them channels of His saving grace to others." The importance of this task can be discerned by the place Paul gave to it when he mentioned the various orders of ministry, placing the evangelist "next to the apostles and prophets and before the pastor and teacher."[2]

Brengle especially emphasized the importance of the itinerant evangelist's role in relation to other Army ministerial functions:

> The Evangelist or Campaigner is the man who probably more directly than any other labors to accomplish this great work [soul-winning]. The Corps Officer, the Divisional Commander, the Departmental Officer, the Commissioner, has many executive and administrative duties which do not bear so directly upon the saving of men as does the work of the Campaigner. Their work is a vitally essential work in preparing the way for and conserving the work of soul-winning, but much that they do bears only indirectly upon the Salvation of men. The Campaigner's work, however, is direct, immediate, unchanging. . . . His sole burden, his one responsibility, is for the souls of men.[3]

Although insisting that evangelists be humble, Brengle held that such persons should "magnify" their office. Possessing no authority to command others or administer great business, the itinerant evangelist ". . . has spiritual authority, the authority that eternal truth bestows."[4] Such evangelistic ministry needs the support of the church. In dealing with the "Campaigner's reception," Brengle indirectly reveals his own yearning for encouragement and support:

> Finally, this lonely man, coming to a Division and Corps, with no power to command, but only to preach and pray, to help and inspire and to seek the lost, should be received as the messenger from God, and supported by love and prayers and understanding sympathy and helped in his mission in every possible way, that Christ may be glorified, souls won. . . and all comrades quickened and sanctified.[5]

Even though soul-winning can take place in a number of forms, Brengle valued preaching as the chief method of evangelism. The effectiveness of such preaching, however, was directly related to the anointing of the Spirit.

> No man is equipped to rightly preach the Gospel, and undertake the spiritual oversight and instruction of souls,

till he has been anointed with the Holy Ghost. . . . But without this Presence great gifts and profound and accurate learning are without avail in the salvation of men. . . . It is fire men need. . . and when they get it, and not until then, will they preach with the Holy Ghost. . . and surely men shall be saved.[6]

Brengle insisted that Spirit-anointed preaching was not foolish. On the contrary, it is reasonable, persuasive, scriptural, and the source of spiritual healing and comfort. It is reasonable, in that "it takes account of man's reason and conforms to the dictates of common sense. . . . God is the Author of man's intellectual powers, and He endowed him with intellectual powers, and He endowed him with reason, and the Holy Spirit respects these powers, and appeals to reason when He inspires a man to preach to his fellows."[7] It is persuasive, not only with regard to the intellect, but also the religious affections. It is scriptural:

The Gospel in not opposed to natural religion and reason, but it has run far ahead of them. It is a revelation from God of facts, of grace and truth, of mercy and love, of a plan of redemption that man could not discover for himself. And this revelation is recorded in the Scriptures. . . . It shows us Jesus Christ and the way by which we come to Him, and through Him get deliverance from sin and become a new creation. . . . The Holy Spirit makes the word alive. . . and He applies it to the heart of the hearers.[8]

And finally, "this preaching is healing and comforting. . . . It warms the heart with love, strengthens faith, and confirms the will in all holy purposes."[9]

For Brengle, the indispensability of the Spirit for preaching is illustrated in the life of the apostle Paul, as evidenced in certain spiritual characteristics:

The preacher must be more than a man--he must be a man plus the Holy Spirit. Paul was such a man. He was full of the Holy Spirit. . . . In the second chapter of the first of Thessalonians, he gives a picture of his character and ministry which were formed and inspired by the Holy Spirit. . . . He was a joyful preacher. . . . He was a bold preacher. . . . He was without guile. . . . He was not a time-server not a covetous man. . . . He was not vainglorious, nor dictatorial, nor oppressive. . . . With all his boldness and faithfulness he was gentle. . . . Finally, Paul was full of self-sacrificing love.[10]

Even apart from preaching, Salvationists have opportunities for witness through word (personal testimony) and deed (lifestyle evangelism). Brengle especially sought to encourage those within the musical forces of the Army to recognize their opportunities and responsibilities in this regard. He believed that Salvation Army music had the chief function of aiding evangelism: "The Salvation Army bands are different from all other bands in that they play for a purpose. The great high purpose of the Salvation Army bands is to glorify God and to blow salvation into the people in the open air. . . . The object of the band is to help us win souls in the open air. . . . Every band ought not only to be a musical organization, but ought to be a praying organization."[11]

In a letter to an Army bandsmen, Brengle noted the rapid development and excellence of Army banding, and added:

> Especially have I prayed that you, each one of you, may be as ambitious to excel in spirituality and the finest Salvationism and Christ-likeness, as you are to excel as instrumentalists, and that you may encourage each other in spiritual things as earnestly and successfully as you do in things musical. . . . So I pray that you may not become standardized in your experience, for that will mean that you all sink to a common dead level of mediocre spirituality, with no passion for souls. . . . I verily believe that the bandsmen of the country, working together, could start such revivals in the Army as we have not known for many years.[12]

That this concern was ongoing, is reflected in a letter written to Bandmaster George Foster, dated August 17, 1935. After expressing regret for not being able to attend the Old Orchard Beach Camp Meeting due to failing health, Brengle wrote of his desire for Army banding to have a soul-winning priority:

> I have been wondering if you couldn't get the band boys to set for themselves a target of twenty-five or fifty souls for the camp meeting, and send those who are not required to play during the prayer meeting, down into the audience to fish? If they went in twos and tackled their man or boy, I believe they could easily lead twenty-five

or fifty or maybe 100 souls to the Lord. . . . I remember twenty-five or thirty years ago, when the Staff Band from New York did some of the best fishing that we had at Old Orchard, and I would like to see all our bandsmen giving themselves up to this kind of work. They play wonderfully. I rejoice every time I think about them, but what a soul-winning brigade they might be if they each and all prayed much about it, and set themselves with full purpose of heart to bring a multitude to Christ.[13]

Brengle not only had a concern for bandsmen to recognize their evangelistic responsibilities, he also had similar words of advice for the choral groups of the Army. In "A Plea for Soul-Winning Songsters," he wrote: "O songsters, I plead with you to pray before you sing and while you sing, asking God that the people may not think of you, nor see you when you sing, but see only Jesus!"[14]

Brengle defended the importance of child evangelism, believing that Jesus' call to children's ministry was marked by "a heart full of tender love and sympathy for the little ones."[15] His suggestions to soul-winners on ministering to children reflect an understanding of the developmental stages of faith-formation:

Children are not hard to reach with the gospel, if the soul-winner will be simple and use common sense in dealing with them. . . . And yet effort must be put forth ceaselessly to win them, and keep them after they are won. . . . The first thing necessary is to believe in the possibility of the conversion of the children. . . . Second, since they can be won, you must make up your mind that you will win them. . . . Above all, you must be simple, and make things very plain for the children. . . . love will help you. . . . But after we have done all, we must remember that they are only lambs, not sheep. . . . that they are in the formative state. . . that they have a personality and individuality of their own; that they are not always willing to take a simple word of their elders, nor to yield to admonition and instruction, but desire to prove their powers.[16]

In summing up his advice to soul-winners with regard to child evangelism, Brengle wrote: ". . . seek help from God. Get all the help you can from others. . . . Study the best books you can find on the subject. . . . Try to put yourself in the place of the child. . . . But, above all, have a heart full of tender love and sympathy for the little ones. . . . They will feel your love and respond to it, and so you can point them to Jesus. . . . "[17] Brengle maintained that little children are not only loved of God and capable of responding to such love, but that such young converts could be effective soul-winners themselves. He wrote: "Again and again, I find that when the children give their hearts to Jesus they become very ardent little workers to win others. . . . Next to the joy of getting the children saved, is the joy of setting them to work, and seeing the gladness that comes to them when they have won a soul."[18]

PREREQUISITES FOR SOUL-WINNING

Brengle believed that there were certain general prerequisites for soul winning, that if followed, would bear fruit:

> If my heart is right with God. . . . exercise unwavering faith. . . . no longer love the world. . . . willing to bear the reproach of Christ. . . . preach the truth. . . . [engage in] much private prayer and Bible study. . . . not shrink from dealing faithfully with souls. . . . wait on God much for a message and get it direct from Him. . . . no longer seek to please men. . . I am bound to see souls saved and sanctified.[19]

Key to such equipping, however, was God's calling. Brengle maintained that the word of the Lord calls, equips, and empowers the obedient Christian to self-sacrificial, world-transforming love, manifest in soul-winning.[20] Such a calling, however, must be responded to, and not resisted. Brengle wrote:

> God chooses His own workmen, and it is the office of the Holy Spirit to call whom He will to preach the Gospel. . . . An no doubt, He *leads* most men by His providence to their life-work; but the call to preach the Gospel is more than a providential leading; it is a distinct and imperative conviction. . . . The man whom God calls cannot safely neglect or despise the call. He will find his mission on earth, his happiness and peace, his power and prosperity, his reward in Heaven, and probably Heaven itself, bound up with that call and dependent upon it. . . . But if he heeds the call, and cheerfully goes where God appoints, God will go with him; he shall nevermore be left alone.[21]

Brengle often likened evangelism to the agricultural metaphor of sowing and reaping. He believed that the "whitened harvest fields," were the result of six forms of "sowing" that the Army had been involved in since its beginning. In this category, he included: "the *tears* shed for a lost world," the Army's "*prayers*. . . for the salvation of the world"; its "*testimonies*. . . to the forgiveness of sins, the witness of the Spirit and the comforts of the Holy Ghost. . . . to the incoming of the Holy Spirit, to love made perfect, to answered prayers, to Divine guidance. . . . to healings. . . . to deliverance from temptation; the "*songs* of the Army," that "soften the heart. . . . interest, alarm, convict, convert, assure, comfort, correct, inspire, guide, instruct, and illumine"; "its *literature* filled with burning messages of love, yearning appeals, faithful warnings, thrilling experiences and patient instructions"; and "the immeasurable influence of *saintly lives* in shops and mills and offices and stores, in mines and kitchens." With such preparatory seed-sowing, "the harvest is at hand, waiting for the reapers."[22] Brengle stressed the present responsibility of "reaping" which requires soul-winners who have volitionally determined to join the "harvest," individuals who have consecrated themselves to this work, and are willing to give of themselves sacrificially to this task.[23]

Thus, obedience to God's call is one of the secrets of successful soul-winning. Elaborating on this "secret," Brengle wrote:

> This obedience must be prompt. . . . Once the soul-winner knows the Master's will he should not delay to fulfill it. . . . This obedience must be exact. . . . This obedience must be courageous. . . . Do you ask how a man can get such a spirit of courageous obedience? I answer by dying. . . to selfish interests, to the love of praise, to the fear of censure, and to the hope of reward in this world, and by a dare-devil faith in the reward that God will give in the world to come; by a steadfast looking unto and following Jesus; by constraining love, and a constant comparison of time with eternity. This obedience must be glad. . . . It is a glad love-service that God calls us to; and once we are wholly His, and the Comforter abides in us, we shall not find it irksome to obey, and by obedience we shall save both ourselves and others to whom the Lord may send us.[24]

Spiritual leadership, as a gift of God, is also to be sought, exercised, and nurtured by those called to be soul-winners. "The soul-winner must have the power of spiritual leadership. . . . [which] is not won nor established by promotion, but by many prayers and tears. Spiritual leaders are not made by man. . . . but only God. . . . It is not long service and experience that makes spiritual leaders, but vigorous spiritual life."[25]

More specifically, however, Brengle viewed the experience of entire sanctification and faithful prayer as requisite for fruitful evangelism. In terms of the former, he firmly maintained that perfect love was the secret to effective and fulfilling ministry. Reflecting on the life and ministry of William Booth, Brengle wrote:

> Our blessed General, now glorified, served the Lord and his fellowmen for sixty-eight years with ever-increasing ardor and flaming zeal, constrained by the love of Christ. It kept him praying, believing, thinking, planning, devising, sacrificing, toiling to the very end. And so it will any man who cultivates it, who does not frustrate it. It will lead us to much prayer. . . . It will lead us to study and think and meditate as to how best we can promote His interests. It will lead us to labor largely and sacrifice freely and always for His dear sake. It will make us patient with our fellow-men, because He died for them. . . .It will make us diligent, patient, joyous students of His word, that we may find out His will and do it. . . . It will give us instant power over the Tempter, for love to Christ will make us hate sin. . . . It will make us soul-winners out of us. . . . Here is the secret of joy and peace and victory— the love of Christ constraining us. How shall we get it, you ask? At His dear feet, in utter self-abandonment to Him and with simple, unquestioning, obedient faith.[26]

When addressing the spiritual prerequisites of the soul-winner, Brengle provides a biblical basis for personal knowledge of Christ in justification, regeneration, adoption, and entire sanctification.

> Every soul-winner. . . has had a definite personal experience of salvation and the baptism of the Holy Ghost, which brings him into close fellowship and tender friendship and sympathy with the Savior. . . . This must be a definite experience, that tallies with the Word

of God. Such only can give the power and assurance which will enable you to lead and win others. . . . The experience that makes a man a soul-winner is twofold: 1. He must know that his sins are forgiven. . . . He must have. . . a restful consciousness that he has been adopted into God's family. . . . 2. He must be sanctified; he must know his heart is cleansed, that. . . all unholy tempers are destroyed by the Baptism of the Holy Ghost.[27]

In reflecting on Acts 14:1, which speaks of the fruitful preaching of Paul and Barnabas in Iconium, Brengle discerned that their homiletical secret was threefold: "their manner," "their matter," and "their spirit." Ultimately, however, their manner and subject matter were conditioned by their "spirit," which was crucial in effectively communicating their message. "The manner may be acceptable and the message true, but if the spirit of the speaker be not right, there will hardly be a 'great multitude' of believers." Brengle understood preaching in a right spirit as a direct result of entire sanctification: "Oh, it was a bright faith and a burning love that set on fire the spirits of these men! And I think this Christlike spirit molded their manner and made them natural and gentle and strong and true and intense with earnestness. . . ."[28] Not only does holiness equip the soul-winner, but it also provides the proper motivation for evangelism. In relating his experience of entire sanctification, Brengle wrote: "The Holy Spirit took possession of my yielded, open heart. Christ was revealed in me and a great passion for the saving and the sanctifying of men burned within me."[29]

Brengle understood the task of evangelism to involve costly discipleship. He described the secret to revival in terms of the soul-winner's humility, self-denial, and willingness to submit to the pathway of the cross: "Some one, no longer trying to save himself or to advance his own interests, dies. . . to self, to the world, to the praise of men, to the ambition for promotion, for place, for power, and lives unto Christ, lives to save men, and the awakening of sinners comes. . . ."[30] For Brengle, holiness makes this costly devotion possible: "So then the cost of winning souls includes the price that must be paid for a pure heart. I must be clean."[31] It is important to note that not only is sanctification a prerequisite for the soul-winner, but it is the ultimate goal of evangelism. Brengle saw the need to lead converts into the pathway of holiness: ". . . but we do not really win them until we constrain them to follow us, as we follow Christ, through death—death to sin, death to the flesh and the world, into newness of life unto Holiness."[32]

When asked if there was a special message for the present age, Brengle replied that holiness, understood as the experience of the love and grace of God by the indwelling presence of the Holy Spirit, was relevant for every age. He understood, however, the importance of holy living in communicating the gospel effectively. Brengle believed that worldwide evangelization was not dependent on a new message, but on holy lives: "we ourselves must be burning, glowing messengers. It is the man even more than the message that wins men."[33] One reason for this, according to Brengle, is that the experience of holiness creates within the soul-winner a love for souls. "Love for Jesus Christ and love toward everybody for His dear sake is Heaven begun below. To this heaven of love He now calls us, and into this heaven of love He now brings us, and through this little heaven He fits us for, and brings us to, the infinite, eternal heaven of love beyond the grave."[34]

Brengle maintained that holiness increases the desire to save souls, in fact, "the zeal of a man with a clean heart, full of the Holy Ghost, increases year by year." Such zeal for the salvation and sanctification of souls leads to practical action, as the sanctified evangelist takes every opportunity to witness to others. "Holiness makes it easy for him to do this. He loves to do it. He finds that as he follows the Spirit, the Lord fills his mouth with truth, and gives him something to say."[35] Thus, for Brengle, the experience of entire sanctification finds its chief expression in holiness evangelism. He maintained that ". . . holiness not only makes us eager for the salvation of sinners, but fills us with unutterable longings for the perfecting of the saints. We want to see 'every man perfect in Christ Jesus.' I have never known anyone to get the blessing, without this desire following."[36]

Recognizing that Kingdom work is beyond human ability, and totally dependent on the presence and power of the Holy Spirit, Brengle wrote:

> When the Holy Spirit is allowed the right of way within us, He will fill our hearts with peace, as he leads us to trust fully in Jesus. He will shed abroad love in our hearts. . . . He will fill us with a passion for righteousness,

which burns like flame, and at the same time fills us with pity and compassion for the unrighteous. He will help us believe for the impossible because we are linked up with Him with whom all things are possible. . . . He will help us to win good success in our work, and at last find ourselves at home for ever in Heaven with the souls we have won for Him.[37]

In this regard, Brengle treated the issue of casting out devils, not so much as the exorcism of demonic spirits, but as the convicting power of the Holy Spirit made manifest through the sanctified soul-winner. He qualified "Satanic possession" as that ". . . which manifests itself in pride, quickness to take offence, jealousy and suspicion, shame of the Cross, covetousness and selfishness, evil temper and ungodly ambition. Surely power to reveal these hiding places of the devil, and to cast him out. . . is needed, and ought to be coveted by every soul-winner. . . . " Brengle further defined the nature, appropriation, and exercise of this power:

1) It is the gift of God. . . . It is none other than the power of the Holy Ghost manifesting itself in perfect love, dwelling in meek, lowly, believing hearts. 2) To have this gift we must have a definite, present, conscious experience of uttermost salvation through faith in and union with Jesus. There is no substitute for faith in this matter of saving men, of dislodging evil and casting out devils. . . . We must *exercise* faith. Passive faith will not do; it must be active. . . . Such faith is perfected in us by the Holy Spirit in response to hearty obedience and in answer to many prayers. [38]

Thus, holiness, understood as the indwelling presence and power of the Holy Spirit, is absolutely essential for Kingdom-building ministry. Although viewing entire sanctification as fundamental to effective evangelistic work, Brengle also realized that an ever-increasing need for power in Christian ministry requires ongoing renewal. He wrote: "To do God's work we must have God's power. The soul-winner receives this power when he is sanctified wholly and filled with the Spirit, and he need never lose it. But while the Holy Spirit abides with the believer, there yet seems to be need for frequent renewals of the power He bestows."[39]

Brengle had much to say about prayer as a prerequisite for effective soul-winning. He believed that "all great soul-winners have been men of much and mighty prayer, and all great Awakenings have been preceded and carried out by persevering, prevailing knee-work in the closet." Brengle illustrated this from the lives of Jesus, Paul, Luther, Knox, Baxter, Wesley, Brainerd, Edwards, Livingstone, Finney, and Booth, claiming that: "God has not changed. He waits to do the will of praying men." Brengle thus exhorted Salvationists to spend time in prayer, if they would be effective evangelists. He noted, however, that there are hindrances to engage in such revival prayer. He understood such to include: "wicked spirits," "sluggishness of the body and mind, caused by sickness, loss of sleep, or too much sleep, overeating," and "failure to respond quickly when. . . led by the Spirit to go to secret prayer."[40] In dealing with how to properly prepare for an evangelistic service, he reminded his readers that the saving presence of Christ in their meetings is not to be presumed upon, but earnestly sought by prayer:

> Now Jesus is ready and willing to go up to every camp Meeting and convention and council and indoor and outdoor Meeting in all the land, and make His personal presence felt by every saint and Soldier, but each one must seek Him. . . . Oh, that we may always make sure that He is with us, and not to take it for granted, else we shall find we have been going on a fool's errand without Him.[41]

Brengle maintained that prayer was an avenue through which spiritual blessing and power were received; hence, the need for constant prayer in evangelistic work. Such prayer must be "definite" and "bold," it must be "importunate, persevering," it must be "for the glory of God, and according to His will. . . . "[42] In answer to the question how a soul-winner should pray, Brengle responded: "In faith, believing, with utter confidence in the sympathy and present help of the Heavenly Father who loves us, of the Savior who has died, but ever lives and intercedes for us before the throne, and of the indwelling Comforter who is ever on our side, waiting to help us. So pray expectantly, and then have watchful patience."[43]

PRACTICAL ADVICE IN SOUL-WINNING[44]

Brengle emphasized synergistic strategies in evangelism, recognizing the divine initiative as well as human responsibility:

> God loves sinners, and the Holy Spirit is always waiting and seeking to find them off guard and surprise them with salvation. . . . To some hearts we must lay siege, and with many arts, wiles and secret prayers, public assaults and tender entreaties, and solemn warnings and steadfast faithfulness, work to win them, and if we do not lose heart and hope, we shall seldom fail. The Lord is with us. Others are like ripe fruit, ready to be picked at any time, only we must be always about the Master's business and not let the ripened fruit spoil for lack of picking.[45]

In soul-winning, Brengle was careful to 'let God be God,' and encouraged others to approach the task of soul-winning unapologetically. In a letter to Lily in 1887, Sam wrote: "But I find that often. . . we drive the sword of truth into them and then we are tempted to say some right thing, something pleasant, agreeable, immediately, to save our own reputation for goodness or cleverness; or we are filled with fear lest we have unnecessarily offended them, instead of trusting God and leaving them alone with their own thundering consciences."[46]

Despite his call to unapologetic evangelism, Brengle's methods evidence sensitivity and Christlike consideration toward those being evangelized. This is illustrated in his article, "How to Win the Jews to Christ" (1929), which is all the more remarkable for its pre-Holocaust sensitivity to the Jewish plight:

> It is not an easy matter for the Jew to accept Christ Jesus as the Messiah. It means for him a much heavier and sharper cross than for the Gentile. Therefore he should be approached: 1) With sympathy and Christ-like love. He has seldom been loved by Christians as he should be loved. He has been despised. He has been hated. He has been feared. He has been snubbed and persecuted, but he has not been loved and sought with Christlike affection. . . . 2) He should be approached in a prayerful spirit and in entire dependence upon the Holy Spirit. . . . 3) He should not be approached with wordy argument, but, rather, with glad testimony to our own

experience of Christ, and he should be urged to seek the experience for himself. . . . Our expectation and hope to win him should not depend primarily upon argument, but upon experience, and our appeal should not be so much to his intellect as to his heart, to his conscience, and his will.[47]

Although urging sensitivity and a measure of accommodation in evangelism, Brengle warned against "misrepresenting God." Soul-winners must maintain a balanced, scriptural representation of God's wrath and mercy:

If we are to win souls and save our own, we must not distort the picture of God's character which we hold up to view. . . . Some religious teachers misrepresent God by making Him utterly savage and cruel. . . others misrepresent God by making Him appear as a sort of goody-goody God, who fawns upon sinners with mawkish sympathy. . . . The truth lies between these two extremes. There is mercy in God, but it is mingled with severity; there is wrath in God, but it is tempered with mercy. The great soul-winners from Bible times till now have recognized this; they have held an even balance between the goodness and the severity of God, because the Bible does so; and the Bible. . . is the only. . . authoritative representation of God.[48]

In evangelistic work, Brengle differentiated between the kind and application of truth needed by unsaved, saved, and sanctified individuals. Soul-winners need spiritual discernment to know what truth is needed, and when such should be applied. Once converted, a person ". . . should be instructed as to the nature and extent of the consecration that is expected of him, and he should be urged and . . . encouraged to make this consecration." Further, the saved individual "should be instructed as to the fact of inbred sin which he will soon find stirring within him, and the importance and possibility of having the enemy cast out. Holiness should be presented to him, not so much as a stern demand of a holy God, as rather his glorious privilege as a child of our Heavenly Father." Brengle explained the relational dynamic of entire sanctification in terms of "yielding to the Heavenly Bridegroom," and "fall[ing] . . . desperately in love with Him by the incoming Holy Spirit." He warned officers to so live out their sanctification, that others will understand full salvation as an "experience of perfect love," rather than a "legal experience."[49]

With regard to leading people into entire sanctification, Brengle gave practical advice of how to encourage people to "make an everlasting and uttermost consecration of their all to God" in seeking and waiting for the experience of entire sanctification: "Show them that they must perfectly submit to God. . . . that they must perfectly trust Him, and rest on His promises now for present cleansing from all sin. That having perfectly submitted to Him, and perfectly trusted Him, they must now keep steadily looking to Him for power to obey, and also for the filling of their hearts with the fire of perfect love."[50] Not only did Brengle encourage others to faithfully preach holiness, he also realized the danger of professionalism in the pulpit. In a letter to Lily written in 1887, he wrote:

> There is a danger of becoming a merely *professional* Holiness teacher, having the form without the power, becoming a man of words, words, words, without any Spirit. . . . The dear Lord has greatly blessed me. . . by showing me that the way to overcome this danger was to pray short, simple, earnest little prayers in public, pray much in private, and to speak what He gave me, and to cease speaking when the Spirit ceased prompting me. This means a close walk with God, and a most careful hearkening to the softest whispers of the Spirit.[51]

Itinerant evangelists ("Specials") were given advice as to "what they should do, avoid, and be." In terms of what a Special should do: 1) "gird and equip himself for his work," 2) "set apart an hour in the early portion of the day to get alone with God and pray," 3) "read," and, 4) "watch and pray and give diligent heed to make his conversation and spirit in private a mighty auxiliary to his public work." In terms of what a Special should avoid: 1) "spiritual, mental and physical indolence," 2) "spiritual pride," 3) "thinking he could be just as successful out of the Army as he can be in it," 4) "gossip," 5) "novels" and too much time reading newspapers, 6) "over-eating," 7) "over-sleeping," 8) "murmuring and complaining," 9) "making hasty judgments," 10) covetousness and anxiety about the future," and, 11) "working beyond his strength." And, in terms of what a Special should be: 1) "a man of God," 2) "an ambassador of heaven," 3) "a watchman

(Ezk 3:17–21)," 4) "a shepherd, who feeds without fleecing the lambs and sheep of Jesus," and, 5) "a thorough Salvationist, a living embodiment, a faithful exponent of the Army's principles."[52]

Another danger the soul-winner must avoid stems from an imbalanced expression of the light and love of holiness. Brengle wrote:

> Sanctification floods the soul with great light and with great love, and thus subjects the possessor to two great and opposite temptations and dangers. If the sanctified man leans to the side of light, he is likely to become critical and faultfinding. . . . On the other hand, if he leans to the side of love, he is likely to be too lenient, too easy. . . . To keep in the middle of the way in a blaze of light without becoming critical and harsh. . . and in fullness of love without being soft and weak. . . is the problem every sanctified soul must solve in order to keep the blessing and be increasingly useful.[53]

In lamenting the decline of the Soldiers' and Friday night Holiness meetings (as means of spiritual nurture), Brengle warned:

> A Holiness meeting is not one in which to club people, or skin them. . . . It is rather a meeting to show them their wondrous heritage in Jesus. You need not condemn them. Just show them what Jesus has for them till they see how far short they fall, and they will condemn themselves and seek the blessing. . . . but where these meetings are neglected, Soldiers become careless, stingy, self-indulgent, ready to neglect duty and make excuses for unfaithfulness; while Officers, feeling that Soldiers are not up to the standard, are likely to become harsh and critical and full of complaints; or else they sink to the level of the Soldiers and become light and frivolous and worldly, and thus the whole tone of the Army is lowered.[54]

Brengle underscored the need for soul-winners to be involved in the nurture and growth of their converts, by means of the motive-power of love: "There is a danger of spending far more effort and care in getting people to the Penitent-form than in keeping them after they are there. Soul-winners are not spiritual incubators, but fathers and mothers in the faith with all the measureless responsibility not only for saving souls, but of keeping them after they are saved."[55] He outlined a number of ways this could be accomplished. Converts need to be visited, to be encouraged to read scripture and other devotional literature, to be taught how to pray, and urged to pray as a regular practice. They are to be taught how to exercise faith in the context of temptation, to engage in spiritual warfare for souls, and they are to be encouraged to pursue holiness. With regard to the latter, Brengle wrote: "They should be patiently, tenderly, firmly led into the experience of sanctification or, as it is otherwise known, 'perfect love.' They must not be allowed to stop at consecration, but pressed on into a definite experience of full salvation."[56] Ultimately, love is the one thing needful for 'keeping the flock,' and soul-winners need to be baptized by holy love in order to 'feed the sheep' with Christlike care.[57]

Although he insisted that a faith-filled and love-inspired and impelled message is essential to effective evangelism, Brengle was also concerned about the demeanor of evangelistic workers after worship services, pointing out that frivolous and jesting behavior by the preacher after the meeting, undermines the effectiveness of the sermon, in that it diminishes the gravity and seriousness of the spiritual atmosphere of the moment. He exhorted officers to allow the Holy Spirit to so control their behavior, "that those who got a blessing in the meeting shall not lose it, but rather have it increased after the meeting."[58]

Brengle also recognized the need to "deal gently" with others. In enumerating the reasons why soul-winners should deal gently with sinners and backsliders, he emphasized the need for holiness as expressed in Christlike compassion. This is only possible as the effectual outworking of the mind of Christ expressing itself in the fruit of the Spirit. Brengle wrote:

> We should deal gently with them in order that we may be like Jesus. . . . lest we ourselves grieve the Spirit and become backsliders. . . . that we may save the backslider. Jesus loves him still, seeks him continually, waits to forgive him and cleanse him and to restore to him. . . . But gentleness is not inconsistent with great firmness and unswerving loyalty to the truth. . . . But how shall one who has not this spirit of perfect gentleness secure it? It is a fruit of the Spirit, and is to be had only at Jesus' feet. . . . it is given to be like Him in these heavenly

tempers and dispositions. 'Let this mind be in you, which was also in Christ Jesus' (Phil 2:5).[59]

Brengle encouraged evangelists not to be discouraged with small numbers in attendance at meetings. In his article entitled, "On Preaching to the Few," he wrote of the potential of those attending such services:

> The smallest crowd may have immeasurable possibilities in it. A Luther, a Wesley, a William Booth may be looking out through the eyes of some little child or some awkward, shy, or mischievous adolescent boy. . . . Sometimes we reach them indirectly. We get some nobody saved and God uses that nobody to reach somebody who becomes 'great in the sight of the Lord.' Let us have no hesitancy in permitting our spiritual imagination to reinforce our faith and enkindle our hope. . . .[60]

Zeal for soul-winning was one result of the experience of entire sanctification. But just as there is a proper evangelistic zeal, Brengle warned against an improper form. He identified various types of zeal which should be avoided: "partial zeal. . . . frequently seen in those who violently attack one kind of sin, while probably they themselves are secretly indulging in some other sin. . . . party zeal. . . takes the form of excessive sectarian and denominational zeal, and makes bigots of men. . . . the zeal of ignorance. . . . being ignorant of God's righteousness, and going about to establish. . . [one's] own righteousness." On the other hand, "true zeal" finds its source in knowledge "from above," and includes "knowledge of the dread condition of the sinner without Christ," and a "knowledge of the unspeakable gift of God, of the possibilities of grace for the vilest sinner. . . . " Such zeal is marked by faithfulness to Christ and the spiritual nurture of souls (characterized as leading others into the experience of holiness). Also, "true zeal is sacrificial," as soul-winners follow in the pathway of the cross.[61]

Brengle's practical advice to soul-winners included suggestions on how best to use time, what to study, how to maintain physical health, and the proper attitude toward money. In terms of time management, he urged soul-winners to make holy use of their time. In spelling this out, Brengle wrote:

> The soul-winner must value time. . . . To redeem time is
> not to be in a feverish hurry, but to make prompt, steady,
> quiet use of the minutes. . . . It takes no more time to ask
> a man about his soul than about his health; but it will
> require more love, and prayer, and holy tact. . . and these
> the soul-winner must have. . . . Finally, if you would
> redeem the time, keep a conscience void of offence, keep
> your soul at white heat with love for Jesus and the dying
> world.[62]

He emphasized the importance of studying scripture, Christian
literature, and the religious experiences of other Christians for
soul-winning.

> No man or woman need hope to be a permanently
> successful soul-winner who is not a diligent student
> of the truth, of the will and ways of God, of men, and
> of methods. . . . The first thing and the last thing to be
> studied is the Bible. . . . He [soul-winner] must become
> full of the thought of God. . . . But the soul-winner must
> not study it simply that he may preach, but that he may
> himself live by it. . . . Besides the Bible the soul-winner
> ought to lay out a course of reading for himself, and stick
> to it, reading a few pages each day. . . . The soul-winner
> should study not only books but men and methods. . . . by
> close, personal, private conversation with, and inquiry
> about the religious experiences of the Christians around
> us.[63]

Brengle also advised soul-winners on the relation of
physical wellness and spiritual vitality concerning soul-winning.
"The soul-winner must take every proper care of his body, yet
without everlastingly coddling. . . and pitying himself. This is
his sacred duty. The body is the instrument through which the
mind and soul work in this world." Brengle gave practical advice
concerning proper rest, diet, and exercise, using John Wesley
and others as models to follow. Not only is the soul-winner's
physical stamina affected by proper care of the body, but there
are also psychological benefits: "The man who never relaxes,
however religious he may be, is likely to become morose, irritable,
impatient, and. . . become melancholy and full of gloom. . . . In
other words, there must be rest. . . . Eating and drinking may not
seem to have anything to do with soul-saving, but nevertheless

they have." For those already suffering from illness or poor health, Brengle shared from his own experience: "Personally, I have suffered much from broken health, exhausted nerves and sleepless nights, and at one time feared lest my work was done; but by prayer and care I have been so far restored to health and strength that I can work six days in the week with all my might, sleep like a kitten, and digest my food fairly well."[64]

In the area of finances, Brengle encouraged evangelists to trust God for their daily provision, and not be distracted from the task of soul-winning:

> The soul-winner to be successful must not be over-anxious about money affairs, but must laugh at the devil and all his fears, and count God faithful, trusting Him to supply all his needs. . . . This freedom from worrying anxiety is the privilege and duty of all soul-winners. . . . The soul-winner must not be anxious about his bread, must beware of covetousness, and must seek to save souls.[65]

REVIVALS

Brengle, as a 'Spiritual Special' promoted religious revivals for most of his ministry. Because of this interest, his writings are replete with references to revivalism.[66] In response to the question of whether there was a special message for soul-winning in the present age, Brengle underscored love-transformed living as the common catalyst of revivals in every age. He discussed the ministries of Martin Luther, George Fox, John Wesley, and William Booth as examples, writing: "Each one of these men first got a definite burning experience of redeeming love and grace, that filled his own heart with peace, with flaming love to God, restful confidence in Jesus, tender compassion for his fellow-men, and then, after diligent searching of Scripture, and after much prayer, he spake as he was moved by the Holy Ghost."[67] Thus, for Brengle, love-transformed persons were the most effective message (and soul-winners) for any age. "Our problem," he wrote, "is not so much to find a message for the age, as to keep the beaming joy, the glory, the radiance and burning love which are found alone in looking long and daily into the face of Jesus. . . joyously embracing the cross and following Him."[68]

Brengle often expressed his conviction that a world-wide revival was possible. In an officers' councils at Old Orchard Beach,

Maine in the summer of 1933, he urged that a revival be sought throughout the Army world. This emphasis became a regular feature in his literary contribution to the *War Cry* and other Army periodicals. In "A Revival In Every Salvation Army Corps" (an article that went through several reprintings), Brengle took his lead from the life and times of the prophet Habakkuk, calling the Army to revival. Reflecting on Habakkuk 3:2, he wrote:

> Shall we not take up his plea? Do we not need, can we not have, a revival in every Corps of the Salvation Army world? Oh, how I want to see it before I die! The need is great! The times are out of joint. The whole world is in the midst of one of the major crises of all historic times. A vast revolution is taking place in economics, in politics, in morals. . . . Everything that can be shaken is being shaken. . . . We need a revival. It is the greatest need of our times. The Church needs it. The Army needs it. The world gropes in darkness and confusion for want of it, and sinners perish without it.[69]

Brengle maintained that such a revival would result in the restoration of a reverent fear of God and a sense of sin, a renewed appreciation for God's moral law,[70] and the manifestation of the love and power of the Holy Spirit. He wrote: "We need a revival that will make men stand in awe of the moral law. . . . we need a revival that will quicken the sense of moral and spiritual responsibility to God where it exists, and restore it where it is lost. We need a revival to reveal to our people the mighty love and energies of the Holy Spirit and their own capacities for service when filled with the Spirit."[71]

Brengle believed that hindrances to revival in the church included spiritual apathy and a lack of spiritual sensitivity:

> There are difficulties in the way of reaching souls today. There is a drift away from organized Christianity. The Church is no longer attractive to masses of people. . . . Again, there is a decay of the sense of sin and the reverent fear of God among men, but this is due to the failure to hear the whole counsel of God proclaimed by Fire-touched lips and hearts aflame with the sense of God's claims and the danger of neglect.[72]

He also viewed an undue emphasis on premillennial eschatology as a hindrance to revival. Although eager with expectation concerning the Second Coming of Christ in the future, Brengle maintained the importance of waiting on the Holy Spirit to reveal Christ in *present* revival. He emphasized that world-wide revival begins with personal revival, by means of the baptism of the Holy Spirit.[73]

Brengle delineated certain conditions that people who want a revival need to consider. He first questioned the motive for wanting a revival: "If you want a revival, what do you want it for? That you may make a good showing on your next inspection?. . . . Do you want it that God's name be hallowed, His Kingdom come and His will be done on earth as it is in Heaven? Do you want it because your heart aches and hurts to see men going heedlessly to hell and destruction. . . ?"[74] He also asked whether those officers who want revival are willing to count the cost:

> If you want revival, what are you willing to do to pay for it? Are you willing to deny yourself and give yourself to earnest, thoughtful. . . prayer, and prolonged, persistent, self-sacrificing, patient labors for it?. . . Will you stir up your love and be a bit more tender in your home and among the people whom you meet? Will you bear a bit more patiently with the things in others that displease you?. . . Will you read the Bible and good books more. . . so that your heart may be full of God's thoughts and so prepared for revival work?. . . Soul winning is not always easy work. You must wrestle with God in prayer, and you must wrestle with sinners in close personal dealing, and you must wrestle with sleepiness and sloth and indifference in yourself if you want a revival.[75]

Thus, divine working in revival requires human cooperation in a synergistic relationship. Brengle was clear on the nature of human responsibility in the preparation for, and spread of, revivals: "Revivals will surely follow when Officers and Soldiers consecrate themselves fully to the Lord and give themselves whole-heartedly and persistently to prayer and personal work for souls. . . . Revivals begin like a fire. . . . If you, my comrade, burst into flame of holy desire and love and faith and prayer and whole-hearted consecrated effort, the revival in your Corps will have begun."[76] In offering advice on how to bring revival to the local church, Brengle exhorted the reader to: "Ask for it, and continue asking. . . . Believe for it, stir up your faith. . . . Believe that the Holy Ghost is working with you. He surely is. Work for it. . . . Be prepared to make sacrifices for it. . . . Don't be discouraged, at least don't yield to discouragement; struggle on, pray on and God will help you and give you victory."[77]

Brengle believed that revivals were especially needed during times of social upheaval and international crisis. For example, he affirmed the need for revivals in war-time, exhorting his readers to meet the conditions that need to be met for revivals to occur. Brengle expressed uncertainty with regard to the outcome of the war (WWI), but rather than attempting to forecast the future, he maintained that:

> Our duty, our solemn, imperative duty, is with the present. The war will not make men better, except as it casts them each upon God. Only by a change of the hearts of men can the world be made better, and only by such a change can they escape 'the wrath to come.' If, then, we love God and our fellow men, our duty is to pray and believe and labor with all our might for the salvation of sinners and the sanctification of believers, and so we shall hasten the coming of 'the new Heaven and new earth, wherein dwelleth righteousness.[78]

What the world needs in every age are Spirit-transformed hearts and lives made possible by revival-fire. Only in this way can social, political, and economic justice be realized:

> The world needs peace, readjustment, disarmament of armies and navies, just treaties, stable governments, unfettered trade, but above all it needs a revival of the reverent fear and love of God, the consciousness of things eternal, the sense of Heaven and Hell, not nebulous and far away, but near about us. It needs a Christian conscience, which makes men sensitive to sin. It needs a revival of pure and undefiled religion. . . . Only the Blood of the Crucified One can make clean the thoughts and imaginations and desires of the deep, sinful heart of man. Only the baptism of fire and the Holy Spirit can purify the nature and fill the heart with love to God and man, and for this we need a revival.[79]

Elsewhere, Brengle wrote about revival as cure for societal ills: "The selfish spirit of the world calls for a revival. The profiteering of greedy capitalists, and the strikes of laborers, regardless of the welfare of consumers; the aged, the infirm and the little children call down the wrath of God upon our generation for the sin of covetousness, and to change this condition of society and avert the righteous and certain wrath of God we need a revival that will fill the hearts of men with reverent consideration for their fellows, with brotherly love for all men, and joy in service and sacrifice for one another."[80]

Brengle not only viewed revival as necessary for the transformation of individual lives and social structures, but for the continued spiritual life and growth of the church. It is only through revival that "the spiritual conquest of the world" is possible, and thus, for Brengle, a special concern of the Army:

> The Salvation Army was born in a revival, its Founder was converted in a revival. . . . the officers and soldiers of the Army are children of revivals, and they will have clearness of vision, fervor of heart, and abounding spiritual life and power only as revivals continue. Without revivals we are as cold and dark, and dead as a furnace without a fire. The surest way to develop the rich, ripe fruit of the spirit in soldiers and officers is to promote revivals.[81]

Spiritual fruit promoted by revival included: "Brotherly love and unity. . . . joy in the Lord. . . . prayerfulness. . . . open windows upon Eternity, upon God, and Heaven and Hell, and sin, and moral responsibility, and duty, and final judgment." Additionally, Brengle maintained that "revivals make men and women and children courageous and daring in the service of the Lord and in efforts to win others to Him. . . . [and] cause hard hearts to open, purse strings to relax and money to flow in God's work. . ."[82] In a similar vein, he elsewhere maintained that:

> Revivals not only result in the salvation of sinners; they bring home backsliders, they stir up careless and lukewarm Christians, they fill the saints with joy, they set up standards for the young people, they make everybody feel the reality and importance of salvation, they shut the mouths of unbelievers, they inspire and train workers, they make gifted young men and women feel it to be worth while to give up pleasure and moneymaking to work for God and their fellow men. They fill earth with

the spirit of Heaven. They open the hearts of men that God may come in.[83]

In the work of evangelism, the fullness of the Holy Spirit equips the soul-winner for spiritual warfare. Such warfare has allies, such as human restlessness apart from God, the human faculty of conscience, other Christians, the reality of death, and the convicting and convincing work of the Holy Spirit. Brengle wrote about these revival allies:

> In every man's breast conscience sits in judgment upon his acts, his choices, his character. . . . and is God's ally and ours in the heart of every man. Good Christian people are our allies. . . . helping to dispel the darkness that envelops sinners. . . . We are not alone in our warfare. Deaths and funerals and open graves are our allies. Through these. . . . men glimpse eternity. . . . Let us appeal to the realities of eternity and press them home. . . upon the attention of our hearers, and we shall go a long way to win them. God the Holy Ghost is our Ally. . . . He is ever whispering to the hearts of men, striving the wills of men, quickening the consciences of men. . . . Let us cooperate with Him, and work in glad and bold confidence, since He is our Helper. He will help us to pray, to believe, and win souls.[84]

Finally, Brengle maintained that "believing, persistent, [and] purposeful prayer was a necessary prerequisite for a revival. He exhorted Salvationists to: ". . . have faith in God! Go to work, serve the Lord, and work as the old-time Salvationists worked. Pray as they prayed, and see whether you shall not have a revival."[85] A more direct affirmation of the place of prayer as a catalyst of revival was discovered among Brengle's papers after his death: "God listens for prayers for a revival and He answers prayer. Revivals always begin in some longing, eager, praying heart or hearts. . . . It is sustained prayer, prayer that holds on, prayer that is repeated again and again through days and weeks and months and years, that brings great revivals."[86] He regularly challenged Salvationists to commit themselves to prayer for revival, believing that ". . . if soldiers and officers throughout the Army world will give themselves up to a year of prayer and Bible searching, the Army world will be swept by such a revival as has not been known."[87] While Brengle encouraged Salvationists to be

programmatic in praying for revival, he clearly understood the
source of all spiritual grace to be found in Christ:

> Again, I say, it is not the numbers present that make a
> successful prayer meeting; it is the presence of Jesus. Two
> or three who get alone with Him, finding Him, hearing
> from Him, getting filled with His Spirit, kindling into
> flame through His touch and going out from their place
> of prayer with His glory in their hearts and reflected in
> their faces, will move Heaven and earth and outwit and
> thwart Hell, while a thousand who come together, sing
> and talk and pray a little, but without getting into close
> grips with Jesus, will accomplish nothing.[88]

Chapter 14

Holiness and the Ethical Dimensions of Brengle's Eschatology

———————

Although the importance of his contribution to the development of Army holiness doctrine is generally acknowledged, what is less well-known are the ways Brengle's holiness priorities influenced other areas of his theology. This chapter explores the effect of Brengle's pneumatology on his eschatological understanding, by examining a variety of passages from primary source materials. Although providing no systematic presentation of his theology, Brengle's numerous writings evidence a characteristic 'sanctified sanity' in his understanding of eschatology.

HOLINESS AND THE ETHICAL KINGDOM

Brengle's holiness theology modified his understanding of the kingdom of God. He came to hold a postmillennial view of eschatology, emphasizing the present reign of Christ, a position characterized by an optimism of grace, which was grounded in the transforming presence and power of the Holy Spirit. He maintained a belief in the present working of the triune God within history, leading to final victory. This perspective was conditioned by his own experience of entire sanctification:

> Many of God's children are longing for Jesus to come in Person, visibly to lead His hosts to victory. But ever since that wonderful morning forty-five years ago when He baptized me with the Holy Ghost and fire, purifying my heart and revealing Himself within me, I have felt that He meant to win His triumphs through dead men

and women--dead to sin, to the world, to its prizes and praises; and alive to Him, filled with His Spirit, indwelt by His presence, burning with His love. . . . I expect the true Vine to show forth all its strength, its beauty, its fruitfulness *through the branches.* I do not expect the love of the Father, the eternal intercession of the risen and enthroned Son, the wise and loving and ceaseless ministry of conviction, conversion, regeneration and sanctification of the Holy Ghost. . . to fail. Jesus is even *now* leading on His hosts to victory, Hallelujah![1]

In a letter dated January 1935, Brengle further delineated his eschatological perspective, marked as it was by an optimism amidst present darkness: "Mind, I do not say that Christ is not coming and that very soon, but do not be carried away with those who are all the time studying the signs. Personally, I feel it very probable that there are mightier revivals to come upon us than the world has yet ever known. . . . I am a pessimistic optimist."[2]

Brengle's eschatology was shaped by the theology of John Wesley, as mediated to him by his teacher/mentor, Daniel Steele, prior to any contact with the Salvation Army. Nonetheless, he shared with William Booth a postmillennial vision for the Army in relation to world-wide revival.[3] The following passage evidences his understanding of the eschatological dimensions of holiness revivalism:

The world and the church look to the Army for spiritual leadership. Large sections of the church have lost spiritual vision and power. Other sections are looking and praying for Jesus to come in Second Advent power and glory to save us. But my own belief is that He is waiting for His people to humble themselves, confess their leanness of soul, reconsecrate themselves for the great task, receive the Holy Ghost, and believe in the Holy Ghost and in the unseen presence of Christ. If we give ourselves day and night to glad, believing, expectant prayer and whole-hearted work for souls, we shall find that He is with us in old-time power.[4]

Brengle understood holiness as the power by which the world would be won for Christ, and he believed that this emphasis was the hallmark of the Salvation Army mission: "To this doctrine and experience the Salvation Army has been committed from the beginning. . . . and one of the chief secrets of its world-conquering power."[5] For him, there were eschatological dimensions to the spread of holiness: "And the whole earth is waiting for the men and women. . . who live in Christ and in whom Christ lives. When the world is filled with such men or controlled by them, then, and only then, will strikes and wars, and bitter rivalries and insane hatreds, and disgusting and hellish evils cease, and the promise and purpose of Christ's coming be fulfilled."[6]

For Brengle, the kingdom of God has come to earth through the work of the Holy Spirit in the experience of entire sanctification, manifest in lives of self-sacrificial love. He wrote:

> The word of the Lord came to multiplied thousands of humble, unknown lads and lassies in kitchens and laundries, in mills and mines and markets, in stores and factories and offices, on shipboard and on farms, and made them mighty in simple faith and burning love and Christlike unselfishness to confound the wisdom and cast down the strength of this world, and to establish the kingdom of heaven upon earth.[7]

Thus, there are personal and social implications to holiness, eschatologically understood, as reflected in Brengle's meditation on Matthew 21:12–13:

> This cleansing of the temple is but a type of His cleansing energies of the world. He came to cleanse men from their sin. Brother, know you not that you are the temple of God!. . . When He came into the world, man was. . . enslaved. . . . But before the impact of His Spirit slavery has vanished from all forward looking nations and will vanish from the earth. Woman is no longer a chattel for her husband but has entered into her rights as a human being. . . . He will yet make the world a temple of God in which all men shall be brothers and the sacrificial love, pure and just, which burned in His heart shall burn in the heart of redeemed humanity.[8]

With regard to the heightened interest in interpreting end-time prophecy characteristic of many premillennial Christians of his day, Brengle wrote: "Personally, I do not consider it profitable to speculate on questions of that character."[9] He felt that Christian preoccupation with prophecy (understood as foretelling the future) undercut the impetus for evangelism.

Writing to his long-time friend, S. Parkes Cadman (well-known radio preacher), Brengle stated: "It seems to me the church is confronted by two great evils, one by much destructive teaching of the so-called modernism, and puerile prophetic teachings of many of the premillennialists the other."[10] Elsewhere, Brengle decried premillennial eschatology as a hindrance to revival: "Other sections [of the church] are looking and praying for Jesus to come in Second Advent power and glory to save us. But my own belief is that He is waiting for His people to humble themselves for the great task [revival], receive the Holy Ghost, and believe in the Holy Ghost and in the unseen presence of Christ."[11] Although acknowledging the fact that anticipation of the promised return of Christ may motivate some to live lives pleasing to God, Brengle emphasized the abiding presence of the triune God, experienced in entire sanctification, as the true motive power for holy living.

> Some people lay great stress upon the second coming of Christ as an incentive to fine and holy living, and I would not minimize this. . . . [but] when the Holy Guest abides within, the Father and the Son are there too; and what finer, and more searching and sanctifying incentive to holy living can one have than this indwelling presence of the Father, Son and Holy Ghost, as Guest of the soul?[12]

Biblical prophecy, for Brengle, was not so much God's blueprint for the future (*contra* dispensationalism), but a summons to ethical living in the present. Illuminated by the Spirit, the sanctified Christian is enabled to understand the present implications of eschatology. Brengle maintained that:

> Many students of prophecy think the prophets have put into our hands a God-given telescope, through which we can peer into the future and foresee the course of all coming history to the utmost bounds of time, and they prepare elaborate charts and write no end of books and make learned mathematical calculations, and often fix dates for the end of all things, but I have never been helped, but rather confused, in trying so to interpret the great prophets. Their value to me ever since God sanctified me has appeared to consist not in the light they throw upon generations yet unborn, but the light they throw upon my own generation.[13]

Thus, rather than foretelling the future, the main purpose of prophecy is to reveal the present implications of God's character and will. About the prophets, Brengle wrote: "Their prophecies are meant to enable me to understand the present, to recognize my own duty, to interpret the will and ways of God to the men of my own generation. . . . There is an element of foretelling in the messages of the prophets, but the infinitely greater element was that of forthtelling, revealing God Himself, His character, His holiness. . . . "[14]

For Brengle, the kingdom of God is not only a future hope, but also a present reality for those who submit to Christ as King, and are indwelt by his Spirit. Despite the forces of evil arrayed against it, the kingdom is being established by means of salvation warfare. In light of the chaos and corruption of the world of his day, Brengle reflected on the words of Isaiah 9:6–7: "Unto us a Child is born, unto us a Son is given; and the government shall be upon His shoulders, and His name shall be called Wonderful, Counselor, the Mighty God, the Everlasting Father, the Prince of Peace. Of the increase of His government and peace there shall be no end." In relation to these verses, he wrote:

> Jesus came and Jesus lives, and Jesus reigns in spite of the fact that there is a rebellion against His government on every hand. The government is on His shoulders. He is bearing the burden. He is in the battle. Oh, the joy of helping Him bear the burden, of standing by His side and under His banner in the battle! We shall win. . . . Wars shall end; tyrannies and oppressions shall perish. Spiritual ignorance and darkness shall pass away like the shadows of night before the rising sun. Sin shall be unmasked and destroyed and Satan overthrown and bound, and the peace and government of Jesus shall surely if slowly prevail. . . . You and I may not live to see it all, but we are hastening it. Every child we lead to Jesus, every sinner we get saved, and every soul we help get sanctified, extends His government and adds a rivulet to the river of His peace, and removes a thorn from the burden on His shoulder. 'We are workers together with God,' and He cannot fail.[15]

Brengle looked forward to the eschatological day of peace prophesied by Isaiah,[16] but saw such as hastened by the faithfulness of the church.

> Every lowly Salvation soldier who loves God and man and follows Jesus in doing good helps to hasten that day. . . . And I thank God for every lowly brother and sister in Christ, every comrade fighting sin, fighting for goodness, battling against worldliness and pride, and folly and indifference. We are on the winning side. We shall conquer though we die, and we hasten the consummation of 'that one far-off, divine event toward which the whole creation moves.'[17]

He thus believed that the establishment of God's kingdom was not without cost: "When the word of the Lord comes to a man it means honor and dignity and joy, but it also may mean sorrow and trial and long and sore discipline, which, if willingly embraced, will mean final and eternal and unspeakable honor and dignity and joy."[18] Brengle maintained that Christ not only calls his followers to self-sacrificial service, but empowers them by his indwelling presence: "He calls them to be good soldiers, counting not their lives dear unto themselves, but to be ready to lay down their lives for His sake, and for the sake of the lost ones who are dear to Him for whom He died. He calls them to lofty endeavor, high adventure, supreme sacrifice, uttermost devotion. He has gone before, and now goes with all who will go with Him."[19]

Brengle also believed that God's kingdom, as a spiritual reality, is established by love, not signs and wonders. Social transformation is thus made possible by the work of the Holy Spirit, changing hearts that have freely responded to Christ's love manifest in Spirit-filled Christians. To those Christians who were discouraged by the increasing depravity of humankind, and a seeming lack of response to the gospel, he wrote:

> His Kingdom is a moral and spiritual kingdom, and is to be won and established by love. . . . and cannot be established by force or spectacular display. I sympathize with those whose hearts are heavy because of the slow progress of His conquests; and I understand how many, discouraged by the apparent hopelessness of winning the world by the preaching and living out of the Gospel, look and long for His second Advent in flaming power

and glory as the only means left for the overthrow of His enemies and the conquest of the world, but personally I look for no such spectacular victory. . . . He will conquer, but only by the Cross. He will come in great power and great glory some wondrous day, but not to change the hearts of men, which can only be done by His Cross. He will come to judge. He forever foreswore the spectacular way, when he refused to cast Himself down from the pinnacle of the temple at Satan's bidding, and chose the lowly, painful way of loving sacrifice.[20]

THE ETHICAL KINGDOM: PRESENT AND FUTURE IMPLICATIONS

The present dimensions of the kingdom of God were, for Brengle, intimately connected to the resurrection life and power of Jesus Christ. When dealing with the doctrine of the resurrection, he rightly viewed the raising of Jesus from the dead not only as signaling his victory over the grave, but also as the source of the believer's resurrection life and hope. Recognizing the essential role this doctrine plays in the Christian gospel, Brengle underscored its evidences (both objective and subjective) and implications. With regard to the former, he wrote:

1. We know it by the testimony of them that saw Him. . . . 2. We know it by the fact that though they were poor and unlearned, despised and hated, and at first bewildered and confounded by the death of their Master, that. . . [they] were joined together in a far stronger more vital and joyous union, after the death of Jesus, than when He was with them in the flesh. 3. We know it by the church dating back to fifty days of the death of Jesus, and built upon the faith that He arose from the dead. . . . 4. But the most vital evidence. . . is that which is given to us individually with the baptism of the Holy Spirit.[21]

Brengle also wrote about the "practical lessons," or implications of Christ's resurrection:

1. The first and plainest lesson we learn is that of immortality. In the presence of the risen Christ we can confidently say, death does not end all. . . . 2. But there is a deeper lesson than this. . . . The apostles labored constantly to make men see and know that the soul, while

yet in the body, may enter into the resurrection power of Jesus and rise and walk with Him in newness of life.[22]

It is important to note this equating of entire sanctification with being "filled with resurrection power and saved to the uttermost." Such resurrection power is available now, bringing freedom from the limitations of the carnal nature. There is a dimension of heaven to be experienced in the present appropriation of holiness, which provides hope for what lies beyond the grave: "We can die to sin and be altogether spiritual and holy, and can live the life of Heaven here upon earth. . . . "[23] The present possibilities of this resurrection life and power involve obligations that can only be fulfilled by the indwelling presence of the Spirit. Christians, as extensions of Christ's incarnation, are empowered by the Spirit of Jesus to manifest his self-sacrificial love to the world. Along these lines, Brengle wrote about the obligation of present holiness:

> Paul tells us that the same power which raised Christ from the dead is in us who believe (Ephesians 1:17–20). . . . Since Jesus rose from the dead and ascended on high, He puts at my disposal the same power to do and suffer His will that His Heavenly Father gave to Him. . . . It is His purpose that we should. . . sustain the same relation to Him now that He sustained to His Heavenly Father in the days of His humanity; that we should be baptized with the same Spirit, and preach with the same authority, and secure the same results, and gain the same final end and eternal victory, and at last sit down with Him on His Throne for evermore. This being so, I am under as much obligation now to be holy, to be empowered by the Spirit. . . as I shall be in Heaven.[24]

In reflecting on the triumph of the 'Second Adam' (Christ), as recorded in Romans 5:12–17 and 1 Corinthians 15:22, Brengle contrasted the death of Abel and the resurrection of Jesus, in order to show how the latter provides moral purpose and hope for the universe: "Looking at the death of Abel there seems to be no moral purpose in the universe. . . . In the resurrection of Jesus we see the supremacy of moral purpose; that this purpose embraces two worlds and cannot be defeated. . .[25] Thus, Jesus' resurrection is the basis of eternal life and hope: "He [Christ] revealed the reconciling, redeeming love of God in His death.

The murderous, blind hate of man could kill Him, but not the love He brought from the Father, that was deathless. But He revealed the power of God unto uttermost, eternal salvation, by His resurrection. . . . Because He lives, hope cannot die."[26]

Despite the optimism of grace evidenced in Brengle's understanding of the present and future dimensions of the kingdom, he was realistic about the ultimate consequences of sin for those who refused to submit to Christ as King in this life. When dealing with the topic of the future state of the wicked, Brengle opposed the "widespread and growing tendency to doubt either the existence of hell or endless punishment of the wicked." He addressed "the old-fashioned Universalist" who maintains that "all men enter into a state of blessedness the moment they die." He also dealt with annihilationism and "conditional universalism." The latter theory, also known as "the doctrine of eternal hope," viewed punishment in the after-life as having a remedial purpose, and that eventually all would be saved.[27] In contrast, Brengle believed in the conscious, endless punishment of the wicked, making his case for the 'biblical' view *versus* the alternative theories:

> The old-fashioned Universalist who believed that all men enter into a state of blessedness the moment they die, whether they be righteous or wicked, has about vanished. But others, with errors even more dangerous, because seemingly more agreeable to natural reason and man's inborn sense of justice, have come to take his place to weaken men's faith in the tremendous sanctions and penalties of God's holy law, and there seems to be a widespread and growing tendency to doubt the existence of Hell, and the endless punishment of the wicked. There are those who believe in annihilation, or extermination, of the wicked. They say there is no eternal Hell, though they do not believe that the wicked enter into a state of happiness after death, but on the contrary are immediately or eventually blotted out of existence. Then there are those who hold the doctrine of 'eternal hope.' They believe that the wicked will be punished after death, possibly for ages, but that in the end they will all be restored to the favor of God and the bliss of the holy. . . . There is something so awful about the old doctrine of endless punishment, and such a seeming

show of fairness about these new doctrines, that they
appeal very strongly to the unsanctified heart, and enlist
on their behalf all the sympathies and powerful impulses
of 'the carnal mind,' which is 'enmity to God, and is not
subject to the law of God. . . . '[28]

As always, Brengle used scripture as his primary religious
authority to establish his position:

In discussing this subject we should stick to the Bible. All
we know about the future state is what God has revealed
and left on record. . . . Human reason as well as human
experience fails us, and we can put no confidence in
the so-called revelations of spiritualism or the dreams
of sects who pretend to be able to probe the secrets of
eternity. So that if the Bible does not settle the question
for us, it cannot be settled. The Bible teaches that there is
to be punishment for the wicked after death, and that this
punishment is one of which they are conscious. . . . The
Bible further teaches that there is to be punishment
for the wicked after death, and that this punishment is
endless.[29]

For Brengle, however, the doctrine of future punishment
had a motivational purpose. He wrote:

Two powerful motives which the Holy Ghost uses to lead
men to accept the Savior and renounce all sin, are the
hope of everlasting blessedness and the fear of eternal
woe. These motives may in time in the heart of a Christian
be swallowed up in a higher motive of love and loyalty to
God, but they always remain as a framework. . . . Such has
always been the effect of the doctrine when proclaimed
in the power and pity and love of the fire-touched lips of
holy men and women. . . But let men. . . begin to tone down
this doctrine, and then old-fashioned Bible conviction for
sin ceases, the instantaneous and powerful conversion of
souls is laughed at, the Holy Ghost is forgotten. . . .[30]

He maintained that Hell was ultimately the result of failure to
receive Christ as Savior and to submit to him as Lord. God as
the "Moral Governor of the universe" is obligated to mete out
punishment for sin, particularly when his redemptive overtures
are met with "determined resistance."[31]

According to Brengle, hell is the necessary result of humanity's sinfulness, by which he means, not only voluntary transgressions of God's moral law, but also self-chosen alienation and estrangement from God: "Hell is not an arbitrary place of torment created by a jealous God. It is the wretchedness, the loneliness, the homelessness, the darkness, the deprivation, wrong-doers inevitably bring upon themselves and into which they eternally fall if they do not turn from unrighteousness and sin."[32] In response to those who object to the eternality of the doctrine of hell, he wrote:

> But some one objects that God is not just to punish a man forever for the sins he commits in the short period of a lifetime. And when he thus speaks of sins he possibly means such gross sins as lying, cheating, swearing, murder, adultery, and such like. But it is not for these sins that men are sent to Hell. . . . Men are sent to Hell by the weight and pull of their self-chosen evil and discordant nature and character, because they will not repent and turn from sin to God. They are filled with unbelief which begets pride and self-will, and are out of harmony with and are in antagonism to God and all His humble, obedient servants. They will not come to Jesus that they may be saved from sin and receive a new heart and life.[33]

Brengle not only underscored the moral nature of God, but also his mercy toward sinners. Unfortunately, those who do not avail themselves of his grace, eventually reap the results of habitual patterns of sinning:

> Not until all His judgments, and warnings, and entreaties and dying love have failed to lead them to repentance and acceptance of the Savior, and they have utterly refused the eternal blessedness of the holy, does God cease to follow sinners with tender mercies. By obstinate sin they come to hate the thing God loves, and to love the thing God hates, and so become as dead to God's will and holiness, and to His plans for them. . . . If sin is such a crime--and the Bible teaches that it is--then God, as the moral Governor of the universe, having provided a perfect way, and done all He could to persuade men to turn from sin now and forever, if He only meets with their determined resistance, is under obligation to place them

under sentence of punishment, to oppose them, and put them away from His holy presence and the society of holy men and angels for evermore, where they can no more breed moral and spiritual pestilence and disturb the moral harmony of God's government and people.[34]

Thus, Brengle believed that a person's choices will find their fulfillment in their final destination. In a letter to his wife, Lily, written in 1912, Sam wrote about the importance and significance of human free will in this regard:

We are on trial to develop moral character. . . . And so with everything, our business, our social relations, everything; everything has good and evil lurking within it, just according as we use or abuse it. And herein lies our greatness, our kingship, our likeness to God: that we can choose; but here also lies our awful and constant danger: that we shall selfishly choose our own will instead of God's will and pleasure. God's will means universal good and well-being; ours means selfishness, narrowness, corruption, loneliness, alienation from God—a dead sea—hell.[35]

Further, Brengle believed that certain choices preclude one's options, as is evident in the verses of an anonymous poem he cited:

Choose I must, and soon must choose,
Holiness, or Heaven lose.
If what Heaven loves I hate,
Shut for me in Heaven's gate.
> Endless sin means endless woe,
> Into endless sin I go,
> If my soul from reason rent,
> Takes from sin its final bent.
As the stream its channel grooves,
And within that channel moves,
So does habit's deepest tide
Groove its bed and there abide.
> Light obeyed increaseth light;
> Light resisted bringeth night.
> Who shall give me will to choose.
> If the love of light I lose.[36]

In affirming the principle that eternal destiny is a culmination of a person's present choices, Brengle wrote: "We are now becoming what we shall ever be—lovers of God and the things of God, or haters of God and the things of God."[37] In fact, he goes as far as to say that people who have, through habitual choices, ended up in Hell, would not be happy in Heaven: "I believe that such a person would possibly be more unhappy in Heaven than in Hell."[38]

It is clear that Brengle's eschatology involved the dreaded specter of "the 'everlasting shame and contempt' and the eternal torments that shall come upon the ungodly." In light of this fate awaiting the unsaved, he consistently urged the unconverted to: "Flee to Jesus. Repent and believe." By repentance, he meant "a godly sorrow for sins, that makes you forsake them and give them all up. . . . that makes you confess them and turn from them forever. Now God says, if you will honestly do this, He will forgive you and make you His child."[39] Brengle maintained that "men and women are always walking along the brink of an abyss into which, if we are not careful, we may fall forever." In the meantime, God is at work by means of prevenient grace, through the agency of his Spirit, not only to make humanity aware of its sinfulness, but also to "make us stop and think of eternal things and not to be careless and indifferent and fooling away precious time and opportunities on the very brink of Hell."[40]

Although Brengle's eschatology took seriously the future and ultimate consequences of life choices, he primarily emphasized the present possibilities of grace to transform the world through the working of the Holy Spirit. Brengle's postmillennial eschatology was influenced by his holiness theology, causing him to view the kingdom of God as partially-realized in this life, by those who have submitted themselves to Christ's reign on earth, and through the presence and power of his Spirit, serve as agents of the New Creation.

Chapter 15

Brengle and the Development of Salvation Army Holiness Theology

The development of Salvation Army holiness doctrine was dramatically influenced by Brengle, who became the major exponent of holiness theology in The Salvation Army. As a product of the late nineteenth century American holiness movement, Brengle's theology moderated the earlier emphases of the British holiness revival, as mediated to William and Catherine Booth by American holiness evangelists in the 1860s. Thus, it is necessary to place Brengle within this theological context in order to demonstrate the importance of his teaching to Army holiness self-understanding.

To properly assess the role of Brengle in shaping Salvation Army holiness doctrine, it is essential to understand the religious milieu of his day and to reflect upon the interpenetration of transatlantic holiness theologies as conveyed through his ministry and message. Being part of the British holiness revival, the Army's theological origins must be examined in light of the priorities of the nineteenth century holiness movement. The holiness emphases of John Wesley and eighteenth century Methodism resurfaced in America during the mid-nineteenth century in both Oberlin and Wesleyan perfectionism. Although finding its roots in Wesley and early Methodism, the British holiness revival was mediated by American perfectionist evangelists, as evidenced in the impact of James Caughey and Phoebe Palmer on the Booths themselves.[1]

Salvation Army historiography has failed to recognize an obvious dependence of the Booths' holiness teaching on the theological emphases of the American holiness movement. This is partly due to the fact that early Salvation Army literature often incorporated parts of others' works without citation, thus leaving the impression of there being no explicit ideological connection. The devotional works of Phoebe Palmer, for example, were republished by the Army press without any mention of her name. This casual approach to documentation has led most Army historians to miss the vital interrelationship between American holiness revivalists and the Booths' fledgling movement.

The American holiness movement gained a wide hearing in Victorian England by communicating an optimism that was attractive to a pessimistic age. An era marked by transition and doubt needed a form of Christianity that would minister to the problems of the day. Practical Christianity was popular to a generation of those who had lost faith in the relevance of their religious institutions. The holiness revival in England was a "revival of hope" in an age of despair.[2] The "new era of American pietism"[3] that characterized the pre-Civil War religious milieu in America was transplanted to England by the nineteenth century holiness movement with an accompanying emphasis on experience rather than doctrine. Practical Christianity was supported by a holiness message that offered both certainty and immediateness to a troubled and burdened people.[4]

William and Catherine Booth were significantly influenced by the American holiness movement through the Palmers' holiness revivals and earlier campaigns by James Caughey in England. The latter not only influenced William Booth's decision to enter into the ministry and his use of revivalistic methods (such as street preaching and the use of the mourner's bench), but above all, Caughey's teaching on the Wesleyan doctrine of holiness made a lasting theological impact on William. Caughey's influence is further substantiated by the fact that, from an early date, the Army included selections from Caughey's works in their publications.[5]

William and Catherine's sanctification experiences date back to 1861, two years after their first known contact with Phoebe Palmer. Their correspondence to one another from this period reflects a direct dependence on Palmer's holiness thought, especially her "altar theology."[6] In addition, her revival preaching provided the impetus for the shy and reserved Catherine Booth to begin her own effective public ministry. Although the Palmers returned to America in 1864, their revival activity proved helpful in paving the way for the 1870s British campaigns of Robert Pearsall and Hannah Whittal Smith, Asa Mahan, William Boardman, Dwight L. Moody, and Ira Sankey. Charles Finney had briefly taken part in the earlier English holiness revival, but his writings had a greater effect than his presence on the propagation of perfectionist revivalism.[7]

Continuing affinity between the Army's holiness theology and American holiness writers is evidenced in the positive reviews of the latter in Army publications. For example, an 1895 *Officer* review of William Arthur's *Tongue of Fire* encouraged every officer to read this classic book carefully to aid in the appropriation and propagation of the experience of holiness.[8] The following year, the same official journal carried a positive review concerning Asa Mahan's views on holiness.[9]

The critical nature of entire sanctification was rooted in John Wesley's teaching on a definite second work of grace. In the nineteenth century holiness revival, however, this crisis experience became more distinct from the Wesleyan emphasis on a critical point in a growth process (although there were exceptions, most notably, Daniel Steele's balanced view of sanctification as a "gradual" and "instantaneous" work).[10]

The blending of American revivalism and perfectionism resulted in a stress on the immediacy and completeness of the "second blessing," received by faith and consecration. The chief advocate of this new interpretation of Wesleyan perfectionism was Phoebe Palmer, who was concerned with the urgency of claiming the biblical promise of the fullness of the Spirit. In what has been called her "altar phraseology,"[11] Palmer insisted that Christ, as the altar, sanctified the gift when such was placed there in a consecrated manner. Thus, faith in God's promise, and active and full consecration, yielded instantaneous sanctification.

Emphasis was placed on the witness of the believer and of the Spirit. The witness of the Spirit did not always accompany the work of entire sanctification but would eventually come to those believers who gave "regular public testimony to what God had done." Nathan Bangs, a Methodist holiness advocate, warned of the dangers involved in claiming a work of the Spirit without the accompanying witness of the Spirit to the completion of this work. The "witness controversy" led others to redefine the nature of the witness, resulting in an emphasis on emotional and physical evidences of the Spirit's presence.[12]

Palmer taught that the "shorter way" of holiness is available to all—by faith. God requires "present holiness" and has made this duty plain. A sacrifice of entire consecration is preliminary to the necessary and attainable state of "purity of intention." Such a sacrifice is acceptable to God only through Christ, the agent of sanctification, by faith. Faith must precede feeling and never be held back by lack of emotion. The promises of God are to be received in the present by the exercise of faith, believing that God is faithful and that His promises are for subjective appropriation.[13] Faith in God's faithfulness and unchanging nature is the guarantee of receiving the "second blessing." She wrote: "The act, on your part, must necessarily induce the promised result on the part of God."[14] Thus, Palmer viewed entire consecration and faith as the "necessary steps" to attaining Christian perfection.[15]

Speaking on the unchangeable government of the "kingdom of grace," Palmer drew out the implications of this fact with regard to faith: "The reason why you were not before blessed . . . was not because God was unwilling to meet you, but wholly from delay on your part in complying with the conditions upon which you were to be received. The *moment* you complied with these, you found the Lord."[16] The principle of appropriating faith was applied to both justification and sanctification. The blood of Christ is efficacious to cleanse from all sin, sanctifying those who "make the required sacrifice" (consecration) by faith. Christian perfection is not only possible in this life, it is also obligatory. It is not only a privilege, it is a duty. It is the "state of supreme love to God; where all the powers of body and mind are perfectly subject to love's control, and ceaselessly offered up to God through Christ." To doubt the attainability and reality of Christian perfection is to de-value the atonement and its effects. Not only has full salvation already been purchased, but it is "already yours" if compliance with the conditions is accompanied by appropriating faith. God commands us to believe and receive, and He would prove unreasonable if the power to be obedient did not accompany the command. "Simple faith," when exercised, appropriates the merits of Christ and makes possible entire sanctification. "You may have this full salvation now—just now."[17]

Palmer was careful to distinguish the seeking of holiness by faith and the seeking of it by works. The correctness of the former approach was evidenced in her three admonitions for those seeking the experience of entire sanctification: "Expect it *by faith*. Expect it *as you are*. Expect it *now*." These three emphases are interconnected ("If you seek it by faith, you must expect it as you are; and if as you are, then expect it now") and are based on the priority of grace and the faithfulness of God.[18]

In her eagerness to advance the theology of holiness, however, Palmer went beyond John Wesley in her propagation of perfection. Wesley's doctrine of perfect love aimed at developing pure, godly intention through the purgation of internal impurities. Palmer, on the other hand, emphasized willful consecration and sudden crisis. She likened entire sanctification to baptism— external evidence to an internal work. Palmer's altar theology emphasized the grace of God in sanctifying every human self-sacrifice placed upon it. Whereas Wesley spoke of the witness of the Spirit to the attainment of perfect love, Palmer believed that the promises in Scripture were witness enough. Once the scriptural conditions were met, the believer could claim by faith the experience of perfect love. All that was necessary to receive was to believe. Unlike Wesley's emphasis on the appropriation of all grace (including holiness) by faith, Phoebe Palmer emphasized the *state* of grace, appropriated and guaranteed by faith in God's promises.[19]

With the development of Wesleyan perfectionism in the nineteenth century holiness movement, the emphasis on the critical nature of sanctification was isolated from Wesley's balanced view of perfect love as a crisis within a growth process. An important catalyst for this theological development was the utilitarian and pragmatic spirit of the age. The revivalists of perfectionism sought to make Christianity practical.[20] Entire sanctification was not a mystical quest. Rather, it was the instantaneous perfecting in love of the believer, fitting one for service. Following in the tradition of Wesley's dictum, "there is no holiness but social holiness," the movement emphasized the transforming power of God's Spirit as the basis for social reform.

The moral strivings of the age were answered by the perfectionist awakening in mid-nineteenth century America, which found its roots in the Wesleyan revival of the previous century.[21]

One crucial point of investigation in discussing Salvation Army holiness theology in relation to the nineteenth century holiness movement is that of sanctifying faith. In contrast to Wesley's emphasis on the assurance of the blessing as a witness of God's Spirit testifying with our spirits, early Salvation Army holiness theology opted for a "naked faith" approach.[22] Once the conditions for entire sanctification (consecration and faith) are fulfilled, holiness can be claimed as complete. In the Army's early years, people were encouraged to ask for the assurance, but the blessing was accepted by "naked faith" prior to any assurance.[23] Representative of such a position was J. A. Wood, whose work, *Perfect Love*, influenced early Salvation Army holiness theology. He believed that in order for faith to be "pure," it must be "naked" (i.e., faith prior to the witness of the Spirit).[24] William Booth concurred: "Remember, the most naked faith is the most efficacious."[25] This emphasis is reflected not only in Booth's teaching but also in other early Army literature, much of which is heavily dependent on the holiness theology of Phoebe Palmer.[26]

The dynamic balance between the immediacy of expectation and the waiting upon God for the assurance of sanctification, as found in Brengle's holiness theology, is not dealt with in early Salvation Army holiness teaching. Although not systematic, the holiness theology of the Army was dominated by members of the Booth family and George S. Railton in the first three decades of the movement's existence. The immediacy of the experience of entire sanctification, appropriated by simple faith, was the predominant teaching. Although Brengle would concur with the receiving of the second blessing by faith alone, he believed that the witness of the Spirit was essential for one to know that the blessing had been given. His writings, especially *Helps to Holiness* and *Heart-Talks on Holiness,* both written prior to the turn of the century, were more "Wesleyan" in that they emphasize the need to wait on the Lord for His witness and assurance.

Thus, it was Brengle's influence that directed The Salvation Army away from the emphases of Phoebe Palmer, and the misuse of her altar theology in popular piety, to a more orthodox Wesleyan expression. Brengle's success in this task is evident in the primary role given to his writings within The Salvation Army from the close of the nineteenth century until recent years. Also noteworthy were the positive reviews given to the works of his mentor, Daniel Steele, as they were republished by the Army in later years.[27] The corrective presented in Brengle's theology not only served to moderate earlier American holiness emphases within the movement, but it also influenced Salvation Army theological development. The interpenetration of these transatlantic theologies, as mediated through the ministry and message of this holiness apostle, helped to center Army holiness theology in the tradition of Wesley, which maintained a balanced tension between active faith and patient waiting in the experience of entire sanctification.

Brengle's pivotal role in the shift toward Wesleyan expression is all the more important in light of the fact that Brengle became the Army's "official" holiness theologian.[28] Evidence for this claim is presented by John Norton, who maintains that Brengle's writings became the Army's definitive statement on sanctification. Norton cites implicit evidence—from the official approval of Brengle's books, to his appointed role as Spiritual Special, to his promotion to the rank of commissioner. Explicit evidence for this claim is based on the incorporation of Brengle's interpretation of holiness into the 1925 *Orders and Regulations for Officers of The Salvation Army.*[29] His articulation of entire sanctification thus served as the basis for Salvation Army holiness self-understanding through most of the twentieth century. Although there would be other official explications of the doctrine of entire sanctification in the first half of the century, doctrinal continuity with Brengle's theology was maintained throughout.[30] In fact, Brengle's understanding of holiness held sway within the Army until the 1969 *Handbook of Doctrine* offered a revised interpretation of sanctification, which was officially set forth by Frederick Coutts.[31]

Conclusion

The importance of Samuel Logan Brengle is not to be underestimated. His teaching further institutionalized Salvation Army holiness doctrine and provided the movement with a practical explication of the same. He understood the experience of entire sanctification as essential to God's saving purposes—a work of God's grace subsequent to regeneration, which is received through identification with Christ's death and resurrection by faith. In the baptism of the Holy Spirit, therefore, the power and presence of the resurrected Christ are mediated to the believing heart, resulting in spiritual communion and fellowship. Understood as union with Christ, entire sanctification equips the believer for effective service. Christ, as Savior and Sanctifier, pardons that He might purify and empower for service. Such heart purity is thus a result of Christ's divine nature imparted to man. Brengle defined holiness as "pure love," and thus the baptism of the Holy Spirit is a "baptism of love." As "perfect deliverance from sin," holiness is a state free from intentional sin, free from doubt or fear, "in which God is loved and trusted with a perfect heart." Christian perfection is not absolute, angelic, or Adamic perfection. Rather, it is relative to the natural limitations of fallen humanity.

Brengle maintained that entire sanctification is available to all believers in this life, and it is not to be equated with growth in grace. It is the uprooting of the sin nature and the instantaneous implanting of the divine nature. Although growth is essential in order to maintain the blessing, the critical nature of entire sanctification is emphasized. He viewed regeneration as partial sanctification. Whereas the Holy Spirit is active in conviction of sin, repentance, faith, forgiveness, assurance of salvation, and empowerment for spiritual warfare in the experience of the believer, such work is understood as preparatory. In regeneration, there is salvation from the voluntary commission of sin and the binding of the "old man."

Thus, entire sanctification is the completion of the work only begun at regeneration. The Holy Spirit, as the agent of assurance, provides knowledge of acceptance with God, salvation, and sanctification. Such assurance ("witness of the Spirit") is to be waited upon by faith. Brengle maintained that perseverance in holiness is conditional, requiring continued "perfect consecration," steadfast faith, communion with the Lord, attention to Scripture, confession of the experience of entire sanctification, self-denial, and dynamic growth in grace.

Having experienced the purifying and empowering presence of the Holy Spirit, Brengle consistently urged others to pursue holiness throughout his life and ministry. He believed that this experience was central to the message and mission of the Army. He also recognized the need for the Army to maintain its commitment to its holiness heritage in order to ensure continued missional integrity and effectiveness. Brengle's importance, however, is to be understood not only in terms of his holiness evangelism but also in light of his influence on the development of Salvation Army holiness doctrine. As the major exponent of holiness theology within The Salvation Army during the late nineteenth and early twentieth centuries, Brengle served to moderate earlier holiness expressions within the movement, re-balancing Army holiness doctrine in the tradition of Wesley. The impact of Brengle's holiness teaching was far-reaching, both within the Army and in the church at large. Throughout the twentieth century his theology served first as the standard for Salvation Army holiness self-understanding and later as the foil for further doctrinal modifications.

After his death, one of the evidences of the enduring influence of Brengle's ministry within the Army was the establishment of an annual National Brengle Institute. During a visit to the United States in 1945, General Albert Orsborn suggested to Commissioner E. I. Pugmire (National Commander) the creation of a "Brengle College," where "scriptural holiness would be taught and retaught," in the hope that "such an institute might become a powerhouse of spiritual energy for The Salvation Army in the United States, and perhaps in the world." Hosted by Commissioner Norman Marshall (Central Territorial

Commander), forty-two delegates from across the country met at Camp Wonderland in Camp Lake, Wisconsin, on August 4, 1947, for the first twenty-one-day Brengle Institute (the location of which was split between Camp Wonderland and the School for Officer Training in Chicago). In the words of Colonel Albert Pepper (Central Training Principal), who served as the director of the institute for its first twelve years: "The institute has been a source of wonderful blessing and inspiration. . . . We were careful not to idolize Commissioner Brengle, but we did hold up his Bible-backed teaching as a guide and his exemplary life as an inspiration."[1] Brengle Institutes began to spread in subsequent years to other countries and have been conducted in most territories of the Army world. These institutes have proven to be occasions of spiritual enrichment and further understanding of the doctrine and experience of holiness.[2]

Earlier generations of Salvationists have understood the significance of Brengle's ministry, especially his literary contribution, as reflected in the following posthumous tribute from the editor of *The Officers' Review:*

> At the age of twenty-seven years Cadet Brengle . . . wrote: "I have been led from the beginning to pray that I might be a blessing . . . to the whole Army." Now that, nearly half a century later, he has been called to his Reward, no one can doubt that his prayer was answered. Apart from the Army's Generals, probably no Officer was known so widely in our ranks, or outside, and his preaching and his writings have enshrined Samuel Brengle in the gratitude and affection of hundreds of thousands.[3]

In 1980, Commissioner Bramwell Tripp wrote in a similar vein about the Brengle legacy:

> But it is through his writings, more than in any other way, that Commissioner Brengle continues to exert a compelling edifying and sacred influence. . . . And so it is, in a way permitted to few mortal men, Samuel Logan Brengle still speaks to our day. Those who heard him speak, who received his private counsel, who felt his hand on the shoulder, who knew first-hand his "sanctified sanity," will never forget him. And those who never knew him, except as a somewhat remote figure in the shadowy

past, know his teaching and his preaching through the various Brengle Institutes and his books.[4]

Although Brengle's influence has been widely felt in days gone by, the question remains—is the Army and the wider Wesleyan-holiness movement in danger of losing the legacy of this holiness apostle out of neglect? Perhaps it is time for a renewed exploration of Brengle's thought in order to rediscover not only the Army's holiness heritage but also the transforming power of divine love as manifest in his life and ministry.

God's Love Immutable

Through God's unchanging, ceaseless years,
His love is burning on,
More quenchless far
Than shining star,
Or glorious flaming sun.
Just now this love doth kindle ours,
Doth make our hearts as one,
To offer praise
Through all our days,
Until our work is done.
And then for ever, evermore,
In mansion bright above,
We'll see His face
Of wondrous grace,
Who saved us by His love.[5]

— Samuel Logan Brengle

Notes

INTRODUCTION

[1]William G. Harris, "Samuel L. Brengle—Salvationist Saint," *War Cry* [NY] (Jun. 6, 1936): 3, 14.

[2]E.g., Clarence W. Hall, *Samuel Logan Brengle: Portrait of a Prophet* (New York: The Salvation Army, 1933); Alice R. Stiles, *Samuel Logan Brengle: Teacher of Holiness* (London: The Salvation Army, 1974); William Clark, *Samuel Logan Brengle: Teacher of Holiness* (London: Hodder and Stoughton, 1980); and Sallie Chesham, *Peace Like a River* (Atlanta: The Salvation Army, 1981). These works do contain some valuable primary source material, but lack the necessary bibliographic information for critical analysis of references.

[3]Herbert A. Wisbey, *Soldiers Without Swords: A History of the Salvation Army in the United States* (New York: Macmillan, 1955), p. v. The sole reference to Brengle reads: "Following the High Council of 1929, American-born officers began to be appointed to top administrative positions. The first American-born commissioner was Samuel Logan Brengle, an evangelist, who as National Spiritual Special had no administrative duties. He had become a lieutenant commissioner in 1926" (p. 186).

[4]Frederick Coutts, *The History of The Salvation Army: Volume 6, 1914–1946* (New York: The Salvation Army, 1979), p. 141; cf. p. 78.

[5]Arch Wiggins, *The History of The Salvation Army: Volume 5, 1904–1914* (New York: The Salvation Army, 1979), pp. 26, 41–42, 89, 129–30, 169, 199–200; Edward H. McKinley, *Marching to Glory: The History of The Salvation Army in the United States, 1880–1992,* 2nd edition (Grand Rapids, MI: Eerdmans, 1995), pp. 41–42, 102, 104, 176, 196–200, 255.

[6]Winston's only reference to Brengle is indirect: "Elizabeth [Swift] married Samuel Brengle, the Army's leading Holiness writer." Diane Winston, *Red-Hot and Righteous: The Urban Religion of The Salvation Army* (Cambridge, MA: Harvard University Press, 1999), p. 80. Although Brengle gets a bit more recognition in Taiz's work, his theological contribution is de-emphasized in favor of a reductionistic sociological analysis of his life. Lillian Taiz, *Hallelujah Lads and Lasses: Remaking The Salvation Army in America, 1880–1930* (Chapel Hill, NC: University of North Carolina Press, 2001), pp. 50, 55–56, 66–67, 154–55.

[7] Samuel L. Brengle, *At the Center of the Circle: Selections From Published and Unpublished Writings of Samuel Logan Brengle*, ed. John D. Waldron (Kansas City: Beacon Hill, 1976); John D. Waldron, "Celebrating the Holy Life: A Fresh Assessment of Samuel Logan Brengle," part 1, *Officer* 36:2 (Feb. 1985): 68. It is interesting to note that the former was not published by the Army but by the Church of the Nazarene press. The latter is also noteworthy in that it represents the first article on Brengle published in *The Officer* after a fifty-year hiatus.

[8] Waldron, "Celebrating the Holy Life," part 1, p. 68.

[9] It is interesting to note that the author disclaims any awareness of hagiography in treatments of Brengle's life: "Certainly, none of Brengle's writing, nor that of his biographers, present him idealistically. . . ." Sallie Chesham, *The Brengle Treasury: A Patchwork Polygon* (Atlanta: The Salvation Army, 1988).

[10] Hall's influence is most strikingly evident in Alice R. Stiles, *Samuel Logan Brengle: Teacher of Holiness* (1974); William Clark, *Samuel Logan Brengle: Teacher of Holiness* (1980); and Sallie Chesham, *Peace Like a River* (1981). Such dependence is due to the fact that Hall's account represents the authorized life of Brengle, the first edition of which was written while the subject was still alive, utilizing primary source materials provided by Brengle that are no longer extant. A later revision, the "memorial edition" (Chicago: The Salvation Army, 1936), filled in the last three years of Brengle's life, while abridging the material from the 1933 edition (with some notable omissions).

[11] R. David Rightmire, "Brengle on Evangelism and the Holy Life," *Word and Deed* 6:1 (Nov. 2003): 5–34; R. David Rightmire, "Holiness and the Ethical Dimensions of Brengle's Eschatology," *Word and Deed* 10:1 (Nov. 2007): 23–38.

[12] Chapter fifteen has been adapted from an article first published by the author as: "Samuel Brengle and the Development of Salvation Army Pneumatology," *Wesleyan Theological Journal* 27:1 and 2 (Spring–Fall 1992): 104–31; and later modified for publication as: "Samuel Logan Brengle and the Development of Pneumatology in The Salvation Army," *Word and Deed* 1:1 (Fall 1998): 29–48. Used by permission.

[13] Heretofore, published listings of Brengle's works have focused solely on his book publications, omitting the nearly 350 article citations found in the bibliography of this volume. For example see R. G. Moyles, *A Bibliography of Salvation Army Literature in English, 1865–1987* (Lewiston, NY: Mellen Press, 1988), pp. 101–2.

CHAPTER 1—SIMPLE FAITH: SEEKING THE BLESSING

[1] Hall, 1936, pp. 15–17; Stiles, p. 3; Chesham, *Peace,* 1981, pp. 13–14; Clark, *Samuel Logan Brengle* [henceforth, *SLB*], pp. 19–20.

[2] Samuel L. Brengle, *Ancient Prophets: With a Series of Occasional Papers on Modern Problems* (London: The Salvation Army, 1930), pp. 46–47.

[3] Hall, 1936, pp. 19–24; Stiles, pp. 4–8; Chesham, *Peace*, p. 15; Clark, *SLB*, pp. 20–23.

[4] Samuel L. Brengle, "The Family Altar: Every Man Priest in His Own Home," *War Cry* [NY] (Feb. 11, 1928): 3.

[5] William D. Woodward, *Life Sketches of Samuel Logan Brengle* (Chicago: Christian Witness, n.d.), p. 8; Hall, 1936, pp. 25–28; Stiles, pp. 9–10; Clark, *SLB*, pp. 23–25. Note from Brengle's own experience the need to *wait* for assurance of salvation, once full consecration had been made.

[6] Samuel L. Brengle, *Fifty Years Before and After: 1885–January Ninth–1935* [pamphlet], National Guard Series, Number One (N.p.: National Association for the Promotion of Holiness, n.d.), pp. 7–8.

[7] Brengle, *Fifty Years*, p. 9; cf. Woodward, pp. 8–9. Over the next several years, Brengle would grow in his realization of something lacking in his spiritual life: "The lack of spiritual power in his life was also something that troubled Sam deeply. Not only was he defeated by the tempter far too frequently, but waves of doubt would often wash over him. . . . Some days he found it well-nigh impossible to believe in God at all. . . . But what troubled him most was the absence of immediacy in his spiritual life. Others could speak in glowing terms of communing with their Lord. . . . Their religion seemed real. . . . Compared with this Brengle felt that his spiritual life was dry and barren." John Larsson, *Spiritual Breakthrough: The Holy Spirit and Ourselves* (London: The Salvation Army, 1983), pp. 2–3.

[8] E.g., Brengle later wrote: "For the next twelve years I had no home . . . but my mother's sweet face was ever before me. . . . Indeed her memory and influence were like a presence ever before and about me and like a flaming shield between me and youth's temptations." Samuel L. Brengle, "Our Mothers," *War Cry* [NY] (May 10, 1924): 5. Cf. Hall, 1936, pp. 29–32; Stiles, pp. 10–11; Clark, *SLB*, pp. 26–27, 30–31.

[9] This Methodist Episcopal school, located in Greencastle, Indiana, would change its name to DePauw University in 1882.

[10] Samuel L. Brengle, "Personal Recollections of Albert J. Beveridge," *War Cry* [NY] (Jun. 11, 1927): 7, 12; Woodward, pp. 9–12; Hall, 1936, pp. 33–38; Stiles, pp. 11–15; Chesham, *Peace*, pp. 21–23; Clark, *SLB*, p. 27.

[11] Quoted in Chesham, *Peace*, p. 24.

[12] Ibid., p. 25.

[13] Woodward, pp. 13–14; Hall, 1936, pp. 39–41; Stiles, p. 15; Clark, *SLB*, pp. 27–29.

[14] Quoted in Stiles, p. 17; cf. Clark, *SLB*, pp. 29–30; Woodward, p. 15.

[15] Woodward, pp. 6, 15–16; Hall, 1936, pp. 42–43.

[16] Samuel L. Brengle, et al., *God as Strategist* (New York: The Salvation Army, 1978): p. 14; cf. Samuel L. Brengle, *Helps to Holiness* (Atlanta: The Salvation Army, 1984), p. 138; Woodward, pp. 20–21.

[17] Daniel Steele (1824–1914) had formerly taught ancient languages at Genesee College and had held the chair of Mental and Moral Philosophy at Syracuse University. He was a leader in the Methodist Episcopal Church and active in the reform movements of his day. Reputed to be a man of scholarly attainments, saintly character, and earnest piety, he authored hundreds of articles on entire sanctification and wrote several books in defense of scriptural holiness (most notably *The Mile-Stone Papers*). Kenneth O. Brown, "Daniel Steele," in *Historical Dictionary of the Holiness Movement,* edited by William Kostlevy (Lanham, MD: Scarecrow Press, 2001), pp. 245–46. For an assessment of Daniel Steele's exegesis of key sanctification texts in the New Testament see J. Prescott Johnson, "Crisis and Consequence: Sanctification and the Greek Tense," *Wesleyan Theological Journal* 37:2 (Fall 2002): 176, 181, 185–87.

[18] Samuel L. Brengle, "From Dawn to Sunrise," part 1, *War Cry* [NY] (Feb. 15, 1896): 10; Samuel L. Brengle, "After Twenty-Nine Years: A Personal Testimony," *Officer* 21:11 (Nov. 1913): 545; Samuel L. Brengle, "An Up-to-Date Testimony to Full Salvation," *War Cry* [NY] (Jan. 14, 1933): 8; Brengle, *Helps to Holiness,* p. 141; Woodward, p. 19; Larsson, pp. 3–4.

[19] Apparently these authors had been recommended to him by Daniel Steele. Note Brengle's contact with Catherine Booth's "matchless little books" prior to his contact with the Army itself. Brengle, "After Twenty-Nine Years," p. 546; Samuel L. Brengle, "After Many Days," *War Cry* [NY] (Nov. 15, 1913): 10. Cf. Eileen Douglas, *Elizabeth Swift Brengle* (London: The Salvation Army, 1922): p. 65.

[20] Samuel L. Brengle, "Impressions of the Army Mother," *War Cry* [NY] (May 13, 1922): 7. Cf. Catherine Booth, *Godliness* (Boston: McDonald and Gill, 1885); Catherine Booth, *Popular Christianity* (Boston: McDonald and Gill, 1888).

[21] Brengle, *God as Strategist,* p. 14; cf. John Coutts, *The Salvationists* (London: Mowbrays, 1977), p. 56; Hall, 1936, pp. 46–47. Some of these student friends also became prominent preachers or teachers (e.g., William Woodward, Charles Jefferson, George Coe, and Doremus Hayes). Woodward, pp. 17–18.

[22] Brengle, "An Up-to-Date Testimony to Full Salvation," p. 8; cf. Samuel L. Brengle, "God Wrought Mightily in My Soul," *War Cry* [NY] (Mar. 29, 1947): 3, 14.

[23] Kate Lee and Samuel L. Brengle, *My Experience of Sanctification* (London: The Salvation Army, n.d.), p. 10; Brengle, *Fifty Years,* pp. 10–11; cf. Chesham, *Peace,* p. 28.

[24] Quoted in Hall, 1936, p. 48.

[25] Brengle, "After Twenty-Nine Years," p. 545; cf. Hall, 1936, p. 47; Stiles, pp. 19–20.

[26] Quoted in Hall, 1936, p. 49; cf. Samuel L. Brengle, *At the Center of the Circle*, p. 9.

[27] Lee and Brengle, p. 10. Elsewhere he wrote: "Slowly the light dawned upon me. I saw that I must consecrate my all to Him. I must take up my cross and unwaveringly follow where He led. I had some confessions to make and this meant inward crucifixion. I could not see the glory [that] was to follow crucifixion. That was hidden from me. But God was faithful." Samuel L. Brengle, "A Definition and an Experience," *War Cry* [NY] (Jul. 11, 1925): 3.

[28] Brengle reflects Wesley's understanding of this verse. In his sermon "Christian Perfection," Wesley wrote: "Now it is evident the Apostle here also speaks of a deliverance wrought in this world . . . from all sin." John Wesley, *Standard Sermons*, vol. 2 (London: Epworth Press, 1921), pp. 150ff.

[29] Samuel L. Brengle, "Ebenezer: 1885–1918," *War Cry* [NY] (Feb. 2, 1918): 16; Brengle, *God as Strategist*, p. 15; Lee and Brengle, p. 11; Brengle, "A Definition and an Experience," p. 3; Brengle, "God Wrought Mightily in My Soul," pp. 3, 14; Samuel L. Brengle, *The Guest of the Soul* (Atlanta: The Salvation Army, 1992), p. 124. Cf. Hall, 1936, pp. 49–50; Stiles, pp. 20–21; Chesham, *Peace*, pp. 30–31; Clark, *SLB*, pp. 32–35; Woodward, pp. 21–22. For a critique of Brengle's interpretation of 1 John 1:9 in relation to his holiness experience, see Dr. William Walker, "The Problem of Holiness," unpublished manuscript of sermon preached at the Bethel Evangelical Church, Detroit, MI, Jul. 19, 1936 (Alexandria, VA: The Salvation Army National Archives), pp. 1–23.

[30] Samuel L. Brengle, Letter from St. Petersburg, FL, to members of the Friday night holiness meeting in Boston, Mar. 1936, published posthumously in "Pennings of a Prophet," *War Cry* [NY] (May 7, 1938): 6.

[31] Brengle, *Helps to Holiness*, pp. ix, 144; Brengle, "A Definition and an Experience," p. 3; Stiles, p. 21; Larsson, p. 4. Note the four-day period of waiting for the religious affections commensurate with the experience of entire sanctification. Cf. Hall, 1933, p. 59, who mistakenly places Brengle's 'glory experience' two days after his experience of entire sanctification.

[32] Samuel L. Brengle, "Full Salvation—My Personal Testimony," *Field Officer* 20:4 (Apr. 1912): 137; Brengle, *God as Strategist*, p. 15; cf. Brengle, *Helps To Holiness*, pp. 144–45.

[33] Quoted in Hall, 1936, p. 53; cf. Stiles, p. 22; Woodward, pp. 23–26.

[34] Samuel L. Brengle, "Looking Backward and Forward after Seventy Years!" *Staff Review* (Jan. 1931): 49. In a sense, Brengle's experience became his message: "He never tired of speaking of the reality of God indwelling the human personality and transforming it to his own likeness. He had the gift of being able to paint the picture of God's glory in the soul of man so vividly that it awakened in his hearers an almost passionate longing for real and immediate

experience of God." Larsson, pp. 5–6; cf. "Staff-Captain Brengle: Our Western Massachusetts D.O.," *War Cry* [NY] (Aug. 24, 1895): 15.

[35] Hall, 1936, p. 54; cf. Stiles, p. 22.

[36] The dating of this encounter is a bit confused in the secondary sources. The only source that provides an exact (albeit erroneous) date is Chesham's *Brengle Treasury* (p. 10), where the event is dated as Jun. 1, 1885 (Brengle's 25th birthday). In both editions of Hall's *Portrait of a Prophet* (1933, p. 55; 1936, p. 70), as well as Chesham's *Peace Like a River* (pp. 32–33), the event is dated as occurring in the fall of 1885. By way of contrast, William Clark refers to the encounter taking place "one fine October day in 1886" (*Samuel Logan Brengle: Teacher of Holiness*, p. 9). This later date is supported by the fact that William Booth's first visit to the United States did not take place until the fall of 1886. See St. John Ervine, *God's Soldier: General William Booth* (NY: Macmillan, 1935), vol. 2, p. 667; Harold Begbie, *The Life of General William Booth, The Founder of The Salvation Army* (New York: Macmillan, 1920), volume 2, p. 67; Edward McKinley, *Marching to Glory: The History of The Salvation Army in the United States*, 2nd ed. (Grand Rapids: Eerdmans, 1995), p. 36.

[37] William Brewer, "Boston," *The Conqueror*, 2:6 (Jul. 1893); Benjamin L. Hartley, *Evangelicals at a Crossroads: Revivalism and Social Reform in Boston, 1860–1910* (London: University Press of New England, 2011), pp. 103, 224.

[38] Quoted in Hall, 1936, p. 55; cf. Woodward, pp. 30–32; Clark, *SLB*, pp. 9–10; Sallie Chesham, *Born to Battle: The Salvation Army in America* (Chicago: Rand McNally, 1965), p. 74; Taiz, p. 50. Brengle had not only read Catherine Booth's books prior to meeting William, but had also heard of the work of The Salvation Army. In an interview about his memories of William Booth, Brengle stated: "The first time I heard of William Booth was through the medium of a newspaper. It was in the year 1878 and I was about seventeen years old at the time. . . . The burden of the article was to ridicule the whole Salvation Army. . . . Five years later while I was studying theology at Boston University, The Salvation Army opened up in the city. Some of my classmates attended the meetings, where they sought and found the blessing of a clean heart. We were, at that time, having a holiness revival in the school, and some of the eager students told us of the wonderful meetings being held at the Salvation Army hall. A little later it was announced that General William Booth was coming to Boston to conduct meetings. It was at one of these meetings I first saw him, and from then on I pronounced him 'God's greatest living man.'" Fletcher Agnew, "'How Could I Help But Love Him?'" *War Cry* [NY] (Apr. 4, 1925): 7, 14.

[39] Samuel L. Brengle, "The Special Campaigner: The Man and His Work," *Staff Review* (Jan. 1927): 16; Brengle, *Ancient Prophets*, p. 65; Woodward, pp. 32–33; Hall, 1936, pp. 57–59; Clark, *SLB*, p. 43. By way of contrast, Lillian Taiz speculates from a socio-historical perspective on Brengle's motivations: "Samuel Brengle, like so many other middle-class men, hoped

to 'succeed grandly in some important work' but confronted a lengthy career path. . . . Within the complex bureaucracy of the Methodist Episcopal church, the young man faced years of 'poor appointments and small memberships.' Yet when Clement Studebaker offered Brengle the pastorate of 'a large and wealthy congregation' in Indiana, giving him opportunity to 'leap over [hurdles confronted] by the average preacher,' the young man rejected the post. Perhaps he recognized that as an employee of Studebaker's church, he could not hope to achieve the independence he associated with success. . . . Reflecting his yearning for independence, Brengle said he preferred the life of an evangelist who 'move[s] about largely care-free. If people do not like him, he does not feel the responsibility of adjusting himself to them, for he soon passes on and hears of them no more.' Brengle believed that his success as an itinerant evangelist would be associated with the numbers of people 'converted and sanctified under his preaching' and not his ability to negotiate social relations within a church bureaucracy." Taiz, pp. 55–56.

[40] Woodward, pp. 33–34; Hall, 1936, pp. 59–61; Chesham, *Treasury*, p. 10; "William McDonald," in William Kostlevy, ed., *Historical Dictionary of the Holiness Movement*, pp. 170–71. The National Camp Meeting Association for the Promotion of Holiness (or National Association) changed its name to the National Association for the Promotion of Holiness (or National Holiness Association) in 1899. Its name was later changed to the Christian Holiness Association in 1971 and then changed again to the Christian Holiness partnership in 1998. Kenneth O. Brown, "Christian Holiness partnership," in Kostlevy, ed., *Historical Dictionary of the Holiness Movement*, pp. 49–50. Brengle's relationship with the National Association would give impetus to the Army's eventual identification with this organization. "In 1960, as part of its celebration of the 100th anniversary of the birth of Samuel Logan Brengle, The Salvation Army became an official denominational member of the National Holiness Association at the latter's annual convention in Asheville, North Carolina." McKinley, p. 255.

CHAPTER 2—EMBODIED HOLINESS ON THE PATHWAY OF DUTY

[1] Captain Annie Shirley opened the Army's work in Boston in Sept. 1884, just after Brengle had started his theological training at the university. Clark, *SLB*, p. 36.

[2] Quoted in Hall, 1933, p. 63; cf. Stiles, p. 23.

[3] Hall, 1933, pp. 62–63.

[4] Hall, 1933, p. 63; Stiles, p. 24; Clark, *SLB*, pp. 36–37.

[5] Hayes was later a professor of New Testament interpretation at Garrett Biblical Institute.

[6] Woodward, pp. 28–29; Hall, 1933, pp. 63–64; Chesham, *Peace*, p. 63.

[7] Quoted in Stiles, p. 24; cf. Woodward, pp. 29–30.

[8] Quoted in Hall, 1933, p. 64; cf. Woodward, p. 30.

[9] Stiles, p. 25; Clark, *SLB,* pp. 37–38. Chesham attributes such resistance to a more intimate relationship chiefly to Elizabeth's frail health but also to the age difference (11 years) between them. *Treasury,* p. 7.

[10] Quoted in Chesham, *Peace,* p. 43. Perhaps this fear of death had something to do with losing four of five siblings in childhood, as well as her own frail condition. Chesham, *Peace,* p. 39.

[11] Hall, 1933, p. 65; Stiles, pp. 29–30.

[12] Samuel L. Brengle, "Mrs. Colonel Brengle: A Sketch of Her Life and Character," part 1, *War Cry* [NY] (May 8, 1915): 10; Clark, *SLB,* pp. 39–40.

[13] Quoted in Hall, 1933, p. 66; cf. Brengle, "Mrs. Colonel Brengle," part 1, p. 10; Chesham, *Peace,* p. 50.

[14] Samuel L. Brengle, "Mrs. Colonel Brengle: A Sketch of Her Life and Character," part 2, *War Cry* [NY] (May 15, 1915): 7; Hall, 1933, pp. 66–67; Stiles, pp. 30–32; Chesham, *Peace,* pp. 50–51; Clark, *SLB,* p. 40.

[15] "Lily knew she had found her place but also that she could never be an officer or do Salvation Army work. She was beyond the age for accepted candidates and was much too frail in health." Chesham, *Peace,* p. 51.

[16] Brengle, "Mrs. Colonel Brengle," part 2, p. 7; Chesham, *Peace,* pp. 51–54; Clark, *SLB,* p. 41; Chesham, *Treasury,* p. 10. While at the training home, Lily became friends with a cadet, Eileen Douglas, who would eventually become international editor of Army publications and writer of spiritual biographies and inspirational literature. Eileen suffered from physical ailments and later lived for fifteen years with the Brengles, while undergoing medical treatment in America. Samuel L. Brengle, "Brigadier Eileen Douglas: An Appreciation," *War Cry* [NY] (May 4, 1918): 6.

[17] Clark, *SLB,* pp. 41–42. Susie would eventually leave the Army to join a religious order within the Roman Catholic Church.

[18] Hall, 1933, pp. 68–69; Chesham, *Peace,* pp. 55–58, 66.

[19] Quoted in Chesham, *Peace,* p. 72.

[20] Quoted in Hall, 1936, p. 62.

[21] Quoted in Hall, 1936, pp. 62–63; cf. Chesham, *Peace,* p. 63.

[22] The certainty of his exclusive commitment to Lily was reaffirmed throughout their marriage, as illustrated in a letter Sam wrote to his wife three years before her death: "If you die, I can't get another wife. I suppose there are several women who would have me, but I wouldn't have them." Letter from Santa Barbara, CA, Jun. 25, 1912 in Clark, *Dearest Lily,* p. 109.

[23] Quoted in Hall, 1936, 64; cf. Clark, *SLB,* pp. 42–43.

[24] Hall, 1936, p. 64; Stiles, p. 29; Clark, *SLB,* p. 44.

[25] Quoted in Chesham, *Peace*, p. 64.

[26] Quoted in Chesham, *Peace*, p. 65.

[27] Hall, 1936, pp. 64–71; Woodward, pp. 34–36; Stiles, pp. 32–35; Chesham, *Peace*, pp. 72–73; Clark, *SLB*, pp. 44–46; Samuel L. Brengle, "Mrs. Colonel Brengle: A Sketch of Her Life and Character," part 3, *War Cry* [NY] (May 22, 1915): 7.

[28] Quoted in Hall, 1936, p. 73; cf. Woodward, pp. 36–37; Stiles, p. 36. This inauspicious beginning fell on Brengle's birthday.

[29] Quoted in Stiles, p. 37; cf. Woodward, pp. 37–39.

[30] Quoted in Hall, 1936, p. 74; cf. Stiles, pp. 37–38.

[31] Brengle, *At the Center of the Circle*, pp. 14–15.

[32] Hall, 1936, p. 75; Stiles, p. 38; Clark, *SLB*, pp. 47–49. In writing to Lily, Sam playfully referred to some of these "lessons in humility," as "scrubology." Woodward, p. 39.

[33] Quoted in Hall, 1936, p. 76; cf. Woodward, pp. 39–40; Clark, *SLB*, pp. 50–52.

[34] Quoted in Hall, 1936, p. 77.

[35] Quoted in Stiles, p. 39.

[36] At this time, he wrote to his wife: "If I had business qualifications, they'd make a D.C. [divisional commander] of me at once." Chesham, *Peace*, p. 74.

[37] Hall, 1936, pp. 76–79; Stiles, pp. 39–40; Chesham, *Peace*, p. 74.

[38] Quoted in Stiles, pp. 40–41.

[39] Quoted in Hall, 1936, p. 83.

[40] Brengle, Letter to Colonel Joseph Atkinson, written from St. Petersburg, FL, Dec. 14, 1935 (Alexandria, VA: The Salvation Army National Archives), p. 1; Hall, 1936, pp. 80–84; Woodward, pp. 41–42; Stiles, pp. 43–44; Clark, *SLB*, pp. 52–54.

[41] Stiles, pp. 44–45; Chesham, *Peace*, pp. 76–80; Clark, *SLB*, pp. 54–55. Due to their son's physical frailty, however, the doctors warned against taking him to Boston in winter. So, George spent the winter months in Amenia being cared for by Lily's family.

[42] Quoted in Hall, 1936, p. 87; cf. Woodward, pp. 43–44.

[43] Quoted in Chesham, *Treasury*, p. 148. The ironic occasion for this letter was the recognition of Brengle as a "distinguished alumnus" of the School of Theology. For full text see Samuel Hewitt (editor), "Letters of Commissioner Samuel Logan Brengle, D.D.," unpublished manuscript (The Salvation Army National Archives, Alexandria, VA; n.d.), pp. 198–99; cf. Brengle, "Personal Recollections of Albert J. Beveridge," pp. 7, 12. It is also to be noted that William McDonald, toward the end of his life, had a change

of heart and confessed to Brengle, "I think that if I were a young man again I would join the Salvation Army." Kenneth O. Brown, Inskip, McDonald, Fowler: "Wholly and Forever Thine": Early Leadership in the National Camp Meeting Association for the Promotion of Holiness (Hazelton, PA: Holiness Archives, 1999), 231; Hartley, *Evangelicals at the Crossroads*, note 62, p. 224.

[44] Letter to Dean Albert Knudson, Boston University School of Theology (Feb. 11, 1936), quoted in Hewitt, pp. 198–99; cf. Samuel L. Brengle, "Pennings of a Prophet: A Field of Service," *War Cry* [NY] (May 14, 1938): 6.

[45] Perhaps part of the premonition about the Boston appointment included a memory of Alice Ferrell Ferris. Many years later, Sam wrote to Lily about running into Alice: "She looked just as she did twenty-six years ago. It took me back to the night I was in No. 1 Boston before I joined the Army, when she was hit in the head with a stone and knocked senseless." Letter from Oakland, CA, Jun. 18, 1912 in Clark, *Dearest Lily*, p. 108.

[46] Hall, 1936, pp. 84–88; Stiles, pp. 45–47; Chesham, *Peace*, pp. 80–81; Clark, *SLB*, pp. 55–56.

[47] George had suffered long-term effects from measles he had contracted as a baby, and Elizabeth (born Nov. 3, 1891) suffered from both polio and tuberculosis during infancy. Chesham, *Peace*, pp. 82–83.

[48] McKinley, p. 41.

[49] Hall, 1936, pp. 88–90; Woodward, pp. 44–45; Stiles, pp. 47–48; Clark, *SLB*, pp. 56–57; Eric Coward, *The Brick and the Book: Samuel Logan Brengle* (London: The Salvation Army, 1948): 1, 8, 16.

[50] Hall, 1936, pp. 90–91; Clark, *SLB*, p. 58. This, and future promotions, reflect the upward mobility possible for educated Army officers. "Single, educated, male and female middle-class Salvationists found themselves promoted quickly into staff or administrative positions. . . . Men like Samuel Brengle . . . quickly moved from field to staff positions." Taiz, pp. 66–67.

[51] Quoted in John D. Waldron, "What Samuel Logan Brengle Had to Say about the Future of The Salvation Army," p. 3; Hall, 1936, p. 93; cf. Clark, *SLB*, pp. 58–62. For an account of Brengle's opening of the Army's work in Laconia, NH, in May 1893, see Edward Carey, "Vignettes of Army History: A Hot Gospel Shot into the Devil's Kingdom," *War Cry* [NY] (Aug. 16, 1980): 5.

[52] "Despite the pleas of such officers as Gifford, Brengle, and even Turk, Ballington resigned in the end . . . and in March 1896 he formed a new organization called the Volunteers of America. It was much like the Army in military style but featured a more democratic form of government." McKinley, p. 102; cf. Woodward, p. 49.

[53] Quoted in Hall, 1936, p. 97.

[54] Brengle, *Ancient Prophets*, p. 66.

[55] John D. Waldron, "Celebrating the Holy Life," part 3, *Officer* 36:4 (Apr. 1985): 148–49.

[56] Hall, 1936, pp. 95–97; Woodward, pp. 49–50; Clark, *SLB*, pp. 62–64.

[57] McKinley, p. 104.

[58] Hall, 1936, p. 99; McKinley, p. 104; Waldron, "Celebrating the Holy Life," part 3, p. 149.

[59] Quoted in Chesham, *Peace*, p. 85; cf. Chesham, *Born to Battle*, pp. 76–77; Waldron, "Celebrating the Holy Life," part 3, p. 149.

[60] Hall, 1936, p. 100; Woodward, p. 51; Clark, *SLB*, pp. 64–66.

[61] Brengle, "Special Campaigner," p. 17; Hall, 1936, p. 108; Woodward, pp. 51–53; Stiles, p. 49; Chesham, *Peace*, pp. 86–87; Coward, p. 9; cf. Taiz, pp. 154–55.

[62] Woodward, pp. 53–54; Clark, *SLB*, pp. 66–68, 92; William Clark, ed., *Dearest Lily* (London: The Salvation Army, 1985), pp. vii–viii.

[63] It is estimated that he delivered more than 25,000 sermons or addresses during his lifetime. "'That Man of God': Commissioner Samuel Logan Brengle," pamphlet prepared for Centenary Meetings, Fredericksburg, IN, 1960.

[64] "Its doctrinal foundation in Wesleyan holiness made it especially congenial to The Salvation Army. The saintly Brengle, still the National Spiritual Special, spoke several times in the college auditorium." McKinley, p. 176. In fact, Brengle recommended Asbury College as one of three schools for American Salvationists to attend. Letter to Brigadier J. N. Parker (Chicago), Mar. 29, 1935, quoted in Hewitt, "Letters."

[65] John D. Waldron, "Celebrating the Holy Life," part 2, *Officer* 36:3 (Mar. 1985): 110–11.

[66] Hall, 1936, pp. 158–62; Stiles, pp. 53–54. It is noteworthy that Brengle was thus the first Army officer to receive a D.D. degree. Wiggins, p. 89.

[67] Hall, 1936, 164; Chesham, *Peace,* p. 128. Dr. D. Willia Caffray, the first woman elder in American Methodism and worldwide holiness evangelist, became a good friend of Brengle's, and they carried on a regular correspondence through the years. For examples see Hewitt, "Letters of Commissioner Samuel Logan Brengle, D.D." In one letter, Brengle acknowledged his indebtedness to Dr. Caffray: "You have stirred me up to greater effort for the distribution of holiness literature, tracts, etc." He also credited her with introducing him to Francis Thompson's "Hound of Heaven," which so impressed him that he committed large portions of it to memory. Kenneth L. Robinson, *From Brass to Gold: The Life and Ministry of Dr. D. Willia Caffray* (University Park, IA: Vennard College, 1971), pp. 201, 334.

CHAPTER 3—INTERNATIONAL MINISTRY: A SPIRITUAL SPECIAL

[1] Accounts of his campaigns across the nation appeared regularly in The *War Cry.* For example, a three-month, six-state tour on the West Coast in 1898, which entailed "several hundred meetings" and "resulted in a total of 564 souls," is recounted in Samuel L. Brengle, "What I Saw Out West," *War Cry* [NY] (Nov. 5, 1898): 4. See also: Samuel L. Brengle, "In the Land of the Setting Sun: Some of Major Brengle's Journeyings and Personal Experiences," *War Cry* [NY] (Oct. 1897): 11.

[2] Quoted in Hall, 1933, p. 215.

[3] Hall, 1933, p. 215.

[4] Quoted in Hall, 1933, p. 216.

[5] Quoted in Hall, 1933, p. 215; cf. Clark, *SLB*, p. 74.

[6] Brigadier Kaleb Swenson sought to reform the Army in Sweden by making the corps self-governing and reinstituting the sacraments. He resisted the autocratic rule of William Booth and was summarily dismissed. A number of officers and soldiers joined Swenson and left to form the "Swedish Salvation Army." Clark, *SLB*, p. 74.

[7] Hall, 1933, p. 217; cf. Clark, *SLB*, pp. 74–75.

[8] Quoted in Hall, 1933, p. 218; cf. Clark, *SLB*, p. 75.

[9] Clark, *SLB*, p. 75; cf. Hall, 1933, p. 219.

[10] Quoted in Hall, 1933, pp. 219–20.

[11] Quoted in Hall, 1933, p. 223.

[12] Hall, 1933, p. 226; cf. Clark, *SLB*, p. 76.

[13] Samuel L. Brengle, "Our Scandinavian Campaign: A Resume," *War Cry* [NY] (Jun. 21, 1906): 10.

[14] Clark, *SLB*, p. 76.

[15] Hall, 1933, p. 228.

[16] Quoted in Hall, 1933, p. 228.

[17] Wiggins relates that ". . . hundreds of men, women and children yielded to Christ, although soul-saving in the country was characteristically slow and difficult. Quite a few Jews became Salvationists, and in certain quarters doctors were so enamored of the Army that they attended Salvationists free of charge." *History*, p. 26.

[18] Hall, 1933, p. 230; cf. Clark, *SLB*, pp. 76–77.

[19] Letter dated Jan. 31, 1907, in Clark, *Dearest Lily*, p. 3.

[20] Letter dated Feb. 4, 1907, in Clark, *Dearest Lily*, p. 3.

[21] Brengle, *The Guest of the Soul*, pp. 9–10; Clark, *Dearest Lily*, p. 1; Clark, *SLB*, p. 77. Cf. William Booth, "Gifts of the Spirit," *War Cry* (Mar. 14, 1885) in John Waldron, ed., *The Most Excellent Way* (n.p.: The Salvation Army, 1978), pp. 1–4.

[22] Quoted in Hall, 1933, p. 233.

[23] Hall, 1933, p. 234.

[24] Quoted in Hall, 1933, pp. 234–35; cf. Clark, *SLB*, p. 78.

[25] Letter dated Feb. 25, 1907, in Clark, *Dearest Lily*, p. 8.

[26] Quoted in Hall, 1933, p. 235.

[27] Letter dated Feb. 18, 1907, in Clark, *Dearest Lily*, p. 7; cf. Clark, *SLB*, p. 79.

[28] Letter from Arendal, Norway, dated Apr. 19, 1907, in Clark, *Dearest Lily*, p. 17.

[29] Brengle, *The Guest of the Soul*, p. 10. In subsequent years, Brengle grew increasingly concerned about the destructive effects of Modernism. When asked by his friend Rev. S. Parkes Cadman (a noted radio preacher) to recommend a book that could counter this influence, Brengle suggested *A Christian Manifesto* by Edwin Lewis (a former leading Modernist). Writing to Rev. Paul S. Reese in 1934, Brengle stated his belief that Lewis' book might be the needed counter-agent that would also serve as a catalyst for an imminent and universal revival: "I have just written Cadman that I think this book of Lewis' is the book he was looking for. . . . I shall not be surprised if a great revival, possibly world-sweeping, is at our doors." Letter to Rev. Paul S. Reese, Kansas City, MO (Dec. 15, 1934). Quoted in Samuel Hewitt (editor), "Letters of Commissioner Samuel Logan Brengle, D.D." Unpublished manuscript (The Salvation Army National Archives, Alexandria, VA; n.d.), pp. 134–35.

[30] Ironically, when approached after the address by a publisher who wanted the manuscript for publication, all Brengle had to show for his testimony to the deity of Christ was a rough outline sketched on the back of an old envelope. Hall, 1933, p. 239. The substance of the address was published as "The Atonement," *War Cry* [NY] (Sept. 14, 1907): 6. The complete form appeared later in two parts: "Meaning of the Atonement," part 1, *Officer* 30:4 (Apr. 1920): 326–31; "Meaning of the Atonement," part 2, *Officer* 30:5 (May 1920): 436–40. It was also reprinted in three parts: "The Necessity of the Atonement," part 1, *Officer* 44:4 (Apr. 1927): 305–8; "The Necessity of the Atonement," part 2, *Officer* 44:5 (May 1927): 427–31; "The Necessity of the Atonement," part 3, *Officer* 44:6 (Jun. 1927): 491–93. In 1934, a revised form of this address appeared as chapter one in Brengle's *The Guest of the Soul*.

[31] Brengle, *The Guest of the Soul*, p. 11.

[32] Hall, 1933, p. 238.

[33] Brengle, *The Guest of the Soul*, p. 35; cf. Hall, 1933, p. 239.

[34] Hall, 1933, p. 240.

35 Quoted in Hall, 1933, p. 241; cf. Clark, *SLB*, pp. 79–81; Wiggins, pp. 41–42.

36 George W. Cooke, "Colonel Brengle in Norway: 225 Souls in Six Days at Hamar," *War Cry* [NY] (Apr. 6, 1907): 16.

37 Letter from Åbo, Finland, dated Oct. 31, 1907, in Clark, *Dearest Lily*, p. 39; cf. p. 29.

38 George W. Cooke, "Colonel Brengle's Chronicles: 240 Souls at Helsingfors," *War Cry* [NY] (Nov. 23, 1907): 4–5.

39 George W. Cooke, "Near the Russian Border: 200 Souls Won for Christ in Colonel Brengle's Meetings in Wiborg," *War Cry* [NY] (Jan. 4, 1908), 11.

40 Hall, 1933, p. 244.

41 Hall, 1933, pp. 245–46; Clark, *SLB*, p. 81.

42 Altogether Brengle visited Denmark three times. The first time was in 1905 when he attended a Danish Congress. He included Denmark in his second European tour in 1906, returning in Feb. 1908. Clark, *Dearest Lily*, p. 47.

43 Quoted in Hall, 1933, p. 249.

44 Hall, 1933, p. 250; Clark, *SLB*, pp. 82–84. Sam wrote a series of letters to Lily, reporting on his condition and progress. See correspondence written from Copenhagen, Denmark, Apr. 7 through May 18, 1908, in Clark, *Dearest Lily*, pp. 53–61.

45 Wiggins maintains that during this time, Brengle "suffered a nervous breakdown." *History*, p. 199.

46 Letter from Amenia, NY, Mar. 12, 1908, in Clark, *Dearest Lily*, pp. 64–65.

47 Letter written from Copenhagen, Denmark, May 5, 1908, in Clark, *Dearest Lily*, p. 60; cf. Hall, 1933, p. 250.

48 Letter written from Copenhagen, Denmark, May 5, 1908, in Clark, *Dearest Lily*, pp. 60–61; cf. Hall, 1933, p. 250.

49 It is estimated that during his six-month campaign in Australia and New Zealand, "he claimed 2,600 converts in his meetings" (800 of which were the result of two months he spent in New Zealand). Wiggins, pp. 129–130, 199–200.

50 Clark, *Dearest Lily*, p. 70; Hall, 1933, p. 252.

51 Clark, *SLB*, pp. 87–89. Brengle explained to Lily what was partly responsible in setting the stage for this reception: "Sydney Buxton, an English missionary, who gave away 700 Japanese copies of *Helps to Holiness,* had been down in New Zealand to a conference . . . and mightily astonished them. . . by talking to them straight on holiness and bowled them over by telling them that if they read a book by a Salvation Army officer entitled *Helps to Holiness*

they could know a great deal more on the subject." Letter from Pakatoa Island, N.Z., Apr. 28, 1910, in Clark, *Dearest Lily*, p. 79. Brengle's campaigns in Timaru, Ashburton, Christchurch, and Wellington are detailed in "Colonel Brengle Campaigning in New Zealand," *War Cry* [NY] (Jun. 4, 1910): 6, 10. A Salvationist reporter wrote: "In the nearly four-weeks campaign on the South Island hundreds have sought the indispensable blessings of pardon and purity. . . . The Colonel's books sold like 'hot cakes.' The trade depot had its usual yearly stock, which was sold out at two corps, and all over the Island the people were clamoring for more books." George W. Cook, "Colonel Brengle under the Southern Cross," *War Cry* [NY] (Jun. 11, 1910): 10.

[52] Throughout Australia, when the pain was too severe for him to endure standing erect, he preached with one foot on a chair. Hall, 1933, p. 256. Despite the physical challenges, Brengle's ministry flourished. In a summary of the campaign in the Australian Commonwealth, New Zealand, and Tasmania, a reporter wrote: "Colonel Brengle remarked the other day that it was one of the most successful campaigns anywhere. . . . Already about 2,200 souls have been at the penitent-form." George W. Cooke, "Colonel Brengle in Tasmania," *War Cry* [NY] (Oct. 15, 1910): 9, 12; cf. "News From Australia: Finish of Colonel Brengle's Seven Months' Campaign—2,600 Souls," *War Cry* [NY] (Dec. 3, 1910): 6.

[53] Quoted in Hall, 1933, p. 257; cf. Clark, *SLB*, pp. 89–90; Clark, *Dearest Lily*, pp. 83–84.

[54] George W. Cooke, "An Asiatic Mission Field: Colonel Brengle Conducts Council With Cingalese Officers," *War Cry* [NY] (Dec. 10, 1910): 6–7.

[55] Quoted in Hall, 1933, p. 258.

[56] Hall, 1933, p. 258; Clark, *SLB*, pp. 84–85.

[57] Letter from Melbourne, Australia, Jul. 23, 1910, in Clark, *Dearest Lily*, pp. 85–86.

[58] Letter from Beaconsfield, Tasmania, Aug. 10, 1910, in Clark, *Dearest Lily*, p. 87.

CHAPTER 4—MANIFOLD TRIALS, MANIFOLD GRACE

[1] Quoted in Woodward, pp. 57–58; cf. Chesham, *Peace*, p. 174.

[2] Quoted in Hall, 1936, p. 210.

[3] Ibid.

[4] Hall, 1936, p. 214; Clark, *SLB*, pp. 82–84.

[5] Earlier, he had been considered for this position, as indicated in Sam's correspondence with Lily: "I spoke to Sharp last night about asking for a change of appointment, and he at once said what so many in all parts of the world have told me, that I ought to be connected with training. He says National Headquarters will not suggest a change because I am in such universal

demand." Letter from Long Beach, CA, Jul. 22, 1912, in Clark, *Dearest Lily*, p. 112.

[6] Coward, *Brick and Book*, p. 15.

[7] Quoted in Chesham, *Peace*, p. 101; cf. Woodward, pp. 58–61; Chesham, *Treasury*, p. 14; Brengle, "Mrs. Colonel Brengle: A Sketch of Her Life and Character," part 3, p. 7.

[8] Samuel L. Brengle, *The Consolation Wherewith He Was Comforted* [pamphlet] (n.p.: The Salvation Army, n.d.), pp. 11, 14. This theme can be seen worked out in other articles, as Brengle related how God's grace proved sufficient through the pain of his wife's death: "And now, what is the secret of all this blessedness, this triumph over the worst that death can do? Some will say, 'It is not natural,' but I. . . say 'It is supernatural.' It is above nature; it is divine. It is Heaven begun below. It is the work of the 'other Comforter' whom Jesus promised should come. . . . The secret is salvation. . . the salvation of our God through repentance, renunciation of sin and faith in a crucified and risen Savior, and the blessing of a clean heart, filled with His Spirit, received and kept by obedient faith." Samuel L. Brengle, "A Word of Thanks and a Personal Testimony," *War Cry* [NY] (May 1, 1915): 10. Cf. Brengle, "Holiness—A Working Experience: In the Hour of Affliction and Death—A Personal Testimony," *Officer* 23:6 (Jun. 1915): 421.

[9] Quoted in Woodward, p. 61.

[10] Hall, 1936, pp. 216–23; Stiles, pp. 56–60; Chesham, *Peace*, pp. 98–101.

[11] Chesham, *Peace*, p. 103; cf. Clark, *SLB*, pp. 92–93.

[12] E.g., Brengle's campaign with Scandinavian Salvationists in the "Western Territory" during which time he spent a month in the Chicago area before proceeding to Minneapolis, Duluth, and other cities. His campaign in Chicago alone resulted in "over 2,000 souls kneeling at the penitent-form." Brengle called this "his greatest campaign in America" to date. Mildred Olson, "Colonel Brengle Has Most Wonderful Campaign He Has Ever Conducted in America," *War Cry* [NY] (Mar. 22, 1919): 8. A few months later, Brengle would write: "This past year has been wonderful. Since the first of January considerably over 3,000 souls have knelt at the penitent-form in my meetings, seeking pardon and purity. Seldom have I seen such manifestations of God's presence and power in my meetings as during these months." Samuel L. Brengle, "June First, 1860–1919," *War Cry* [NY] (Jun. 28, 1919): 10; Samuel L. Brengle, *Love-Slaves* (Atlanta: The Salvation Army, 1982), pp. 128–29.

[13] Brengle, "My Day of Days: A Testimony Written on Jan. 9, 1923," *War Cry* [NY] (Feb. 3, 1923): 3.

[14] Chesham, *Peace*, p. 134. It was during this period of frail health and recuperation that Brengle gained a new appreciation of nature as God's creation ("mysticism in nature"). Samuel L. Brengle, "The Mystic, Wondrous Universe in My Back Yard," *Staff Review* (Oct. 1925): 140–44.

[15] Quoted in Chesham, *Peace*, p. 137.

[16] Quoted in Hall, 1933, p. 355. It is interesting to note that although Brengle became increasingly involved in the issues raised by the reform movement, including the eventual deposition of General Bramwell Booth, chapter 44 ("Reform") was omitted in subsequent editions of Hall's *Portrait of a Prophet* (e.g., the 1936 "Memorial Edition").

[17] Quoted in Hall, 1933, p. 356.

[18] The writer specified his points of complaint: 1) "The perpetuation of power in one man or in one family cannot continue without instigating a revolt that will end either in the dissolution of the Army or in a final paralysis of any initiative on the part of its soldiers." 2) He denounced the "disesteem and contumely" to which leading officers and some of the most promising men in the rank and file had been treated. 3) The writer took unqualified exception to the methods of appointing the General's successor. 4) He charged the General with "particularly offensive nepotism." 5) He demanded that the leadership of the Army should be committed to a Governing Council. F. A. MacKenzie, *The Clash of the Cymbals: The Secret History of the Revolt in The Salvation Army* (New York: Brentano's, 1929), pp. 46–48; cf. Hall, 1933, p. 356. For full text of manifesto, see Appendix: "The First Blast of a Trumpet," in MacKenzie, pp. 172–80. Although the origin of this manifesto has never been established, Ervine claimed, "It was undoubtedly issued in the United States, but there is textual evidence to show that it was either inspired by Booth-Tucker or written by someone who had access to the opinions he had expressed in his correspondence and was subsequently to elaborate in *The Two Wise Mice*." St. John Ervine, *God's Soldier: General William Booth*, vol. 2 (New York: Macmillan, 1935), pp. 888–89; cf. McKinley, pp. 196–97.

[19] For text of "Atwood" Bulletins see Ervine, pp. 1105–13; cf. Hall, 1933, p. 357; Frank Smith, *The Betrayal of Bramwell Booth: The Truth about The Salvation Army Revolt* (London: Jarrolds, 1929), pp. 51–53. The first issue of *The International Salvationist,* edited by "W. L. Atwood" appeared in January 1928, "published" on mimeograph paper. The identity of this "Atwood" is far from clear, Brengle even writing in June of 1927 that he had never met anyone who knew this mystery person. Ervine, p. 889. For text of "Atwood's" *International Salvationist,* no. 1, Jan. 1928, see Ervine, pp. 1114–20.

[20] Brengle, Letter to "My Dear Comrade," written from Arlington, NJ, Jun. 1, 1927 (Alexandria, VA: The Salvation Army National Archives), pp. 1–14; cf. Hall, 1933, p. 358; Smith, pp. 53–54, 56–57; John Larsson, *1929: A Crisis That Shaped The Salvation Army's Future* (London: Salvation Army, 2009): pp. 69–70.

[21] Quoted in Hall, 1933, p. 359. "On September 3, 1927, Commissioner Brengle, who, in the previous June, had never seen or heard of 'Atwood,' warned Bramwell Booth that the man was the agent of his implacable enemies. . . . He wrote . . . 'believe me, unless a number of devoted men over here are utterly mistaken, he is the tool of ruthless, determined, unspiritual group who must be reckoned with.'" Ervine, pp. 903–04. Brengle's perception of the locus of

the problem was not shared by all, in that many believed that it was Bramwell Booth who ". . . had turned a benevolent autocracy into a tyranny. The feeling against him was deepened by his action on certain issues, which was held to be contrary to the spirit of . . . Salvation Army regulations. The points raised may be divided into four: 1) emoluments; 2) alleged nepotism; 3) excessive use of authority; 4) allowing undue family influence to prevail in decisions relating to Army matters." MacKenzie, p. 50.

[22] MacKenzie, p. 72.

[23] MacKenzie, pp. 73–74; cf. Smith, p. 63. For full text of Eva's "Fifteen Points" see MacKenzie, pp. 181–84. For Bramwell's response to his sister, dated Nov. 1927, see MacKenzie, pp. 185–92. For Eva's response to Bramwell's response, dated Feb. 9, 1928, see MacKenzie, pp. 193–212.

[24] MacKenzie, pp. 86–96. For text of Bramwell's letter to Territorial Commanders, dated Apr. 23, 1928, see MacKenzie, pp. 213–15. For text of 1904 Supplementary Deed Poll, see Ervine, pp. 1078–90.

[25] Quoted in Hall, 1933, p. 360; cf. Clark, *SLB*, p. 134.

[26] MacKenzie, pp. 96–99; cf. Smith, pp. 17–18. The Founder had always considered the Army as his creation to shape and control. His autocratic methods were tempered, to a degree, by a pragmatic spirit that took advantage of the gifts and creativity of his subordinates. Bramwell had helped his parents govern the Army and, with their passing, saw the mantle of leadership as his birthright. Unfortunately, he not only lacked the charisma of his father, but his autocratic leadership style became increasingly threatened by the gifts and abilities of others under his command. Thus, he and his immediate family perceived the calling of a High Council as an act of usurpation, a challenge to their divinely ordained authority. MacKenzie, pp. 100–2.

[27] For further details regarding the significance of this council, and Brengle's role in it, see Larsson, 1929, pp. 125, 161, 173, 184, 186, 199, 200, 215, 220, and 229.

[28] MacKenzie, pp. 106–7. For a contrasting perspective, see Frank Smith's *Betrayal of Bramwell Booth,* a self-acclaimed "defense of General Bramwell Booth against the unwarrantable and un-Christian attack made upon him by the 'High Council' of The Salvation Army." Smith wrote: "Like all revolts this public expression of disloyalty was the result of long and careful planning. The breakdown in health of General Bramwell Booth was not the cause of it. But this breakdown did give those who were engineering the 'revolt' their opportunity" not only to undermine the General's authority but also "to create prejudice against the members of his family" (*Betrayal,* pp. 17–18, 88).

[29] Hall, 1933, pp 360–61.

[30] MacKenzie, p. 122.

[31] Letter to Colonel Jenkins, written from Sunbury Court, England, Jan. 14, 1929 (Alexandria, VA: The Salvation Army National Archives), pp. 5–6.

[32] MacKenzie, p. 122. Despite these attempts to convey affection, Frank Smith castigated the Council as spiritually insensitive, stating that "the spirit of God could have had no part or lot in either the drawing up of such a resolution. . . ." He further questions whether its members "possessed the spirit of Christ which they profess to have." Smith goes so far as to characterize the Council as "the Sunbury Soviet," whose deliberations are secretive, deceptive, and "farcical," while the General and his family are portrayed as courteous, loving, prayerful, and without guile. Smith, pp. 108–14.

[33] Chesham, *Born to Battle,* p. 195. Other members of this party were: Commissioners James Hay, George Mitchell, John Cunningham; Lt. Commissioner William Haines; and, Colonel Annie Trounce. All but Hay and Haines were chosen because of their affection for the General. Note that Yamamuro had written the only biography of Bramwell Booth that had been published to date (Catherine Bramwell-Booth published her *Bramwell Booth* in 1933). Ervine, p. 975.

[34] Hall, 1933, p. 361; Clark, *SLB*, p. 136.

[35] P. W. Wilson, *General Evangeline Booth of The Salvation Army* (New York: Charles Scribner's Sons, 1948), p. 214. Cf. MacKenzie, p. 127.

[36] MacKenzie, p. 136; cf. Ervine, p. 984; Smith, pp. 17–18, 51.

[37] Brengle, Letter to Colonel Jenkins, Jan. 14, 1929, p. 10.

[38] MacKenzie, pp. 132–33.

[39] McKinley, p. 200.

[40] Quoted in Wilson, pp. 215–16; cf. Brengle, Letter to Colonel Jenkins, Jan. 14, 1929, p. 25.

[41] Waldron, "Celebrating the Holy Life," part 3, p. 149. By way of contrast, Brengle's position was understood as a defection by some. For example, Ervine presents him as an unwitting turncoat: "Commissioner Brengle . . . who had been regarded as one of the Booths' firmest hopes until he had made a half-turn from his General by voting for the request that he should resign, now turned completely away. He had been induced to believe that Bramwell Booth had threatened the Army with a lawsuit, and in the darkening afternoon of Wednesday he announced his defection from his General's side." Ervine, pp. 984–85.

[42] "The High Council Official Bulletin," *War Cry* [NY] (Feb. 2, 1929): 8.

[43] Writing to staff officers, Commissioner Edward Higgins (Chief of the Staff) stated: "It seems unthinkable that General Booth could have adopted this course of action, and the only charitable construction I can place upon it is that he is in too enfeebled a condition to fully appreciate the seriousness of his action." MacKenzie, p. 147.

[44] Brengle, Letter to Colonel Jenkins, Jan. 15, 1929, p. 1. Cf. MacKenzie, pp. 137–38, 153, 157–58; McKinley, p. 200. In a prior letter to

Colonel Walter Jenkins (National Chief Secretary, U.S.), dated Jan. 14, 1929, Brengle expressed concern with regard to the choice of a successor to Bramwell Booth. He indicated that Evangeline was a logical choice but questioned whether she would be physically able to embark on this path at age sixty-three. Margaret Troutt, *The General Was a Lady: The Story of Evangeline Booth* (Nashville: A. J. Holman, 1980), pp. 212–13.

[45] An example of Brengle's influence on American church leaders is evident in his response to a cable from Dr. Cadman, former president of the Federated Churches of Christ in America. Wiring Brengle during the High Council, Cadman had written: "The transition in government of the Army at this time from an autocracy to a constitutional form of direction and to steps leading up to this by the High Council have been watched with deepest interest and sympathy by the churches of America. . . . I join with millions of Americans in wishing for the High Council Divine wisdom and direction in the selection of the successor and the policies to be adopted in the new regime." Brengle's response was gracious and optimistic: "Grateful for cable. The practical unanimity of spirit, the dignity of procedure, the firmness, mingled with kindness, of the High Council in facing difficulties is commended by best British thought." Samuel L. Brengle, "Reply to Rev. Dr. S. Parkes Cadman's Message to the High Council," *War Cry* [NY] (Feb. 9, 1929): 2.

[46] Quoted in Chesham, *Peace*, p. 173; cf. Clark, *SLB*, pp. 131, 139.

[47] Quoted in Chesham, *Treasury*, p. 150.

[48] Hall, 1933, pp. 362–65; Clark, *SLB*, pp. 139–42.

[49] The Commander's address of appreciation concerning Brengle included the following remarks: "The Commissioner has lived his life and performed his service with an eye so single to the glory of God that either the praise or the blame of any man is of little worth to him. . . . While closely allied to all of us by a thousand bonds, he stands out a figure alone! He stands out because he has stood. He has stood for every purpose embraced in his calling. . . . He has stood up for the Gospel of Jesus Christ. . . . He has stood up for The Salvation Army. . . . He has stood up for its authority . . . defending its methods. . . faithfully supporting in word and deed its leaders. . . . He has stood before the whole world bright in the light of an unstinted, undiminishing devotion to God. . . . Commissioner Brengle has stood always for the good of others. . . . [He] stands a glistening example for holy literature . . . [his] pen has moved the world. . . . Commissioner Brengle has stood up as one of the world's greatest preachers. . . . He has sought the salvation of the people, not his own glory. . . . He has called upon God to help him. Prayer has been the breath of his life, the pulse of his soul, the well from which has drawn the glistening waters of his daily salvation, and the Redeemer's fullness of power." Evangeline Booth, "He Stands Out a Figure Alone," *War Cry* [NY] (Oct. 17, 1931): 9, 13. For a biographical sketch written on the occasion of Brengle's retirement, see "Commissioner Samuel L. Brengle: A Character Sketch of a Salvation Army Saint," *War Cry* [NY] (Oct. 17, 1931): 3, 14.

50 Quoted in Chesham, *Peace*, pp. 180–81; cf. Letter to Rev. Edward Mallory, Boston (Nov. 11, 1931), quoted in Samuel Hewitt (editor), "Letters of Commissioner Samuel Logan Brengle, D.D." Unpublished manuscript (The Salvation Army National Archives, Alexandria, VA; n.d.), p. 120. This letter, to one of Brengle's closest friends (with whom he stayed in Old Orchard Beach, Maine, and St. Petersburg, Florida), reveals that Brengle was hoping to be able to accept invitations to minister in Korea, China, and Japan in the following year.

51 Samuel L. Brengle, "Retired: A Valedictory Message," *War Cry* [NY] (Oct. 17, 1931): 12.

52 The receptivity of the attendees to his ministry is attested by the fact that although only scheduled to speak three times, he was pressed into service twelve times during the conference. Robinson, pp. 200–1.

53 Letter to Rev. Dr. John Paul, Chicago Evangelistic Institute (Sept. 18, 1933). Quoted in Hewitt, "Letters of Commissioner Samuel Logan Brengle, D.D.," pp. 127–29. Similar sentiments were shared in a letter to D. Willia Caffray (1933) quoted in Robinson, pp. 200–1.

54 Letter to Rev. S. Parkes Cadman, Brooklyn, NY (Apr. 10, 1934), quoted in Hewitt, "Letters of Commissioner Samuel Logan Brengle, D.D.," pp. 118–19; Samuel L. Brengle, "A Revival in Every Salvation Army Corps," *Officers' Review* 2:6 (Nov.–Dec. 1933): 481–87; cf. Samuel L. Brengle, "A World-Wide Revival," reproduced in Allen Satterlee (editor), "Pentecost and Beyond: Collected Writings of Commissioner Samuel Logan Brengle." Unpublished manuscript (The Salvation Army National Archives, Alexandria, VA; n.d.), pp. 6–16.

55 "Commissioner Brengle Awarded Order of the Founder by the General," *War Cry* [NY] (Nov. 2, 1935): 13; Stiles, pp. 61–62; Clark, *SLB*, pp. 143–46.

56 Quoted in Clark, *SLB*, p. 146. For full text of commendation see "Commissioner Brengle Awarded Order of the Founder by the General," p. 13.

57 Samuel L. Brengle, "Retired," *Staff Review* (Jul. 1924): 202–3. Reprinted in *Officer* 39:4 (Oct. 1924): 266–68.

58 Chesham, *Peace*, p. 147.

59 "A Lamp of Remembrance," *War Cry* [NY] (May 4, 1940): 7, 14.

60 Brengle, Letter to Colonel Joseph Atkinson, Boston, from Grove Farm, Poughquag, NY, Aug. 3, 1935 (Alexandria, VA: The Salvation Army National Archives), pp. 1–2. Cf. Samuel L. Brengle, "Light at Evening Time," *War Cry* [NY] (May 9, 1936): 6.

61 Letter to Commissioner Gunpei Yamamuro, Tokyo, Feb. 27, 1936, quoted in Chesham, *Treasury*, p. 184.

62 Quoted in Hall, 1936, p. 246; cf. "Letter to General Evangeline Booth," Feb. 17, 1936, in Chesham, *Treasury*, p. 183; Woodward, p. 62.

[63] Quoted in Chesham, *Peace*, pp. 184–85; cf. Brengle, "Pennings of a Prophet," [published posthumously] *War Cry* [NY] (May 7, 1938): 6.

[64] Brengle, Letter to Colonel Joseph Atkinson, Aug. 12, 1935, pp. 1–2.

[65] Quoted in Chesham, *Peace*, p. 188.

[66] Quoted in William G. Harris, "'This Man of God': Funeral Service of Commissioner Brengle," *War Cry* [NY] (Jun. 6, 1936): 13. Harris also notes: "She [Evangeline Booth] and Samuel L. Brengle were dear friends. Perhaps no one save these two know what Brengle has meant to the Army and to herself in sane judgment, sound counsel and advice, charged with a spiritual dynamic." (p. 13).

[67] Quoted in Harris, "This Man of God," p. 13.

[68] Commissioner Alexander M. Damon, "Bulletin! Commissioner Samuel Logan Brengle in Heaven," Territorial Headquarters, New York, May 20, 1936 (Alexandria, VA: The Salvation Army National Archives), p. 1; Hall, 1933, pp. 248–51; Stiles, pp. 55–56, 62–63; cf. Clark, *SLB*, pp. 147–48. A memorial service was held on May 31, 1936, at Brengle's home corps in Mount Vernon, New York, which included the reading of his favorite Psalm (103rd) and a tribute by his son, George. "In Memoriam: Colonel Barrett Conducts Impressive Service for the Late Commissioner Brengle," *War Cry* [NY] (Jun. 13, 1936): 10, 11.

[69] *The Salvation Army Yearbook, 1936* (London: The Salvation Army, 1937), p. 10. This sentiment is supported by the reflection of Frederick Coutts: "The Commissioner's personal influence had always been greater than any rank he held or appointment he was given." *The History of The Salvation Army*, p. 141. For a biographical tribute published within weeks of Brengle's death see William G. Harris, "Samuel L. Brengle—Salvationist Saint," *War Cry* [NY] (Jun. 6, 1936): 3, General Evangeline Booth also noted Brengle's ongoing legacy: "The Commissioner's writings, not less than his personal evangelism, have made his name a household word throughout the Army. He was a profuse writer, and thousands of Salvationists have found the way to Christ through his books and articles. These were like his preaching—simple, direct, explanatory and amply illustrated. . . . In a very real sense, even now that he has ceased to preach orally, Commissioner Brengle will go on, through these products of his sanctified pen, speaking to this and to succeeding generations." Evangeline Booth, "An Apostle of the Penitent-Form: An Unsurpassed Exponent of the Doctrine of Holiness," *War Cry* [NY] (Jun. 20, 1936): 9. Through the years, Brengle's living legacy has been noted by many. E.g., Bramwell Tripp, "A Godly, Gracious Influence for More Than a Century," *War Cry* [NY] (May 10, 1980): 21.

Chapter 5—Communicating Holiness: Methods and Materials

[1]Quoted in James McGraw, "The Preaching of Samuel Logan Brengle," *Preacher's Magazine* (Feb. 1956): 7; cf. William Kostlevy, "Ridout, George W.," in *Historical Dictionary of the Holiness Movement*, pp. 217–18.

[2]Brengle, "Special Campaigner," p. 21; Brengle, *Ancient Prophets*, p. 73; cf. McGraw, p. 8.

[3]Quoted in Hall, 1936, p. 114; cf. Woodward, *Life Sketches,* pp. 54–55.

[4]Samuel L. Brengle, "A Great Little Book on Prayer" (review of Samuel Chadwick's *The Path of Prayer*), *Officers' Review* 1:5 (Sept.–Oct. 1932): 395.

[5]Samuel L. Brengle, "The Hebrew Prophets and the Life of Today," *Staff Review* (Oct. 1927): p. 390; Brengle, *Ancient Prophets*, p. 1. Cf. "How to Study the Bible," chapter 24 in Samuel L. Brengle, *Heart-Talks on Holiness* (Atlanta: The Salvation Army, 1988), pp. 102–5.

[6]Samuel L. Brengle, *Resurrection Life and Power* (Atlanta: The Salvation Army, 1981), p. 150; cf. Hall, 1936, pp. 184–86. Some of Brengle's favorite songs were: "O Love That Will Not Let Me Go," "Take the Name of Jesus with You," "O Boundless Salvation," "There Is a Name I Love to Hear," "Rescue the Perishing," "Tell Me the Story of Jesus," "I'll Follow Thee of Life the Giver," and "Blessed Assurance." Chesham, *Peace*, pp. 131–32.

[7]Samuel L. Brengle, "The Army Song Book as a Manual of Devotion," *War Cry* [NY] (Jul. 17, 1915): 16; Samuel L. Brengle, *Resurrection Life and Power* (Atlanta: The Salvation Army, 1981), p. 151.

[8]Quoted in Hall, 1936, p. 119.

[9]Samuel L. Brengle, "How Much Do You Read—and What?" *Officers' Review* 6:1 (Jan.–Feb. 1937): 50 [Published posthumously, this article is Brengle's last contribution to *The Officers' Review*]. The breadth of Brengle's reading is attested to by the fact that 813 titles from his personal library were donated to the Training School in New York after his death, the majority of which were theological in nature. See unpublished list: "Commissioner Brengle's Books," Salvation Army School for Officer Training, Suffern, NY; n.d. In recognition of this gift, the library at the Training School was dedicated by Commissioner Alexander Damon as the Brengle Memorial Library on Jun. 2, 1938. "A Brengle Memorial," *War Cry* [NY] (May 21, 1938): 8.

[10]Brengle, "How Much Do You Read—and What?" p. 47.

[11]Quoted in McGraw, p. 8.

[12]Hall, 1936, pp. 115–17; Stiles, pp. 50–51.

[13]Quoted in Hall, 1936, p. 118.

[14]Brengle, "Special Campaigner," p. 20; Brengle, *Ancient Prophets*, p. 72. For an assessment of the Army's use of various media in promoting its

missional objectives, see Winston, *Red-Hot and Righteous* (1999). It is not surprising that Winston has virtually nothing to say about Brengle in her book about the Army in America (one reference on p. 80), due to the fact that he didn't utilize the very means that she analyzes.

[15]Letter from Minneapolis, MN, Mar. 15, 1912, in Clark, *Dearest Lily*, p. 104.

[16]Four of these soloists who also served as officer assistants were George Cooke, Walter Mabee, Earl Lord, and Wesley Bouterse.

[17]Hall, 1936, pp. 120–22; Stiles, p. 51; Chesham, *Peace*, p. 121.

[18]"On the Platform with Colonel Brengle: A Typical Soul-Battle Described," *War Cry* [NY] (Feb. 7, 1914): 6.

[19]Quoted in Hall, 1936, p. 123.

[20]Quoted in Clark, *SLB*, p. 156.

[21]Samuel L. Brengle, "Profound," *Field Officer* 13:9 (Sept. 1905): Reprinted as "On Saying Something Profound," *Officer* 37:3 (Sept. 1923): 238, 250.

[22]Hall, 1936, p. 124.

[23]Quoted in Hall, 1936, pp. 125–26; cf. Stiles, p. 51.

[24]Foreword, Hall, 1936, p. vi.

[25]Quoted in Hall, 1936, p. 127.

[26]McKinley, p. 42; cf. McGraw, p. 9. E.g., Samuel L. Brengle, "Incidents Picked Up Along the Way," *War Cry* [NY] (Oct. 19, 1918): 7.

[27]Letter from Milwaukee, WI, Mar. 25, 1912, in Clark, *Dearest Lily*, p. 105.

[28]Clark, *Dearest Lily*, p. x. That Lily's concern was primarily with regard to Sam's health and stamina is reflected in a letter she wrote to him while on an overseas campaign: "My darling boy, that outsider wrote an admirable article about Colonel Brengle, but I noted that he spoke of his 'frail form.' Where is that boasted fat? . . . If you would only quit your self-indulgence, and bring me home thirty-five pounds more husband." Letter from Amenia, NY, Apr. 14, 1910, in Clark, *Dearest Lily*, p. 94.

[29]Letter from Gisborne, New Zealand, Apr. 22, 1910, in Clark, *Dearest Lily*, p. 78.

[30]Letter from Amenia, NY, Mar. 30, 1910, in Clark, *Dearest Lily*, pp. 93–94.

[31]Letter from Brisbane, Australia, Jun. 7, 1910, in Clark, *Dearest Lily*, pp. 82–83.

[32]Quoted in Hall, 1936, pp. 127–28.

[33]Hall, 1936, pp. 128–29; Stiles, pp. 51–52; Clark, *SLB*, p. 14; cf. Coward, p. 10.

[34]"Staff-Captain Brengle: Our Western Massachusetts D.O.," *War Cry* [NY] (Aug. 24, 1895): 15.

[35]Evangeline Booth, "An Apostle of the Penitent-Form: An Unsurpassed Exponent of the Doctrine of Holiness," *War Cry* [NY] (Jun. 20, 1936): 9.

[36]Hall, 1936, pp. 131–34; Stiles, p. 52; Chesham, *Peace*, p. 122; Coward, p. 10.

[37]Commissioner Alexander M. Damon, "Bulletin! Commissioner Samuel Logan Brengle in Heaven," p. 1. His effectiveness in this regard was captured in the following tribute: "Commissioner Brengle was . . . an Apostle of the Penitent-Form. Like the Founder, he was an unwavering believer in public confession and could persuade people to accept the truth with whom others had failed." Evangeline Booth, "An Apostle of the Penitent-Form," p. 9.

[38]Samuel L. Brengle, "Correspondence: Problems of the Sunday Night Prayer Meeting," *Staff Review* (Apr. 1928): 197. It is obvious that such means had their limits: "I am not a musician, but I am persuaded that we often hurt our Prayer Meetings by too free a use of band instruments. They often drown out the words we sing, and make it next to impossible to deal effectively with seekers at the penitent-form." Ibid., p. 198.

[39]Hall, 1936, p. 135; Stiles, p. 53.

[40]Brengle, "Correspondence: Problems of the Sunday Night Prayer Meeting," p. 198. Cf. Hall, 1936, p. 138.

[41]Samuel L. Brengle, *The Soul-Winner's Secret* (Atlanta: The Salvation Army, 1988), pp. 78–87; Samuel L. Brengle, "They Are Only Lambs," *War Cry* (Feb. 2, 1985): 20–21; Chesham, *Peace*, p. 160.

[42]Samuel L. Brengle, "Conversion of Young People," *War Cry* [NY] (Jan. 2, 1915): 11.

[43]Samuel L. Brengle, "The Children, the Children, Oh, the Children," *War Cry* [NY] (Jul. 19, 1919): 2–3.

[44]Samuel L. Brengle, *Can Little Children Be Really Saved?* (New York: The Salvation Army, 1937), pp. 11, 28. This pamphlet was a reprint of "Can Little Children Be Really Saved?" *Officer* 29:3 (Sept. 1919): 233–36.

[45]Brengle, *Can Little Children Be Really Saved?*, p. 23.

[46]Waldron, "Celebrating the Holy Life," part 1, pp. 69–71.

[47]Quoted in Chesham, *Peace*, p. 162. On his campaigns, Brengle often put the "band boys" to work in "dealing personally with the unsaved" during the prayer meeting. E.g., W. Scott Potter, "The Staff Band at Poughkeepsie," *War Cry* [NY] (Jun. 17, 1899): 4.

[48]Chesham, *Peace*, pp. 164–65.

[49]Brengle, *Ancient Prophets*, p. 154.

[50] Hall, 1933, p. 336; Clark, *SLB*, pp. 124–30. For collections of letters see Clark, *Dearest Lily*; Hewitt, "Letters," comprising letters of Brengle's later years, made available by his daughter, Elizabeth (Mrs. H. Chester Reed), after her father's death.

[51] Quoted in Waldron, "Celebrating the Holy Life," part 1, p. 71. See Sallie Chesham's *Peace Like a River* for numerous quotes from his follow-up letters.

[52] Quoted in Chesham, *Peace*, p. 172.

[53] "Samuel L. Brengle and 'The Officers' Review,'" *Officers' Review* 5:4 (Jul.–Aug. 1936): 303.

[54] John C. Izzard with Henry Gariepy, *Pen of Flame: The Life and Poetry of Catherine Baird* (Alexandria, VA: The Salvation Army, 2002), pp. 35–36, 39–42, 48–49, 107.

[55] Hall, 1936, pp. 165–71, 192–93.

[56] Hall, 1933, p. 332. His writing has been likened to that of John Bunyan, in terms of its experiential basis, and to that of Thomas à Kempis, in terms of its "colloquial and simple language." See Hall, 1933, p. 334.

[57] Letter to General Bramwell Booth, Dec. 9, 1925, quoted in Hewitt, "Letters," p. 6; cf. Hall, 1933, p. 332. Occasionally, however, Brengle indulged in meditative poetry when the demands of his ministry permitted. E.g., "The Sea," *War Cry* [NY] (Dec. 4, 1915): 1; "'It Is I, Be Not Afraid,'" *War Cry* [NY] (Jan. 6, 1917): 10; "God's Love Immutable," *Officers' Review* 5:4 (Jul.–Aug. 1936): 296; cf. Hall, 1933, pp. 333–34. In this regard, it is interesting to note his mentoring influence on the literary development of Catherine Baird. Izzard, *Pen of Flame*, pp. 35–36, 39–42.

[58] Quoted in Hall, 1933, p. 332.

[59] Quoted in Hall, 1933, p. 333; "Samuel L. Brengle and 'The Officers' Review,'" *Officers' Review* 5:4 (Jul.–Aug. 1936): 303.

[60] After 1925, however, he had more time to devote to his writing, resulting in the publication of several of his longer works. Chesham, *Peace*, p. 155.

[61] Letter from Copenhagen, Denmark, Feb. 13, 1908, in Clark, *Dearest Lily*, p. 49.

[62] Woodward, p. 47.

[63] Quoted in Chesham, *Peace*, p. 156.

[64] Clark, *SLB*, pp. 116–17.

[65] Hall, 1933, p. 335; "Samuel L. Brengle and 'The Officers' Review,'" *Officers' Review* 5:4 (Jul.–Aug. 1936): 303.

[66] Quoted in Hall, 1933, p. 336. Cf. Letter to Rev. S. Parkes Cadman, Brooklyn, NY (Apr. 10, 1934). Quoted in Hewitt, "Letters," p. 119.

[67] Brengle, *Fifty Years Before and After*, pp. 6–7. For original publication see "Fifty Years of Holy Living!" *War Cry* [NY], part 1 (Jan. 12, 1935): 4; part 2 (Jan. 19, 1935): 4.

[68] Hall, 1933, pp. 342–44. Cf. "'Samuel L. Brengle: Portrait of a Prophet': A Preliminary Notice" *Officers' Review* 3:1 (Jan.–Feb. 1934): 37; Woodward, p. 46; Clark, *SLB*, p. 116; Chesham, *Treasury*, p. 14; Coward, pp. 8–9.

[69] Quoted in Hall, 1933, p. 345.

[70] Hall, 1933, pp. 346–49; Clark, *SLB*, pp. 121–24; Coward, p. 9.

[71] Hall, 1933, pp. 349–50.

[72] *When the Holy Ghost Is Come* was the first volume of the new Liberty Library. Wiggins, *History*, p. 169.

[73] Cf. "'Love-Slaves': Colonel Samuel L. Brengle's Latest Book," *Officer* 37:6 (Dec. 1923): 447–50. The reviewer finds the book helpful in that it is "'not an elaborate treatise' but full of thoughts that should suggest many helpful addresses to a busy Field Officer and start him forth on a new campaign" (p. 447). See also: "*Love-Slaves:* New Book by Colonel Samuel L. Brengle," *War Cry* [NY] (Jan. 5, 1924): 5. Another reviewer described the book as "a modern interpretation and exposition of the Sermon on the Mount . . . under three heads: the Agenda, the things to be done, the life to be lived; the Credenda, the things to be believed . . . [and] the Propaganda, a combination of [a] religion of faith and action." Wallace Winchell, "*Love-Slaves,* by Colonel S. L. Brengle," *War Cry* [NY] (Jul. 5, 1924): 12.

[74] *Ancient Prophets* has been likened to "ripened wisdom in pleasant capsules." See Hall, 1933, p. 351.

[75] Quoted in Chesham, *Peace*, p. 157.

[76] Quoted in Chesham, *Peace*, pp. 217–18.

[77] Letter from Champaign, IL, Jan., 9, 1923, in Clark, *Dearest Lily*, pp. 142–43.

CHAPTER 6—BRENGLE THE MAN

[1] Quoted in Hall, 1933, p. 178; cf. Coward, pp. 11–12.

[2] Hall, 1936, p. 142. Perhaps this is why Brengle is almost silent on sacramental issues, as well.

[3] Evangeline Booth, "An Apostle of the Penitent-Form," p. 9.

[4] Hall, 1936, p. 142. Cf. Waldron, "Celebrating the Holy Life," part 2, pp. 110–11.

[5] Hall, 1933, p. 181.

[6] Quoted in Hall, 1936, p. 146; cf. Coward, p. 11; Daniel Steele, *Love Enthroned: Essays on Evangelical Perfection* (New York: Eaton and Mains,

1902), pp. 400–6. "Emotion, he claimed, could be 'a fire, warming and useful when correctly applied, but destructive and demoralizing when out of control.' As a consequence, his own preaching did not 'excite a fever of enthusiasm,' but rather aimed 'to incite to earnest heart-scrutiny . . . deep penitence and soul-satisfaction.' Emotional and expressive religion, he argued, led the 'little people' into a shallow experience." Taiz, pp. 154–55. Elsewhere, Brengle encouraged seekers after holiness to enter into this "perpetual covenant" with both heart and head. Samuel L. Brengle, *Heart-Talks on Holiness* (Atlanta: The Salvation Army, 1988), p. 68.

[7] Letter from Amenia, NY, Jul. 21, 1909, in Clark, *Dearest Lily*, p. 123.

[8] Brengle, *When the Holy Ghost Is Come*, p. 44.

[9] Hall, 1933, p. 183; cf. Frederick Coutts, *The Call to Holiness* (London: The Salvation Army, 1977), pp. 10–11.

[10] Hall, 1933, p. 184.

[11] Hall, 1936, pp. 146–47.

[12] Brengle, *Helps to Holiness*, p. 130.

[13] Hall, 1936, pp. 146–47. Cf. Waldron, "Celebrating the Holy Life," part 2, pp. 110–11.

[14] Pastor and radio preacher of Central Congregational Church, Brooklyn, N.Y., and a former president of the Federal Council of Churches of America.

[15] Hall, 1933, pp. 185–86.

[16] Quoted in Hall, 1933, p. 270; cf. Coward, p. 12.

[17] Earl Lord, "I Sang For Brengle," quoted in Chesham, *Treasury*, p. 137. For examples of his sense of humor see Clark, *SLB*, pp. 154–55; Woodward, pp. 55–56. Cf. Hall, 1936, pp. 192–93; Hall, 1933, pp. 276–78.

[18] Quoted in Hall, 1933, p. 271; cf. McKinley, p. 42.

[19] Coward, pp. 10, 12.

[20] Hall, 1933, p. 272.

[21] Quoted in Hall, 1933, p. 275.

[22] Ibid.

[23] Earl Lord, "I Sang for Brengle," quoted in Chesham, *Treasury*, p. 137; cf. Chesham, *Peace*, p. 126. On occasion, as time permitted, he liked to run. Glenn Ryan recalls an encounter with Brengle in Chicago, when the near-sixty-year-old saint asked if there was any place he could do some running, "explaining [that] there were benefits in running and lifting the heels high that were not in other exercises." Ryan also recounts Brengle's ill-fated attempts to get overweight officers to engage in physical exercise. "Brengle—A Jogger:

Reminisces about The Salvation Army's Prophet of Holiness," *War Cry* [NY] (Oct. 13, 1979): 10–11.

[24] Brengle, *Helps to Holiness*, pp. 53–54.

[25] This is especially pronounced in Sallie Chesham's *Peace Like a River*. As John Waldron writes: "The book *Peace Like a River* brings the reader into the intimate circle of this idyllic marriage and the subsequent happy family life. The effect of Lily on Samuel Brengle's life can hardly be over-estimated." Waldron, "Celebrating the Holy Life," part 2, p. 112.

[26] Hall, 1936, pp. 202, 203, 205; Clark, *SLB*, p. 92. The warmth of their correspondence throughout their marriage bears witness to their ongoing intimacy. For example, in a letter written by Sam to Lily from Oakland, CA, on Sept. 22, 1911, he declared: "Say, I'm in love, hopelessly in love and altogether in love. No help for me! I never expect to get over it." Clark, *Dearest Lily*, p. 101. In another letter, Sam wrote to Lily: "I'm in love still. Haven't got over [it] yet, and only a little deeper in since I wrote you yesterday." Letter from Waterloo, IA, Mar. 21, 1913, in Clark, *Dearest Lily*, p. 114. At one point he described himself as "the fondest lover in America." Quoted in Coward, p. 14.

[27] Letter from Amenia, NY, Jan. 24, 1908, in Clark, *Dearest Lily*, p. 63.

[28] Samuel L. Brengle, "Holiness—A Working Experience: In the Hour of Affliction and Death—A Personal Testimony," *Officer* 23:6 (Jun. 1915): 422; cf. Brengle, *The Consolation Wherewith He Was Comforted*, p. 13; Brengle, "Mrs. Colonel Brengle: A Sketch of Her Life and Character," part 3, p. 7.

[29] Letter from Rockhampton, Australia, Jun. 22, 1910, in Clark, *Dearest Lily*, p. 84.

[30] Letter from Amenia, NY, Jul. 7, 1910, in Clark, *Dearest Lily*, p. 97.

[31] Letter from Christiania, Norway, Mar. 7, 1907, in Clark, *Dearest Lily*, p. 9; cf. Coward, p. 14.

[32] Letter from Lun, Finland, Sept. 29, 1907, in Clark, *Dearest Lily*, pp. 32–34.

[33] Letter from Amenia, NY, Jan. 31, 1908, in Clark, *Dearest Lily*, p. 64.

[34] Quoted in Clark, *Dearest Lily*, p. 116; cf. Coward, p. 14.

[35] Brengle, *Ancient Prophets*, p. 48.

[36] Samuel L. Brengle, "A Father's Letters to His Corps Cadet Boy at School," *War Cry* [NY] (May 13, 1916): 6.

[37] Letter from Amenia, NY, May 6, 1909, in Clark, *Dearest Lily*, p. 122.

[38] Letter from Launceston, Tasmania, Aug. 19, 1910, in Clark, *Dearest Lily*, p. 135.

[39] Letter from Amenia, NY, Sept. 29, 1909, in Clark, *Dearest Lily*, pp. 124–25.

[40] Letter from "Home," Oct. 8, 1908, in Clark, *Dearest Lily*, p. 147.

[41] This is indicated in the following excerpts from Sam's correspondence with his daughter: "My precious girlie . . . read your Bible and pray before going to bed and if your room-mate should prove to be unconverted, you should try to get her saved. It will be beautiful, if you can win some souls this winter. . . ." Letter from Amenia, NY, Sept. 21, 1908, in Clark, *Dearest Lily*, p. 145. "Bless you! Go on testifying and the Lord may give you a revival, my darling. . . . These schools need revivals. They used to have them and the Lord may use you to start one at your school. Pray for this my darling." Letter from "Home," Oct. 9, 1908, in Clark, *Dearest Lily*, p. 147. Cf. Chesham, *Peace*, pp. 89–93; Clark, *Dearest Lily*, pp. x–xi.

[42] Letter from Amenia, NY, Apr. 26, 1910, in Clark, *Dearest Lily*, p. 96.

[43] Letter from S. S. Mahens en route to Sydney, May 18, 1910, in Clark, *Dearest Lily*, p. 80. Sam further comforted Lily with a reminder of their having consecrated George to God from the time of his conception, writing: "I wrote George a long letter yesterday and a brief one today. . . . I wish he'd preach. I don't think God wants him for a lawyer. I got a good deal of comfort yesterday in recalling the fact that the act of union which resulted in his conception was preceded by prayer and consecration and from the moment we knew he was formed within you and that you had him beneath your heart, he was given to God and followed by renewed consecrations and vows and prayers, and that all his life-long we have dedicated him to God and sought to train him for the Lord. . . ." Letter from Warren, PA, Sept. 27, 1912, in Clark, *Dearest Lily*, p. 113.

[44] Letter from Amenia, NY, Jun. 16, 1910, in Clark, *Dearest Lily*, pp. 96–97.

[45] Letter from Melbourne, Australia, Jul. 25, 1910, in Clark, *Dearest Lily*, p. 130.

[46] Ibid., pp. 130–31.

[47] Despite such expressions of parental disappointment, George continued to respect his father, writing: "I doubt that any man ever walked more humbly with his God, or saw more clearly that in God's sight it is fundamentals that count." George Brengle, "Tribute to His Father," quoted in Chesham, *Treasury*, p. 190.

[48] Quoted in Clark, *Dearest Lily*, p. viii.

[49] Clark, *SLB*, pp. 92–101; cf. Clark, *Dearest Lily*, p. viii.

CHAPTER 7—HOLINESS AS GIFT AND INHERITANCE

[1] Brengle, "After Twenty-Nine Years," pp. 545–46.

[2] Samuel L. Brengle, "The Baptism of the Spirit: Is It Accompanied by the Gift of Tongues?" *War Cry* [NY] (Aug. 26, 1939): 3, 9.

[3] Brengle, "An Up-to-Date Testimony to Full Salvation," p. 8. It is noteworthy that another Salvation Army holiness exponent, Gunpei Yamamuro of Japan, expressed his experience of entire sanctification in terms of the rising sun metaphor. R. David Rightmire, *Salvationist Samurai: Gunpei Yamamuro and the Rise of The Salvation Army in Japan* (Lanham, MD: Scarecrow Press, 1997), pp. 38–39.

[4] Samuel L. Brengle, "A Testimony—January 9, 1885–1922," *War Cry* [NY] (Feb. 4, 1922): 5.

[5] Samuel L. Brengle, "My Day of Days: A Testimony Written on January 9, 1923," *War Cry* [NY] (Feb. 3, 1923): 3. Cf. Steele, *Love Enthroned*, p. 101.

[6] Brengle, *Heart-Talks on Holiness*, pp. 47, 49, 94; Clark, *SLB*, pp. 102–3.

[7] Samuel L. Brengle, "My Personal Testimony," *War Cry* [NY] (Jun. 18, 1932): 4. The importance of testifying to the experience of entire sanctification in a literary manner on the anniversary of the event was modeled for Brengle by his mentor, Daniel Steele. E.g., see the latter's *The Mile-Stone Papers: Doctrinal, Ethical, and Experimental on Christian Progress* (Minneapolis: Bethany Fellowship, 1966), pp. 213–16.

[8] Samuel L. Brengle, "Fifty Years of Holy Living!" part 1, *War Cry* [NY] (Jan. 12, 1935): 4.

[9] Larsson, p. 87.

[10] Brengle views the work of Christ as providing the basis for entire sanctification. He interprets 1 John 3:5, 8 as presenting a twofold purpose of Christ's manifestation to the world: to take away sin (v. 5), and to destroy the works of Satan (v. 8). The former results in the justification and regeneration of the believer; the latter, in entire sanctification. Brengle, *Heart-Talks on Holiness*, pp. 1–2.

[11] "Loving God," quoted in Chesham, *Treasury*, p. 48.

[12] Brengle, *The Guest of the Soul*, p. 46.

[13] Samuel L. Brengle, "Holiness: Reasons Why Everybody Should Be Entirely Sanctified," *War Cry* [NY] (Jan. 28, 1888): 11.

[14] Brengle, *At the Center of the Circle*, pp. 23–24.

[15] Samuel L. Brengle, *The Way of Holiness* (Atlanta: The Salvation Army, 1988), pp. 5–8. Cf. Daniel Steele, *The Gospel and the Comforter* (Apollo, PA: West Publishing, 1897), p. 246.

[16] Brengle, "Holiness: Reasons Why Everybody Should Be Entirely Sanctified," 11.

[17] Brengle, *At the Center of the Circle*, p. 50; Samuel L. Brengle, *Wait on the Lord: Selections from the Writings of Commissioner Samuel L. Brengle*, edited and revised by John D. Waldron (New York: The Salvation Army, 1960), p. 11.

[18] Brengle, *The Guest of the Soul*, p. 58. Cf. Steele, *The Mile-Stone Papers*, pp. 121–22.

[19] Brengle, *The Guest of the Soul*, pp. 58–67.

[20] Brengle, "Holiness: Reasons Why Everybody Should Be Entirely Sanctified," 11.

[21] Brengle, *The Soul-Winner's Secret*, p. 55.

[22] Brengle, "Holiness: When We Get It and How," *War Cry* [NY] (Feb. 11, 1888): 7; Brengle, *Helps to Holiness*, pp. 6–8.

[23] Support for viewing Pentecost as paradigmatic for a definite second work of grace is found in: Brengle, *Helps to Holiness*, pp. 8–9; cf. Steele, *Love Enthroned*, pp. 120–21.

[24] Brengle, *Heart-Talks on Holiness*, pp. 4–5; cf. Clark, *SLB*, pp. 107–8.

[25] So here there is no paradox, the two aspects of the life of holiness do not deny but supplement each other. Clark, *SLB*, pp. 103–6.

[26] Samuel L. Brengle, "Fifty Years of Holy Living!" part 2, *War Cry* [NY] (Jan. 19, 1935): 4; Lee and Brengle, p. 14; Brengle, *Fifty Years Before and After*, p. 18. Cf. "Loving God," quoted in Chesham, *Treasury*, p. 49.

[27] Such misrepresentation is reflected in John Coutts' interpretation of Brengle's holiness theology, which he views as antiquated and in need of rebalancing in the light of other emphases: "As years and generations go by, the thinkers and teachers of one generation begin to seem more and more irrelevant to the learners of the next. Thus it was with the Army, and its traditional idea of holy living . . . for even if the inward experience is by definition beyond words, each generation of believers must struggle to find some language in which to convey it. Brengle's encounter with God . . . was understood by him as 'the baptism of the Holy Spirit.' Among Salvationist of the 1950s, to . . . whom the idea of a 'second blessing' was . . . outdated, some new interpretation was called for." The re-articulation found its voice in the teaching of John's father, Frederick Coutts, whose *The Call to Holiness* answers the question of whether the experience of holiness is gained instantly or gradually. The answer he gives is that the life of holiness is both a crisis and a process (which curiously, differs little from Brengle's teaching). John Coutts, in preferring his father's restatement of the doctrine of holiness, and characterizing such as embodying "the devout middle-of-the-road scholarship of British biblical theologians as C. H. Dodd and T. W. Manson," seems unaware of his own presuppositional biases for things modern and British. John Coutts, *Salvationists*, pp. 54–59

[28] Samuel L. Brengle, "Holiness: When We Get It and How," *War Cry* [NY] (Feb. 11, 1888): 7; Brengle, *Helps to Holiness*, pp. 5–6.

[29] Quoted in Clark, *SLB*, p. 107.

[30] This is similar to Frederick Coutts' emphasis on both crisis and process: "In the initial act of surrender I receive of the fullness of the Spirit according to my capacity to receive. But that capacity grows with receiving." Frederick Coutts, *The Call to Holiness* (London: The Salvation Army, 1977), p. 36. Cf. Jonathan Raymond, "The Journey Toward Holiness," *War Cry* (Feb. 2, 2002): 14–15. Although Coutts emphasizes both crisis and process, the crisis is seen as only a "gateway experience to growth in holiness." John Larsson, in *Spiritual Breakthrough*, views this increased emphasis on process as signaling a major shift in Salvation Army holiness theology, as illustrated in the more recent editions of the Army's official *Handbook of Doctrine*. Until 1969 the editions devoted about seven thousand words to the crisis experience and only about two hundred words to the process. But in the handbook published in 1969, a different pattern emerges. The chapter heading changes from 'Entire Sanctification' to simply 'Sanctification,' and the proportion of words dealing with the crisis and the process is reversed" (Larsson, p. 57). In a later abridgment of Army doctrine, critical aspects of holiness are seen primarily in relation to "the response God requires," namely, our consecration. Although there is mention of the gift of the Holy Spirit as a "life changing power," characterized by the "grace of love," the divine work of heart purification is muted. *The Doctrine We Adorn: An Abridged Study of Salvation Army Doctrines* (London: The Salvation Army, 1982), pp. 98–103. As Larsson rightly notes, "there is a great deal to be said for this emphasis on the process. . . . But whether the interpretation of the crisis as simply the gateway to the mountain trail of holiness fully accounts for the kind of experience Samuel Brengle knew on 9 January 1885 needs consideration." (Larsson, pp. 57–58).

[31] Samuel L. Brengle, "Holiness and the Mistaken Lieutenant," *War Cry* [NY] (Jan. 21, 1933): 6. Although emphasis on "maturity" following "purity" is evident in some of Brengle's later writings, this in no way represents a de-emphasis of the critical dimensions of entire sanctification. Rather, it is a concern to further delineate the growth in grace that follows and presupposes the blessing of a clean heart. For opposing view, see Michael Reagan, "Crisis in Process: The Holiness Teaching of Samuel Logan Brengle" (M.A. Thesis, California State University Dominguez Hills, Spring 1997), pp. 89–90.

[32] Brengle, *The Soul-Winner's Secret*, p. 48. Cf. Steele, *The Gospel and the Comforter*, p. 247.

[33] Samuel L. Brengle, "Is Temper Destroyed or Sanctified?" *Field Officer* 11:6 (Jun. 1903): 207; Brengle, *When the Holy Ghost Is Come*, pp. 133–36; Clark, *SLB*, pp. 108–11; cf. Steele, *The Mile-Stone Papers*, pp. 101–2, 105, 109–10. Elsewhere Brengle insists that holiness as Christlikeness is antithetical to an argumentative spirit. "Don't argue . . . It is natural to the 'carnal mind' to resent opposition. But we are to be 'spiritually minded' . . . We are impatient of contradiction, and are hasty in judging men's motives and condemning all who do not agree with us . . . Now , I am strongly

inclined to believe that this is one of the last fruits of the carnal mind which grace ever subdues." Brengle, *Helps to Holiness*, pp. 65, 68.

[34] Brengle, *Heart-Talks on Holiness*, p. 57.

[35] In contrast to views of positional sanctification (John Darby and the Plymouth Brethren), progressive sanctification (John Calvin and Reformed theology), sanctification at death, or purgatorial sanctification (Roman Catholic doctrine), Brengle (in line with John Wesley) held to the view of critical sanctification, in which the believer is instantly and entirely sanctified. This crisis involves the death of the 'old man' and the impartation of the fullness of the Holy Spirit. Brengle, *Heart-Talks on Holiness*, pp. 1–4, 13–15; cf. Brengle, *Wait on the Lord*, p. 5.

[36] Samuel L. Brengle, "Holiness: How to Keep It," *War Cry* [NY] (Sept. 29, 1894): 5.

[37] Brengle, *Helps to Holiness*, pp. 138–39.

[38] Brengle, *The Way of Holiness*, pp. 16–17.

[39] Brengle, *When the Holy Ghost Is Come*, p. 14. Although Brengle maintained that there is victory over Satan for the entirely sanctified, spiritual warfare continues on a different front: "But while Christ has set this sanctified man at liberty, and he no longer has to fight against his old worldly passions and fleshly appetites, yet he has a continual warfare with Satan to keep this liberty. . . . He must fight to hold fast his faith in the Holy Spirit's sanctifying and keeping power." Brengle, *Helps to Holiness*, p. 20.

[40] Brengle, "Holiness: Reasons Why Everybody Should Be Entirely Sanctified," 11.

[41] Brengle, "Holiness: When We Get It and How," *War Cry* [NY] (Feb. 11, 1888): 7. Although Brengle does not prefer the term "eradication," the metaphors he employs imply the same thing, although such should not be misconstrued as "sinless perfection." Cf. Reagan, pp. 56–57.

[42] "A Matter of Definition" [Letter to Rev. Charles G. Trumbull, Editor of *Sunday School Times*, Philadelphia, PA, written on Apr. 6, 1934], quoted in Chesham, *Treasury*, p. 54. See also: Hewitt, "Letters of Commissioner Brengle," p. 130.

[43] "A Matter of Definition," quoted in Chesham, *Treasury*, pp. 54–55; cf. Steele, *The Mile-Stone Papers*, p. 99. See also: Hewitt, "Letters of Commissioner Brengle," pp. 130–31.

[44] Samuel L. Brengle, "Holiness: Is It Real?" *War Cry* [NY] (Sept. 15, 1894): 12.

[45] Samuel L. Brengle, "Sanctification," *War Cry* [NY] (Mar. 6, 1937): 4.

[46] Samuel L. Brengle, "The Amazing Transformation," *War Cry* [NY] (Jun. 6, 1981): 2.

[47] Brengle, "Is Temper Destroyed or Sanctified?" p. 207; Samuel L. Brengle, "Temper," *War Cry* [NY] (Jan. 10, 1903): 10; Brengle, *When the Holy Ghost Is Come*, pp. 149–50.

[48] Brengle, *At the Center of the Circle*, p. 11; Brengle, *Wait on the Lord*, 22. It is interesting to note that although holiness was seen as the "privilege of all believers," not all of the Army's early leadership encouraged the preaching of the same to the "simple folk." This is evident in a letter from Sam to Lily, written from Copenhagen, Denmark, on May 2, 1908: "I have a letter, a regular brain-teaser from [George Scott] Railton. . . . He agrees with me in my doctrine of the Holy Spirit, but thinks we should not mention the Holy Ghost to simple folk. He does not . . . and then he wonders why God does not give him results such as Finney saw! He emasculates the gospel and then wonders why it is barren." Quoted in Clark, *Dearest Lily*, p. 59.

[49] Samuel L. Brengle, "A Chat with Paul," *War Cry* [NY] (Jan. 28, 1933): 6.

[50] Brengle, "Offenses against the Holy Ghost," *War Cry* [NY] (Apr. 22, 1911): 6–7; Brengle, *When the Holy Ghost Is Come*, pp. 82–83.

[51] Samuel L. Brengle, "Officers Who Burn and Shine," *Officer* 38:2 (Feb. 1924): 140; Samuel L. Brengle, "A Burning and Shining Light: A Homily on Red-Hot Religion," *War Cry* [NY] (Sept. 22, 1928): 12; Brengle, *Resurrection Life and Power*, pp. 85–86.

[52] Samuel L. Brengle, "No Time to Be Holy!" *War Cry* [NY] (May 8, 1943): 4.

[53] Brengle, *The Guest of the Soul*, p. 48; Brengle, *At the Center of the Circle*, pp. 11–12. By way of contrast, Hall records: "When on one occasion he overheard a zealous comrade heckling another with: 'Take it or leave it, brother, it is holiness or hell!', Brengle interrupted the exhortation to say, 'Not so. No justified soul will be in hell. But the justified man must walk in the light he has, or he will backslide. And walking in the light will eventually lead him to take the step that will give him a clean heart as well as a justified soul.'" Hall, 1933, p. 187.

[54] Brengle, "God's House of Flesh and Blood," p. 686.

[55] Samuel L. Brengle, "The Holiness Standard of The Salvation Army in Teaching and Practice," *Officer* 23:3 (Mar. 1915): 145; Brengle, *Love-Slaves*, pp. 68–69; Brengle, *Wait on the Lord*, p. 4.

[56] Samuel L. Brengle, "Importance of the Doctrine and Experience of Holiness to Spiritual Leaders," part 1, *War Cry* [NY] (Aug. 19, 1911): 7; Brengle, *When the Holy Ghost Is Come*, pp. 138–41.

[57] Samuel L. Brengle, "Importance of the Doctrine and Experience of Holiness to Spiritual Leaders," part 2, *War Cry* [NY] (Aug. 26, 1911): 11; Brengle, *When the Holy Ghost Is Come*, pp. 144–47.

[58] Brengle, "Importance of the Doctrine and Experience of Holiness to Spiritual Leaders," part 2, p. 11; Brengle, *When the Holy Ghost Is Come*, pp. 144–47.

CHAPTER 8—ETHICAL DIMENSIONS OF HOLINESS

[1] Brengle used a variety of terms to express the multi-dimensional nature of the experience of entire sanctification. It is noteworthy that unlike many exponents of the holiness message in the nineteenth and early twentieth centuries, who preferred to use structural terminology (e.g., "second work of grace" and "second blessing"), Brengle primarily used ethical ("perfect love" and "Christlikeness"), ceremonial ("heart purity" and "clean heart"), and dynamic ("baptism of the Holy Spirit" and "fullness of the Holy Spirit") categories to express the varied nuances of the doctrine and experience of entire sanctification. In this regard, Brengle reflects the influence of John Wesley and John Fletcher (mediated to him by his theological mentor, Daniel Steele).

[2] Brengle, *The Soul-Winner's Secret*, pp. 54–58; cf. Brengle, *The Guest of the Soul*, pp. 81–82.

[3] Brengle, *The Way of Holiness*, p. 4; Brengle, *At the Center of the Circle*, p. 72.

[4] Ibid.

[5] Lee and Brengle, p. 14.

[6] Samuel L. Brengle, "Jesus Christ's Training of Paul," *Staff Review* (Jul. 1925): 122.

[7] Brengle, "Pentecost," pp. 4, 14; "Pentecost," quoted in Chesham, *Treasury*, pp. 58–59.

[8] Samuel L. Brengle, "The Meaning of a 'Clean Heart': The Heart— Its Natural Condition as Described by Scripture, and Exemplified in Human Nature and Conduct," paper 1, *Officer* 7:5 (May 1899): 175.

[9] Samuel L. Brengle, "No Time to Be Holy!" *War Cry* [NY] (May 8, 1943): 4.

[10] Brengle, "The Meaning of a 'Clean Heart': Can the Natural State of the Heart Be Altered?" paper 2, *Officer* 7:6 (Jun. 1899): 214.

[11] Samuel L. Brengle, "Purity before Power: The Holy Ghost Cleanses When He Comes," *War Cry* [NY] (Nov. 8, 1924): 6; Brengle, *When the Holy Ghost Is Come*, pp. 31–36.

[12] Brengle, "Commissioner Brengle's Last Whitsun Message," p. 205.

[13] Brengle, *When the Holy Ghost Is Come*, pp. 37–43.

[14] Quoted in Chesham, *Treasury*, pp. 56–57.

[15] Samuel L. Brengle, *Helps to Holiness*, pp. ix–x; cf. Samuel L. Brengle, "My Testimony," *War Cry* [NY] (Jan. 31, 1891): 11; Samuel L. Brengle, "Full Salvation—My Personal Testimony," *Field Officer* 20:4 (Apr. 1912): 137.

[16] "Loving God," quoted in Chesham, *Treasury*, pp. 47–48.

[17] Brengle, *At the Center of the Circle*, p. 21.

[18] Samuel L. Brengle, *Helps to Holiness*, pp. 1–2; cf. Brengle, "Holiness: Reasons Why Everybody Should Be Entirely Sanctified," *War Cry* [NY] (Jan. 28, 1888): 11. Cf. Steele, *The Mile-Stone Papers*, p. 247.

[19] Samuel L. Brengle, *When the Holy Ghost Is Come*, p. 8.

[20] Samuel L. Brengle, "A Perfect Heart," *War Cry* [NY] (Dec. 1, 1906): 6. Reprinted as "A Perfect-Hearted People," *Officer* 44:3 (Mar. 1927): 187; Brengle, *The Guest of the Soul*, pp. 81–82.

[21] Brengle, "A Perfect-Hearted People," pp. 187–90; cf. Brengle, *The Guest of the Soul*, pp. 82–86.

[22] Samuel L. Brengle, "Love-Slaves," *Officer* 33:2 (Aug. 1921): 124–25; Samuel L. Brengle, *Love-Slaves* (Atlanta: The Salvation Army, 1923), pp. 1–3. Cf. Steele, *Love Enthroned*, p. 359.

[23] Brengle, "Love-Slaves," p. 126; Brengle, *Love-Slaves*, pp. 5–6.

[24] Brengle, *Heart-Talks on Holiness*, p. 12.

[25] Samuel L. Brengle, *The Way of Holiness*, p. 1. Elsewhere he wrote: "Holiness is the sum of all Divine virtues. . . . Holiness is wholeness. Holiness is healthiness, and what holiness is in God, so it is in man. It is inherent in God. It is His nature. It is imparted in man. We are made partakers of the Divine nature when we, with penitent hearts, renounce our own righteousness and trusting only in Christ, affectionately, unreservedly and forever yield our free wills to Him. He purifies our hearts. . . . He sheds abroad His love in our hearts. He comes and makes His abode with us and in us. He sanctifies us wholly, and fills us with the Spirit." Samuel L. Brengle, "A Definition and an Experience," *War Cry* [NY] (Jul. 11, 1925): 3.

[26] Brengle, *The Way of Holiness*, pp. 2–3.

[27] Brengle, "The Holiness Standard," p. 148; cf. Brengle, *Love-Slaves*, pp. 73–74.

[28] Samuel L. Brengle, "The Heart of Jesus," *War Cry* [NY] (Sept. 1, 1888): 2; Brengle, *Helps to Holiness*, pp. 35–36.

[29] Samuel L. Brengle, "Pentecost," *War Cry* [NY] (Jun. 4, 1938): 4, 14; "Pentecost," quoted in Chesham, *Treasury*, p. 58. Cf. Steele, *Love Enthroned*, pp. 126–27.

[30] Brengle, *Helps to Holiness*, pp. 89–90.

[31] Brengle, *Resurrection Life and Power*, pp. 5–6, 12–13.

[32] Samuel L. Brengle, "The Mystic, Wondrous Universe in My Back Yard," *Staff Review* (Oct. 1925): 140; Brengle, *The Guest of the Soul*, p. 118.

[33] Samuel L. Brengle, "Paul's Secret: Alive in Christ," *Staff Review* (Apr. 1925): 151–58; Brengle, *Resurrection Life and Power*, pp. 47–57.

[34] Samuel L. Brengle, "A Corps Cadet's Testimony, with Some Observations," *War Cry* [NY] (Oct. 6, 1928): 12.

[35] Brengle, Letter to Colonel Joseph Atkinson, Aug. 12, 1935, p. 2.

[36] Samuel L. Brengle, "Union with Jesus," *War Cry* (Jan. 21, 1905): 6–7; Brengle, *Heart-Talks on Holiness*, pp. 61–68.

[37] Brengle, "The Holy Guest of the Soul," p. 59.

[38] Brengle, *Heart-Talks on Holiness*, pp. 51, 53.

[39] Brengle, *Resurrection Life and Power*, p. 121.

[40] Letter from Amenia, NY, Jan. 23, 1910, in Clark, *Dearest Lily*, p. 129.

[41] Brengle, *Helps to Holiness*, p. 25

[42] Ibid., pp. 89–90.

[43] Samuel L. Brengle, "The Holy Guest of the Soul," *Staff Review* (Feb. 1930): 57–58.

[44] "Loving God," quoted in Chesham, *Treasury*, p. 49.

[45] Samuel L. Brengle, "God's House of Flesh and Blood," *Officer* 25:10 (Nov. 1917): 685.

[46] Ibid., pp. 685–86.

[47] Samuel L. Brengle, "Mary's Christmas, Your Christmas and Mine," *War Cry* [NY] (Dec. 3, 1927): 6, 14.

[48] Samuel L. Brengle, "Who Is the 'Christ in You'?" *War Cry* [NY] (Mar. 24, 1979): 5.

[49] Brengle, *The Guest of the Soul*, pp. 44–45.

[50] Samuel L. Brengle, "Pentecost and Beyond—A Whitsuntide Message," *Staff Review* (May 1931), reproduced in Satterlee, "Pentecost and Beyond," pp. 1–5.

[51] Samuel L. Brengle, "'The Way to Pentecost'" (review of Samuel Chadwick's *Way to Pentecost*), *Officers' Review* 2:2 (Mar.–Apr. 1933): 127.

Chapter 9—Heart Holiness: Misconceptions and Hindrances

[1] Brengle, *When the Holy Ghost Is Come* (Atlanta: The Salvation Army, 1909), p. 11.

[2] Samuel L. Brengle, Letter to "My Dear Comrades," written from St. Petersburg, FL, Apr. 24, 1936 (Alexandria, VA: The Salvation Army National Archives), p. 1; cf. Samuel L. Brengle, "Commissioner Brengle's Last Whitsun Message," *Officers' Review* 6:3 (May–Jun. 1937): 205.

[3] Brengle, "The Meaning of a 'Clean Heart': How to Obtain a Clean Heart and to Know It," paper 3, *Officer* 7:7 (Jul. 1899): 257.

[4] Ibid.

[5] Samuel L. Brengle, "Preparing His House," *War Cry* [NY] (Mar. 5, 1910): 11; Brengle, *When the Holy Ghost Is Come*, p. 11.

[6] Samuel L. Brengle, "From Dawn to Sunrise," part 1, *War Cry* [NY] (Feb. 15, 1896): 10.

[7] Ibid.

[8] Samuel L. Brengle, "From Dawn to Sunrise," part 2, *War Cry* [NY] (Feb. 22, 1896): 2.

[9] Brengle, *The Way of Holiness*, p. 3. Cf. Steele, *Love Enthroned*, pp. 26–30.

[10] Brengle, "Preparing His House," p. 11; Brengle, *When the Holy Ghost Is Come*, p. 13. Cf. Steele, *Love Enthroned*, p. 62.

[11] "Holiness," quoted in Chesham, *Treasury*, p. 169; cf. Brengle, *Heart-Talks on Holiness*, pp. 7–11.

[12] "Emotionality," quoted in Chesham, *Treasury*, p. 36. Cf. Lee and Brengle, p. 15.

[13] Brengle, "The Holiness Standard," p. 149; cf. Brengle, *Love-Slaves*, p. 75.

[14] "God Enthroned in Your Life," quoted in Chesham, *Treasury*, p. 31.

[15] Lee and Brengle, p. 15.

[16] Clark, *Dearest Lily*, p. 78.

[17] Brengle, *Helps to Holiness*, p. 2; cf. Brengle, *The Guest of the Soul*, pp. 81–82.

[18] Brengle, "Holiness: Reasons Why Everybody Should Be Entirely Sanctified," 11. Brengle's understanding of the difference between sins and infirmities can be traced back to his theological mentor, Daniel Steele, who followed Wesley in this regard: "Infirmities are failures to keep the law of perfect obedience given to Adam in Eden. This law no man on earth can keep, since sin has impaired the powers of universal humanity. Sins are offences against the law of love, the law of Christ. . . . Refusal to love with the whole heart is the ground of condemnation, and not inevitable failures in keeping the law of Adamic perfection. . . . Infirmities are an involuntary outflow from our imperfect moral organization. Sin is always voluntary. Infirmities have their ground in our physical nature, and they are aggravated by intellectual

deficiencies. But sin roots itself in our moral nature. Infirmities entail regret and humiliation. Sin always produces guilt. Infirmities in well-instructed souls do not interrupt communion with God. . . . Many infirmities are without remedy as long as we are in the body. Sins, by the keeping power of Christ, are avoidable through every hour of our regenerate life. . . . A thousand infirmities are consistent with perfect love to God and man, but not one sin. Hence it is evident that sins are incompatible with perfection; and that unnoticed and involuntary errors or faults, are not. . . . Not only sin properly so-called (that is, a voluntary transgression of a known law) but sin improperly so-called (that is, an involuntary transgression of a Divine law, known or unknown) needs the Atoning Blood. I believe there is not such perfection in this life as excludes these involuntary transgressions, which I apprehend to be naturally consequent on the ignorance and mistakes inseparable from mortality. Therefore, 'sinless perfection' is a phrase I never use." Daniel Steele, "Sin or Infirmity," *Officer* 36:5 (May 1923): 403–6; Daniel Steele, *The Mile-Stone Papers,* pp. 33–34, 38–39. Cf. Steele, *Love Enthroned,* pp. 80–90.

[19] Samuel L. Brengle, "Holiness: What It Is Not and What It Is," *War Cry* [NY] (Jan. 7, 1899): 7; Brengle, *Heart-Talks on Holiness,* pp. 7–11.

[20] Samuel L. Brengle, "Importance of the Doctrine and Experience of Holiness to Spiritual Leaders," part 1, *War Cry* [NY] (Aug. 19, 1911): 7; Brengle, *When the Holy Ghost Is Come,* pp. 138–41. Cf. Steele, *Love Enthroned,* pp. 120–21.

[21] Brengle, *Ancient Prophets,* pp. 155–56.

[22] Brengle, *The Guest of the Soul,* p. 46.

[23] Brengle, "Commissioner Brengle's Last Whitsun Message," p. 205; cf. Samuel L. Brengle, Letter to "My Dear Comrades," written from St. Petersburg, FL, Apr. 24, 1936 (Alexandria, VA: The Salvation Army National Archives), p. 1; "Way of the Spirit," quoted in Chesham, *Treasury,* p. 55.

[24] Samuel L. Brengle, "Hindrances to Full Salvation," *War Cry* [NY] (May 8, 1897): 6; Brengle, *Heart-Talks on Holiness,* pp. 20–25.

[25] Samuel L. Brengle, "Offenses against the Holy Ghost," *War Cry* [NY] (Apr. 22, 1911): 6–7; Brengle, *When the Holy Ghost Is Come,* pp. 78–80.

[26] Brengle, "Offenses Against the Holy Ghost," pp. 6–7; Brengle, *When the Holy Ghost Is Come,* pp. 80–81.

[27] Quoted in Hall, 1936, p. 148.

[28] Brengle, *Helps to Holiness,* p. 96.

CHAPTER 10—THE APPROPRIATION OF HOLINESS

[1] Brengle, "Pentecost," pp. 4, 14; "Pentecost," quoted in Chesham, *Treasury,* pp. 58–59. Brengle, at times, provided briefer outlines, as indicated in the following examples: "1. Get converted—now! 2. Consecrate yourself. Present your body a living sacrifice. Lay aside every weight and sin. Do it now. 3. Believe unwaveringly. Look for the baptism of the Holy Spirit." Brengle,

"Loving God," quoted in Chesham, *Treasury*, p. 48. "This unspeakable blessing is provided for by our compassionate Heavenly Father through the shed blood of our Lord Jesus Christ, and is received through a complete renunciation of all sin, an uttermost consecration to all the known will of God, importunate prayer and child-like faith." Brengle, "Holiness: What It Is Not and What It Is," p. 7.

2 Brengle, *The Way of Holiness*, pp. 9–15.

3 Samuel L. Brengle, "A Stirring Appeal for Purity in Heart and Life," *War Cry* [NY] (Oct. 20, 1900): 6; Brengle, *The Guest of the Soul*, pp. 87–88. Cf. Steele, *Love Enthroned*, p. 358.

4 Brengle, "Fifty Years of Holy Living!" part 1, p. 4.

5 Brengle, *Helps to Holiness*, p. 10; cf. "Where Do Men Receive the Fullness of the Holy Spirit?" quoted in Chesham, *Treasury*, p. 67.

6 Brengle, "Love-Slaves," p. 127; Brengle, *Love-Slaves*, pp. 7–8.

7 Brengle, "The Meaning of a 'Clean Heart,'" paper 3, p. 258; cf. Steele, *Love Enthroned*, pp. 209–10; Steele, *The Mile-Stone Papers*, pp. 114–17; William Booth, "A Pure Heart: LXX—How Can I Get a Pure Heart?" *Field Officer* 9:7 (Jul. 1901): 327–29.

8 Brengle, "The Meaning of a 'Clean Heart,'" paper 3, p. 259; cf. Brengle, *Helps to Holiness*, pp. 91, 112. Brengle, *When the Holy Ghost Is Come*, pp. 16–17.

9 Brengle, *Fifty Years*, pp. 9–11.

10 Brengle, *At the Center of the Circle*, p. 36. The Christological focus of such identification is obvious: "It was not by self-assertion and self-seeking, but by self-surrender, self-denial that Jesus won resurrection life and power. Let us learn from Him the secret of resurrection life and power through self-denial." Samuel L. Brengle, "Did the Resurrection Hang upon Self-Denial?" *War Cry* [NY] (Apr. 7, 1928): 11.

11 Lee and Brengle, p. 16. Cf. Steele, *Love Enthroned*, pp. 368, 371.

12 Brengle, *Resurrection Life and Power*, pp. 121–22.

13 Samuel L. Brengle, "Sanctification vs. Consecration," *Officers' Review* 5:4 (Jul.–Aug. 1936): 289; cf. Brengle, *Helps to Holiness*, p. 127. Brengle maintained that Christians should "not be allowed to stop at consecration, but pressed on into a definite experience of full salvation." He also noted that it was at this point that Finney failed in his early ministry, as the latter led his hearers through stages of repentance and consecration but failed to offer them the hope of sanctification. According to Brengle, mere renunciation of sin and consecration to God left the believer in bondage to self, still waiting for divine deliverance and cleansing. Brengle, *The Soul-Winner's Secret*, pp. 72–73.

14 Samuel L. Brengle, "Which Class Are You?" *War Cry* [NY] (Dec. 11, 1976): 10.

[15]"Jubilation!" [Letter to Rev. C. W. Butler in Cleveland, OH, Jan. 9, 1936], quoted in Chesham, *Treasury*, p. 56.

[16]Brengle, *Helps to Holiness*, p. 114. Elsewhere, he wrote about the role of faith in the appropriation of holiness: ". . . I must trust Him to purify my whole being, to sanctify me wholly and fill me with the Holy Spirit. And if I believe, He can and will do the wonder work of grace in me. He will make me holy; He will perfect me in love. . . . Just keep on trusting, thanking, praising and obeying Him, and peace and victory will come." Samuel L. Brengle, "An Open Letter to a Young Man Seeking Spiritual Help," *War Cry* [NY] (Aug. 27, 1927): 7.

[17]Samuel L. Brengle, "Some of My Experiences in Teaching Holiness," *War Cry* [NY] (Oct. 12, 1889): 11; Brengle, *Helps to Holiness*, pp. 103–4; cf. Brengle, *At the Center of the Circle*, pp. 21–22.

[18]Brengle, *Heart-Talks on Holiness*, pp. 13–14.

[19]"Two Kinds of Faith," quoted in Chesham, *Treasury*, p. 32.

[20]Brengle, *Resurrection Life and Power*, p. 46. Cf. Steele, *Love Enthroned*, p. 330.

[21]Letter to Miss Martha Tarbell, Editor of Guide for International Sunday School Lessons, Oct. 28, 1935, quoted in Chesham, *Treasury*, pp. 186–87.

[22]Brengle, *Helps to Holiness*, pp. 112–13; Brengle, *At the Center of the Circle*, p. 36. Cf. Steele, *Love Enthroned*, p. 382.

[23]Brengle, *Heart-Talks on Holiness*, p. 93.

[24]Ibid., p. 94.

[25]Samuel L. Brengle, "Hindrances in Obtaining the Blessing," *War Cry* [NY] (Jan. 12, 1889): 10; Samuel L. Brengle, "Seeking the Blessing: A Dialogue," *Field Officer* 14:2 (Feb. 1906): 44–45. Elsewhere, he identified "the preoccupation of the mind, failure to apprehend the importance of the experience, self-will, [and] self-conceit" as further hindrances to holiness. Samuel L. Brengle, "Practical Hindrances to Holiness," *Officer* 6:12 (Dec. 1898): 363.

[26]Brengle, "Hindrances in Obtaining the Blessing," p. 10; Brengle, *Helps to Holiness*, pp. 12–16. It is noteworthy that in correcting misunderstandings about holiness, Brengle consistently underscored the ethical dimensions of entire sanctification, emphasizing holiness as renewal in image of Christ, manifest in purity and perfect love.

[27]Samuel L. Brengle, "The Whisperer—Fight!" *War Cry* [NY] (Sept. 22, 1917): 9.

[28]Lee and Brengle, p. 16.

[29]Brengle, *Heart-Talks on Holiness*, pp. 15–17.

[30] Samuel L. Brengle, "The Witness of the Spirit," *War Cry* [NY] (May 21, 1910): 10; Brengle, *When the Holy Ghost Is Come*, pp. 23–27; cf. Steele, *The Gospel and the Comforter*, pp. 117, 127–28. Elsewhere, Brengle outlined several conditions with regard to receiving or maintaining such assurance. "The witness of the Spirit is dependent on our faith. God does not give it to those who do not believe in Jesus. . . . We must not get our attention off Jesus, and the promises of God in Him, and fix it upon the witness of the Spirit. . . . The witness may be brightened by diligence in the discharge of duty, by frequent seasons of glad prayer, by definite testimony to salvation and sanctification, and by stirring up our faith; the witness may be dulled by neglect of duty, by sloth in prayer, by inattention to the Bible, by indefinite, hesitating testimony and by carelessness. . . . But the witness will be lost if we willfully sin or persistently neglect to follow where He leads. . . . If lost, it may be found again by prayer and faith and a dutiful taking up of the cross which has been laid down." Brengle, "The Witness of the Spirit," p. 10; Brengle, *When the Holy Ghost Is Come*, pp. 27–29.

[31] Brengle, *When the Holy Ghost Is Come*, p. 29.

[32] Brengle, *Helps to Holiness*, pp. 30, 33.

[33] Ibid., p. 24.

[34] Larsson, pp. 99–100.

[35] Brengle, *Helps to Holiness*, pp. 61–63; cf. Chesham, *Peace*, pp. 204–5. Elsewhere Brengle maintained that: "We should never tell people they are saved [or sanctified]; but rather, we should intelligently point out the way of salvation to them, and persistently urge them to press hard along the way till God Himself notifies them that their faith is accepted of Him." Brengle, "From Dawn to Sunrise," part 1, p. 10.

[36] Brengle, *Heart-Talks on Holiness*, pp. 90–92.

[37] Samuel L. Brengle, "The Secret of Power," *War Cry* [NY] (Jan. 12, 1929): 12; Brengle, *Helps to Holiness*, pp. 38–40; Brengle, *At the Center of the Circle*, p. 13. Cf. Steele, *Love Enthroned*, p. 388.

[38] Brengle, "The Holiness Standard," pp. 150–51.

[39] Brengle, *Helps to Holiness*, pp. 124–25; Brengle, "Sanctification vs. Consecration," p. 291.

[40] Brengle, *Helps to Holiness*, p. 125; Brengle, "Sanctification vs. Consecration," p. 292.

[41] Brengle, *Helps to Holiness*, pp. 126–27; Brengle, "Sanctification vs. Consecration," p. 293.

[42] Brengle, *At the Center of the Circle*, pp. 74–75.

[43] Samuel L. Brengle, "Your Own Soul," *War Cry* [NY] (Dec. 20, 1890): 14; Brengle, *Helps to Holiness*, p. 49.

CHAPTER 11—MAINTAINING HOLINESS

[1] Brengle, "The Meaning of a 'Clean Heart': How to Keep a Clean Heart," paper 5, *Officer* 7:9 (Sept. 1899): 347–49; Samuel L. Brengle, "The Meaning of a Clean Heart," *Officer* 34:6 (Jun. 1922): 494–96; Brengle, *Heart-Talks on Holiness,* pp. 31–35. Brengle later delineated a shorter list of means by which holiness is kept: "I have been asked the secret of keeping the Blessing, and I can only reply: Keep in the will of God, obey Him, seek Him daily, waiting at His gates. Read the Bible regularly. Never neglect secret prayer. Keep testifying to the grace of God bestowed upon you. Help others." Lee and Brengle, p. 11; Brengle, "Fifty Years of Holy Living!" part 1, p. 4. For variations on these themes see Brengle, *The Way of Holiness,* pp. 35–39; Brengle, *Heart-Talks on Holiness,* p. 78; Brengle, "Loving God," quoted in Chesham, *Treasury,* p. 48; Brengle, *At the Center of the Circle,* p. 19.

[2] Samuel L. Brengle, "The Maintenance of Our Consecration: 'I Counted' and 'I Count,'" *Officer* 22:10 (Oct. 1914): 657; cf. Brengle, *Love-Slaves,* p. 35.

[3] Brengle, "The Maintenance of Our Consecration," pp. 658–59; cf. Brengle, *Love-Slaves,* pp. 36–40.

[4] Brengle, "Ebenezer: 1885–1918," p. 16.

[5] Lee and Brengle, pp. 11–12; Brengle, *Fifty Years,* pp. 13–14.

[6] Brengle, *At the Center of the Circle,* p. 31. Cf. Steele, *Love Enthroned,* pp. 174–76; 398–99.

[7] Samuel L. Brengle, "The Lost Blessing Found: A Word to Sorrowful Souls," *War Cry* [NY] (Sept. 21, 1918): 2.

[8] Lee and Brengle, p. 12.

[9] Brengle, *The Way of Holiness,* pp. 35–39.

[10] In response to a young man who wanted him to write a book on "the temptations of the sanctified soul," Brengle suggested the reading of his published works, writing: "I think you will find that they are very 'plain, outspoken, honest, concrete, down-on-the-earth' books. . . . I commend to you especially *Helps to Holiness* and *Heart-Talks on Holiness.*" Samuel L. Brengle, "Write Another Book," *War Cry* [NY] (Jun. 24, 1967): 10–11.

[11] Samuel L. Brengle, "An Open Letter to a Young Comrade," *War Cry* [NY] (Mar. 28, 1936): 6; Brengle, "Write Another Book," pp. 10–11.

[12] Quoted in Chesham, *Peace,* pp. 177–78. This letter is indicative of the fact that Brengle's simplicity of gospel communication was not due to an inability to think at a deeper theological level. His friendship with Dr. S. Parkes Cadman, pastor of Park Avenue Church in New York, resulted in scholarly literary exchanges on several spiritual issues.

[13] Samuel L. Brengle, "Holiness: Temptations of a Sanctified Man," part 1, *War Cry* [NY] (Apr. 14, 1888): 14; Brengle, *Helps to Holiness,* pp. 18–20.

[14] Samuel L. Brengle, "Holiness: Temptations of a Sanctified Man," part 2, *War Cry* [NY] (Apr. 21, 1888): 14; Brengle, *Helps to Holiness*, pp. 21–22.

[15] Chesham, *Peace*, p. 179.

[16] Brengle, "The Holiness Standard," p. 150.

[17] Brengle, "The Whisperer—Fight!" p. 9. Reprinted as "Fight the Satanic Whisperer," *Officer* 27:3 (Sept. 1918): 230–31; Brengle, *Resurrection Life and Power*, pp. 124–26.

[18] Brengle, *Helps to Holiness*, pp. 114–15.

[19] Ibid., pp. 27–28; Brengle, *At the Center of the Circle*, pp. 81–82.

[20] Brengle, *Helps to Holiness*, pp. 30–31.

[21] Ibid., p. 28.

[22] Samuel L. Brengle, "Stooping to Conquer," *Field Officer* 13:8 (Aug. 1905): 285.

[23] Brengle, "My Testimony," *War Cry* [NY] (Jan. 31, 1891): 11; Brengle, "Full Salvation—My Personal Testimony," p. 138.

[24] Lee and Brengle, p. 13.

[25] Brengle, "Holiness and Temptation," *Officer's Review* (May–Jun., 1936) reproduced in Satterlee, "Pentecost and Beyond," pp. 93–94.

[26] Samuel L. Brengle, "Dealing with Officers on Their Failures in Holiness," *Staff Review* (Apr. 1924): 119. Cf. Brengle, *Heart-Talks on Holiness*, p. 78.

[27] Samuel L. Brengle, "Another Chance for You: A Test of Love," *War Cry* [NY] (Apr. 14, 1894): 3; Brengle, *Helps to Holiness*, pp. 107–8, 110.

[28] Brengle, "Ebenezer: 1885–1918," p. 16.

[29] Quoted in Chesham, *Peace*, p. 215. Elsewhere, Brengle wrote: "John Fletcher, whom Mr. Wesley thought was the holiest man who had lived since the days of the Apostle John, lost the blessing five times before he was finally established in the grace of holiness, and Mr. Wesley declared that he was persuaded from his observation, that people usually lose the blessing several times before they learn the secret of keeping." Samuel L. Brengle, "Holiness: How to Keep It," *War Cry* [NY] (Sept. 29, 1894): 5; Brengle, *Helps to Holiness*, p. 118.

[30] Brengle, "Can One Who Has Lost the Blessing of Full Salvation Be Restored?" *Officer* 27:4 (Oct. 1918), p. 314. Cf. Brengle, *Helps to Holiness*, p. 76.

[31] Samuel L. Brengle, "Can One Who Has Lost the Blessing of Full Salvation Be Restored?" pp. 313–14. Cf. Brengle, *Resurrection Life and Power*, p. 105.

[32] Brengle, "Holiness and Temptation," *Officer's Review* (May–Jun., 1936), reproduced in Satterlee, "Pentecost and Beyond," pp. 91–99.

[33] Samuel L. Brengle, "How to Get and Keep the Fire!" *Field Officer* 15:6 (Jun. 1907): 212.

[34] Brengle, "The Holiness Standard," pp. 147–48; Brengle, *Love-Slaves*, pp. 72–73.

[35] Brengle, "The Holiness Standard," p. 152; Brengle, *Love-Slaves*, pp. 79–80; cf. Waldron, *Privilege of All Believers*, p. 114.

[36] Brengle, "The Holiness Standard," p. 149.

[37] Ibid.

[38] Brengle promoted the reading of holiness literature, stating that: "We shall not have to go outside the Army to secure such literature. The Army has a library of books and papers on this subject, and they are plain, simple, scriptural, and full of thrill, passion, compelling power of life and experience." Brengle, "The Holiness Standard," p. 149; cf. Brengle, *Love-Slaves*, p. 76.

[39] Brengle, "The Holiness Standard," p. 149.

CHAPTER 12—THE FRUIT OF HOLINESS

[1] Brengle, *When the Holy Spirit Is Come*, pp. 133–36. Cf. "Evidences of Perfect Love," in Steele, *Love Enthroned*, pp. 250–65.

[2] Brengle, "The Meaning of a Clean Heart: The Outcome, or Result, of Having Clean Heart" paper 4, *Officer* 7:8 (Aug. 1899): 302–4. Cf. Brengle, *Heart-Talks on Holiness*, pp. 26–30; cf. Steele, *The Mile-Stone Papers*, pp. 218–23.

[3] Samuel L. Brengle, "When the Comforter Is Come," *War Cry* [NY] (Jun. 10, 1916): 5; Brengle, *Resurrection Life and Power*, pp. 122–23.

[4] Brengle, *When the Holy Ghost Is Come*, pp. 38–39; quoted in Chesham, *Peace*, p. 202.

[5] Brengle, *The Way of Holiness*, pp. 22–23.

[6] Samuel L. Brengle, "The Blessedness of the Pentecostal Baptism," *Staff Review* (Apr. 1930): 190–93; cf. Brengle, *The Guest of the Soul*, pp. 48–54, 57; Brengle, *Wait on the Lord*, p. 11. Although Brengle maintained that the fruit of the Spirit are given to the believer at regeneration, he understood that the perfection of such fruit required a deeper work. Hence, there is no inconsistency in Brengle's early and late statements concerning the fruit of the Spirit, as claimed by Reagan, "Crisis in Process," pp. 79–81.

[7] Brengle, *Helps to Holiness*, pp. 99–100; cf. Chesham, *Peace*, p. 197.

[8] Samuel L. Brengle, "Ebenezer: 1885–1918," *War Cry* [NY] (Feb. 2, 1918): 16; Brengle, *God as Strategist*, p. 15; Lee and Brengle, p. 11; Brengle, "A Definition and an Experience," p. 3; Brengle, "God Wrought Mightily in My Soul," pp. 3, 14; Brengle, *The Guest of the Soul*, p. 124.

[9] Brengle, "Commissioner Brengle's Last Whitsun Message," p. 205.

[10] Brengle, "'The Terror of the Lord,'" p. 238.

[11] Samuel L. Brengle, "'The Terror of the Lord,'" *Officer* 24:4 (Apr. 1916): 237–38; Brengle, *Love-Slaves*, pp. 82–83.

[12] Samuel L. Brengle, "'Put Up Thy Sword into the Sheath,'" *War Cry* [NY] (Feb. 11, 1905): 6. Reprinted as "The Sheathed Sword: A Law of the Spirit," *War Cry* [NY] (Jul. 29, 1911): 6; Brengle, *When the Holy Ghost Is Come*, pp. 122–23.

[13] Samuel L. Brengle, "Meekness of Heart," *War Cry* [NY] (Feb. 4, 1922): 6; Brengle, *When the Holy Ghost Is Come*, p. 59.

[14] Brengle, *When the Holy Ghost Is Come*, pp. 59–60.

[15] Brengle, *The Way of Holiness*, p. 19.

[16] Samuel L. Brengle, "Be Faithful, Be Loving," *War Cry* [NY] (Dec. 30, 1916): 3.

[17] Brengle, *At the Center of the Circle*, p. 37; cf. Samuel L. Brengle, "Officers Who Burn and Shine," *Officer* 38:2 (Feb. 1924): 138, 140.

[18] Quoted in Chesham, *Treasury*, p. 34.

[19] Samuel L. Brengle, Letter to "My Dear Comrades," written from St. Petersburg, FL, Apr. 24, 1936 (Alexandria, VA: The Salvation Army National Archives), p. 1; Brengle, "Way of the Spirit," quoted in Chesham, *Treasury*, p. 55.

[20] Samuel L. Brengle, "Hope and Power of His Resurrection," *War Cry* [NY] (Apr. 15, 1922): 11; Brengle, *Resurrection Life and Power*, pp. 6–7.

[21] Brengle, "Holiness: Reasons Why Everybody Should Be Entirely Sanctified," p. 11.

[22] Samuel L. Brengle, "The Power of Pentecost," *War Cry* [NY] (Feb. 18, 1922): 6.

[23] Brengle, "Holiness: Reasons Why Everybody Should Be Entirely Sanctified," p. 11.

[24] Brengle, *The Way of Holiness*, pp. 6–7.

[25] Brengle, *Helps to Holiness*, pp. 44, 46.

[26] Brengle, *The Guest of the Soul*, pp. 102, 104.

[27] Brengle, *When the Holy Ghost Is Come*, pp. 45–50.

[28] Brengle, *The Way of Holiness*, p. 31.

[29] Brengle, *Heart-Talks on Holiness*, p. 76.

[30] Brengle, *Love-Slaves*, pp. 96–97.

[31] Samuel L. Brengle, "Four Kinds of Self-Denial," *War Cry* [NY] (Apr. 14, 1917): 13.

[32] Brengle, *Resurrection Life and Power*, p. 58; cf. Brengle, "Officers Who Burn and Shine," p. 140.

³³Samuel L. Brengle, "Victory through the Holy Spirit over Suffering," *War Cry* [NY] (Aug. 5, 1911): 6; *War Cry* [NY] (Nov. 26, 1921): 6; Brengle, *When the Holy Ghost Is Come*, pp. 127–32.

³⁴Brengle, "Victory through the Holy Spirit over Suffering," p. 6.

³⁵Samuel L. Brengle, "The Lord's Own Prayer," *Staff Review* (Jan. 1925): 21; Brengle, *At the Center of the Circle*, pp. 38–39.

³⁶Samuel L. Brengle, "The Seamless Coat of Jesus," *Officer* 50:2 (Feb. 1930): 92.

³⁷Brengle, "The Family Altar: Every Man Priest in His Own Home," p. 3.

³⁸Brengle, *At the Center of the Circle*, p. 39.

³⁹Ibid., p. 42.

⁴⁰Brengle, *Helps to Holiness*, p. 25.

⁴¹Brengle, *The Guest of the Soul*, pp. 46–47.

⁴²Samuel L. Brengle, "Praying in the Spirit," *War Cry* [NY] (May 20, 1911): 10; Brengle, *When the Holy Ghost Is Come*, p. 95.

⁴³Brengle, *The Way of Holiness*, pp. 53–55.

CHAPTER 13—EVANGELISM AND THE HOLY LIFE

¹Samuel L. Brengle, "The Cost of Saving Souls," *Staff Review* (Jul. 1926): 270.

²Samuel L. Brengle, "The Special Campaigner: The Man and His Work." *Staff Review* (Jan. 1927): 18–19.

³Samuel Logan Brengle, *Ancient Prophets: With a Series of Occasional Papers on Modern Problems* (London: Salvation Army, 1930), pp. 69–70.

⁴Brengle, *Ancient Prophets*, pp. 71, 75.

⁵Ibid, p. 76.

⁶Samuel L. Brengle, "Preaching," *War Cry* [NY] (Jul. 15, 1911): 10; Samuel Logan Brengle, *When the Holy Ghost Is Come* (Atlanta: Salvation Army, 1982), pp. 106–14.

⁷Samuel L. Brengle, "Preaching," *War Cry* [NY] (Jul. 15, 1911): 10; Brengle, *When the Holy Ghost Is Come*, pp. 106–14. In a letter to Adam Kanice, Old Concord, PA, Feb. 1, 1936, Brengle writes on the importance of liberal arts education in developing such rational powers: "First, the processes of education exercise the faculties of the mind. The study of mathematics and logic exercises the logical faculties. The study of history broadens one's perspective. The study of poetry and fiction develops the imagination. The study of the best literature enlarges one's vocabulary and powers of expressing ideas, all of which is helpful to right thinking, and gives a person knowledge and facts to

think about. . . . The study of philosophy, of morals and of ethics and religion gives one correct standards of life and conduct which purifies the mind and enables it to think straight and true. The study of languages exercises the critical faculties and memory and gives us a firmer and wider grasp of our own language and meaning of many words, without which we cannot think. Above all, true education acquaints us with the best thoughts and methods of thinking of the great thinkers of the ages. . . . Above all, get that blessed spiritual education that comes from sitting at the feet of Jesus and acquainting yourself with the Holy Scriptures and being filled with the Holy Spirit." Samuel L. Brengle, "Education," quoted in Sallie Chesham, *The Brengle Treasury: A Patchwork Polygon* (Atlanta: Salvation Army, 1988), p. 100.

[8] Samuel L. Brengle, "Preaching," *War Cry* [NY] (Jul. 15, 1911): 10; Brengle, *When the Holy Ghost Is Come*, pp. 106–14.

[9] Ibid.

[10] Samuel L. Brengle, "Characteristics of the Anointed Preacher," *War Cry* [NY] (Jun. 3, 1911): 6; Brengle, *When the Holy Ghost Is Come*, pp. 97–104. Cf. Samuel L. Brengle, "Paul—A Model Preacher," *Field Officer* 17:5 (May 1909): 161–64.

[11] Samuel L. Brengle, "Our Salvationist Bandsmen," *War Cry* [NY] (Jun. 16, 1923): 7.

[12] Samuel L. Brengle, "A Letter to Army Bandsmen," *War Cry* [NY] (Apr. 23, 1932): 6.

[13] Samuel L. Brengle, "Letter Shows Brengle Spirit," *War Cry* [NY] (Sept. 10, 1955): 3.

[14] Samuel L. Brengle, "A Plea for Soul-Winning Songsters," *War Cry* [NY] (Aug. 15, 1931): 7.

[15] Samuel L. Brengle, "Your Commission," *War Cry* [NY] (Nov. 23, 1901): 2.

[16] Samuel L. Brengle, *The Soul Winner's Secret* (Atlanta: Salvation Army, 1988), pp. 78–83.

[17] Ibid., p. 86.

[18] Brengle, "Can Little Children Be Really Saved?" p. 236.

[19] Samuel L. Brengle, "'Ifs' of a Soul-Winner," *War Cry* (Feb. 25, 1888): 15.

[20] Brengle, *Soul-Winner's Secret*, pp. 101–4.

[21] Samuel L. Brengle, "The Holy Spirit's Call to the Work," *War Cry* [NY] (Jul. 22, 1911): 6; Brengle, *When the Holy Ghost Is Come*, pp. 115, 119.

[22] Samuel L. Brengle, "Whitened Harvest Fields," *Officer* 27:2 (Aug. 1918): 101–3; Reprinted from *War Cry* [NY] (Oct. 3, 1914): 11; cf. Samuel L. Brengle, *Love-Slaves* (Atlanta: Salvation Army, 1982), pp. 105–8.

[23] Brengle, *Love-Slaves*, pp. 109–10.

[24] Samuel L. Brengle, "The Soul-Winner's Obedience," *War Cry* [NY] (Apr. 8, 1899): 2; Brengle, *Soul-Winner's Secret*, pp. 6–10.

[25] Samuel L. Brengle, "Spiritual Leadership," *War Cry* [NY] (Sept. 16, 1899): 6; Brengle, *Soul-Winner's Secret*, pp. 22–23, 25, 27.

[26] Samuel L. Brengle, "Constrained by Love," *Field Officer* 20:11 (Nov. 1912): 414.

[27] Samuel L. Brengle, "The Personal Experience of the Soul-winner," *War Cry* [NY] (Mar. 11, 1899): 6; Brengle, *Soul-Winner's Secret*, pp. 1–3.

[28] Samuel L. Brengle, "So Spake," *Field Officer* 10:3 (Mar. 1902): 108–10; Brengle, *Soul-Winner's Secret*, pp. 92–96.

[29] Brengle, "Special Campaigner," p. 16. Cf. Samuel L. Brengle, "Looking Backward and Forward After Seventy Years!" p. 49.

[30] Samuel L. Brengle, "The Cost of Saving Souls," *Staff Review* (Jul. 1926): 266.

[31] Ibid, p. 268.

[32] Ibid, p. 267.

[33] Samuel Brengle, "Is There a Special Message for the Present Age?" *Staff Review* (Jan. 1929) reproduced in Allen Satterlee (editor), "Pentecost and Beyond: Collected Writings of Commissioner Samuel Logan Brengle" (Unpublished manuscript located at The Salvation Army National Archives, Alexandria, VA; n.d.), pp. 27–33.

[34] Samuel L. Brengle, "Love for Souls: Two Portraits—Which is Yours?" *Field Officer* 12:6 (Jun. 1904): 202. In this same article, Brengle juxtaposes two portraits of officers. First, "the Officer who has lost his love for souls," and second, "the Officer who has love for souls." The former is characterized as: "1). . . light and foolish and treacherous, or impatient and quick to take offence. . . . 2) His chief thought in the meetings will probably be concerning the collection. . . . 3) He no longer shouts for joy, has lost his delight in secret prayer, and is too busy to read his Bible. . . . 4) If people try his patience, or treat him ill, he frets about it, grieves the Spirit, and so quenches love, which decays from neglect. . . . 5) Since he has lost his love, he has lost light and wisdom, and so walks in darkness and knows not wither he goes, doing no end of harm, both to himself and to others. . . . The Officer who has love for souls is just the opposite of all this. . . . 1) He is generous and patient toward all men. He does not take offence, but loves and prays for those who may ill-treat him. . . . 2) He has no time to worry and think anxiously about his salary, and he will often almost forget the collection in his eagerness to win souls. 3) He studies and plans and works and prays continually to reach the hearts of the people. . . . 4) His love grows by exercise, and he exercises it upon the people who try his patience, treat him ill, and talk unkindly or untruthfully about him. . . . 5) He walks in the light, and so does not stumble, has fellowship with Jesus, is guided by the inward moving. . . of the Holy Spirit, and is full of humility and power and glory." Brengle, "Love for Souls," pp. 202–3.

[35] Samuel L. Brengle, "Holiness and Zeal for Souls," *Officer*, 31:6 (Dec. 1920): 525. In this regard, Brengle reminded his readers of two truths: "1) Most sinners hope that someone will speak to them about their souls. . . . 2) When God moves us to speak to people, we may be sure that He has been dealing with their hearts and preparing the way for us" (pp. 525–26).

[36] Brengle, "Holiness and Zeal for Souls," p. 526.

[37] Samuel L. Brengle, "A Business Too Big For Us," *Officer* 37:1 (Jul. 1923): 72.

[38] Samuel L. Brengle, "Power to Cast Out Devils," *Field Officer* 13:7 (Jul. 1905): 273–74.

[39] Brengle, *Soul-Winner's Secret*, pp. 48–49.

[40] Samuel Brengle, "Soul-Winners: Their Prayers," *War Cry* [NY] (Feb. 2, 1895): 3. Reprinted as "The Prayers of Soul-Winners," *Officer* (May 1897): 140–41; and as "Prayer—The Soul-Winner's Secret," *Officer* 30:2 (Feb. 1920): 123–25. Samuel L. Brengle, "Prayer That Kindles Flaming Revivals," *War Cry* [NY] (Jan. 11, 1919): 3; Samuel L. Brengle, *Helps To Holiness* (Atlanta: Salvation Army, 1984), p. 84. Samuel L. Brengle, "Ask Largely," *War Cry* [NY] (Apr. 20, 1940): 7, 14; Brengle, *Helps To Holiness*, pp. 80–81.

[41] Samuel L. Brengle, "How to Prepare for the Meeting," *Officer* 30:3 (Mar. 1920): 267–68; Samuel L. Brengle, *Heart Talks On Holiness* (Atlanta: Salvation Army, 1988), pp. 108–9.

[42] Samuel L. Brengle, "Prayer," *War Cry* [NY] (Aug. 19, 1899): 4; Brengle, *Soul-Winner's Secret*, pp. 11–15; Brengle, "Prayer," *War Cry* [NY] (Oct. 10, 1936): 5. General Evangeline Booth requested that this chapter from *The Soul-Winner's Secret* be printed in every *War Cry* around the world in recognition of the Universal Day of Prayer and Reconciliation, Oct. 11, 1936.

[43] Samuel L. Brengle, "How Soul-Winners Should Pray," *Officers' Review* 3:2 (Mar.–Apr. 1934): 120.

[44] Although practical advice abounds in Brengle's writings, it is especially focused on evangelism in "The Soul-Winner's Secret," a multi-part series which first appeared in *The War Cry* [NY], and eventually in a book of the same title. For the *War Cry* series see "The Personal Experience of the Soul-winner," (Mar. 11, 1899): 6; "The Soul-Winner's Obedience," (Apr. 8, 1899): 2; "The Zeal of the Soul-Winner," (Apr. 15, 1899): 2 and (Apr. 22, 1899): 7; "The Studies of the Soul-Winner," (May 13, 1899): 3 and (May 20, 1899): 5; "Finance," (Jun. 24, 1899): 6; "The Health of the Soul-Winner," (Jul. 8, 1899): 7 and (Jul. 29, 1899): 2; "Prayer," (Aug. 19, 1899): 4; "'Redeeming the Time,'" (Sept. 2, 1899): 13; "Spiritual Leadership," (Sept. 16, 1899): 6. The book form of *The Soul-Winner's Secret* was part of the Army's "Red-Hot Library." For a review of this book, that gives qualified support for Brengle's ideas see "Our Bookshelf: 'The Soul-Winner's Secret,'" *Field Officer* 11:11 (Nov. 1903): 430.

[45] Samuel L. Brengle, "Winning a Soul," *War Cry* [NY] (Feb. 20, 1909): 7.

[46] Samuel L. Brengle, "Commissioner Brengle Writes. . . " *Officers' Review* 4:5 (Sept.–Oct. 1935): 419.

[47] Samuel L. Brengle, "How to Win the Jews to Christ," *Officer* 49:5 (Nov. 1929): 359–60.

[48] Samuel L. Brengle, "Misrepresenting God," *War Cry* [NY] (Mar. 7, 1925): 6; Brengle, *Love-Slaves*, pp. 50–51.

[49] Samuel L. Brengle, "The Kind of Truth Needed for the Holiness Meeting," *Officer* 6:6 (Jun. 1898): 183; Brengle, *Soul-Winner's Secret*, pp. 66–68.

[50] Samuel L. Brengle, "How To Get People Sanctified Wholly," *Officer* 6:8 (Aug. 1898): 238.

[51] Samuel L. Brengle, "Commissioner Brengle Writes. . . " *Officers' Review* 4:5 (Sept.–Oct. 1935): 419.

[52] Samuel L. Brengle, "Specials: What They Should Do, Avoid, and Be," *Field Officer* 11:10 (Oct. 1903): 390–91; reprinted in *Officer* 35:3 (Sept. 1922): 227–28.

[53] Brengle, *Soul-Winner's Secret*, pp. 99–100.

[54] Samuel L. Brengle, "Soldiers' and Holiness Meetings," *Field Officer* 11:7 (Jul. 1903): 250.

[55] Brengle, *Soul-Winner's Secret*, p. 70.

[56] Brengle, *Soul-Winner's Secret*, pp. 71–72. The failure to encourage believers to move beyond consecration to entire sanctification is illustrated from the early ministry of Charles Finney, who emphasized disciplined renunciation of sin and obedient consecration to God, without an equal emphasis on "the faith that receives." The result of this was "groaning bondage under the law of sin and death." Finney later came to realize through his own holiness experience, that after total consecration has been made, the believer needs to wait on the divine heart-cleansing power of the Holy Spirit (pp. 73–74).

[57] Brengle, *Soul-Winner's Secret*, p. 77.

[58] Samuel L. Brengle, "After the Meeting," *Field Officer* 11:8 (Aug. 1903): 307; Brengle, *Soul-Winner's Secret*, pp. 97–98.

[59] Samuel L. Brengle, "Deal Gently," *War Cry* [NY] (May 11, 1901): 2; Brengle, *Soul-Winner's Secret*, pp. 88–91.

[60] Samuel L. Brengle, "On Preaching to the Few," *War Cry* [NY] (Sept. 10, 1960): 3.

[61] Samuel L. Brengle, "The Zeal of the Soul-Winner," *War Cry* [NY] (Apr. 15, 1899): 2 and (Apr. 22, 1899): 7; Brengle, *Soul-Winner's Secret*, pp. 16–20.

[62] Samuel L. Brengle, "'Redeeming the Time,'" *War Cry* [NY] (Sept. 2, 1899): 13; Brengle, *Soul-Winner's Secret*, pp. 28–32.

[63] Samuel L. Brengle, "The Studies of the Soul-Winner," *War Cry* [NY] (May 13, 1899): 3 and (May 20, 1899): 5; Brengle, *Soul-Winner's Secret*, pp. 34–35, 37–39.

[64] Samuel L. Brengle, "The Health of the Soul-Winner," *War Cry* [NY] (Jul. 8, 1899): 7 and (Jul. 29, 1899): 2; Brengle, *Soul-Winner's Secret*, pp. 40–47.

[65] Samuel L. Brengle, "Finance," (Jun. 24, 1899): 6; Brengle, *Soul-Winner's Secret*, pp. 59–63.

[66] It is noteworthy that Brengle's "revival" articles were reprinted regularly after his death, especially in the *War Cry*.

[67] Samuel L. Brengle, "Correspondence: Is There a Special Message For the Present Age?" *Staff Review* (Jan. 1929): 119.

[68] Ibid., p. 122.

[69] Samuel L. Brengle, "A Revival In Every Salvation Army Corps," *Officers' Review* 2:6 (Nov.–Dec. 1933): 482; cf. Samuel L. Brengle, "A World-Wide Revival," *Officer's Review* (Nov.–Dec., 1933) reproduced in Satterlee, "Pentecost and Beyond," p. 8.

[70] Brengle exhorted soul-winners to declare the inevitability of divine retribution. He wrote: "The majesty of God's law can be measured only by the terrors of His judgments. God is rich in mercy, but He is terrible in wrath. . . . If men do not accept His mercy, they shall be overtaken by wrath. God's law cannot be broken with impunity. . . . Judgement follows wrong-doing as night follows day. And this should be preached and declared continually and everywhere. It should not be preached harshly, as though we were glad of it. . . . It should be preached soberly, earnestly, tearfully, intelligently, as a solemn, certain, awful fact to be reckoned with in everything we think and say and do." Samuel L. Brengle, "'The Terror of the Lord.'" *Officer* 24:4 (Apr. 1916): 237. Reprinted in *War Cry* [NY] (May 20, 1916): 11.

[71] Brengle, "A Revival In Every Salvation Army Corps," p. 483.

[72] Samuel L. Brengle, "The Great Call To Go For Souls," *War Cry* [NY] (Mar. 5, 1921): 5; Samuel L. Brengle, *Resurrection Life and Power* (Atlanta: Salvation Army, 1981), pp. 74–76. Elsewhere, Brengle laments the fact that ". . . after two thousand years the followers of Jesus, to whom He offers the resources of 'all power in Heaven and in earth,' have made no larger conquests and taken possession of so small a portion of the earth in His name! And why is this so? It is due in part to the sloth, the inertia, the deadening weight of ignorance with which the heralds of the Gospel must contend. . . . But worse. . . is the sin of the heart, the depravity of nature, that makes men resist the light. . . . The great mass of men in all lands do not want 'this Man' to rule over them; they do not hunger and thirst after righteousness. . . . But into this deadness, this darkness and indifference and sin. . . Jesus has bidden His friends to go with light, with love, with power from on high. . . . " Samuel L. Brengle, "The Other Side of Christmas," *War Cry* [NY] (Dec. 4, 1926): 6, 14.

[73] Brengle, "A World-Wide Revival," *Officer's Review* (Nov.–Dec., 1933) reproduced in Satterlee, "Pentecost and Beyond," pp. 6–16.

[74] Samuel L. Brengle, "Who Wants A Revival?" *Officer* 47:1 (Jul. 1928): 21.

[75] Brengle, "Who Wants A Revival?" pp. 21–22.

[76] Brengle, "A Revival In Every Salvation Army Corps," pp. 485, 487.

[77] Samuel L. Brengle, "Why Not Revival In Your Corps?" *War Cry* [NY] (Jan. 1, 1916): 6.

[78] Samuel L. Brengle, "Can We Have Revivals in War Time?" *War Cry* [NY] (Mar. 2, 1918): 9, 12.

[79] Samuel L. Brengle, "Needed—A Revival," *War Cry* [NY] (Dec. 3, 1932): 6.

[80] Samuel L. Brengle, "We Need a Revival!" *War Cry* [NY] (Jan. 8, 1949): 4.

[81] Samuel L. Brengle, "'The World For God' Campaign," *War Cry* [NY] (Feb. 29, 1936): 4.

[82] Samuel L. Brengle, "A Flaming Revival," *War Cry* [NY] (Jan. 18, 1919): 9.

[83] Brengle, "We Need a Revival!" p. 14.

[84] Samuel L. Brengle, "The Great Call To Go For Souls," *War Cry* [NY] (Mar. 5, 1921): 5; Brengle, *Resurrection Life and Power*, pp. 74–76.

[85] Samuel L. Brengle, "How Believing, Persistent, Purposeful Prayer Brought a Revival," *War Cry* [NY] (Apr. 18, 1936): 6.

[86] Samuel L. Brengle, "Pennings of a Prophet: Sustained Prayer For Revival," *War Cry* [NY] (Apr. 23, 1938): 6.

[87] Ibid, p. 14. An example of Brengle's call to revival prayer can be found in the following plan: "What a grand chance!. . . . A Seventy-Day Battle for Souls! Why not a half or all-night of prayer for souls every seven days of the seventy? Ten all-nights of prayer! If only ten people united in prayer and really prayed, mighty things would happen. If only one or two wrestled with God for ten nights out of the seventy, God would make bare His arm and work wonders. That would be getting out of the ruts. That would be something new, it would be a novelty that would interest all Heaven and make a stir in Hell, and something would happen on our battlefields on earth." Samuel L. Brengle, "Why Omit Prayer?" *War Cry* [NY] (Jan. 23, 1926): 7.

[88] Samuel L. Brengle, "Ten Half-Nights of Prayer in Seventy Days," *War Cry* [NY] (Jan. 30, 1926): 7.

CHAPTER 14—HOLINESS AND THE ETHICAL DIMENSIONS OF BRENGLE'S ESCHATOLOGY

[1] Samuel L. Brengle, "Looking Backward and Forward After Seventy Years!" *Staff Review* (Jan. 1931): 47; Brengle, *The Guest of the Soul* [originally published in 1934] (Atlanta: The Salvation Army, 1992), p. 112.

[2] Quoted in Sallie Chesham, *Peace Like a River* (Atlanta: The Salvation Army, 1981), p. 191.

[3] For Wesley's postmillennial perspective see Randy L. Maddox, "Nurturing the New Creation: Reflections on a Wesleyan Trajectory," in *Wesleyan Perspectives on the New Creation*, edited by M. Douglas Meeks (Nashville: Kingswood Books, 2004), pp. 34–42. Daniel Steele was also a strong supporter of postmillennial eschatology. Steele's *Antinomianism Revived* (1887) took to task the doctrines of Calvinism and premillennialism that were popular among the Bible and Prophecy movement of his day. Kenneth O. Brown, "Daniel Steele," in *The Historical Dictionary of the Holiness Movement*, edited by William Kostlevy (Lanham, MD: Scarecrow Press, 2001), p. 246. For an in-depth assessment of Booth's eschatological understanding, see Andrew S. Miller III, "The Good Time Coming": The Impact of William Booth's Eschatological Vision," Master's Thesis, Asbury Theological Seminary, Dec. 2005.

[4] Samuel L. Brengle, "A Revival In Every Salvation Army Corps," *Officers' Review* 2:6 (Nov.–Dec., 1933): 486.

[5] Samuel Logan Brengle, *Love-Slaves* [originally published in 1923] (Atlanta: The Salvation Army, 1982), p. 70.

[6] Brengle, *Love-Slaves*, p. 17.

[7] Brengle, *The Soul-Winner's Secret* [originally published in 1903] (Atlanta: The Salvation Army, 1988), p. 103.

[8] Samuel L. Brengle, "Pennings of a Prophet: Cleansing the Temple," *War Cry* [NY] (May 21, 1938): 6.

[9] Letter to Mrs. Samuel Martin, Morris Run, PA, Mar. 5, 1935, quoted in Sallie Chesham, *The Brengle Treasury* (Atlanta: The Salvation Army, 1988), p. 186.

[10] Letter to Rev. S. Parkes Cadman, Brooklyn, NY (Apr. 10, 1934). Quoted in Samuel Hewitt (editor), "Letters of Commissioner Samuel Logan Brengle, D.D." Unpublished manuscript (Salvation Army National Archives, Alexandria, VA; n.d.), p. 119.

[11] Brengle, "A World-Wide Revival," *Officer's Review* (Nov.–Dec., 1933) reproduced in Allen Satterlee (ed.), "Pentecost and Beyond: Collected Writings of Commissioner Samuel Logan Brengle," Unpublished manuscript (Alexandria, VA: The Salvation Army National Archives, n.d.), p. 15.

[12] Brengle, *Guest of the Soul*, p. 65.

[13] Samuel Logan Brengle, *Ancient Prophets: With a Series of Occasional Papers on Modern Problems* [originally published in 1929] (London: The Salvation Army, 1930), p. 7.

[14] Brengle, *Ancient Prophets*, p. 8.

[15] Samuel L. Brengle, "His Shoulders," *War Cry* [NY] (Nov. 15, 1924): 3, 13.

[16] The establishment of Christ's kingdom involves not only spiritual warfare in the present, but also his ultimate victory over all evil, and the full consummation God's good purposes: "He has a program. He is not a muddled, uncertain leader. He knows where He is going, to war with 'principalities and powers, and rulers of the darkness of this world.' His goal is ultimate victory, the overthrow of the foolish and abominable idolatries; torturing superstitions; political, ecclesiastic, economic, and social despotisms; every debasing, shameful, enslaving vice; and every proud and haughty thing that would exalt itself against the knowledge of God and His Christ. And when victory is won, he is going home to the throne and to a universal dominion of righteousness, holiness, love, joy, and peace forevermore. Hallelujah!" Samuel Logan Brengle, *At the Center of the Circle: Selections of Published and Unpublished Writings of Samuel Logan Brengle*, edited by John D. Waldron (Kansas City: Beacon Hill Press, 1976), p. 40.

[17] Samuel L. Brengle, "The Triumphs of Peace as Foreseen by Prophets and Poets," *War Cry* [NY] (Nov. 13, 1926): 5.

[18] Samuel L. Brengle, "When the Word of God Comes," *War Cry* [NY] (Jul. 25, 1903): 2; Samuel L. Brengle, *Resurrection Life and Power* [originally published in 1925] (Atlanta: The Salvation Army, 1981), p. 133.

[19] Brengle, *At the Center of the Circle*, p. 40.

[20] Samuel L. Brengle, "The Disappointed Angels," *War Cry* [NY] (Dec. 22, 1917): 13; Brengle, *Resurrection Life and Power*, pp. 90–91.

[21] Samuel L. Brengle, "The Resurrection," *War Cry* [NY] (Mar. 29, 1902): 7. Reprinted as "Lessons of the Resurrection," *War Cry* [NY] (Mar. 26, 1910): 10; Brengle, *Resurrection Life and Power*, pp. 10–11.

[22] Brengle, "The Resurrection," p. 7; Brengle, *Resurrection Life and Power*, pp. 12–13.

[23] Ibid.

[24] Samuel L. Brengle, *Heart-Talks On Holiness* [originally published in 1897] (Atlanta: The Salvation Army, 1988), pp. 95–97.

[25] Samuel L. Brengle, "The Death of Abel; the Resurrection of Jesus," *War Cry* [NY] (May 30, 1925): 5.

[26] Samuel L. Brengle, "Resurrection Life and Hope," *War Cry* [NY] (Apr. 16, 1927): 7, 14.

[27] Samuel L. Brengle, "Future Punishment: Is It Endless?" *War Cry* [NY] (Dec. 31, 1892): 2.

[28] Samuel L. Brengle, "Future Punishment: Is It Endless?" p. 2; Samuel L. Brengle, "Hell: What the Bible Says About Future Punishment," [Part 1] *Officer* 27:6 (Dec. 1918): 507; cf. Brengle, *Love-Slaves*, pp 19–20.

[29] Brengle, "Hell: What the Bible Says About Future Punishment," [Part 1] pp. 508–9; cf. Brengle, *Love-Slaves*, pp. 2–21, 23.

[30] Brengle, "Hell: What the Bible Says About Future Punishment," [Part 1] p. 510; Brengle, "Future Punishment: Is It Endless?" p. 2; Brengle, *Love-Slaves*, pp. 25–27.

[31] Brengle, "Future Punishment: Is It Endless?" p. 2.

[32] Samuel L. Brengle, "Did Lincoln Believe in Hell?" *War Cry* [NY] (Feb. 13, 1926): 7.

[33] Samuel L. Brengle, "Hell: What the Bible Says About Future Punishment," [Part 2] *Officer* 28:1 (Jan. 1919): 58; cf. Brengle, *Love-Slaves*, pp. 27–28.

[34] Brengle, "Hell: What the Bible Says About Future Punishment," [Part 2] pp. 58–59; Brengle, *Love-Slaves*, pp. 28–30.

[35] Letter from Redlands, CA, Jul. 12, 1912 in William Clark (ed.), *Dearest Lily: A Selection of the Brengle Correspondence* (London: The Salvation Army, 1985), p. 110.

[36] Brengle, "Hell: What the Bible Says About Future Punishment," [Part 2] p. 60; Brengle, *Love-Slaves*, p. 33.

[37] Brengle, *Resurrection Life and Power*, p. 27.

[38] Brengle, "Hell: What the Bible Says About Future Punishment," [Part 2] p. 59; Brengle, *Love-Slaves*, p. 31.

[39] Samuel L. Brengle, "One Look At a Man From Hell," *War Cry* [NY] (Jan. 23, 1892): 10.

[40] Brengle, "Pennings of a Prophet," *War Cry* [NY] (May 7, 1938): 6.

CHAPTER 15—BRENGLE AND THE DEVELOPMENT OF SALVATION ARMY HOLINESS THEOLOGY

[1] See John Kent, *Holding the Fort: Studies in Victorian Revivalism* (London: Epworth Press, 1978), pp. 325–28.

[2] Walter E. Houghton, *The Victorian Frame of Mind* (New Haven: Yale University Press, 1980), pp. 63ff.

[3] Perry Miller, *The Life of the Mind in America: From the Revolution to the Civil War* (New York: Harcourt, Brace and World, 1965), p. 93.

[4] Melvin E. Dieter, *The Holiness Revival of the Nineteenth Century* (Metuchen, NJ: Scarecrow Press, 1980), pp. 201–5, 211.

[5] E.g., James Caughey, "Holiness: Your Remedy," *War Cry* [London] (Mar. 6, 1880). For Caughey's influence on the Booths, see Roger Green, *The Life and Ministry of William Booth, Founder of The Salvation Army* (Nashville: Abingdon Press, 2005), note 36, pp. 237–38. Cf. Kent, *Holding the Fort*, pp. 325ff.; Richard Carwardine, *Transatlantic Revivalism: Popular Evangelicalism in Britain and American 1790–1865* (London: Greenwood Press, 1978), pp. 102ff.; Dieter, pp. 60–61.

[6] See Frederick de Lautour Booth-Tucker, *The Life of Catherine Booth,* 2 vols. (New York: Fleming Revell, 1892), 1:206, 208–9; Kent, *Holding the Fort,* pp. 326–27. In addition, some Salvation Army doctrinal language and hymnody are directly borrowed from Phoebe Palmer. See *The Doctrines and Discipline of The Salvation Army* (London: The Salvation Army, 1881); *Songs of The Salvation Army* (London: The Salvation Army, 1878), "Holiness Section" nos. 445–84; *Holiness Hymns* (London: The Salvation Army, 1880), nos. 4, 32; Kent, *Holding the Fort,* pp. 336–40.

[7] The legacy bequeathed to the British holiness revival by American perfectionist evangelists and writings would eventually feed back into the home movement with the beginning of The Salvation Army's work in the United States in 1880. Dieter, *Holiness Revival*, pp. 60–61, 156; Kent, *Holding the Fort*, p. 295ff.

[8] "The Tongue of Fire," *Officer* 3:5 (May 1895): 144.

[9] Commissioner Nicol, "Review of *Misunderstood Texts* by Asa Mahan," *Officer* 4:7 (Jul.–Aug. 1896): 202.

[10] Daniel Steele, *Love Enthroned*, p. 337.

[11] Actually, Palmer's "altar theology" is directly derived from the writings of Adam Clarke. See Phoebe Palmer, *Entire Devotion to God* (London: The Salvation Army, n.d.), pp. 40–41; Kent, *Holding the Fort*, pp. 321–22; Kevin Lowery, "A Fork in the Wesleyan Road: Phoebe Palmer and the Appropriation of Christian Perfection," *Wesleyan Theological Journal* 36:2 (Fall 2001): 193–95.

[12] Dieter, *Holiness Revival*, pp. 33–34; Melvin E. Dieter, "Wesleyan-Holiness Aspects of Pentecostal Origins," in Vinson Synan, *The Holiness-Pentecostal Movement in the United States.* Grand Rapids: Eerdmans Publishing Co., 1971), pp. 62–63. Cf. John Peters, *Christian Perfection and American Methodism* (Nashville: Abingdon, 1956), p. 113.

[13] Phoebe Palmer, *The Way of Holiness, with Notes by the Way; Being a Narrative of Religious Experience Resulting from a Determination to Be a Bible Christian* (New York: Lane and Scott, 1850), pp. 19, 22–24, 31, 38, 40–41.

[14] Phoebe Palmer, *Faith and Its Effects; Fragments From My Portfolio* (New York: W. C. Palmer, 1854), pp. 101–4.

[15] Lowery, "A Fork in the Wesleyan Road," p. 193; cf. Thomas Oden, ed., *Phoebe Palmer: Selected Writings* (New York: Paulist Press, 1988), p. 130–145.

[16] Palmer, *Faith and Its Effects*, p. 41.

[17] Ibid., pp. 34–35, 41, 52–53, 58.

[18] Ibid., pp. 285–86.

[19] Charles E. Jones, *Perfectionist Persuasion: The Holiness Movement and American Methodism, 1867–1936* (Metuchen, NJ: Scarecrow Press, 1974), pp. 5–6; cf. Ivan Howard, "Wesley Versus Phoebe Palmer: An Extended Controversy," *Wesleyan Theological Journal* 6:1 (Spring 1971): 31–40; Charles E. White, *The Beauty of Holiness: Phoebe Palmer as Theologian, Revivalist, Feminist, and Humanitarian* (Grand Rapids: Zondervan, 1986), pp. 125–44.

[20] The utilitarian spirit of the holiness revival is evident in the terminology employed by its leaders (e.g., James Caughey's *Christianity in Earnest*, William Boardman's "gospel efficiency," and Phoebe Palmer's *Faith and Its Effects*).

[21] Timothy Smith, *Revivalism and Social Reform: American Protestantism on the Eve of the Civil War* (Baltimore: Johns Hopkins University Press, 1980), pp. 145–46.

[22] Cf. James Caughey, *Earnest Christianity Illustrated* (Boston: J. P. Magee, 1855), pp. 198–99, 202; Kent, *Holding the Fort*, p. 323.

[23] See "Subject Notes," *Officer* 1:3 (Mar. 1893): 88.

[24] J. A. Wood, *Perfect Love: Or Plain Things for Those Who Need Them*, 36th ed. (London: The Salvation Army, 1902), pp. 64, 75.

[25] William Booth, "Letter from William Booth to the Brethren and Sisters Laboring for Jesus in Connection with the Dunedin Hall Christian Mission, Edinburgh," *East London Evangelist* 1 (Apr. 1, 1869): 105.

[26] See "Sanctification," *The Christian Mission Magazine*, 8 (Feb. 1876), 35–36; cf. Phoebe Palmer, *Entire Devotion to God*, p. 40. This book was printed by the Army and used as a primer for the teaching of entire sanctification within the movement.

[27] E.g., "Mile-Stone Papers, A Book for the Head and the Heart," *Officer* 30:4 (Oct. 1919): 322–24; "Holiness Vindicated in Scripture and Experience," [Review of Daniel Steele's *Difficulties Removed in the Way of Holiness*] *Officer* 30:5 (Nov. 1919): 444–45.

[28] John Norton claims that neither William nor Bramwell Booth had the time to write a systematic theology of holiness, but that they found their man for the job in Brengle. "The Doctrine of Sanctification in The Salvation Army: Samuel Logan Brengle," part 3, *Journal of Aggressive Christianity* 2 (Aug./Sept. 1999): 3.1.

[29] Norton, 3.2, "The Doctrine of the Second Blessing," n. 68. Actually, evidence for Brengle's influence can be dated much earlier. For example, see "Holiness: Theory and Practice" *Officer* 2:3 (Mar. 1894): 65–69, in which the author interprets the Army's official "Doctrines and Discipline" in a manner that reflects Brengle's influence.

[30] Cf. T. H. Howard, *Standards of Life and Service* (London: The Salvation Army Book Dept., 1909), pp. 8–14, 28–29, 40–48, 71–72, 98, 100, 102, 104, 113–22, 123, 126, 152, 154; Frederick St. George de Latour Booth-Tucker, ed., *The Successful Soul-Winner: A Summary of Finney's Revival Lectures* (London: Salvationist Publishing and Supplies, 1926), pp. 22–23, 26, 35, 63, 68, 85, 110; *Orders and Regulations for Officers of The Salvation Army* (London: International Headquarters, 1936), pp. 140–41, 203, 208, 209, 212, 215, 217; *Orders and Regulations for Soldiers of The Salvation Army* (London: International Headquarters, 1950), pp. 8–9, 10–11; and the "old edition" of *The Salvation Army Handbook of Doctrine* (1927), pp. 103–6, 124–26, 128–38, 145–47.

[31] During the 1960s, the foundations of Salvation Army holiness doctrine underwent modification. The chief protagonist in this development was Frederick Coutts, whose *Call to Holiness* (1957) sought to re-balance Brengle's emphasis on the critical nature of entire sanctification with an equal stress on the process of holiness following the second blessing. Coutts borrowed Brengle's definition of holiness as "Christ in you" and developed the progressive implications of such communion between God and man. Both Brengle and Coutts emphasized experience; however Coutts, instead of talking of the elimination of the sin nature, preferred to speak of the redirection of the will toward the good. For a further discussion of this shift in emphasis and subsequent development of Army holiness doctrine, see R. David Rightmire's *Sacraments and The Salvation Army: Pneumatological Foundations* (Metuchen, NJ: Scarecrow Press, 1990), pp. 263–66. Cf. John Norton, 3.2, "The Doctrine of the Second Blessing," n. 70. Norton further interprets this shift in holiness theology as one that "brings Salvation Army teaching much closer to a reformed understanding of sanctification" (in its Keswick form), representing "a modification under Calvinist influence of the Wesleyan position of sanctification." Norton, 4.2, "The Doctrine of Holiness."

CONCLUSION

[1] Quoted from Orsborn and Pepper in Bramwell Tripp, "A Godly, Gracious Influence for More than a Century," *War Cry* (May 10, 1980): 21; Chesham, *Peace*, p. 219.

[2] Chesham, *Born to Battle*, p. 238. Lt. Colonel Mina Russell, having known Commissioner Brengle and having taught at the first "Brengle College," participated in Brengle Institutes in England, Finland, Canada, Brazil, East Africa, Ghana, Japan, Korea, Australia, Hong Kong, and the Philippines. Clark, *SLB*, pp. 150–53; videotaped interview of Mina Russell by William Francis at the 50th anniversary of the Brengle Institute, Chicago, 1997.

³"Samuel L. Brengle and 'The Officers' Review,'" *Officers' Review* 5:4 (Jul.–Aug. 1936): 303. For a biographical tribute that underscores Brengle's legacy, see Harris, "Samuel L. Brengle—Salvationist Saint," p. 3.

⁴Tripp, p. 21. Similar words of appreciation of Brengle's legacy were written more recently by John Larsson: "Brengle knew that something important had happened to him, but he could have no inkling of how momentous the events of that morning were to prove to the course of his life. He could not have known that the gusts of the Spirit now released in his life were soon to blow him from the comparative lull of the Boston Theological Seminary where he was studying, right into the storm center of the early-day Salvation Army warfare, that he would almost be killed in a hooligan attack, that during his convalescence he would begin to write of his personal experience of God, and that his writings would lead him to be hailed as a prophet and a saint within the Army." *Spiritual Breakthrough*, p. 1.

⁵Samuel L. Brengle, "God's Love Immutable," *Officers' Review* 5:4 (Jul.–Aug. 1936): 296.

Bibliography

BOOKS AND PAMPHLETS

Begbie, Harold. *Life of William Booth, The Founder of The Salvation Army*, 2 vols. New York: Macmillan, 1920.

Booth, Catherine Mumford. *Godliness*. Boston: McDonald and Gill, 1885.

_____. *Popular Christianity*. Boston: McDonald and Gill, 1888.

Booth, William. *Purity of Heart*. London: Salvation Army Book Room, 1902.

Booth-Tucker, Frederick de Lautour. *The Life of Catherine Booth*, 2 vols. New York: Fleming Revell, 1892.

_____, ed. *The Successful Soul-Winner: A Summary of Finney's Revival Lectures*. London: Salvationist Publishing and Supplies, 1926.

Brengle, Samuel Logan. *Ancient Prophets: With a Series of Occasional Papers on Modern Problems* [originally published in 1929]. London: The Salvation Army, 1930.

_____. *At the Center of the Circle: Selections from Published and Unpublished Writings of Samuel Logan Brengle*. Edited by John D. Waldron. Kansas City: Beacon Hill, 1976.

_____. *Can Little Children Be Really Saved?* [pamphlet]. New York: The Salvation Army, 1937.

_____. *The Consolation Wherewith He Was Comforted* [pamphlet]. N.p.: The Salvation Army, n.d.

_____. *The Cost of Saving Souls* [pamphlet]. London: The Salvation Army, n.d.

_____. *Fifty Years Before and After: 1885–January Ninth–1935* [pamphlet]. N.p.: National Association for the Promotion of Holiness, n.d.

_____, et al. *God as Strategist* [originally published in 1942]. New York: The Salvation Army, 1978.

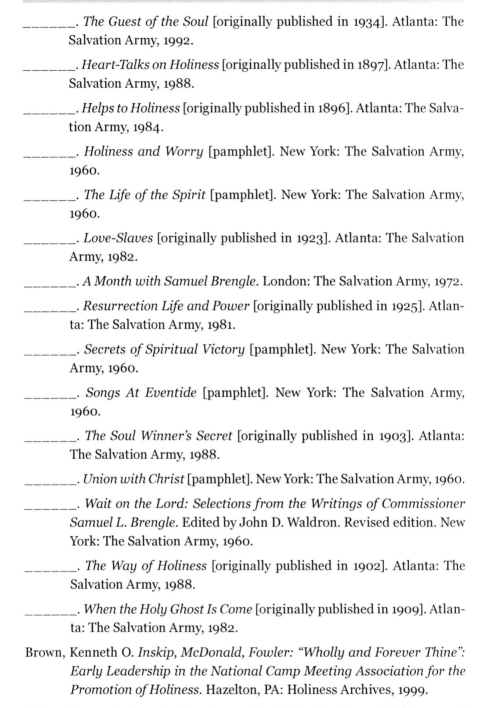

_____. *The Guest of the Soul* [originally published in 1934]. Atlanta: The Salvation Army, 1992.

_____. *Heart-Talks on Holiness* [originally published in 1897]. Atlanta: The Salvation Army, 1988.

_____. *Helps to Holiness* [originally published in 1896]. Atlanta: The Salvation Army, 1984.

_____. *Holiness and Worry* [pamphlet]. New York: The Salvation Army, 1960.

_____. *The Life of the Spirit* [pamphlet]. New York: The Salvation Army, 1960.

_____. *Love-Slaves* [originally published in 1923]. Atlanta: The Salvation Army, 1982.

_____. *A Month with Samuel Brengle*. London: The Salvation Army, 1972.

_____. *Resurrection Life and Power* [originally published in 1925]. Atlanta: The Salvation Army, 1981.

_____. *Secrets of Spiritual Victory* [pamphlet]. New York: The Salvation Army, 1960.

_____. *Songs At Eventide* [pamphlet]. New York: The Salvation Army, 1960.

_____. *The Soul Winner's Secret* [originally published in 1903]. Atlanta: The Salvation Army, 1988.

_____. *Union with Christ* [pamphlet]. New York: The Salvation Army, 1960.

_____. *Wait on the Lord: Selections from the Writings of Commissioner Samuel L. Brengle*. Edited by John D. Waldron. Revised edition. New York: The Salvation Army, 1960.

_____. *The Way of Holiness* [originally published in 1902]. Atlanta: The Salvation Army, 1988.

_____. *When the Holy Ghost Is Come* [originally published in 1909]. Atlanta: The Salvation Army, 1982.

Brown, Kenneth O. *Inskip, McDonald, Fowler: "Wholly and Forever Thine": Early Leadership in the National Camp Meeting Association for the Promotion of Holiness*. Hazelton, PA: Holiness Archives, 1999.

Callen, Barry. *God As Loving Grace: The Biblically Revealed Nature and Work of God*. Nappanee, IN: Evangel Publishing House, 1996.

Carwardine, Richard. *Transatlantic Revivalism: Popular Evangelicalism in Britain and America, 1790–1865*. London: Greenwood Press, 1978.

Caughey, James. *Earnest Christianity Illustrated*. Boston: J. P. Magee, 1855.

Chesham, Sallie. *Born to Battle: The Salvation Army in America*. Chicago: Rand McNally, 1965.

_____. *The Brengle Treasury: A Patchwork Polygon*. Atlanta: The Salvation Army, 1988.

_____. *Peace Like a River*. Atlanta: The Salvation Army, 1981.

Choy, Leona. *Powerlines: What Great Evangelicals Believed about the Holy Spirit—1850–1930*. Camp Hill, PA: Christian Pub., 1990.

Clark, William, ed. *Dearest Lily: A Selection of the Brengle Correspondence*. London: The Salvation Army, 1985.

_____. *Samuel Logan Brengle: Teacher of Holiness*. London: Hodder and Stoughton, 1980.

Coutts, Frederick. *The Call to Holiness*. London: The Salvation Army, 1957.

_____. *The History of The Salvation Army: Volume 6, 1914–1946* [originally published in 1973]. New York: The Salvation Army, 1979.

Coutts, John. *The Salvationists*. London: Mowbrays, 1977.

Coward, Eric. *The Brick and the Book: Samuel Logan Brengle*. London: The Salvation Army, 1948.

Dieter, Melvin E. *The Holiness Revival of the Nineteenth Century*. Metuchen, NJ: Scarecrow Press, 1980.

_____. "Wesleyan-Holiness Aspects of Pentecostal Origins," in Vinson Synan, *The Holiness-Pentecostal Movement in the United States*. Grand Rapids: Eerdmans Publishing Co., 1971.

The Doctrine We Adorn: An Abridged Study of The Salvation Army Doctrines. London: The Salvation Army, 1982.

The Doctrines and Discipline of The Salvation Army. London: The Salvation Army, 1881.

Douglas, Eileen. *Elizabeth Swift Brengle*. London: The Salvation Army, 1922.

Ervine, St. John. *God's Soldier: General William Booth*. Volume 2. New York: Macmillan, 1935.

Farthing, Peter (ed.). *Samuel Logan Brengle: Heart for God*. Sydney, Australia: Salvation Army, 2009.

Gariepy, Henry. *Christianity in Action: The International History of the Salvation Army*. Grand Rapids: Eerdmans, 2009.

Hall, Clarence W. *Samuel Logan Brengle: Portrait of a Prophet*. New York: The Salvation Army, 1933. Revised Memorial Edition. Chicago: The Salvation Army, 1936.

Hartley, Benjamin L. *Evangelicals at the Crossroads: Revivalism and Social Reform Boston, 1860–1910*. London: University Press of New England, 2011.

Holiness Hymns. London: The Salvation Army, 1880.

Hostetler, Bob (ed.) *Take Time to Be Holy: 365 Daily Inspirations To Bring You Closer to God* [Selected writings of S. L. Brengle, revised and "updated" for the contemporary reader]. Phoenix: Tyndale House Publishers, 2013.

Houghton, Walter E. *The Victorian Frame of Mind*. New Haven: Yale University Press, 1980.

Howard, T. H. *Standards of Life and Service*. London: The Salvation Army Book Dept., 1909.

Izzard, John C., with Henry Gariepy. *Pen of Flame: The Life and Poetry of Catherine Baird*. Alexandria, VA: The Salvation Army, 2002.

Jones, Charles E. *Perfectionist Persuasion: The Holiness Movement and American Methodism, 1867–1936*. Metuchen, NJ: Scarecrow Press, 1974.

Kent, John. *Holding the Fort: Studies in Victorian Revivalism*. London: Epworth Press, 1978.

Kostlevy, William, ed. *Historical Dictionary of the Holiness Movement*. Lanham, MD: Scarecrow Press, 2001.

Larsson, John. *1929: A Crisis That Shaped The Salvation Army's Future*. London: Salvation Army, 2009.

_____. *Spiritual Breakthrough: The Holy Spirit and Ourselves*. London: The Salvation Army, 1983.

Lee, Kate and Samuel L. Brengle. *My Experience of Sanctification*. London: The Salvation Army, n.d.

MacKenzie, F. A. *The Clash of the Cymbals: The Secret History of the Revolt in The Salvation Army*. New York: Brentano's Ltd., 1929.

McKinley, Edward H. *Marching to Glory: The History of The Salvation Army in the United States, 1880–1992.* 2nd edition. Grand Rapids, MI: Eerdmans, 1995.

Miller, Perry. *The Life of the Mind in America: From the Revolution to the Civil War.* New York: Harcourt, Brace and World, 1965.

Moyles, R. G. *A Bibliography of The Salvation Army Literature in English (1865–1987).* Lewiston, NY: Mellen Press, 1988.

Orders and Regulations for Officers of The Salvation Army. London: The Salvation Army, 1936.

Orders and Regulations for Soldiers of The Salvation Army. London: The Salvation Army, 1950.

Palmer, Phoebe. *Entire Devotion to God: A Present to a Christian Friend.* London: The Salvation Army, n.d.

_____. *Faith and Its Effects; Fragments from My Portfolio.* New York: W. C. Palmer, 1854.

_____. *Phoebe Palmer: Selected Writings.* Edited by Thomas Oden. New York: Paulist Press, 1988.

_____. *The Way of Holiness, With Notes by the Way; Being a Narrative of Religious Experience Resulting from a Determination to Be a Bible Christian.* New York: Lane and Scott, 1850.

Peters, John. *Christian Perfection and American Methodism.* New York: Abingdon Press, 1956.

Rightmire, R. David. *Sacraments and The Salvation Army: Pneumatological Foundations.* Metuchen, NJ: Scarecrow Press, 1990.

_____. *Salvationist Samurai: Gunpei Yamamuro and the Rise of The Salvation Army in Japan.* Lanham, MD: Scarecrow Press, 1997.

Robinson, Kenneth L. *From Brass to Gold: The Life and Ministry of Dr. D. Willia Caffray.* University Park, IA: Vennard College, 1971.

The Salvation Army Handbook of Doctrine. London: The Salvation Army, 1927.

The Salvation Army Handbook of Doctrine. London: The Salvation Army, 1969.

The Salvation Army Yearbook, 1936. London: The Salvation Army, 1937.

The Salvation Army Yearbook, 1947. London: The Salvation Army, 1948.

The Salvation Army Yearbook, 1957. London: The Salvation Army, 1958.

The Salvation Army Yearbook, 1960. London: The Salvation Army, 1961.

Smith, Frank. *The Betrayal of Bramwell Booth: The Truth about The Salvation Army Revolt.* London: Jarrolds, 1929.

Smith, Timothy. *Revivalism and Social Reform: American Protestantism on the Eve of the Civil War.* Baltimore: Johns Hopkins University Press, 1980.

Songs of The Salvation Army. London: The Salvation Army, 1878.

Steele, Daniel. *The Gospel and the Comforter.* Apollo, PA: West Publishing, 1897.

_____. *Love Enthroned: Essays on Evangelical Perfection* [originally published in 1875]. New York: Eaton and Mains, 1902.

_____. *The Mile-Stone Papers: Doctrinal, Ethical, and Experimental on Christian Progress* [originally published in 1878]. Minneapolis: Bethany Fellowship, 1966.

_____. *A Substitute for Holiness, or Antinomianism Revived* [originally published in 1887]. New York: Garland Publishing, 1984.

Stiles, Alice R. *Samuel Logan Brengle: Teacher of Holiness.* London: The Salvation Army, 1974.

Taiz, Lillian. *Hallelujah Lads and Lasses: Remaking The Salvation Army in America, 1880–1930.* Chapel Hill, NC: University of North Carolina Press, 2001.

"That Man of God": Commissioner Samuel Logan Brengle [pamphlet prepared in connection with Centenary Meetings at Fredericksburg, IN, 1960]. Chicago: The Salvation Army, 1960.

Troutt, Margaret. *The General Was a Lady: The Story of Evangeline Booth.* Nashville: A. J. Holman, 1980.

Waldron, John D., ed. *The Most Excellent Way.* N.p.: The Salvation Army, 1978.

_____, ed. *The Privilege of All Believers: Selected Articles by Various Officers of The Salvation Army from 1880–1980.* Toronto: The Salvation Army, 1981.

Wesley, John. *Standard Sermons.* Edited by Edward Sugden. Vol. 2. London: Epworth Press, 1921.

White, Charles E. *The Beauty of Holiness: Phoebe Palmer as Theologian, Revivalist, Feminist, and Humanitarian*. Grand Rapids: Zondervan, 1986.

Wiggins, Arch. *The History of The Salvation Army: Volume 5, 1904–1914* [originally published in 1968]. New York: The Salvation Army, 1979.

Wilson, P. W. *General Evangeline Booth of The Salvation Army*. New York: Charles Scribner's Sons, 1948.

Winston, Diane. *Red-Hot and Righteous: The Urban Religion of The Salvation Army*. Cambridge, MA: Harvard University Press, 1999.

Wisbey, Herbert A. *Soldiers Without Swords: A History of The Salvation Army in the United States*. New York: Macmillan, 1955.

Wood, J. A. *Perfect Love: Or Plain Things for Those Who Need Them*, 36th ed. London: The Salvation Army, 1902.

Woodward, William D. *Life Sketches of Samuel Logan Brengle*. Chicago: Christian Witness, n.d.

Wynkoop, Mildred Bangs. *A Theology of Love: The Dynamic of Wesleyanism*. Kansas City, MO: Beacon Hill, 1972.

ARTICLES

"A Book for the Head and the Heart: A Review." *Field Officer* 9:9 (Sept. 1901): 386–89.

Booth, Evangeline. "An Apostle of the Penitent-Form: An Unsurpassed Exponent of the Doctrine of Holiness." *War Cry* [NY] (Jun. 20, 1936): 9.

_____. "He Stands Out a Figure Alone." *War Cry* [NY] (Oct. 17, 1931): 9, 13.

Booth, William. "Letter from William Booth to the Brethren and Sisters Laboring for Jesus in Connection with the Dunedin Hall Christian Mission, Edinburgh." *East London Evangelist* 1 (Apr. 1, 1869): 105.

"A Brengle Memorial." *War Cry* [NY] (May 21, 1938): 8.

Brengle, Samuel Logan. "About the Future of The Salvation Army." *Staff Review* (Apr. 1928): 183–89.

_____. "After Many Days." *War Cry* [NY] (Nov. 15, 1913): 10.

_____. "After the Meeting." *Field Officer* 11:8 (Aug. 1903): 307.

_____. "After Twenty-Nine Years: A Personal Testimony." *Officer* 21:11 (Nov. 1913): 545–46.

_____. "All Ye That Labor." *War Cry* [NY] (Sept. 2, 1899): 2.

_____. "The Amazing Transformation." *War Cry* [NY] (Jun. 6, 1981): 2.

_____. "The Angels' Song of Peace." *War Cry* [NY] (Dec. 21, 1918): 4.

_____. "Another Chance for You: A Test of Love." *War Cry* [NY] (Apr. 14, 1894): 3.

_____. "Apples of Gold in Pictures of Silver." *War Cry* [NY] (Dec. 11, 1899): 10.

_____. "Apples of Gold in Pictures of Silver." *War Cry* [NY] (Jan. 25, 1890): 13.

_____. "Are You a Patriot?" *War Cry* [NY] (Jul. 2, 1898): 3.

_____. "The Army Song Book as a Manual of Devotion." *War Cry* [NY] (Jul. 17, 1915): 16.

_____. "Ask Largely." *War Cry* [NY] (Apr. 20, 1940): 7, 14.

_____. "At Eventide: A Message for Retired Warriors." *Officer* 49:3 (Sept. 1929): 191.

_____. "The Atonement." *War Cry* [NY] (Sept. 14, 1907): 6.

_____. "The Baptism of the Spirit: Is It Accompanied by the Gift of Tongues?" *War Cry* [NY] (Aug. 26, 1939): 3, 9.

_____. "The Battle Is the Lord's!: A Word of Encouragement to Common Folk Engaged in Spiritual Warfare." *War Cry* [NY] (Nov. 28, 1942): 4.

_____. "Be Faithful, Be Loving." *War Cry* [NY] (Dec. 30, 1916): 3.

_____. "The Bible." *War Cry* [NY] (Dec. 12, 1925): 10.

_____. "The Blessedness of the Pentecostal Baptism." *Staff Review* (Apr. 1930): 187–93.

_____. "The Blessing That Overflows." *War Cry* [NY] (Sept. 16, 1911): 11. Reprint of Chapter 21 ("The Overflowing Blessing") from *When the Holy Ghost Is Come* (1909).

_____. "Bob Ingersoll's Funeral Sermon." *War Cry* [NY] (Aug. 12, 1899): 5.

_____. "Brigadier Eileen Douglas: An Appreciation." *War Cry* [NY] (May 4,1918): 6.

_____. "A Burning and Shining Light: A Homily on Red-Hot Religion." *War Cry* [NY] (Sept. 22, 1928): 12.

_____. "A Business Too Big for Us." *Officer* 37:1 (Jul. 1923): 71–72.

_____. "Can Little Children Be Really Saved?" Part 1: *Officer* 29:3 (Sept. 1919): 233–36; Part 2: *Officer* 29:5 (Nov. 1919): 470. Reprinted in *War Cry* [NY]. Part 1 (Oct. 25, 1924): 10; Part 2 (Nov. 8, 1924): 10.

_____. "Can One Who Has Lost the Blessing of Full Salvation Be Restored?" *Officer* 27:4 (Oct. 1918): 313–16.

_____. "Can We Have Revivals in War Time?" *War Cry* [NY] (Mar. 2, 1918): 9, 12. Reprinted in *War Cry* [NY] (Oct. 9, 1943): 5, 14.

_____. "Can You Feed Yourself, or Must You Be Fed with a Spoon?" *War Cry*, [NY] (Aug. 13, 1927): 7, 12.

_____. "Characteristics of the Anointed Preacher." *War Cry* [NY] (Jun. 3, 1911): 6.

_____. "A Chat with Paul." *War Cry* [NY] (Jan. 28, 1933): 6.

_____. "The Children, the Children, Oh, the Children." *War Cry* [NY] (Jul. 19, 1919): 2–3.

_____. "Christianity and World Peace." *War Cry* [NY] (Jan. 9, 1926): 5, 9.

_____. "Christmas, and Nothing to Give." *War Cry* [NY] (Dec. 15, 1934): 3.

_____. "The Christmas Song of the Angels." *Officer* 29:6 (Dec. 1919): 543–45.

_____. "Christ's Constraining Love." *War Cry* [NY] (Jan. 31, 1920): 7.

_____. "Comforted." *War Cry* [NY] (Jan. 14, 1905): 3. Reprinted in *War Cry* [NY] (Jan. 3, 1925): 15.

_____. "Commissioner Brengle Writes." *Officers' Review* 4:5 (Sept.–Oct. 1935): 419–22.

_____. "Commissioner Brengle's Last Whitsun Message." *Officers' Review* 6:3 (May–Jun. 1937): 205.

_____. "Confessing Other People's Sins, and the Vision That Saves." *War Cry* [NY] (Apr. 25, 1914): 6.

_____. "Constrained by Love." *Field Officer* 20:11 (Nov. 1912): 414.

_____. "Conversion of Young People." *War Cry* [NY] (Jan. 2, 1915): 11.

_____. "A Corps Cadet's Testimony, with Some Observations." *War Cry* [NY] (Oct. 6, 1928): 12.

_____. "Correspondence: Is There a Special Message for the Present Age?" *Staff Review* (Jan. 1929): 113–22.

_____. "Correspondence: Problems of the Sunday Night Prayer Meeting." *Staff Review* (Apr. 1928): 196–98.

_____. "The Cost of Saving Souls." *Staff Review* (Jul. 1926): 265–70.

_____. "The Cure for Discouragement." *War Cry* [NY] (Feb. 9, 1946): 4. Reprinted in *War Cry* [NY] (Dec. 6, 1952): 4.

_____. "The Danger of Middle Age." *War Cry* [NY] (Mar. 4, 1911): 6.

_____. "Deal Gently." *War Cry* [NY] (May 11, 1901): 2.

_____. "Dealing with Officers on Their Failures in Holiness." *Staff Review* (Apr. 1924): 113–20.

_____. "Death." *War Cry* [NY] (Feb. 6, 1904): 11.

_____. "The Death of Abel—The Resurrection of Jesus." *War Cry* [NY] (Apr. 22, 1916): 6. Reprinted in *War Cry* [NY] (Apr. 2, 1932): 3.

_____. "A Definition and an Experience." *War Cry* [NY] (Jul. 11, 1925): 3.

_____. "Despise Not the Day of Small Things." *Officer* 49:5 (Nov. 1929): 434.

_____. "Did Lincoln Believe in Hell?" *War Cry* [NY] (Feb. 13, 1926): 7.

_____. "Did the Resurrection Hang Upon Self-Denial?" *War Cry* [NY] (Apr. 7, 1928): 11, 14.

_____. "The Disappointed Angels." *War Cry* [NY] (Dec. 22, 1917): 13.

_____. "Disentangled and Separate." *Staff Review* (Oct. 1924): 295–300.

_____. "Divorce and Remarriage." *War Cry* [NY]. Part 1 (Aug. 2, 1913): 13; Part 2 (Aug. 9, 1913): 13.

_____. "Do Not Be Deceived by Wet Propaganda." *War Cry* [NY] (Apr. 12, 1930): 3.

_____. "Don't Be a Baby!" *Officer* 33:4 (Oct. 1921): 272–74.

_____. "Earth's Grave Yards—Eternity's Grain Fields." *War Cry* [NY] (Apr. 3, 1915): 6.

_____. "Ebenezer: 1885–1918." *War Cry* [NY] (Feb. 2, 1918): 16.

_____. "Encourage One Another." *Field Officer* 19:10 (Oct. 1911): 391–92.

_____. "Entrusted with a Great Sorrow." *War Cry* [NY] (Apr. 25, 1936): 6.

_____. "The Family Altar: Every Man Priest in His Own Home." *War Cry* [NY] (Feb. 11, 1928): 3.

_____. "A Father's Letters to His Corps Cadet Boy at School." *War Cry* [NY] (May 13, 1916): 6.

_____. "A Few B's for The Salvation Army Officers." *Officer* 24:7 (Jul. 1916): 454.

_____. "Fifty Years of Holy Living!" *War Cry* [NY]. Part 1 (Jan. 12, 1935): 4; Part 2 (Jan. 19, 1935): 4. Reprinted as *Fifty Years Before and After* [pamphlet] (N.p.: National Association for the Promotion of Holiness, n.d.).

_____. "Fifty-Seven—My Testimony." *War Cry* [NY] (Jun. 23, 1917): 7.

_____. "Fight the Satanic Whisperer." *Officer* 27:3 (Sept. 1918): 230–31.

_____. "The First Christmas." *War Cry* [NY] (Dec. 22, 1902): 2. Reprinted in *War Cry* [NY] (Dec. 25, 1920): 4; *War Cry* [NY] (Dec. 2, 1922): 5; *War Cry* [NY] (Dec. 18, 1943): 4.

_____. "A Flaming Revival." *War Cry* [NY] (Jan. 18, 1919): 9. Reprinted in *War Cry* [NY] (Mar. 16, 1940): 7, 14; and as "Christ for the Nation!" in *War Cry* [NY] (Jan. 20, 1945): 5, 14.

_____. "Flee! Follow! Fight!" *War Cry* [NY] (May 2, 1936): 6.

_____. "Four Kinds of Self-Denial." *War Cry* [NY] (Apr. 14, 1917): 13.

_____. "The Frankness of Jesus: A Message to the Young People." *War Cry* [NY] (Feb. 5, 1916): 10.

_____. "From Dawn to Sunrise." *War Cry* [NY]. Part 1 (Feb. 15, 1896): 10; Part 2 (Feb. 22, 1896): 2.

_____. "Full Salvation—My Personal Testimony." *Field Officer* 20:4 (Apr. 1912): 137–38.

_____. "Future Punishment: Is It Endless?" *War Cry* [NY] (Dec. 31, 1892): 2.

_____. "Gideon's Band." *War Cry* [NY] (Feb. 16, 1895): 11.

_____. "The Giving of Thanks." *War Cry* [NY] (Nov. 22, 1902): 6.

_____. "God Our Helper! A Word for the New Year." *War Cry* [NY] (Jan. 5, 1918): 7.

_____. "God Wrought Mightily in My Soul." *War Cry* [NY] (Mar. 29, 1947): 3, 14. Reprinted in *War Cry* [NY] (Jul. 14, 1951): 6.

_____. "God's House of Flesh and Blood." *War Cry* [NY] (Sept. 15, 1917): 9. Reprinted in *Officer* 25:10 (Nov. 1917): 685–88.

_____. "God's Love Immutable." *Officers' Review* 5:4 (Jul.–Aug. 1936): 296.

_____. "The Great Call to Go for Souls." *War Cry* [NY] (Mar. 5, 1921): 5.

_____. "A Great Little Book on Prayer." *Officers' Review* 1:5 (Sept.–Oct. 1932): 395–98.

_____. "Growing Older Gladly: A Personal Testimony." *Officer* 25:7 (Aug. 1917): 458.

_____. "Guidance." *War Cry* [NY]. Part 1 (Dec. 31, 1921): 6; Part 2 (Jan. 7, 1922): 6; Part 3 (Jan. 14, 1922): 6.

_____. "Have Faith in God." *War Cry* [NY] (May 22, 1937): 2.

_____. "Hearing God." *War Cry* [NY] (Apr. 3, 1943): 5, 14.

_____. "The Heart of Jesus." *War Cry* [NY] (Sept. 1, 1888): 2.

_____. "The Hebrew Prophets and the Life of Today." *Staff Review* (Oct. 1927): 390–96.

_____. "Hell: What the Bible Says about Future Punishment." Part 1: *Officer* 27:6 (Dec. 1918): 507–10; Part 2: *Officer* 28:1 (Jan. 1919): 58–60.

_____. "Hindrances in Obtaining the Blessing." *War Cry* [NY] (Jan. 12, 1889): 10.

_____. "Hindrances to Full Salvation." *War Cry* [NY] (May 8, 1897): 6.

_____. "His Shoulders." *War Cry* [NY] (Nov. 15, 1924): 3, 13.

_____. "Hold Fast." *War Cry* [NY] (May 26, 1917): 7.

_____. "Holiness—A Working Experience: In the Hour of Affliction and Death—A Personal Testimony." *Officer* 23:6 (Jun. 1915): 419–22.

_____. "Holiness and Temptation." *Officers' Review* (May–Jun. 1936). Reprinted in *War Cry* (Mar. 23, 1985): 15.

_____. "Holiness and the Mistaken Lieutenant." *War Cry* [NY] (Jan. 21, 1933): 6.

_____. "Holiness and Worry." *War Cry* [NY] (Jul. 22, 1922): 5.

_____. "Holiness and Zeal for Souls." *Officer* 31:6 (Dec. 1920): 525–26.

_____. "Holiness: How to Keep It." *War Cry* [NY] (Sept. 29, 1894): 5.

_____. "Holiness: Is It Real?" *War Cry* [NY] (Sept. 15, 1894): 12.

_____. "Holiness: Reasons Why Everybody Should Be Entirely Sanctified." *War Cry* [NY] (Jan. 28, 1888): 11.

_____. "The Holiness Standard of The Salvation Army in Teaching and Practice." *Officer* 23:3 (Mar. 1915): 145–52. Reprinted in *War Cry* [NY] (Jul. 3, 1915): 3, 7. Reprinted as "Maintaining the Holiness Standard." *Officer* 50:6 (Jun. 1930): 441–51. Reprinted as "The Holiness Standard." *War Cry*. Part 1 (Feb. 9, 1985): 15; Part 2 (Feb. 16, 1985): 15.

_____. "Holiness: Temptations of a Sanctified Man." Part 1: *War Cry* [NY] (Apr. 14, 1888): 14; Part 2: *War Cry* [NY] (Apr. 21, 1888): 14.

_____. "Holiness: What It Is Not and What It Is." *War Cry* [NY] (Jan. 7, 1899): 7.

_____. "Holiness: When We Get It and How." *War Cry* [NY] (Feb. 11, 1888): 7.

_____. "Holy Covetousness." *War Cry* [NY] (Jan. 7, 1905): 4. Reprinted in *Officer* 29:1 (Jul. 1919): 13–15.

_____. "The Holy Guest of the Soul." *Staff Review* (Feb. 1930): 56–60.

_____. "The Holy Spirit and Sound Doctrine." *War Cry* [NY] (May 6, 1911): 10.

_____. "The Holy Spirit's Call to the Work." *War Cry* [NY] (Jul. 22, 1911): 6.

_____. "Hope and Power of His Resurrection." *War Cry* [NY] (Apr. 15, 1922): 11.

_____. "How a Nobody Became a Somebody and Suddenly Eclipsed Everybody." *War Cry* [NY] (Dec. 8, 1917): 2.

_____. "How Believing, Persistent, Purposeful Prayer Brought a Revival." *War Cry* [NY] (Apr. 18, 1936): 6.

_____. "How Much and What Do You Read?" *War Cry* [NY] (Jan. 11, 1930): 12. Reprinted as "How Much Do You Read—and What?" *Officers' Review* 6:1 (Jan.–Feb. 1937): 47–50.

_____. "How Soul-Winners Should Pray." *Officers' Review* 3:2 (Mar.–Apr. 1934): 119–20.

_____. "How to Be Holy and Happy: An Open Letter Concerning Games." *War Cry* [NY] (Oct. 13, 1928): 12.

_____. "How to Bear Grief." *War Cry* [NY] (Jun. 20, 1914): 5.

_____. "How to Get and Keep the Fire!" *Field Officer* 15:6 (Jun. 1907): 212.

_____. "How to Get People Sanctified Wholly." *Officer* 6:8 (Aug. 1898): 238.

_____. "How to Keep Sweet." *War Cry* [NY] (Sept. 14, 1918): 11.

_____. "How to Prepare for the Meeting." *Officer* 30:3 (Mar. 1920): 266–68.

_____. "How to Win the Jews to Christ." *War Cry* [NY] (Dec. 1, 1928): 12. Reprinted in *Officer* 49:5 (Nov. 1929): 359–61.

_____. "If Thou Knewest the Gift and Who?" *War Cry* [NY] (Dec. 5, 1925): 8. Reprinted in *War Cry* [NY] (Dec. 19, 1931): 13; and as "'If Thou Knewest the Gift.'" *War Cry* [NY] (Dec. 21, 1940): 8–9.

_____. "'Ifs' of a Soul-Winner." *War Cry* (Feb. 25, 1888): 15.

_____. "Importance and Benefits of Bible Study." *War Cry* [NY]. Part 1 (May 24, 1902): 2; Part 2 (May 31, 1902): 7.

_____. "Importance of the Doctrine and Experience of Holiness to Spiritual Leaders." *War Cry* [NY]. Part 1 (Aug. 19, 1911): 7; Part 2 (Aug. 26, 1911): 11.

_____. "Impressions of the Army Mother." *War Cry* [NY] (May 13, 1922): 7.

_____. "Impressions of the I. C. C." *War Cry* [NY] (Aug. 15, 1914): 9.

_____. "In God's School." *War Cry* [NY] (Jun. 17, 1899): 2.

_____. "In Sight of Port." *War Cry* [NY] (Aug. 4, 1906): 7.

_____. "Is Death a Mystery?" *War Cry* [NY] (May 31, 1924): 5. Reprinted in *War Cry* [NY] (Dec. 8, 1928): 12.

_____. "Is Temper Destroyed or Sanctified?" *Field Officer* 11:6 (Jun. 1903): 207–9.

_____. "Is the Baptism with the Holy Ghost a Third Blessing?" *War Cry* [NY] (Apr. 30, 1910): 7, 11; Reprinted in *Officer* 49:4 (Oct. 1929): 265–74.

_____. "Is There a Special Message for the Present Age?" *Staff Review* (Jan. 1929).

_____. "'It Is I, Be Not Afraid.'" *War Cry* [NY] (Jan. 6, 1917): 10.

_____. "Jesus Christ's Training of Paul." *Staff Review* (Jul. 1925): 19–24.

_____. "Jesus, God's Christmas Gift to Men: An Answer to Skeptics." *War Cry* [NY] (Dec. 14, 1929): 12.

_____. "Jesus Lost at the Jerusalem Congress." *War Cry* [NY] (May 10, 1930): 12.

_____. "Jonah, the Fleeing Prophet." *War Cry* [NY] (Nov. 18, 1905): 8.

_____. "Jonah's Second Chance." *War Cry* [NY] (Dec. 16, 1905): 9.

_____. "June First, 1860–1919." *War Cry* [NY] (Jun. 28, 1919): 10.

_____. "Killing in Battle: Is It Murder?: An Answer to a Question of Conscience." *War Cry* [NY] (Jan. 31, 1942): 5.

_____. "The Kind of Truth Needed for the Holiness Meeting." *Officer* 6:6 (Jun. 1898): 183–84. Reprinted in *War Cry* [NY] (Jan. 14, 1899): 5.

_____. "King David's Use of the Bible." *War Cry* [NY] (Dec. 22, 1900): 10.

_____. "The Law of Individual and World Freedom." *War Cry* [NY] (Jul. 6, 1918): 2.

_____. "The Leakage of Spiritual Power." *Officer* 25:3 (Mar. 1917): 205–6.

_____. "Lessons of the Resurrection." *War Cry* [NY] (Mar. 26, 1910): 10.

_____. "Letter Shows Brengle Spirit." *War Cry* [NY] (Sept. 10, 1955): 3.

_____. "A Letter to Army Bandsmen." *War Cry* [NY] (Apr. 23, 1932): 6.

_____. "Letting Truth Slip." *War Cry* [NY] (Mar. 9, 1895): 5.

_____. "The Life of the Spirit: An Early Morning Experience." *War Cry* [NY] (Jan. 22, 1916): 3.

_____. "The Life of the Spirit: The Perils of Maturity in Life." *War Cry* [NY] (Jan. 29, 1916): 11.

_____. "Light and Letters on Books." *Staff Review* 6:1 (Jan. 1926): 63–67.

_____. "Light at Evening Time." *War Cry* [NY] (May 9, 1936): 6.

_____. "'Light of the World' or Electric Light, Which?" *War Cry* [NY] (Jun. 2, 1928): 12.

_____. "Looking Backward and Forward After Seventy Years!" *Staff Review* (Jan. 1931): 47.

_____. "The Lord's Own Prayer." *Staff Review* (Jan. 1925): 16–22.

_____. "The Lost Blessing Found: A Word to Sorrowful Souls." *War Cry* [NY] (Sept. 21, 1918): 2.

_____. "Love for Souls: Two Portraits—Which Is Yours?" *Field Officer* 12:6 (Jun. 1904): 202–3.

_____. "Love-Slaves." *Officer* 33:2 (Aug. 1921): 124–27. Reprinted in *War Cry* [NY] (Aug. 27, 1921): 12.

_____. "Magnify Your Office." *Field Officer* 20:3 (Mar. 1912): 95–96.

_____. "Maintaining the Holiness Standard." *Officer* 50:6 (Jun. 1930): 441–51. Reprint of "The Holiness Standard of The Salvation Army in Teaching and Practice." *Officer* 23:3 (Mar. 1915): 145–52.

_____. "The Maintenance of Our Consecration: 'I Counted' and 'I Count.'" *Officer* 22:10 (Oct. 1914): 657–60. Reprinted in *War Cry* [NY] (Nov. 13, 1915): 7.

_____. "A Man in Christ, or the Sons of God Unveiled." *War Cry* [NY] (Dec. 23, 1916): 17. Reprinted as "'A Man in Christ': The Sons of God Unveiled." *Officer* 25:2 (Feb. 1917): 123–27; and as "A Man in Christ, or the Soul of God Unveiled." *War Cry* [NY] (Dec. 17, 1938): 4, 14.

_____. "Martyrs of Progress." *War Cry* [NY] (May 27, 1899): 4.

_____. "Mary's Christmas, Your Christmas and Mine." *War Cry* [NY] (Dec. 3, 1927): 6, 14.

_____. "The Master Workman." *War Cry* [NY] (May 15, 1909): 11. Reprinted as "Jesus—The Workingman." *War Cry* [NY] (Sept. 2, 1916): 9.

_____. "The Meaning of a 'Clean Heart': The Heart—Its Natural Condition as Described by Scripture, and Exemplified in Human Nature and Conduct." Paper 1: *Officer* 7:5 (May 1899): 175–76; "Can the Natural State of the Heart Be Altered?" Paper 2: *Officer* 7:6 (Jun. 1899): 214–16; "How to Obtain a Clean Heart and to Know It." Paper 3: *Officer* 7:7 (Jul. 1899): 257–59; "The Outcome, or Result, of Having a Clean Heart." Paper 4: *Officer* 7:8 (Aug. 1899): 302–4; "How to Keep a Clean Heart." Paper 5: *Officer* 7:9 (Sept. 1899): 347–49.

_____. "The Meaning of a Clean Heart." *Officer* 34:6 (Jun. 1922): 494–96.

_____. "Meaning of the Atonement." Part 1: *Officer* 30:4 (Apr. 1920): 326–31; Part 2: *Officer* 30:5 (May 1920): 436–40. Reprinted in three parts as "The Necessity of the Atonement." Part 1: *Officer* 44:4 (Apr. 1927): 305–8; Part 2: *Officer* 44:5 (May 1927): 427–31; Part 3: *Officer* 44:6 (Jun. 1927): 491–93.

_____. "Meekness of Heart." *War Cry* [NY] (Feb. 4, 1922): 6.

_____. "A Minister's Success or Failure." *War Cry* [NY] (Jun. 18, 1938): 6.

_____. "Misrepresenting God." *War Cry* [NY] (Mar. 7, 1925): 6.

_____. "More Than Conquerors!" *War Cry* [NY] (Apr. 8, 1916): 11.

_____. "Mrs. Colonel Brengle: A Sketch of Her Life and Character." *War Cry* [NY]. Part 1 (May 8, 1915): 10; Part 2 (May 15, 1915): 7; Part 3 (May 22, 1915): 7.

_____. "My Day of Days: A Testimony Written on January 9, 1923." *War Cry* [NY] (Feb. 3, 1923): 3.

_____. "My Friend: An Appreciation." *War Cry* [NY] (Nov. 28, 1925): 7.

_____. "My Personal Testimony." *War Cry* [NY] (Jun. 18, 1932): 4, 14.

_____. "My Testimony." *War Cry* [NY] (Jan. 31, 1891): 11.

_____. "The Mystery of Death's Archery." *War Cry* [NY] (Aug. 4, 1928): 12.

_____. "The Mystic, Wondrous Universe in My Back Yard: For Tired and Retired Officers." *Staff Review* (Oct. 1925): 140–44.

_____. "Needed—A Revival." *War Cry* [NY] (Dec. 3, 1932): 6.

_____. "The New 'Handbook of The Salvation Army Doctrine.'" *Staff Review* (Apr. 1923): 119–25.

_____. "A New Year's Message." *War Cry* [NY] (Jan. 19, 1918): 16.

_____. "Notes and Comments." *Staff Review* (Jul. 1926): 364–67.

_____. "No! Is the Answer." *War Cry* [NY] (May 17, 1930): 12.

_____. "No Substitute." *Field Officer* 15:9 (Sept. 1907): 344.

_____. "No Time to Be Holy!" *War Cry* [NY] (Feb. 11, 1933): 6. Reprinted in *War Cry* [NY] (May 8, 1943): 4; *War Cry* [NY] (Feb. 2, 1952): 5; *War Cry* [NY] (Mar. 16, 1957): 5, 14; *War Cry* [NY] (Aug. 3, 1957): 5, 14; *War Cry* [NY] (Mar. 8, 1958): 5, 14.

_____. "Offenses against the Holy Ghost." *War Cry* [NY] (Apr. 22, 1911): 6–7.

_____. "Officers Who Burn and Shine!" *Officer* 38:2 (Feb. 1924): 137–40.

_____. "On Growing Older Gladly." *Officer* 29:2 (Aug. 1919): 127–29.

_____. "On Saying Something Profound." *Officer* 37:3 (Sept. 1923): 237–38, 250. Reprint of "Profound." *Field Officer* 13:9 (Sept. 1905): 387–88.

_____. "On Preaching to the Few." *War Cry* [NY] (Sept. 10, 1960): 3.

_____. "One Look at a Man from Hell." *War Cry* [NY] (Jan. 23, 1892): 10.

_____. "An Open Letter to a Broken-Hearted Mother." *War Cry* [NY] (Jul. 15, 1933): 12.

_____. "An Open Letter to a Deeply Afflicted Comrade." *War Cry* [NY] (Mar. 11, 1922): 7.

_____. "An Open Letter to a Young Comrade." *War Cry* [NY] (Mar. 28, 1936): 6.

_____. "An Open Letter to a Young Man Seeking Spiritual Help." *War Cry* [NY] (Aug. 27, 1927): 7.

_____. "The Other Side of Christmas." *War Cry* [NY] (Dec. 4, 1926): 6, 14.

_____. "Ought." *War Cry* [NY] (Mar. 7, 1936): 9, 14. Reprinted in *War Cry* [NY] (Feb. 24, 1940): 7, 14.

_____. "Ought We to Pray for Money?" *Officer* 24:5 (May 1916): 302–3.

_____. "Our Mothers." *War Cry* [NY] (May 10, 1924): 5.

_____. "Our Salvationist Bandsmen." *War Cry* [NY] (Jun. 16, 1923): 7.

_____. "Our Scandinavian Campaign: A Resume." *War Cry* [NY] (Jun. 21, 1906): 10.

_____. "Paul—A Model Preacher." *Field Officer* 17:5 (May 1909): 161–64.

_____. "Paul's Secret: Alive in Christ." *Staff Review* (Apr. 1925): 151–58. Reprinted in *War Cry* [NY] (Dec. 4, 1943): 4, 14.

_____. "Pennings of a Prophet." *War Cry* [NY] (May 7, 1938): 6.

_____. "Pennings of a Prophet: A Field of Service." *War Cry* [NY] (May 14, 1938): 6.

_____. "Pennings of a Prophet: Cleansing the Temple." *War Cry* [NY] (May 21, 1938): 6.

_____. "Pennings of a Prophet: Dare to Be a Daniel!" *War Cry* [NY] (Apr. 30, 1938): 6, 14.

_____. "Pennings of a Prophet: Sustained Prayer for Revival." *War Cry* [NY] (Apr. 23, 1938): 6, 14.

_____. "Pennings of a Prophet: The Atonement." *War Cry* [NY]. Part 1 (Mar. 19, 1938): 6, 14; Part 2 (Mar. 26, 1938): 6, 14; Part 3 (Apr. 2, 1938): 6, 14; Part 4 (Apr. 9, 1938): 6, 14.

_____. "Pentecost." *War Cry* [NY] (Jun. 4, 1938): 4, 14.

_____. "Pentecost and Beyond: A Whitsuntide Message." *Staff Review* (May 1931).

_____. "A Perfect Heart." *War Cry* [NY] (Dec. 1, 1906): 6. Reprinted as "A Perfect-Hearted People." *Officer* 44:3 (Mar. 1927): 187–90.

_____. "Personal Recollections of Albert J. Beveridge." *War Cry* [NY] (Jun. 11, 1927): 7, 12.

_____. "A Plea for Soul-Winning Songsters." *War Cry* [NY] (Aug. 15, 1931): 7.

_____. "The Power of Pentecost." *War Cry* [NY] (Feb. 18, 1922): 6.

_____. "Power to Cast Out Devils." *Field Officer* 13:7 (Jul. 1905): 273–74.

_____. "Practical Hindrances to Holiness." *Officer* 6:12 (Dec. 1898): 363.

_____. "Prayer." *War Cry* [NY] (Oct. 10, 1936): 5.

_____. "Prayer That Kindles Flaming Revivals." *War Cry* [NY] (Jan. 11, 1919): 3.

_____. "Prayer—The Soul-Winner's Secret." *Officer* 30:2 (Feb. 1920): 123–25.

_____. "The Prayers of Soul-Winners." *Officer* (May 1887).

_____. "Praying for Money." *War Cry* [NY] (Apr. 15, 1916): 7.

_____. "Praying in the Spirit." *War Cry* [NY] (May 20, 1911): 10.

_____. "Preaching." *War Cry* [NY] (Jul. 15, 1911): 10.

_____. "Preparing His House." *War Cry* [NY] (Mar. 5, 1910): 11.

_____. "Profound." *Field Officer* 13:9 (Sept. 1905): 387–88. Reprinted as "On Saying Something Profound," *Officer* 37:3 (Sept. 1923): 237–38, 250.

_____. "Puffed Up!" *War Cry* [NY] (Jul. 11, 1936): 9, 14.

_____. "Purity before Power: The Holy Ghost Cleanses When He Comes." *War Cry* [NY] (Nov. 8, 1924): 6.

_____. "Put Up Thy Sword into the Sheath." *War Cry* [NY] (Feb. 11, 1905): 6. Reprinted as "The Sheathed Sword: A Law of the Spirit." *War Cry* [NY] (Jul. 29, 1911): 6.

_____. "The Reasonableness of the Christian Faith." *Staff Review* (Jul. 1931): 239.

_____. "Recent Acts of the Holy Spirit." *War Cry* [NY] (Jul. 10, 1915): 11.

_____. "Red-Hot Religion." *War Cry* [NY] (Nov. 17, 1928): 12.

_____. "'Redeeming the Time!' January 9th, 1885–1919." *War Cry* [NY] (Feb. 8, 1919): 3.

_____. "The Relation of the Word of God to Religious Experience." *Staff Review* (Jul. 1927): 354–62.

_____. "Reply to Rev. Dr. S. Parkes Cadman's Message to the High Council." *War Cry* [NY] (Feb. 9, 1929): 2.

_____. "The Resurrection." *War Cry* [NY] (Mar. 29, 1902): 7. Reprinted as "Lessons of the Resurrection." *War Cry* [NY] (Mar. 26, 1910): 10.

_____. "Resurrection Life and Hope." *War Cry* [NY] (Apr. 16, 1927): 7, 14.

_____. "Retired!" *Staff Review* (Jul. 1924): 202–6. Reprinted in *Officer* 39:4 (Oct. 1924): 265–71.

_____. "Retired: A Valedictory Message." *War Cry* [NY] (Oct. 17, 1931): 12.

_____. "A Revival in Every Salvation Army Corps." *Officers' Review* 2:6 (Nov.–Dec. 1933): 481–87. Reprinted as "A Revival in Every Corps." *War Cry* [NY] (Mar. 26, 1949): 2; *War Cry* [NY] (Feb. 16, 1957): 2; *War Cry* [NY] (Sept. 20, 1958): 2; *War Cry* [NY] (Feb. 21, 1959): 2; *War Cry* [NY] (Dec. 29, 1962): 5, 7.

_____. "The Rising Tide of Atheism and Our Defense against It." *Staff Review* (Jan. 1928): 63–69.

_____. "Robbery? I Wonder." *War Cry* [NY] (Apr. 16, 1932): 8.

_____. "Salvation—A Personal Revelation of God to the Individual Soul." *Officer* 36:2 (Feb. 1923): 159–63.

_____. "Sanctification." *War Cry* [NY] (Mar. 6, 1937): 4.

_____. "Sanctification vs. Consecration." *Officers' Review* 5:4 (Jul.–Aug. 1936): 289–98.

_____. "The Seamless Coat of Jesus." *Staff Review* (Jan. 1926): 13–17. Reprinted in *Officer* 50:2 (Feb. 1930): 89–96.

_____. "The Secret of Power." *War Cry* [NY] (Jan. 12, 1929): 12.

_____. "The Secret Society of the Sons of God." *Field Officer* 17:7 (Jul. 1909): 241–43.

_____. "Secrets of Spiritual Victory: Minding Your Own Business." *War Cry* [NY] (Aug. 17, 1907): 6; reprinted in *War Cry* [NY] (Jun. 3, 1916): 7.

_____. "Seeking the Blessing: A Dialogue." *Field Officer* 14:2 (Feb. 1906): 44–45.

_____. "Self-Denial and the Resurrection." *War Cry* [NY] (Mar. 27, 1937): 7.

_____. "The Sin against the Holy Ghost." *War Cry* [NY] (Mar. 25, 1911): 6.

_____. "The Sin of Unbelief." *War Cry* [NY] (Aug. 25, 1951): 5, 14.

_____. "Sins against Chastity the Most Heinous of All Sins against Mankind—A Reply to a Critic." *War Cry* [NY] (Jul. 23, 1921): 6.

_____. "Sixty Years! Hail to Another Sixty!" *War Cry* [NY] (Sept. 9, 1925): 2.

_____. "Slaves or Freemen, Which?" *War Cry* [NY] (Jul. 5, 1919): 3. Reprinted in *War Cry* [NY] (Jun. 30, 1923): 7.

_____. "So Spake." *Field Officer* 10:3 (Mar. 1902): 108–10.

_____. "Sold for Ten Dollars." *War Cry* [NY] (Jan. 2, 1926): 8.

_____. "Soldiers' and Holiness Meetings." *Field Officer* 11:7 (Jul. 1903): 250.

_____. "Some Good Things That May Come out of the War." *War Cry* [NY] (Jul. 27, 1918): 6–7. Abridged and reprinted in *War Cry* [NY] (Jan. 17, 1942): 4.

_____. "Some of My Experiences in Teaching Holiness." *War Cry* [NY] (Oct. 12, 1889): 11.

_____. "Songs at Eventide." *War Cry* [NY] (Sept. 25, 1915): 9.

_____. "The Soul-Winner's Secret." Multi-part series in *War Cry* [NY], "The Personal Experience of the Soul-Winner" (Mar. 11, 1899): 6; "The Soul-Winner's Obedience" (Apr. 8, 1899): 2; "The Zeal of the Soul-Winner" (Apr. 15, 1899): 2 and (Apr. 22, 1899): 7; "The Studies of the Soul-Winner" (May 13, 1899): 3 and (May 20, 1899): 5; "Finance" (Jun. 24, 1899): 6; "The Health of the Soul-Winner" (Jul. 8, 1899): 7 and (Jul. 29, 1899): 2; "Prayer" (Aug. 19, 1899): 4; "Redeeming the Time" (Sept. 2, 1899): 13; "Spiritual Leadership" (Sept. 16, 1899): 6.

_____. "Soul-Winners: Their Prayers." *War Cry* [NY] (Feb. 2, 1895): 3.

_____. "Sowing before Reaping." *War Cry* [NY] (Apr. 25, 1925): 5.

_____. "Speaking with Tongues and the Everlasting Sign." *Officer* 21:9 (Sept. 1913): 431–33. Reprinted as "The Gift of Tongues." *Officer* 24:2 (Feb. 1916): 107–10; and "Speaking with Tongues and the Everlasting Sign." *War Cry* [NY] (Nov. 18, 1922): 5; *Officer* 36:1 (Jan. 1923): 49–51.

_____. "The Special Campaigner: The Man and His Work." *Staff Review* (Jan. 1927): 16–22.

_____. "Specials: What They Should Do, Avoid, and Be." *Field Officer* 11:10 (Oct. 1903): 390–91. Reprinted in *Officer* 35:3 (Sept. 1922): 227–28; *Officer* 52:4 (Apr. 1931): 339–41.

_____. "Spiritual Dangers: 'Wind of Doctrine.'" *Field Officer* 12:7 (Jul. 1904): 242–44.

_____. "Standing Up for One's Higher Rights." *Officer* 40:2 (Feb. 1925): 130.

_____. "Startling Statement about a Most Subtle Sin." *War Cry* [NY] (Dec. 18, 1920): 4.

_____. "A Stirring Appeal for Purity in Heart and Life." *War Cry* [NY] (Oct. 20, 1900): 6.

_____. "Stooping to Conquer." *Field Officer* 13:8 (Aug. 1905): 284–86.

_____. "A Subtle Sin." *Officer* 32:1 (Jan. 1921): 36–39.

_____. "Temper." *War Cry* [NY] (Jan. 10, 1903): 10.

_____. "Temptation." *War Cry* [NY] (Jun. 19, 1943): 4, 14.

_____. "Ten Half-Nights of Prayer in Seventy Days." *War Cry* [NY] (Jan. 30, 1926): 7.

_____. "The Terror of the Lord." *Officer* 24:4 (Apr. 1916): 237–38. Reprinted in *War Cry* [NY] (May 20, 1916): 11.

_____. "A Testimony—January 9, 1885–1922." *War Cry* [NY] (Feb. 4, 1922): 5.

_____. "That Automobile Accident: An Attempt at Interpretation and Testimony." *War Cry* [NY] (Aug. 30, 1924): 5. Reprinted in *Officer* 39:5 (Nov. 1924): 375–80.

_____. "They Are Only Lambs." *War Cry* (Feb. 2, 1985): 20–21.

_____. "A Thirteenth Century Salvationist: St. Francis of Assisi." *Staff Review* (Oct. 1931): 319–26.

_____. "Three Reasons for Self-Denial." *Field Officer* 21:2 (Feb. 1913): 59–60. Reprinted in *War Cry* [NY] (Apr. 5, 1913): 3.

_____. "To Elijah under the Juniper Tree: A Letter to a Depressed Officer." *Officer* 48:6 (Jun. 1929): 505–7.

_____. "The Trial of Faith Wrought into Experience." *Staff Review* (May 1929): 199–204.

_____. "Triumph!" *War Cry* [NY] (Apr. 11, 1936): 6.

_____. "The Triumphs of Peace as Foreseen by Prophets and Poets." *War Cry* [NY] (Nov. 13, 1926): 5.

_____. "Trying the Spirits." *War Cry* [NY] (Aug. 21, 1909): 10.

_____. "Union with Jesus." *War Cry* [NY] (Jan. 21, 1905): 6–7.

_____. "Unitarianism at the Other Side of the Trinity, and the Sin Against the Holy Spirit." *War Cry* [NY] (Jul. 12, 1919): 2.

_____. "An Up-to-Date Testimony to Full Salvation." *War Cry* [NY] (Jan. 14, 1933): 8.

_____. "Victory through the Holy Spirit over Suffering." *War Cry* [NY] (Aug. 5, 1911): 6. Reprinted in *War Cry* [NY] (Nov. 26, 1921): 6.

_____. "The War and Belief in God." *War Cry* [NY] (Apr. 22, 1944): 4, 14.

_____. "The Way of Death." *War Cry* [NY] (Feb. 27, 1926): 7.

_____. "The Way to Pentecost" (review of Samuel Chadwick's *The Way to Pentecost*). *Officers' Review* 2:2 (Mar.–Apr. 1933): 127–30.

_____. "We Need a Revival!" *War Cry* [NY] (Jan. 8, 1949): 4, 14. Reprinted in *War Cry* [NY] (Jan. 10, 1953): 5, 14; *War Cry* [NY] (Nov. 26, 1955): 5, 14; *War Cry* [NY] (Jan. 11, 1958): 5, 14; *War Cry* [NY] (Jan. 16, 1960): 5, 14. Reprinted as "Revival Is Our Need." *War Cry* [NY] (Oct. 12, 1957): 5, 14.

_____. "Were the Angels Mistaken?" *War Cry* [NY] (Dec. 20, 1919): 11.

_____. "What about My Future?" *War Cry* [NY] (Sept. 21, 1907): 7; Reprinted in *Field Officer* 15:10 (Oct. 1907): 363–65.

_____. "What about the Future of The Salvation Army?" *Officer* (Oct. 2001): 4–5.

_____. "What Are Your Talents?: Encouraging Advice to Bandsmen." *War Cry* [NY] (Nov. 6, 1915): 7.

_____. "What Do You Expect?" *Officer* 34:2 (Feb. 1922): 104–5.

_____. "What I Saw Out West." *War Cry* [NY] (Nov. 5, 1898): 4.

_____. "What Is Holiness?" *War Cry* [NY] (Jul. 8, 1922): 5.

_____. "What of the Army's Present and Future?" *Staff Review* (Jan. 1929): 81–86.

_____. "What We Believe." *War Cry* [NY]. Part 1 (Dec. 10, 1921): 7; Part 2 (Dec. 17, 1921): 16.

_____. "Whatsoever a Man Soweth." *War Cry* [NY] (Nov. 17, 1917): 9.

_____. "When the Comforter Is Come." *War Cry* [NY] (Jun. 10, 1916): 5.

_____. "When the Word of God Comes." *War Cry* [NY] (Jul. 25, 1903): 2.

_____. "Where Is Your Faith?: A Word to Workers in the Flesh-and-Blood Campaign." *War Cry* [NY] (Oct. 14, 1916): 8, 12.

_____. "Which Class Are You?" *War Cry* (Dec. 11, 1976): 10.

_____. "The Whisperer—Fight!" *War Cry* [NY] (Sept. 22, 1917): 9. Reprinted as "Fight the Satanic Whisperer," *Officer* 27:3 (Sept. 1918): 230–31; Brengle, *Resurrection Life and Power*, pp. 124–26.

_____. "Whitened Harvest Fields." *War Cry* [NY] (Oct. 3, 1914): 11. Reprinted in *Officer* 27:2 (Aug. 1918): 101–4; in *War Cry* [NY] (Nov. 23, 1918): 11; and in *War Cry* [NY] (Sept. 20, 1919): 9. Also reprinted as "Sowing before Reaping." *War Cry* [NY] (Apr. 25, 1925): 5.

_____. "Who among Us Is of the Tribe of Diotrephes?" *Staff Review* (Oct. 1930): 317–24. Reprinted in *Officer* 52:3 (Mar. 1931): 221–27, 252.

_____. "Who Is He?" *War Cry* [NY] (Jan. 29, 1910): 10–11.

_____. "Who Is the 'Christ In You'?" *War Cry* (Mar. 24, 1979): 5.

_____. "Who Wants a Revival?" *Officer* 47:1 (Jul. 1928): 21–22.

_____. "Who's Quitting the Ship?" *Field Officer* 19:6 (Jun. 1911): 201–2. Reprinted in *Officer* 48:4 (Apr. 1929): 314–16.

_____. "Why Deny Myself?" *War Cry* [NY] (Mar. 13, 1937): 2.

_____. "Why Not Revival in Your Corps?" *War Cry* [NY] (Jan. 1, 1916): 6.

_____. "Why Omit Prayer?" *War Cry* [NY] (Jan. 23, 1926): 7.

_____. "Winning a Soul." *War Cry* [NY] (Feb. 20, 1909): 7.

_____. "The Witness of the Spirit." *War Cry* [NY] (May 21, 1910): 10. Reprinted in *War Cry* [NY] (Apr. 28, 1923): 16.

_____. "A Word of Cheer to a Comrade Tempted to Feel Useless." *War Cry* [NY] (Jul. 12, 1930): 12.

_____. "A Word of Thanks and a Personal Testimony." *War Cry* [NY] (May 1, 1915): 10.

_____. "'The World for God' Campaign." *War Cry* [NY] (Feb. 29, 1936): 4.

_____. "A World in Travail: A Wartime Meditation in 1918." *Officer* (Mar. 1918).

_____. "The World War and Belief in God." *War Cry* [NY]. Part 1 (Jan. 8, 1916): 6; Part 2 (Jan. 15, 1916): 6.

_____. "A World-Wide Revival." *Officers' Review* (Nov.–Dec. 1933).

_____. "Write Another Book." *War Cry* [NY] (Jun. 24, 1967): 10–11.

_____. "You." *Officer* 33:3 (Sept. 1921): 215–16. Reprinted in *War Cry* [NY] (Jul. 30, 1921): 5.

_____. "Your Commission." *War Cry* [NY] (Nov. 23, 1901): 2.

_____. "Your Own Soul." *War Cry* [NY] (Dec. 20, 1890): 14. Reprinted in *War Cry* [NY] (Mar. 23, 1929): 12.

Brewer, William. "Boston," *The Conqueror*. 2:6 (Jul. 1893): 253.

Brown, Kenneth O. "Christian Holiness Partnership," pp. 49–50. In *Historical Dictionary of the Holiness Movement*. Edited by William Kostlevy. Lanham, MD: Scarecrow Press, 2001.

_____. "Steele, Daniel." pp. 245–46. In *Historical Dictionary of the Holiness Movement*. Edited by William Kostlevy. Lanham, MD: Scarecrow Press, 2001.

Carey, Edward. "Vignettes of Army History: A Hot Gospel Shot into the Devil's Kingdom." *War Cry* (Aug. 16, 1980): 5.

Caughey, James. "Holiness: Your Remedy." *War Cry* [London] (Mar. 6, 1880)

"Colonel Brengle Campaigning in New Zealand." *War Cry* [NY] (Jun. 4, 1910): 6, 10.

"Commissioner Brengle Awarded Order of the Founder by the General." *War Cry* [NY] (Nov. 2, 1935): 13.

"Commissioner S. L. Brengle at Central Ohio Divisional Young People's Camp." *War Cry* [NY] (Aug. 27, 1927): 12.

"Commissioner Samuel Logan Brengle: Centenary 1860–1960" (cover story). *War Cry* [Chicago] (Jun. 4, 1960)—selected articles and pictures, pp. 2–9, 12–15, 18.

Cooke, George W. "An Asiatic Mission Field." *War Cry* [NY] (Dec. 10, 1910): 6–7.

_____. "Colonel Brengle in California." *War Cry* [NY] (Aug. 5, 1911): 5.

_____. "Colonel Brengle in Norway: 225 Souls in Six Days at Hamar." *War Cry* [NY] (Apr. 6, 1907): 16.

_____. "Colonel Brengle in Tasmania." *War Cry* [NY] (Oct. 15, 1910): 9, 12.

_____. "Colonel Brengle under the Southern Cross." *War Cry* [NY] (Jun. 11, 1910): 10.

_____. "Colonel Brengle's Chronicles: 240 Souls at Helsingfors." *War Cry* [NY] (Nov. 23, 1907): 4–5.

_____. "Near the Russian Border: 200 Souls Won for Christ in Colonel Brengle's Meetings in Wiborg." *War Cry* [NY] (Jan. 4, 1908): 11.

"A Fisher of Men: Being a Few 'High Spots' in the Life of a Great Holiness Preacher." *War Cry* [NY] (Jul. 3, 1926): 11, 15.

Flagg, Deborah. "Samuel Logan Brengle: A Life Aflame for God." *War Cry* (Feb. 17, 1996): 22.

Harris, William G. "Commissioner Samuel L. Brengle: A Character Sketch of a Salvation Army Saint." *War Cry* [NY] (Oct. 17, 1931): 3, 14.

_____. "Samuel L. Brengle—Salvationist Saint." *War Cry* [NY] (Jun. 6, 1936): 3, 14.

_____. "'This Man of God': Funeral Service of Commissioner Brengle." *War Cry* [NY] (Jun. 6, 1936): 13.

"The High Council Official Bulletin." *War Cry* [NY] (Feb. 2, 1929): 8.

Hill, Fred. "Holiness and Depression 1: The Condition." *Officer* 38:6 (Jun. 1987): 257–60.

_____. "Holiness and Depression 2: How Brengle Needed Help with Depression." *Officer* 38:7 (Jul. 1987): 299–302.

_____. "Holiness and Depression 3: Help through Counseling." *Officer* 38:8 (Aug. 1987): 355–58.

_____. "Stress: A Christian Approach." *Salvationist*. Part 5 (Oct. 27, 2001): 17; Part 7 (Nov. 17, 2001): 17.

"Holiness: Theory and Practice." *Officer* 2:3 (Mar. 1894): 65–69.

"Holiness Vindicated in Scripture and Experience." *Officer* 30:5 (Nov. 1919): 444–45.

Howard, Ivan. "Wesley Versus Phoebe Palmer: An Extended Controversy." *Wesleyan Theological Journal* 6:1 (Spring 1971): 31–40.

"In Memoriam: Colonel Barrett Conducts Impressive Service for the Late Commissioner Brengle." *War Cry* [NY] (Jun. 13, 1936): 10, 11.

Johnson, J. Prescott. "Crisis and Consequence: Sanctification and the Greek Tense." *Wesleyan Theological Journal* 37:2 (Fall 2002): 172–93.

Keller, Mabel G. "Opening Weekend at Old Orchard." *War Cry* [NY] (Aug. 30, 1930): 5.

"'Love-Slaves': Colonel Samuel L. Brengle's Latest Book." *Officer* 37:6 (Dec. 1923): 447–50.

"'Love-Slaves': New Book by Colonel Samuel L. Brengle." *War Cry* [NY] (Jan. 5, 1924): 5.

Lowery, Kevin. "A Fork in the Wesleyan Road: Phoebe Palmer and the Appropriation of Christian Perfection." *Wesleyan Theological Journal* 36:2 (Fall 2001): 187–222.

Maddox, Randy. "Nurturing the New Creation: Reflections on a Wesleyan Trajectory," pp. 34–42. In *Wesleyan Perspectives on the New*

Creation. Edited by M. Douglas Meeks. Nashville: Kingswood Books, 2004.

"Mile-Stone Papers, A Book for the Head and the Heart." *Officer* 30:4 (Oct. 1919): 322–24.

"New Crest Books Release Spotlights the Salvation Army Poet Catherine Baird." *War Cry* 122:6 (Mar. 16, 2002): 9.

"News from Australia." *War Cry* [NY] (Dec. 3, 1910): 6.

Nicol (Commissioner). Review of *Misunderstood Texts* by Asa Mahan. *Officer* 4:7 (Jul.–Aug. 1896): 202.

Norton, John. "The Doctrine of Sanctification in The Salvation Army: Samuel Logan Brengle." Part 3: *Journal of Aggressive Christianity* 2 (Aug.–Sept. 1999).

O'Brien, Glen. "Why Brengle? Why Coutts? Why Not?" *Word and Deed* (Nov. 2010): 5–24.

Olson, Mildred. "Colonel Brengle Has Most Wonderful Campaign He Has Ever Conducted in America." *War Cry* [NY] (Mar. 22, 1919): 8.

"On the Platform with Colonel Brengle: A Typical Soul-Battle Described." *War Cry* [NY] (Feb. 7, 1914): 6.

"Our Bookshelf: 'The Soul-Winner's Secret.'" *Field Officer* 11:11 (Nov. 1903): 430.

"Portrait of a Prophet" (cover story). *War Cry* [Chicago] (Dec. 15, 1973): 2–9.

Potter, W. Scott. "The Staff Band at Poughkeepsie." *War Cry* [NY] (Jun. 17, 1899): 4.

Pritchett, Wayne. "Holiness for Our Times: A Salvationist Response to 'Re-Minting Christian Holiness.'" *Officer* (Jun. 1999): 25–29.

Raymond, Jonathan. "The Journey toward Holiness." *War Cry* 122:3 (Feb. 2, 2002): 14–15.

Rhemick, John. "Salvation Story: A Salvationist Handbook of Doctrine" [Review]. *Word and Deed* 2:2 (Spring 2000): 56–60.

Rightmire, R. David. "Brengle and the Future of The Salvation Army: Organizational Assessment and Conditions for Success," *Word and Deed* 7:2 (May 2005): 61–75.

_____. "Brengle on Evangelism and the Holy Life," *Word and Deed* 6:1 (Nov. 2003): 5–34.

_____. "Holiness and the Ethical Dimensions of Brengle's Eschatology," *Word and Deed* 10:1 (Nov. 2007): 23–38.

_____. "Samuel Brengle and the Development of the Salvation Army Pneumatology." *Wesleyan Theological Journal* 27: 1 and 2 (Spring–Fall 1992): 104–31.

_____. "Samuel Logan Brengle." In *Historical Dictionary of the Holiness Movement*, p. 27. Edited by William Kostlevy. Lanham, MD: Scarecrow Press, 2001.

_____. "Samuel Logan Brengle and the Development of Pneumatology in The Salvation Army." *Word and Deed* 1:1 (Fall 1998): 29–48.

Ryan, Glenn. "Brengle—A Jogger: Reminisces about The Salvation Army's Prophet of Holiness." *War Cry* (Oct. 13, 1979): 10–11.

"Samuel L. Brengle and 'The Officers' Review.'" *Officers' Review* 5:4 (Jul.–Aug. 1936): 303.

"'Samuel L. Brengle: Portrait of a Prophet': A Preliminary Notice." *Officers' Review* 3:1 (Jan.–Feb. 1934): 36–37.

"Sanctification." *The Christian Mission Magazine* 8 (Feb. 1876): 35–36.

"Staff-Captain Brengle: Our Western Massachusetts D.O." *War Cry* [NY] (Aug. 24, 1895): 15.

"The Status of Field Versus Staff Officers: Some Views on a Vital Problem." *Staff Review* (Apr. 1930): 109–15.

Steele, Daniel. "Sin or Infirmity." *Officer* 36:5 (May 1923): 403–6.

"Subject Notes." *Officer* 1:3 (Mar. 1893): 88.

"The Tongue of Fire." *Officer* 3:5 (May 1895): 144.

Tripp, Bramwell. "A Godly, Gracious Influence for More Than a Century." *War Cry* (May 10, 1980): 21.

Waldron, John D. "Celebrating the Holy Life: A Fresh Assessment of Samuel Logan Brengle" Part 1: *Officer* 36:2 (Feb. 1985): 68–72; Part 2: *Officer* 36:3 (Mar. 1985): 109–12; Part 3: *Officer* 36:4 (Apr. 1985): 148–50.

_____, ed. "The Privilege of All Believers: Holiness and Temptation." *War Cry* (Mar. 23, 1985): 15.

_____, ed. "The Privilege of All Believers: The Holiness Standard." *War Cry*. Part 1 (Feb. 9, 1985): 15; Part 2 (Feb. 16, 1985): 15.

Winchell, Wallace. "Love-Slaves, by Colonel S. L. Brengle." *War Cry* [NY] (Jul. 5, 1924): 12.

Unpublished Sources

Antill, David E. "Brengle in Boston: A Brief Introduction to Some of the Significant Events of Samuel Logan Brengle's Time in Boston." Paper prepared for the 125th anniversary commemoration celebration of Brengle's sanctification in Boston, Jan. 8–11, 2010.

Brengle, Samuel Logan. "The Danger of Middle Age." Unpublished paper, n.d.

_____. Letters to Colonel Jenkins (NY) from Sunbury Court, England; January 14 and 15, 1929. The Salvation Army National Archives, Alexandria, VA.

_____. Letters to Colonel Joseph Atkinson (Boston) from Grove Farm, Poughquag, NY; August 3 and 12, 1935. The Salvation Army National Archives, Alexandria, VA.

_____. Letter to Colonel Joseph Atkinson (Boston) from St. Petersburg, FL; Dec. 14, 1935. The Salvation Army National Archives, Alexandria, VA.

_____. Letter to "My Dear Comrade," from Arlington, NJ; Jun. 1, 1927. The Salvation Army National Archives, Alexandria, VA.

"Commissioner Brengle's Books." Typewritten list of volumes donated posthumously to Training School in New York (forming the basis of the Brengle Memorial Library). The Salvation Army School for Officer Training, Suffern, NY; n.d.

Damon, Commissioner Alexander M. "Bulletin! Commissioner Samuel L. Brengle in Heaven." The Salvation Army Territorial Headquarters, New York (May 20, 1936).

Hewitt, Samuel Alexander, ed. "Letters of Commissioner Samuel Logan Brengle, D.D." Unpublished manuscript. The Salvation Army National Archives, Alexandria, VA; n.d.

Himes, William. "Brengle: Portrait of a Prophet." A musical drama by William Himes (music and lyrics), Fran Anderson (original script), and Ken Jernberg (new script) for Central Territorial Holiness Celebration (1997).

Hobgood, W. Edward. "My Life's Ambition." Musical on the life of S. L. Brengle. Atlanta: Salvation Army Southern Territory, 2008.

Miller, Andrew S. "'The Good Time Coming': The Impact of William Booth's Eschatological Vision," Master's Thesis, Asbury Theological Seminary, Dec., 2005.

Reagan, Michael. "Crisis in Process: The Holiness Teaching of Samuel Logan Brengle." Master of Arts Thesis, California State University Dominguez Hills, Spring 1997.

Rightmire, R. David. "Transitions in Salvation Army Holiness Theology: A Historical Assessment." Paper presented at the Joint Meeting of the American Academy of Religion and Society of Biblical Literature, Baltimore, Nov. 23, 2013.

Russell, Mina. Videotaped Interview by William Francis at the 50th Anniversary Brengle Institute, Chicago, 1997.

Satterlee, Allen, ed. "Pentecost and Beyond: Collected Writings of Commissioner Samuel Logan Brengle." Unpublished manuscript. The Salvation Army National Archives, Alexandria, VA; n.d.

Waldron, John D. "What Samuel Logan Brengle Had to Say About the Future of The Salvation Army." Unpublished paper presented at the Territorial History Conference, Sept. 14, 1975. The Salvation Army National Archives, Alexandria, VA.

Walker, William. "The Problem of Holiness." Unpublished manuscript of sermon preached at Bethel Evangelical Church, Detroit, MI, Jul. 19, 1936. The Salvation Army National Archives, Alexandria, VA.

Index

D

Drummond, Henry 59

E

Edinburgh, Scotland 15
Edwards, Jonathan 69, 182
Egleston Square Church 9
England 18, 20–21, 23, 39, 81, 212
entire sanctification xvii, 4, 6, 14, 17, 21, 23, 42, 70, 72, 76, 93–95, 99–107,
　　115–116, 121–127, 131–143, 145–147, 151, 153–157, 161, 164–166,
　　168–169, 171, 178–181, 184, 188, 197–199, 204, 213–217, 219–220,
　　229, 257, 260, 276, 284
eschatology xvii
　　ethical dimensions 197–198, 200, 209
　　postmillennial 197, 209, 279
　　premillennial 191, 200
ethical dimensions of holiness 109, 111, 165, 171, 197, 200, 203, 266
evangelism (soul-winning) xvii, 171–196

F

faith 7–9, 15, 17, 21, 31, 35–37, 41–43, 55, 57–58, 60, 65–66, 73–74, 76,
　　80, 83, 96, 99–101, 106–107, 110, 113, 116, 121–122, 125–126, 128,
　　131–135, 137–140, 142–143, 145, 148–154, 161–162, 164–167, 170, 173,
　　175–178, 181–182, 186–188, 193, 195, 199, 203, 205, 212–217, 219–220
Fénelon 75
Fifty Years Before and After 69
Finland. *See* Campaigns
Finney, Charles 55, 61, 125, 182, 213, 265, 276
Fletcher, John 6, 27, 269
Florida 27, 54
Foster, George 174
Founder, of The Salvation Army. *See* Booth, William
Fox, George 166, 190
Francis, of Assisi 166
French, George 26
fruit of the Spirit 99, 101, 270
fullness of the Spirit 96, 115, 159, 213, 257
full salvation 96–98, 123–124, 128, 137, 148, 185, 187, 265
Fundamentalism 73

G

Garrett Biblical Institute 27, 231
Gauntlett, S. Carvosso 56
Glasgow, Scotland 15
glorification 96
Guest of the Soul, The 71

guidance 17, 23, 45, 66–67, 161, 170, 177

H

Hall, Clarence ix, xiii, xvi, 29–30, 32, 35, 67, 70, 73–75, 78, 225
Handbook of Doctrine (Salvation Army) 217
Harris, William G. 66
Harvard Law School 81
Hawaii/Hawaiian Islands 29, 39
Hayes, Doremus A. 14
Haymarket Square 15
health 15, 18, 23, 47–48, 51, 80, 174, 188–189, 232, 239–242, 248
heart purity 94, 109–111, 113, 127, 132, 151, 166, 219, 260
Heart-Talks on Holiness 68, 70, 216
heaven 9, 19, 45, 52, 64, 95–96, 106, 112, 114, 119, 122, 133, 138, 140–141,
    163, 170, 176, 180–181, 185, 192–194, 199, 204, 208–209
hell 15, 20, 98, 106, 112, 141, 154, 192–195, 205–209
Helps to Holiness xi, 23, 38, 68–70, 216, 238–239
Helsingfors. *See* Campaigns, Finland
Higgins, Edward J. 27, 50, 54–56, 59, 243
High Council (1929) 46–49, 225, 242
hindrances to heart holiness xvii, 128, 137, 171, 182, 191, 266
Hinman, Professor 4
holiness ix, xi–xii, 261
    advocate 5, 34, 66, 119, 213, 263
    appropriation of 36, 96, 131–143, 181–196, 204–209, 213–215, 266
    as crisis/critical dimension 26, 99–101, 153, 193, 213, 215, 256
    as process/progressive dimension 57, 60, 96, 99–101, 109, 121, 124,
        134, 136, 142, 256, 284
    camp meeting 10, 27, 174, 182
    Christlikeness 71, 109, 115, 162, 257
    heritage 99, 106, 145, 155, 160, 186, 220, 222, 256, 282, 284
    meeting 7, 24, 36, 229
    movement 6, 69, 75–76, 211–212, 215–216, 222
    standard 7, 21, 115, 125, 155–156, 164, 168, 220, 270
Holland. *See* Campaigns, Netherlands
Holy Guest 116, 138, 200
Holy Spirit (Ghost) xvi, 6, 21, 24, 30–31, 34, 70, 74, 80, 93–95, 98–99,
    103–105, 107, 111–113, 117–118, 122–125, 134, 138–143, 151, 156, 159,
    162, 165–166, 173, 177, 178, 180–181, 190, 193, 195, 197, 200, 206, 240
Horner, Rebecca Anne 1
humility 5, 7, 19, 67, 76, 77, 99, 111, 113, 126, 146, 162, 166, 169, 179, 233

I

Indiana 1, 2, 4–5, 10, 25, 231
Indiana Asbury University. *See* DePauw University
International Congress 29

CPSIA information can be obtained at www.ICGtesting.com
Printed in the USA
LVOW11s0538081114

412663LV00006B/6/P